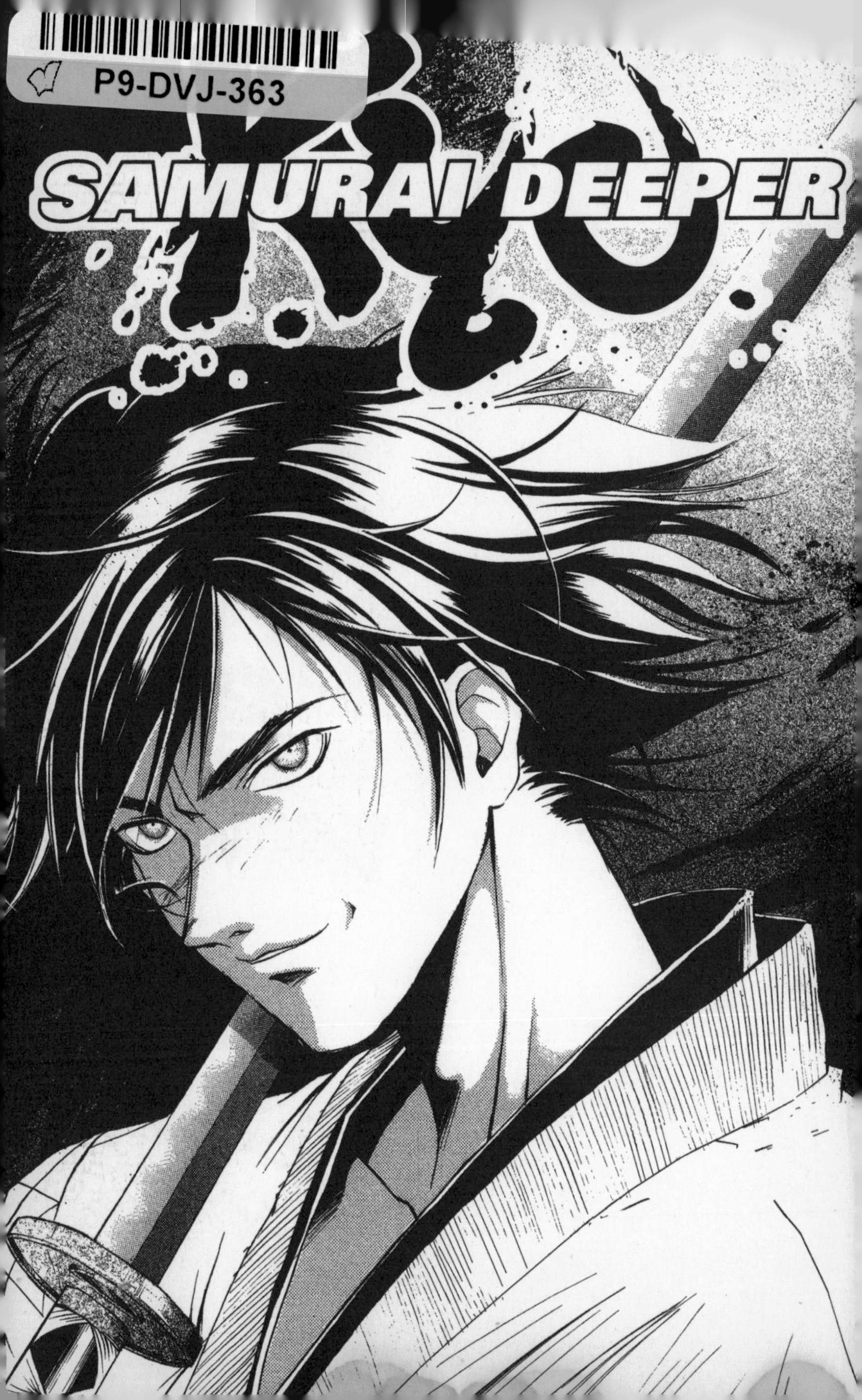
SAMURAI DEEPER

SAMURAI DEEPER KYO

Vol. 1

by Akimine Kamijyo

TOKYOPOP®

Los Angeles • Tokyo

Samurai Deeper Kyo Vol. 1
created by Akimine Kamijyo

Translation - Takako Maeda
Additional Translation - Yukiko Nakamura & Dan Danko
English Adaptation - Dan Danko
Associate Editor - Steve Grest
Retouch and Lettering - Miyuki Ishihara
Cover Artist - Aaron Suhr

Editor - Jake Forbes
Digital Imaging Manager - Chris Buford
Pre-Press Manager - Antonio DePietro
Production Managers - Jennifer Miller and Mutsumi Miyazaki
Art Director - Matt Alford
Managing Editor - Jill Freshney
VP of Production - Ron Klamert
President and C.O.O. - John Parker
Publisher and C.E.O. - Stuart Levy

A  **TOKYOPOP**® Manga

TOKYOPOP Inc.
5900 Wilshire Blvd. Suite 2000
Los Angeles, CA 90036

E-mail: info@TOKYOPOP.com
Come visit us online at www.TOKYOPOP.com

ISBN: 1-59182-225-4

First TOKYOPOP printing: June 2003
10 9 8 7
Printed in the USA

SAMURAI DEEPER

TABLE OF CONTENTS

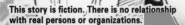

EDITOR'S NOTE:

Samurai Deeper KYO is a historical fantasy that takes place four years after the battle of Sekigahara, during the very beginning of the Edo era. Many of the events, places and even a few characters are based on facts, but the story is first and foremost a fantasy, so liberties have been taken with history.

For the English edition, many terms unique to this era have been retained. For readers familiar with Edo Japan and samurai culture, these may already be known to you, but should you encounter any terms you're not familiar with, there is a glossary at the back of the book that defines them.

Names are listed in traditional Japanese fashion, family name first. Also, name suffixes have been retained where they were used in the original work. "-san" at the end of a name is the equivalent of Mr./Ms. and indicates politeness between two people of relatively equal standing. "-sama" shows greater respect and is used when addressing people of much higher standing. We hope that these additions enhance your reading of *Samurai Deeper KYO*.

Now, on to the story…

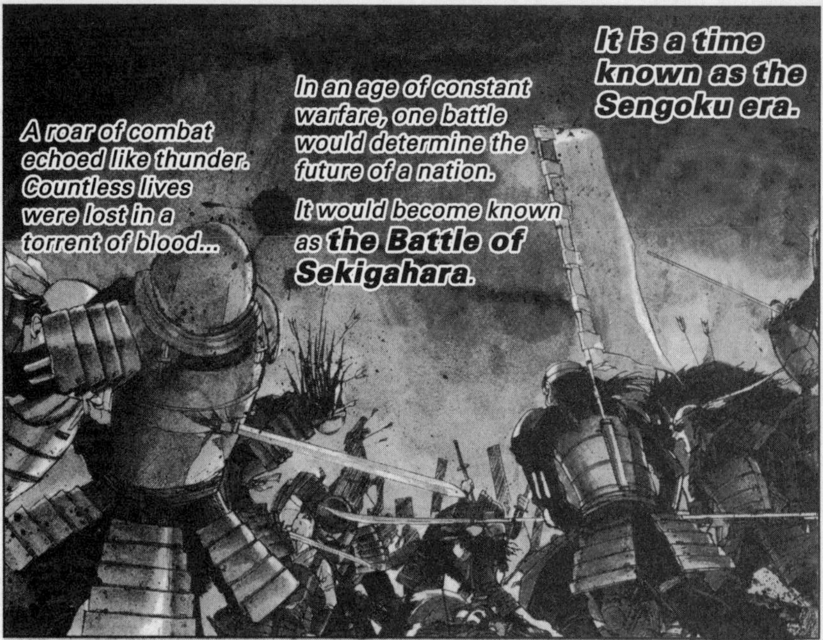
It is a time known as the Sengoku era.
In an age of constant warfare, one battle would determine the future of a nation.
It would become known as the Battle of Sekigahara.
A roar of combat echoed like thunder. Countless lives were lost in a torrent of blood...

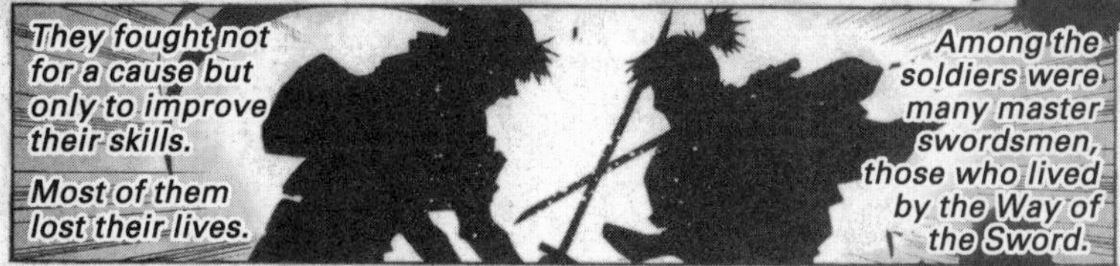
Among the soldiers were many master swordsmen, those who lived by the Way of the Sword.
They fought not for a cause but only to improve their skills.
Most of them lost their lives.

But among the many brave warriors to be forgotten by history...

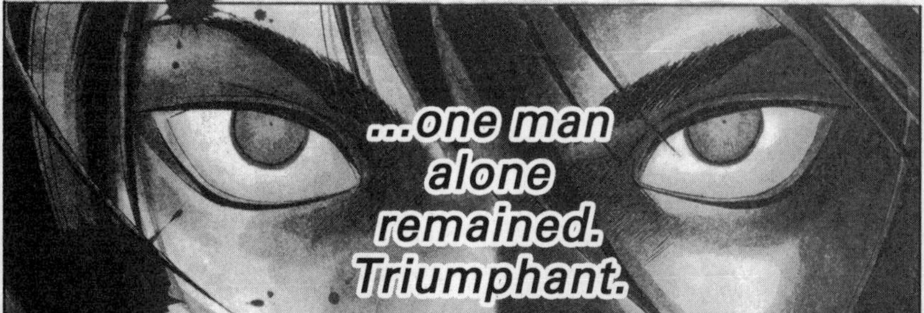
...one man alone remained. Triumphant.

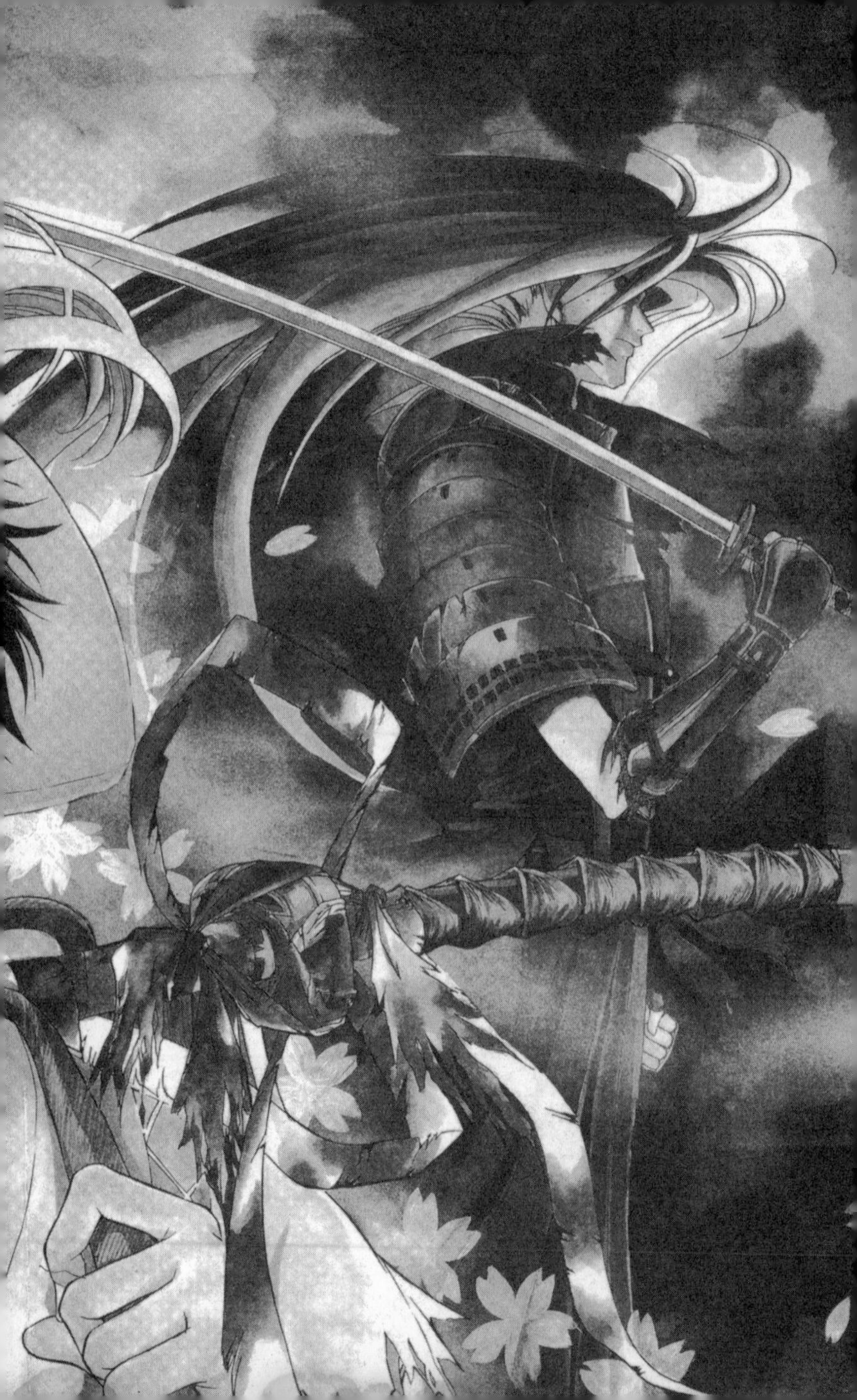

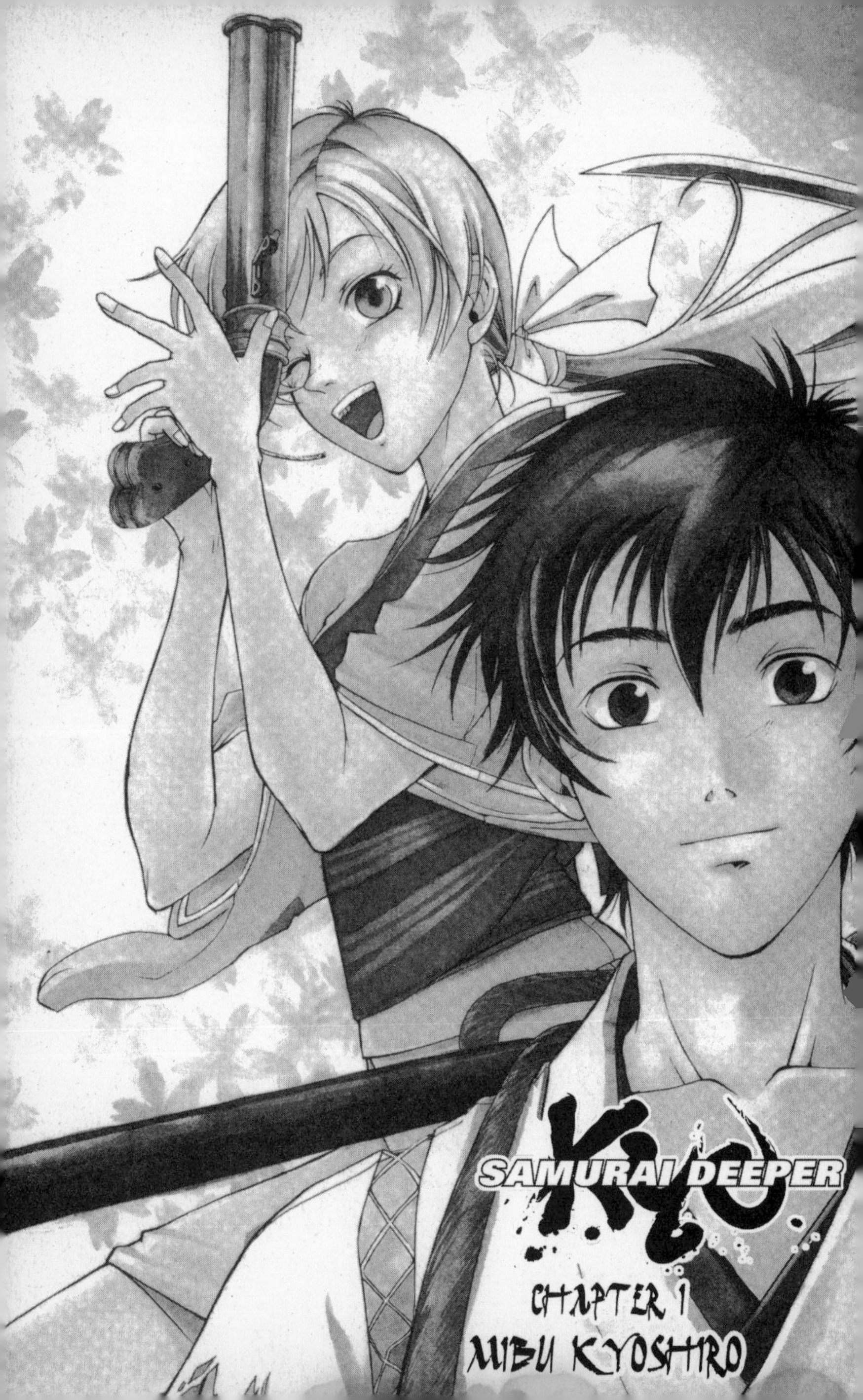
SAMURAI DEEPER
KYO
CHAPTER 1
MIBU KYOSHIRO

Stray hair

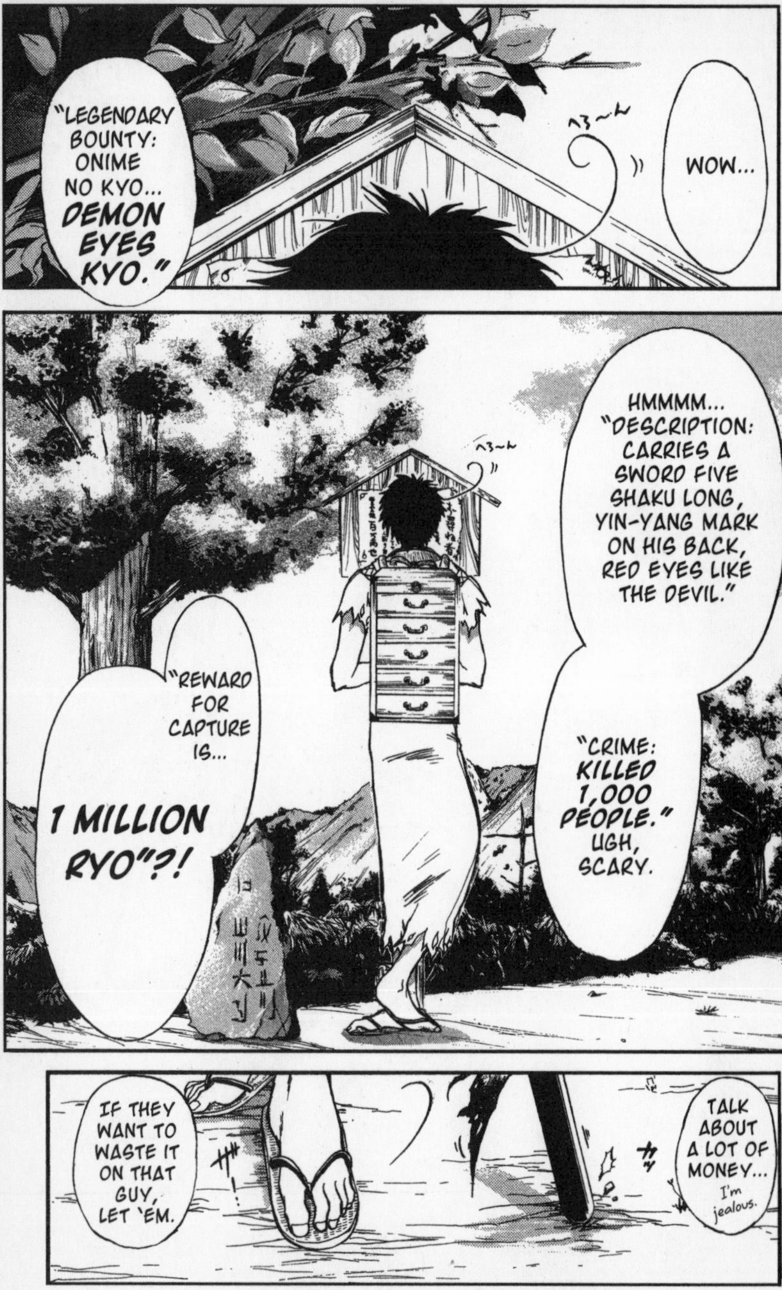
WOW...
"LEGENDARY BOUNTY: ONIME NO KYO... DEMON EYES KYO."
HMMMM... "DESCRIPTION: CARRIES A SWORD FIVE SHAKU LONG, YIN-YANG MARK ON HIS BACK, RED EYES LIKE THE DEVIL."
"CRIME: KILLED 1,000 PEOPLE." UGH, SCARY.
"REWARD FOR CAPTURE IS...
1 MILLION RYO"?!
TALK ABOUT A LOT OF MONEY...
I'm jealous.
IF THEY WANT TO WASTE IT ON THAT GUY, LET 'EM.

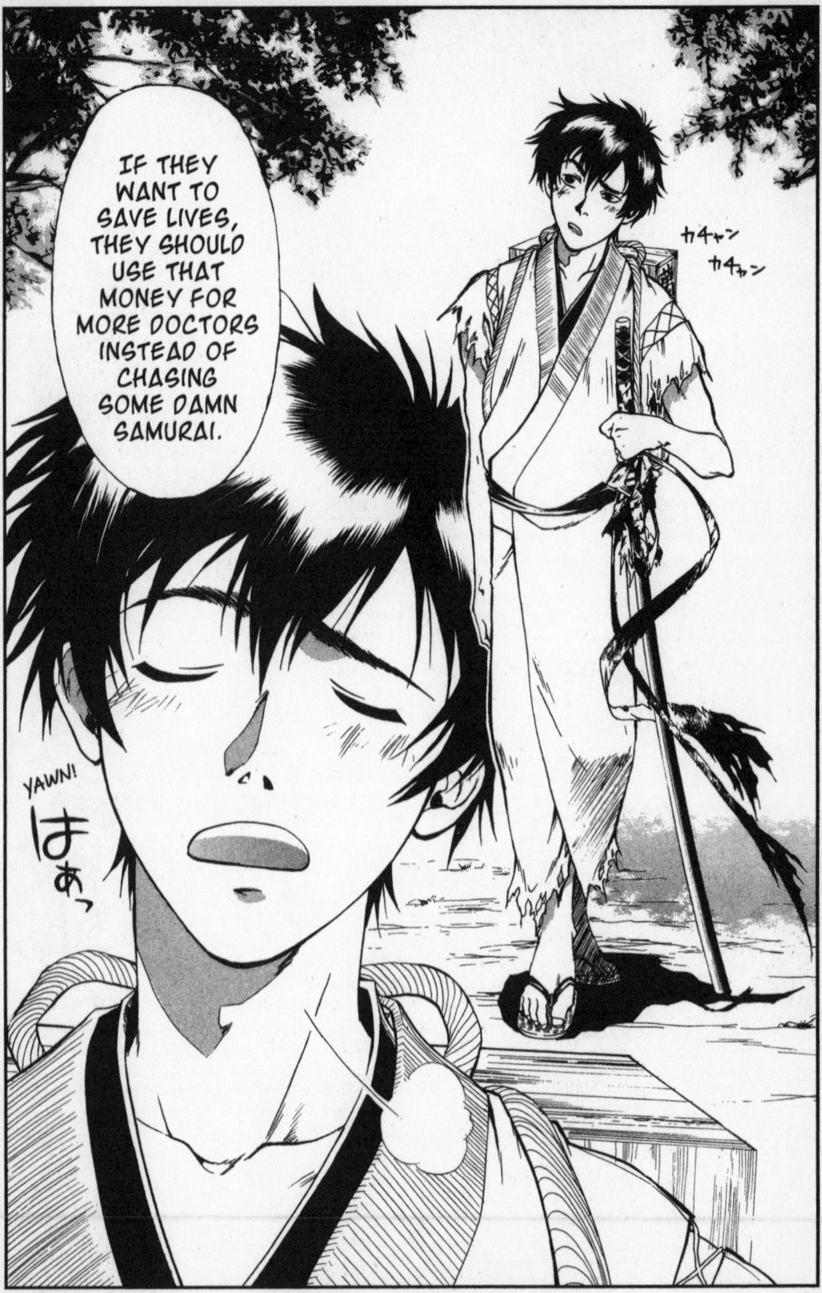
IF THEY WANT TO SAVE LIVES, THEY SHOULD USE THAT MONEY FOR MORE DOCTORS INSTEAD OF CHASING SOME DAMN SAMURAI.
カチャン カチャン
YAWN!
はぁっ

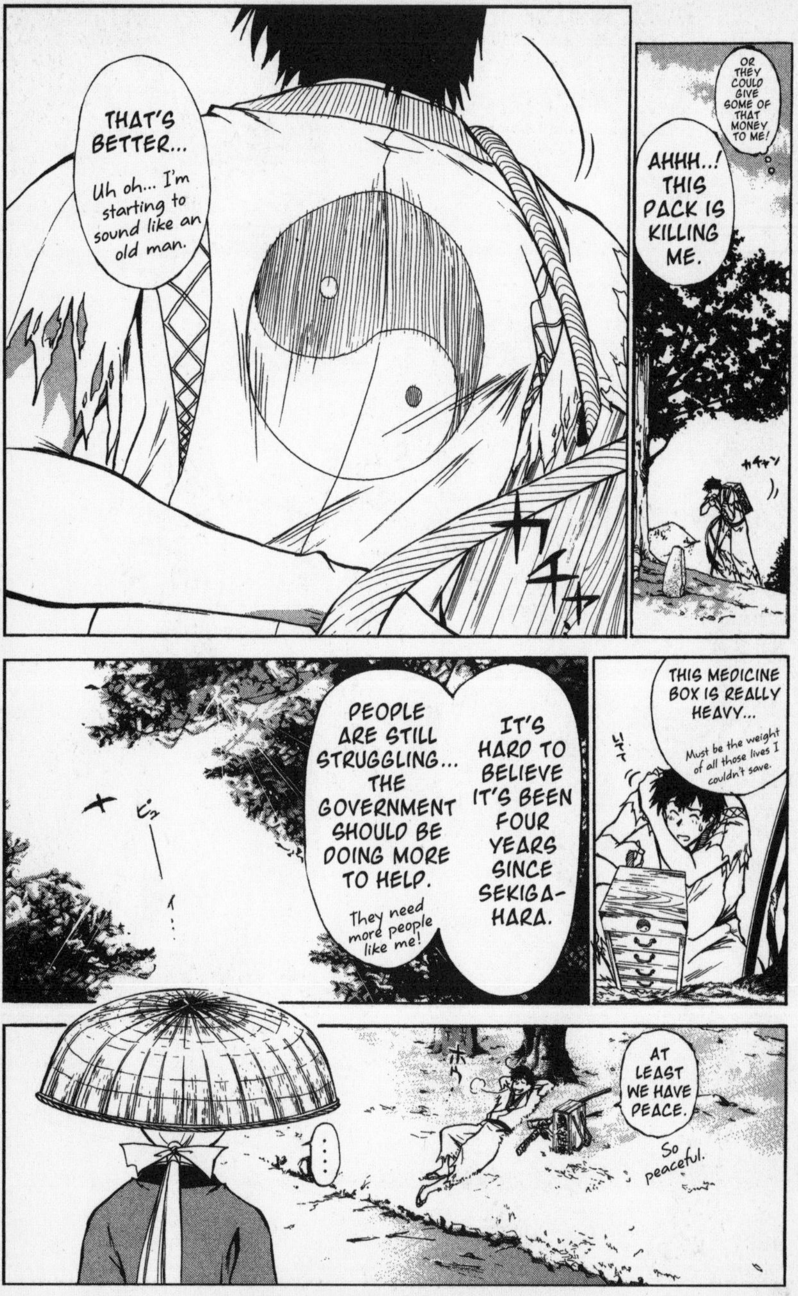
AHHH..! THIS PACK IS KILLING ME.
OR THEY COULD GIVE SOME OF THAT MONEY TO ME!
THAT'S BETTER...
Uh oh... I'm starting to sound like an old man.
THIS MEDICINE BOX IS REALLY HEAVY...
Must be the weight of all those lives I couldn't save.
IT'S HARD TO BELIEVE IT'S BEEN FOUR YEARS SINCE SEKIGAHARA.
PEOPLE ARE STILL STRUGGLING... THE GOVERNMENT SHOULD BE DOING MORE TO HELP.
They need more people like me!
AT LEAST WE HAVE PEACE.
So peaceful.
....

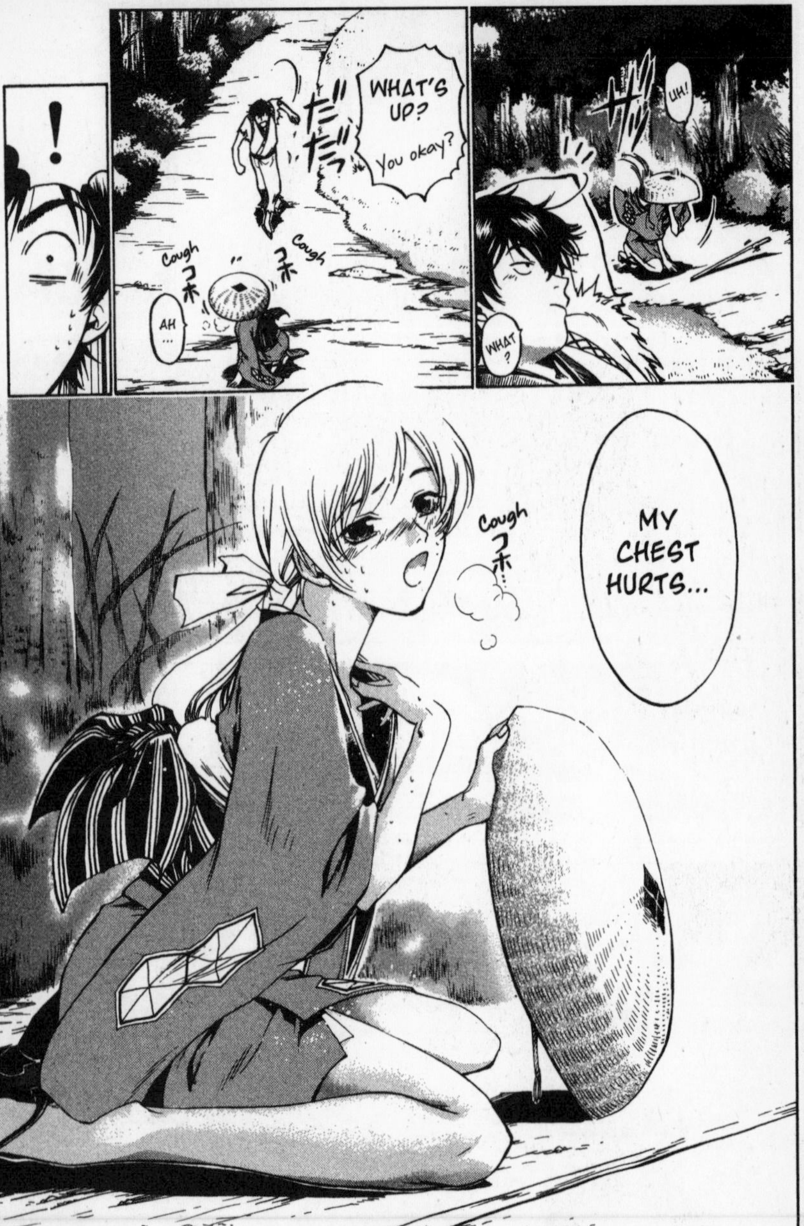
UH!
WHAT ?
WHAT'S UP?
You okay?
Cough
コホ
Cough
コホ
AH ...
!
Cough
コホ...
MY CHEST HURTS...

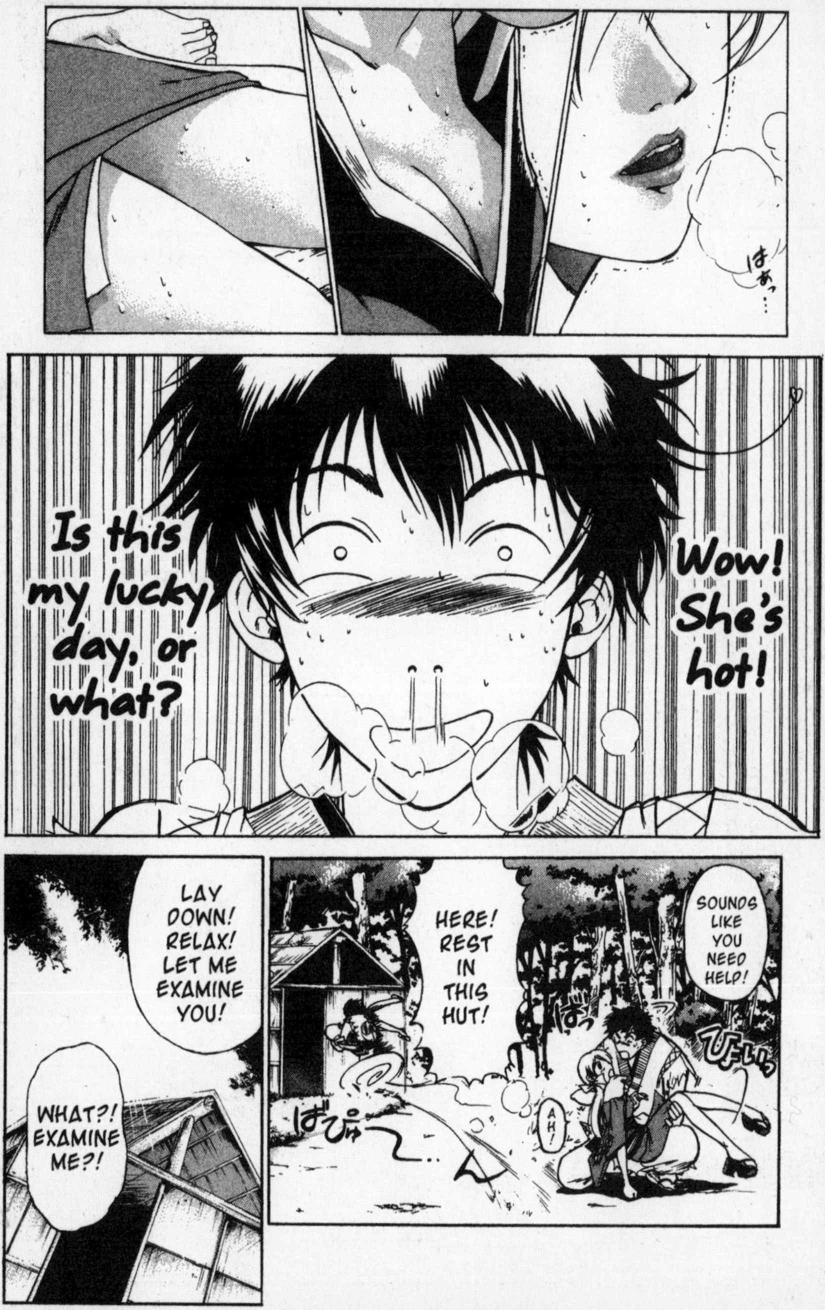
はあっ…
Wow! She's hot!
Is this my lucky day, or what?
SOUNDS LIKE YOU NEED HELP!
AH!
ぱっ
HERE! REST IN THIS HUT!
LAY DOWN! RELAX! LET ME EXAMINE YOU!
WHAT?! EXAMINE ME?!

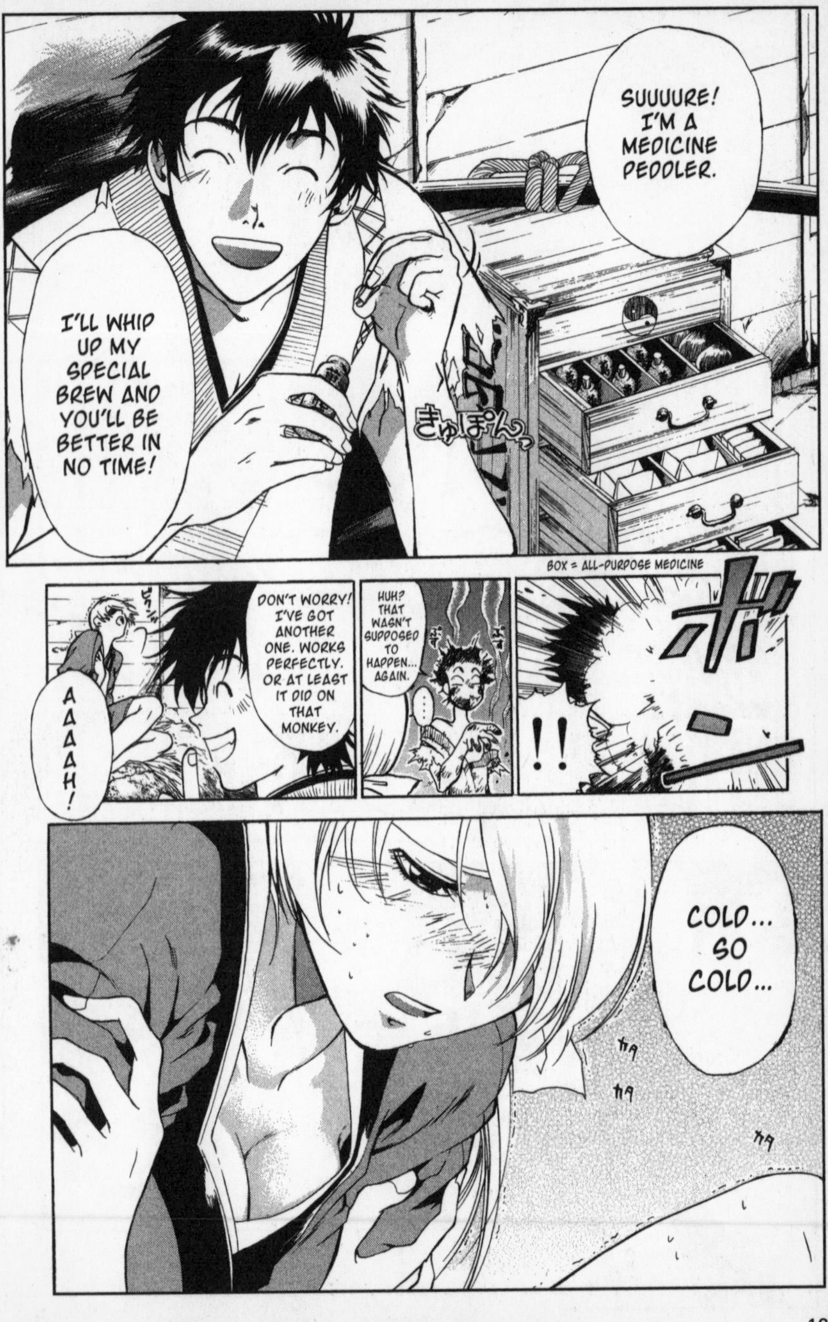

SUUUURE! I'M A MEDICINE PEDDLER.
I'LL WHIP UP MY SPECIAL BREW AND YOU'LL BE BETTER IN NO TIME!
きゅぽんっ
BOX = ALL-PURPOSE MEDICINE
!!
HUH? THAT WASN'T SUPPOSED TO HAPPEN... AGAIN.
...
DON'T WORRY! I'VE GOT ANOTHER ONE. WORKS PERFECTLY. OR AT LEAST IT DID ON THAT MONKEY.
AAAAAH!
COLD... SO COLD...

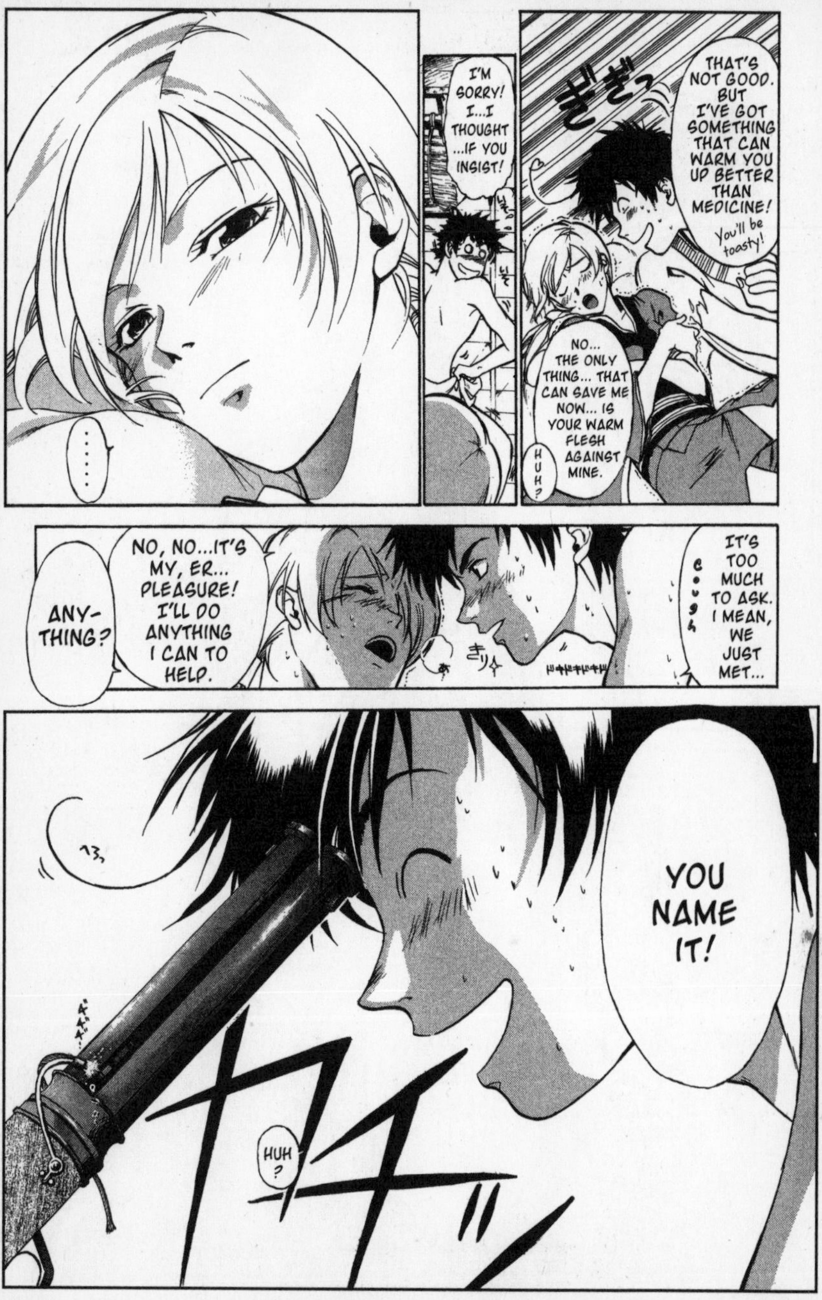
ぎぎっ
THAT'S NOT GOOD. BUT I'VE GOT SOMETHING THAT CAN WARM YOU UP BETTER THAN MEDICINE!
You'll be toasty!
NO... THE ONLY THING... THAT CAN SAVE ME NOW... IS YOUR WARM FLESH AGAINST MINE.
HUH?
I'M SORRY! I...I THOUGHT ...IF YOU INSIST!
......
IT'S TOO MUCH TO ASK. I MEAN, WE JUST MET...
cough
NO, NO...IT'S MY, ER... PLEASURE! I'LL DO ANYTHING I CAN TO HELP.
ANYTHING?
YOU NAME IT!
HUH?

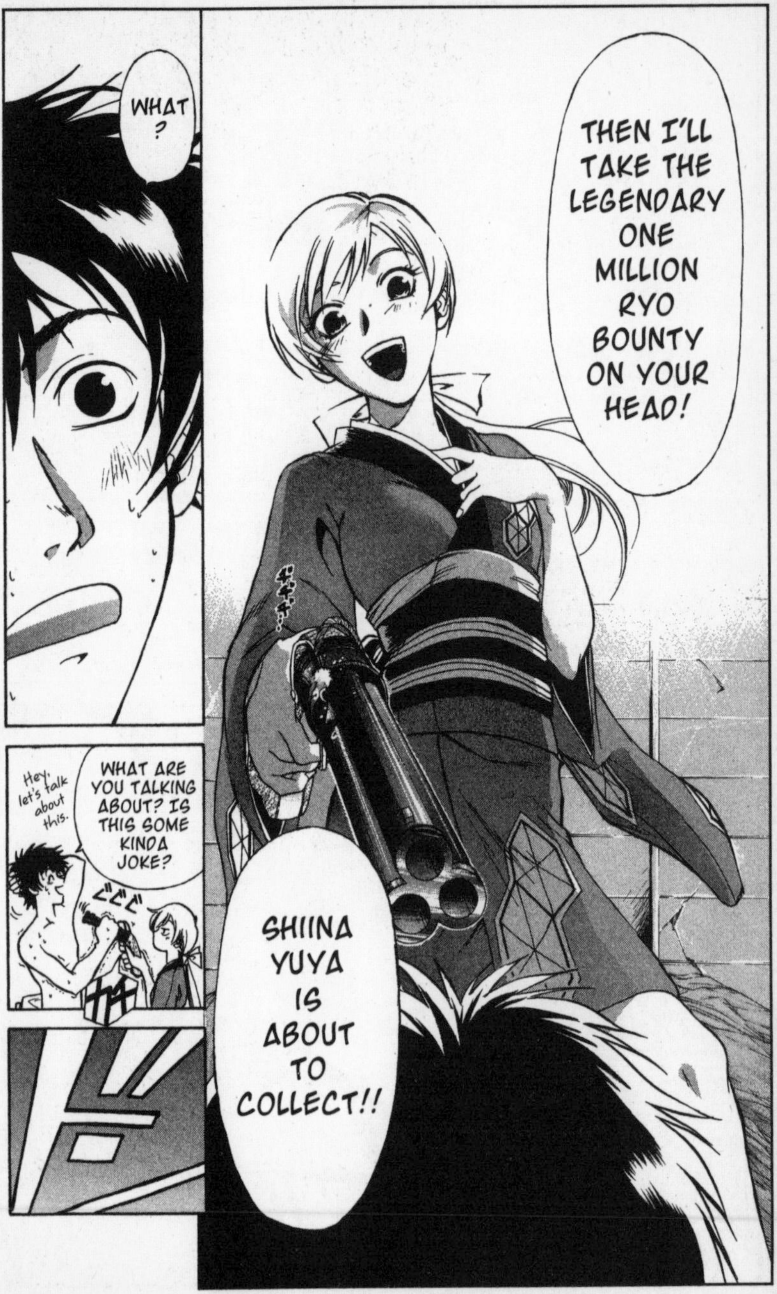
THEN I'LL TAKE THE LEGENDARY ONE MILLION RYO BOUNTY ON YOUR HEAD!
WHAT?
WHAT ARE YOU TALKING ABOUT? IS THIS SOME KINDA JOKE?
Hey, let's talk about this.
SHIINA YUYA IS ABOUT TO COLLECT!!

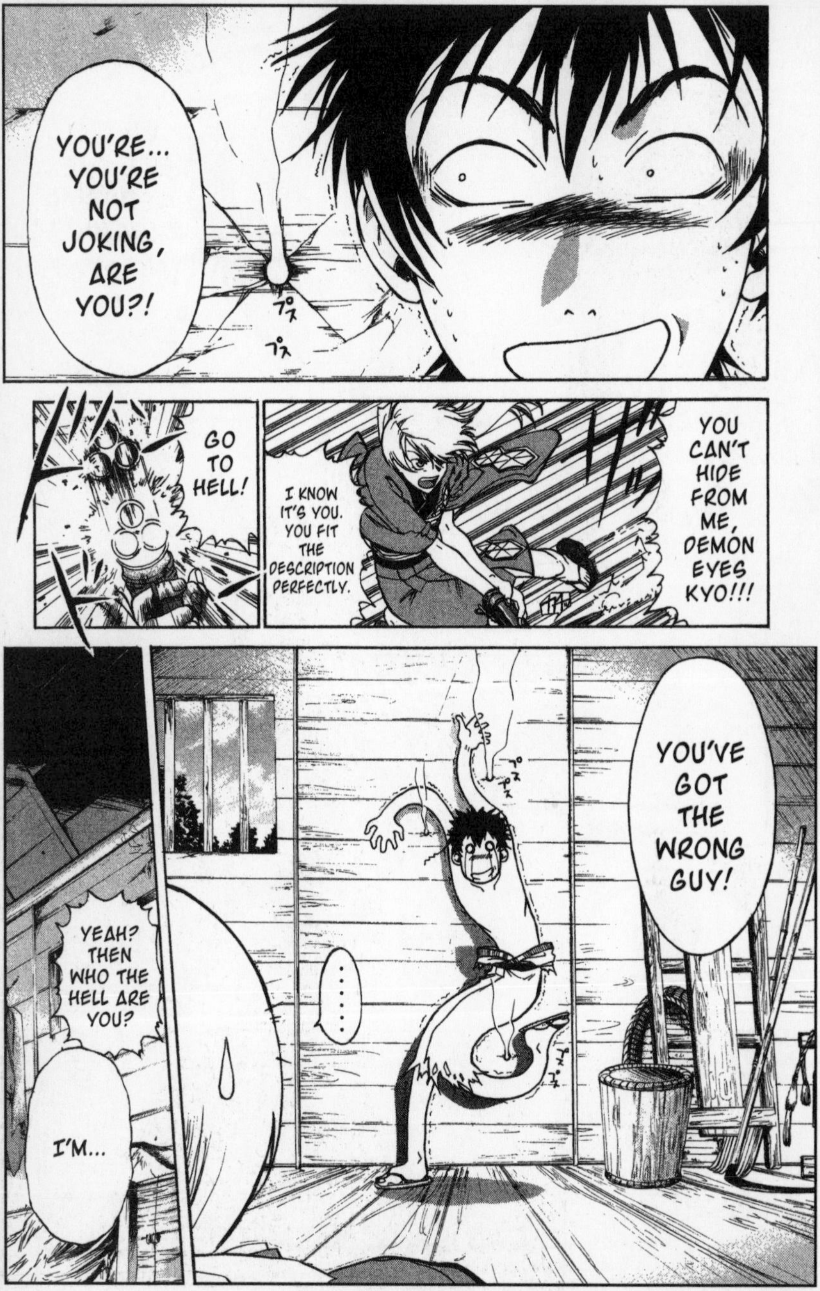
YOU'RE... YOU'RE NOT JOKING, ARE YOU?!
プス
プス
YOU CAN'T HIDE FROM ME, DEMON EYES KYO!!!
I KNOW IT'S YOU. YOU FIT THE DESCRIPTION PERFECTLY.
GO TO HELL!
YOU'VE GOT THE WRONG GUY!
......
YEAH? THEN WHO THE HELL ARE YOU?
I'M...

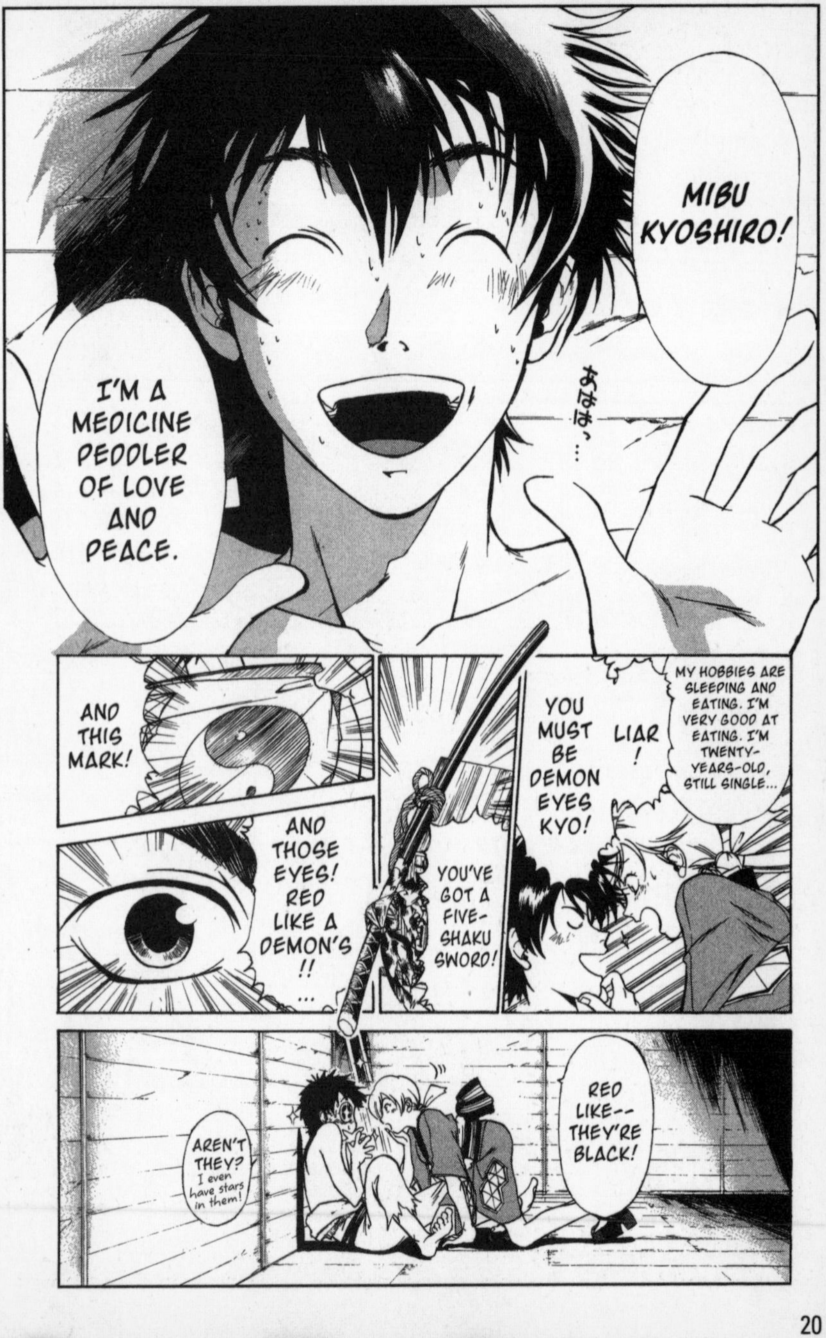
MIBU KYOSHIRO!
あはは…
I'M A MEDICINE PEDDLER OF LOVE AND PEACE.
MY HOBBIES ARE SLEEPING AND EATING. I'M VERY GOOD AT EATING. I'M TWENTY-YEARS-OLD, STILL SINGLE...
LIAR!
YOU MUST BE DEMON EYES KYO!
YOU'VE GOT A FIVE-SHAKU SWORD!
AND THIS MARK!
AND THOSE EYES! RED LIKE A DEMON'S!! ...
RED LIKE-- THEY'RE BLACK!
AREN'T THEY? I even have stars in them!

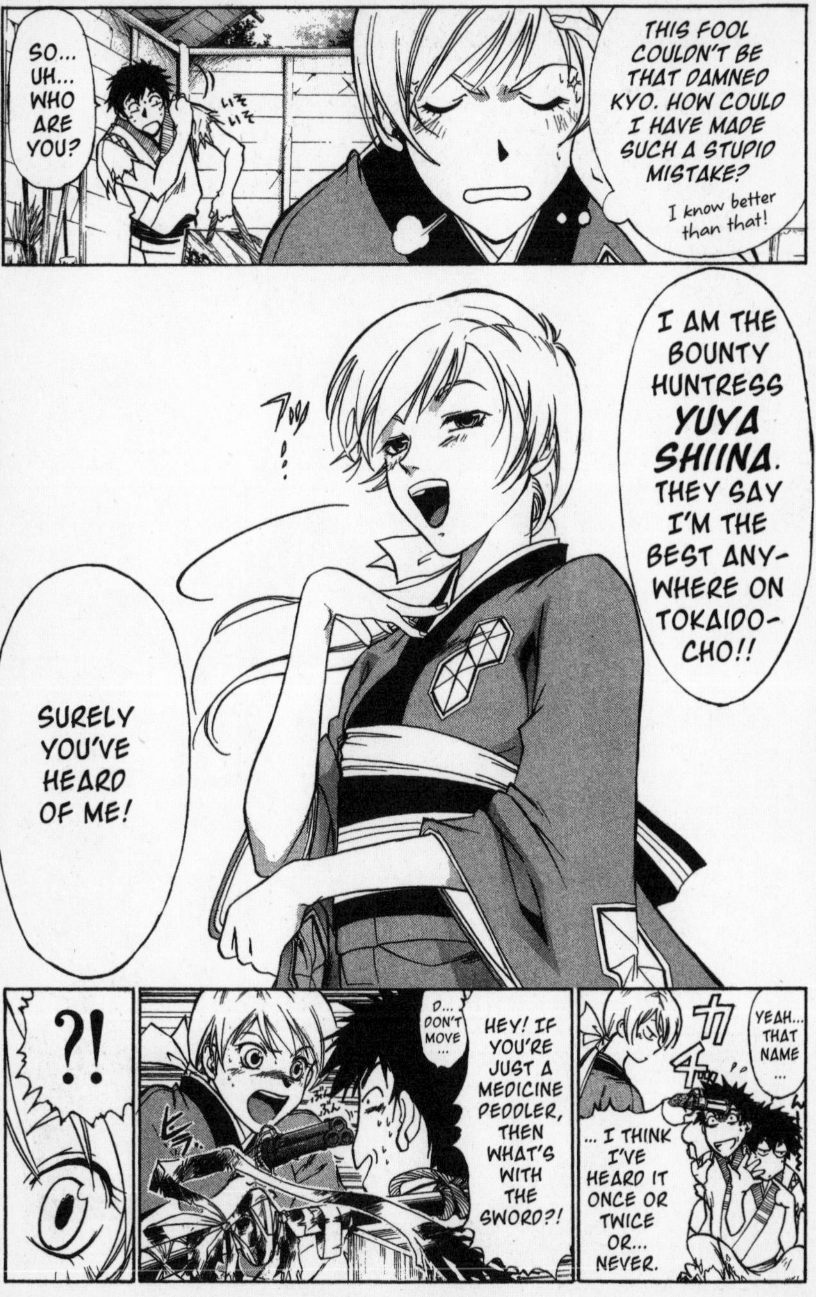
THIS FOOL COULDN'T BE THAT DAMNED KYO. HOW COULD I HAVE MADE SUCH A STUPID MISTAKE?
I know better than that!
SO... UH... WHO ARE YOU?
I AM THE BOUNTY HUNTRESS YUYA SHIINA. THEY SAY I'M THE BEST ANY-WHERE ON TOKAIDO-CHO!!
SURELY YOU'VE HEARD OF ME!
YEAH... THAT NAME ...
... I THINK I'VE HEARD IT ONCE OR TWICE OR... NEVER.
HEY! IF YOU'RE JUST A MEDICINE PEDDLER, THEN WHAT'S WITH THE SWORD?!
D... DON'T MOVE ...
?!

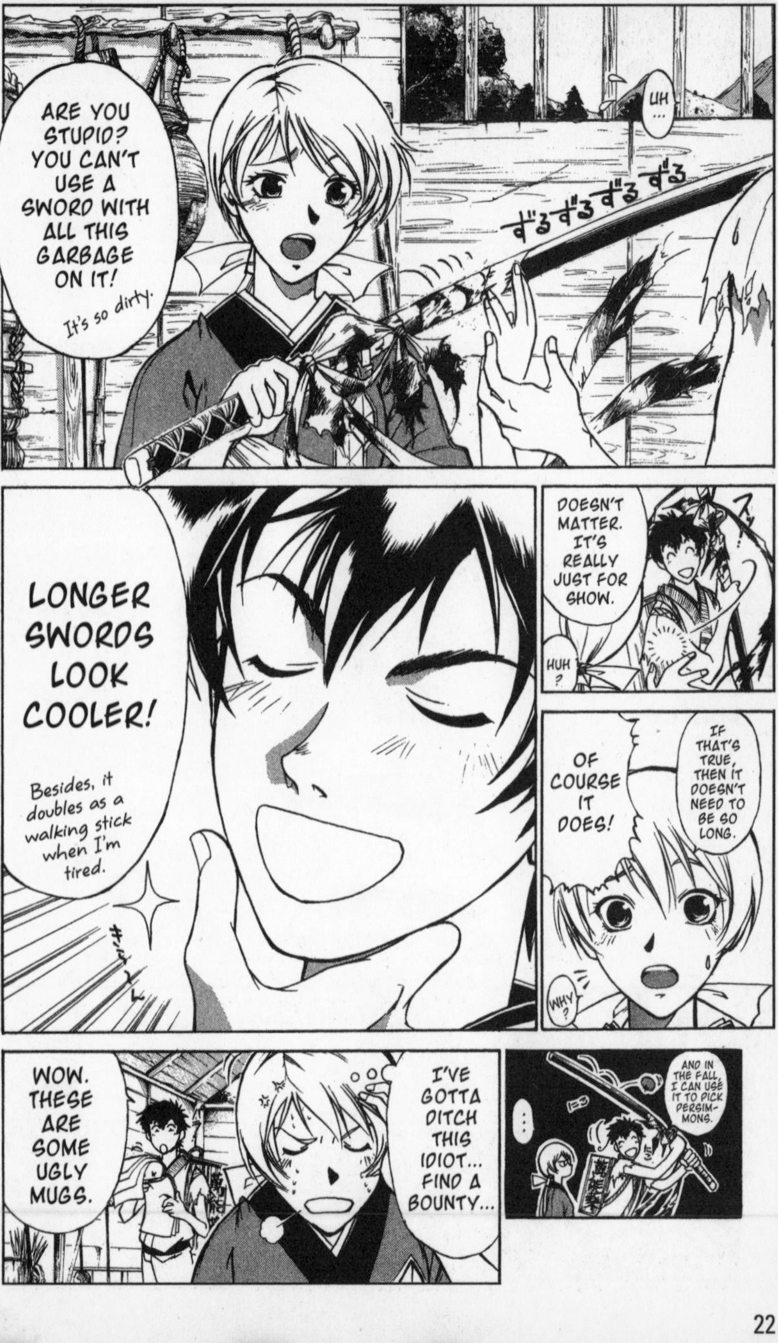
UH ...
ずるずるずるずる
ARE YOU STUPID? YOU CAN'T USE A SWORD WITH ALL THIS GARBAGE ON IT!
It's so dirty.
DOESN'T MATTER. IT'S REALLY JUST FOR SHOW.
HUH ?
IF THAT'S TRUE, THEN IT DOESN'T NEED TO BE SO LONG.
OF COURSE IT DOES!
WHY ?
LONGER SWORDS LOOK COOLER!
Besides, it doubles as a walking stick when I'm tired.
AND IN THE FALL, I CAN USE IT TO PICK PERSIMMONS.
...
I'VE GOTTA DITCH THIS IDIOT... FIND A BOUNTY...
WOW. THESE ARE SOME UGLY MUGS.

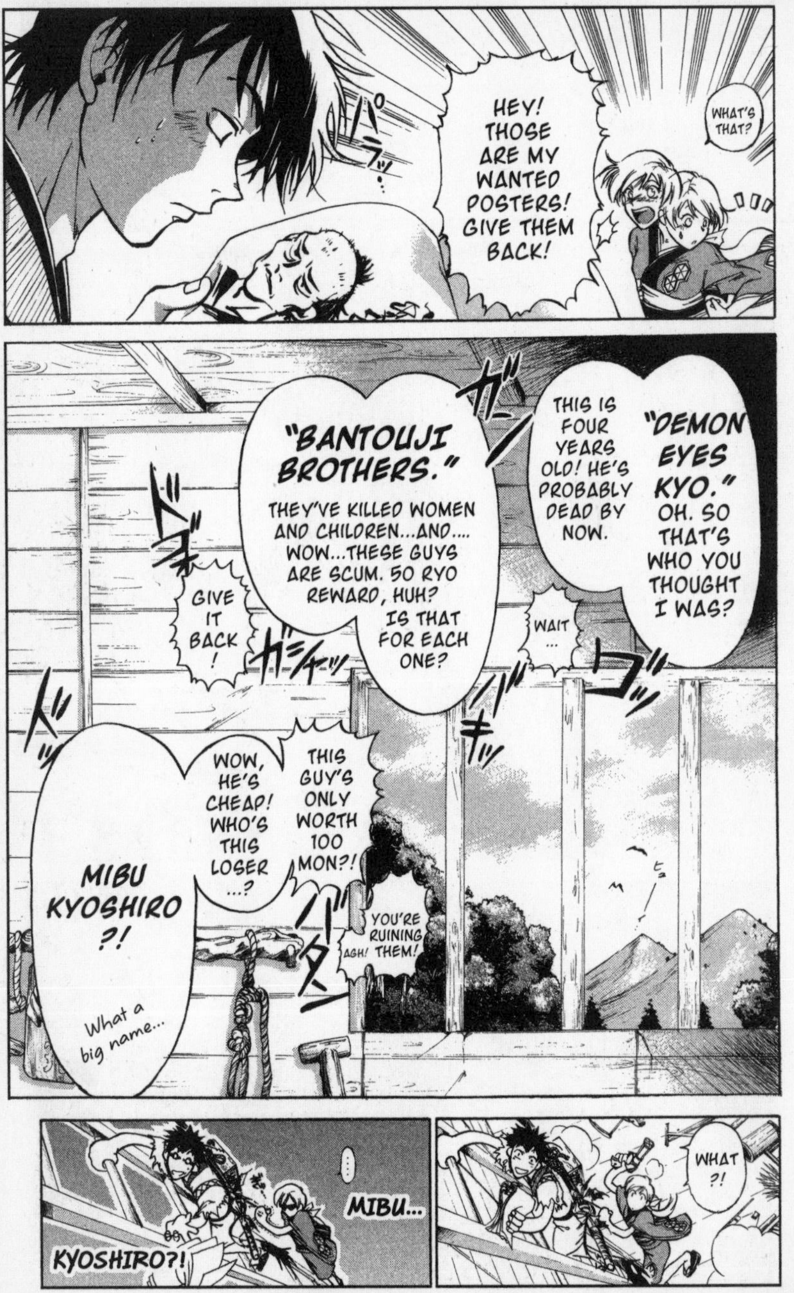
WHAT'S THAT?
HEY! THOSE ARE MY WANTED POSTERS! GIVE THEM BACK!
"DEMON EYES KYO." OH. SO THAT'S WHO YOU THOUGHT I WAS?
THIS IS FOUR YEARS OLD! HE'S PROBABLY DEAD BY NOW.
WAIT...
"BANTOUJI BROTHERS."
THEY'VE KILLED WOMEN AND CHILDREN...AND.... WOW...THESE GUYS ARE SCUM. 50 RYO REWARD, HUH?
IS THAT FOR EACH ONE?
GIVE IT BACK!
THIS GUY'S ONLY WORTH 100 MON?!
WOW, HE'S CHEAP! WHO'S THIS LOSER ...?
YOU'RE RUINING THEM!
AGH!
MIBU KYOSHIRO ?!
What a big name...
WHAT ?!
...
MIBU...
KYOSHIRO?!

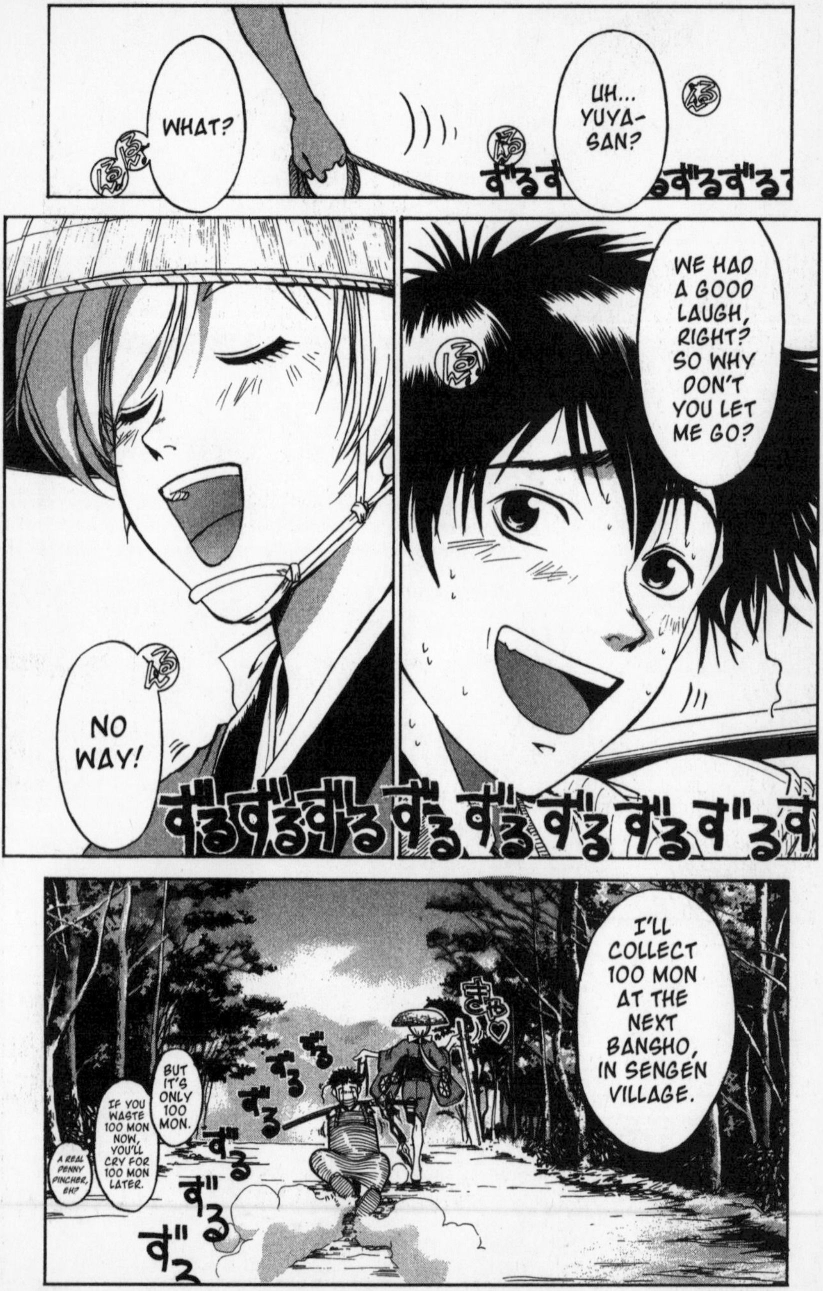
UH... YUYA-SAN?
WHAT?
WE HAD A GOOD LAUGH, RIGHT? SO WHY DON'T YOU LET ME GO?
NO WAY!
I'LL COLLECT 100 MON AT THE NEXT BANSHO, IN SENGEN VILLAGE.
BUT IT'S ONLY 100 MON.
IF YOU WASTE 100 MON NOW, YOU'LL CRY FOR 100 MON LATER.
A REAL PENNY PINCHER, EH?

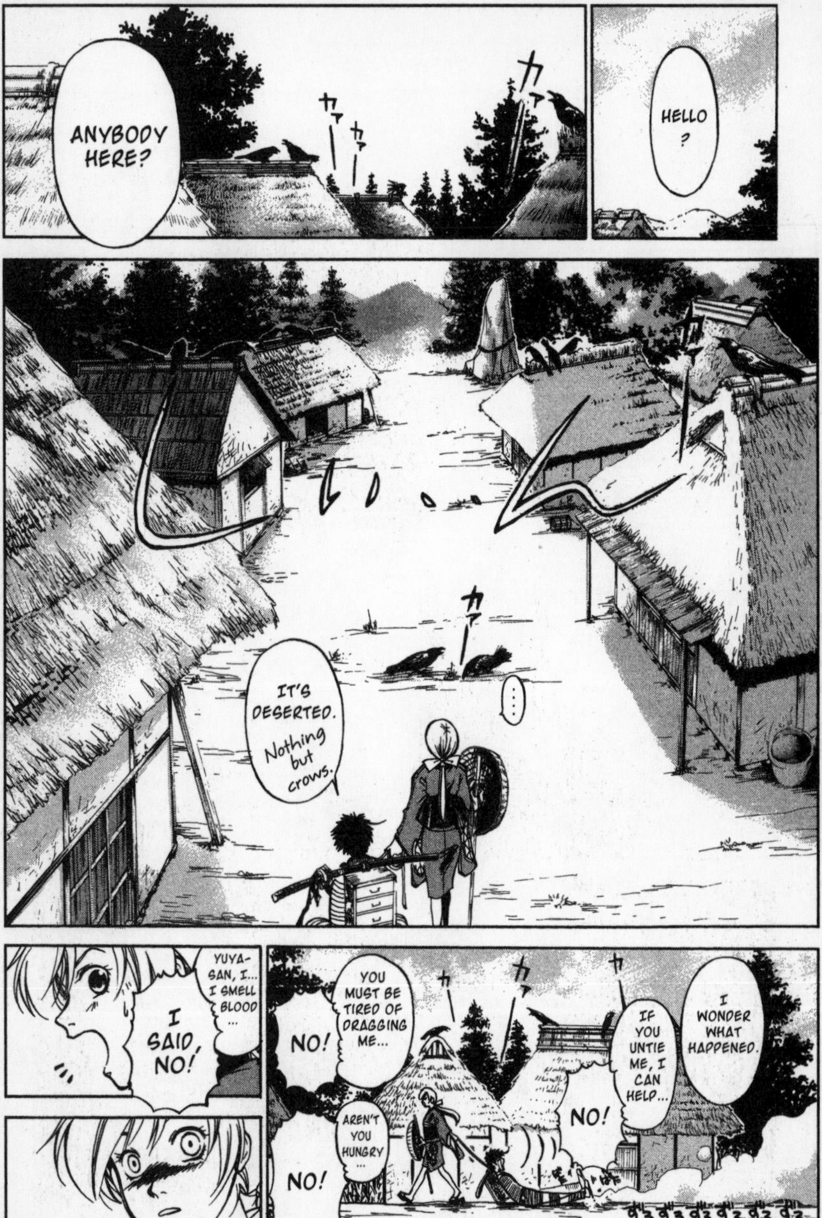
HELLO ?
カァー
カァー
カァー
ANYBODY HERE?
カァー
IT'S DESERTED. Nothing but crows.
...
I WONDER WHAT HAPPENED.
IF YOU UNTIE ME, I CAN HELP...
NO!
YOU MUST BE TIRED OF DRAGGING ME...
NO!
AREN'T YOU HUNGRY...
NO!
ずるずるずるずるずるずる
YUYA-SAN, I... I SMELL BLOOD...
I SAID, NO!

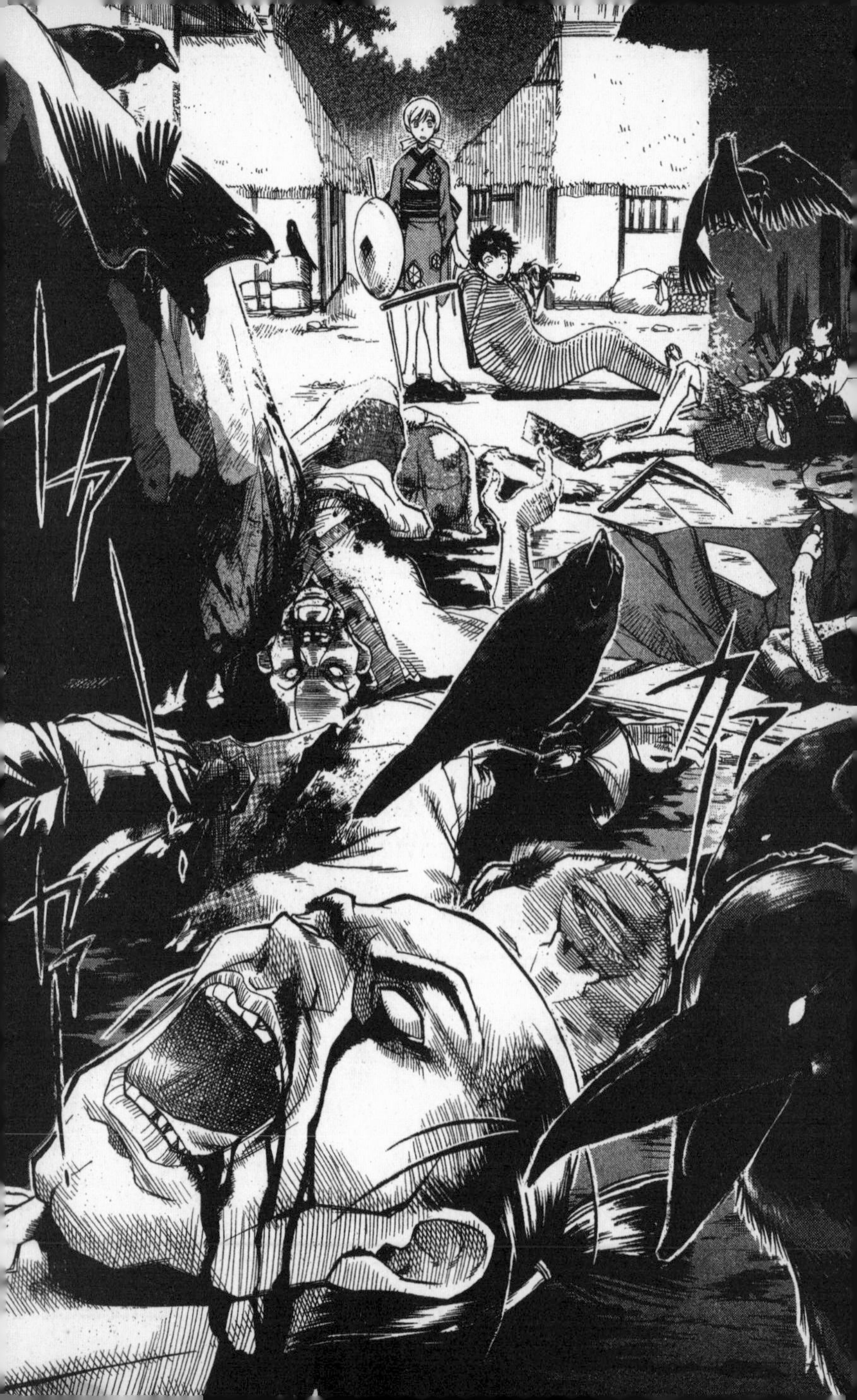

カァ
カァ
カァ

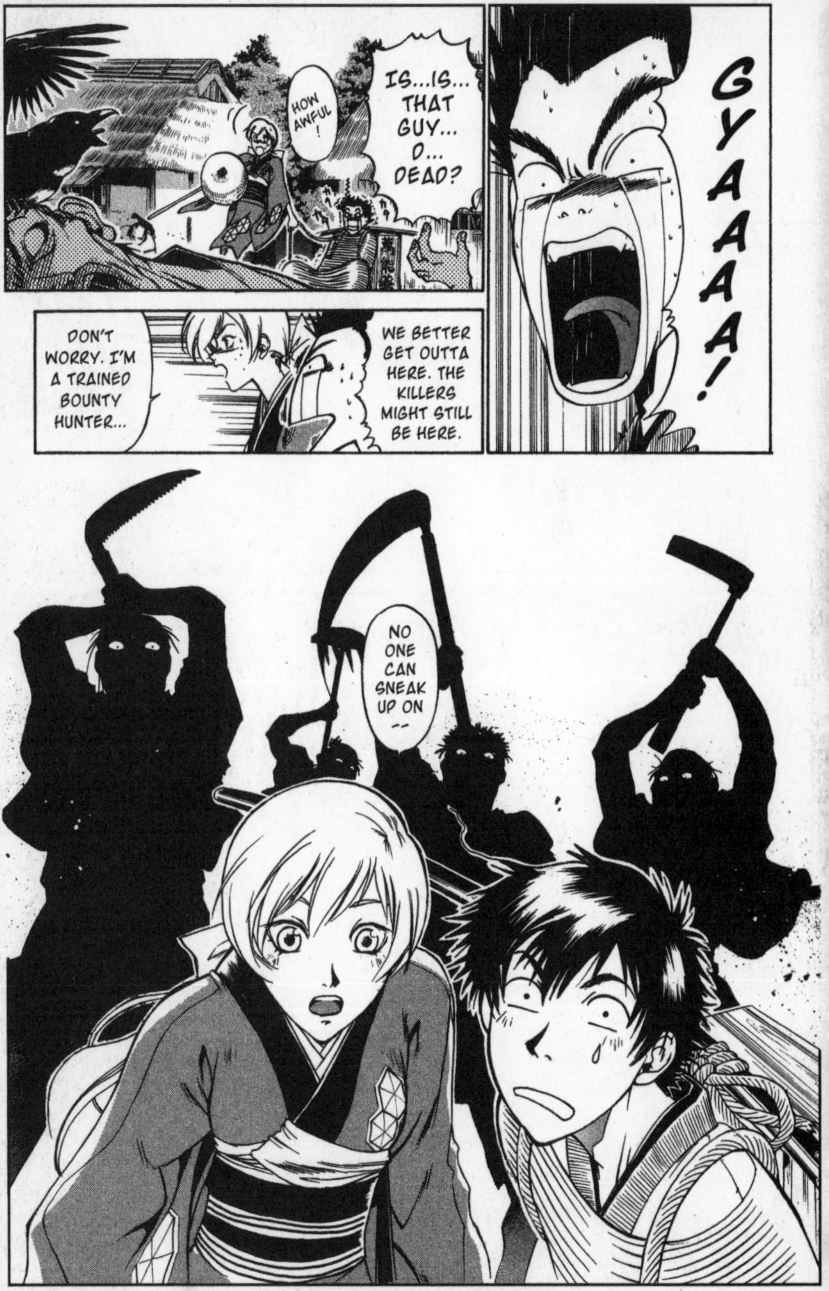
GYAAAAA!
IS...IS... THAT GUY... D... DEAD?
HOW AWFUL!
WE BETTER GET OUTTA HERE. THE KILLERS MIGHT STILL BE HERE.
DON'T WORRY. I'M A TRAINED BOUNTY HUNTER...
NO ONE CAN SNEAK UP ON --

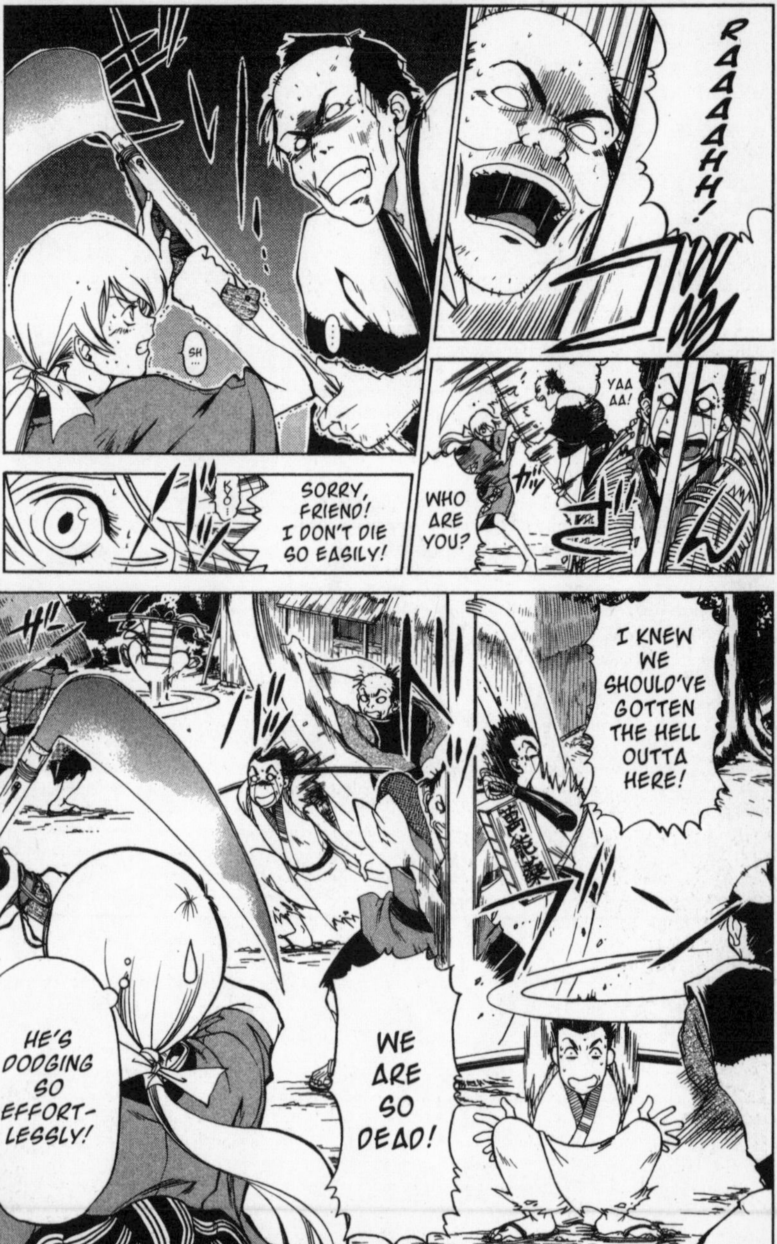
RAAAAAHH!
SH...
...
YAA AA!
WHO ARE YOU?
SORRY, FRIEND! I DON'T DIE SO EASILY!
I KNEW WE SHOULD'VE GOTTEN THE HELL OUTTA HERE!
WE ARE SO DEAD!
HE'S DODGING SO EFFORTLESSLY!

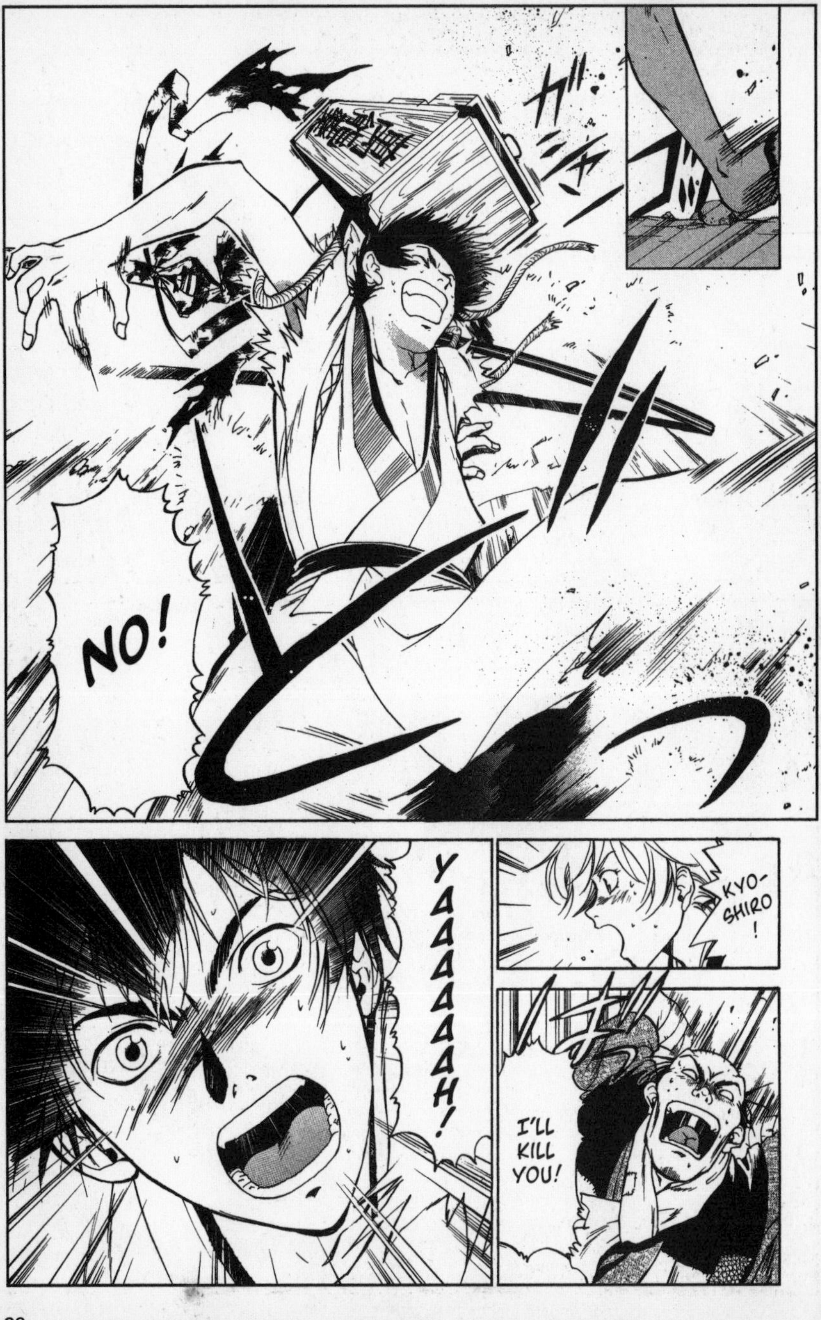
NO!
KYO-SHIRO!
I'LL KILL YOU!
YAAAAAAH!

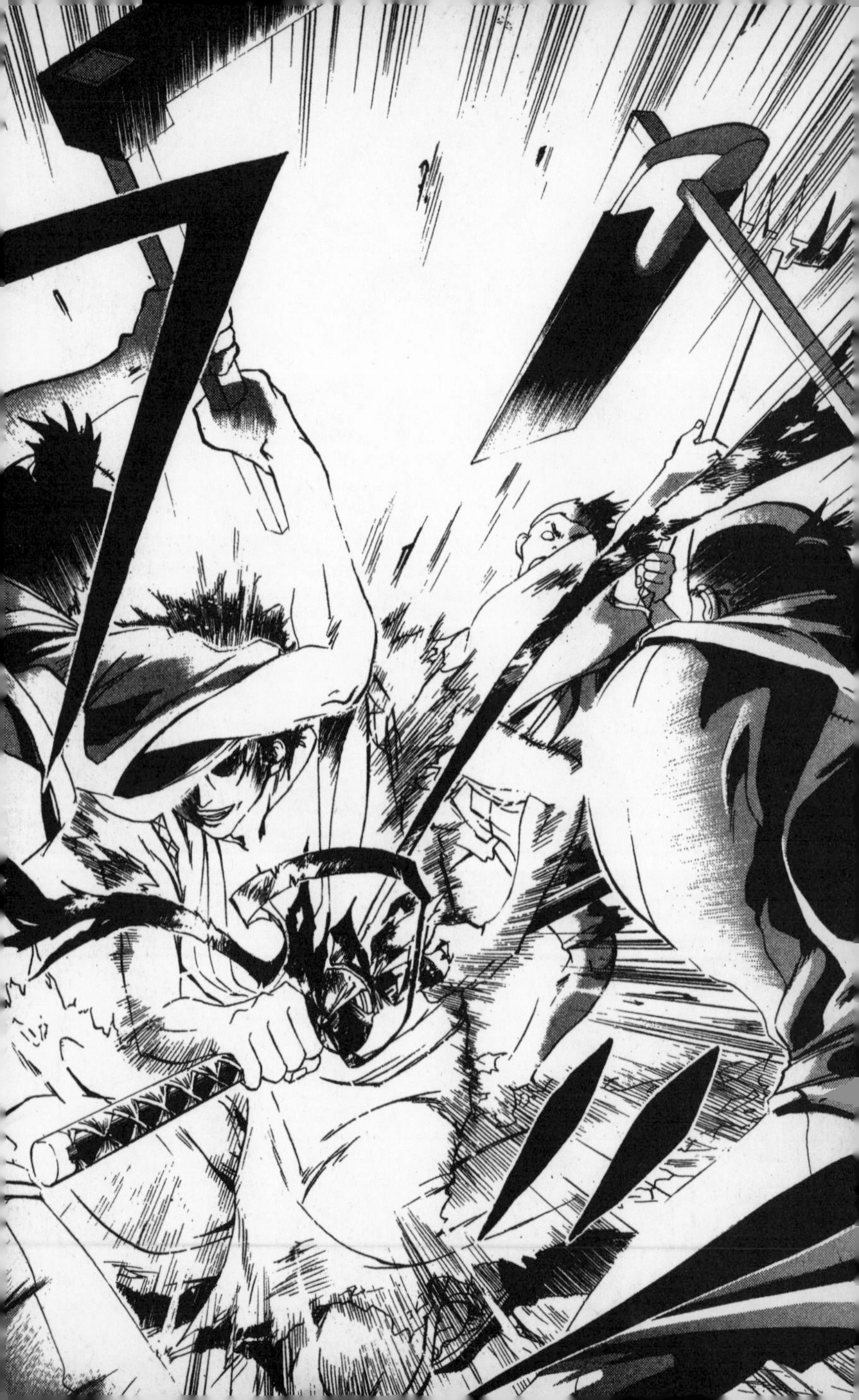

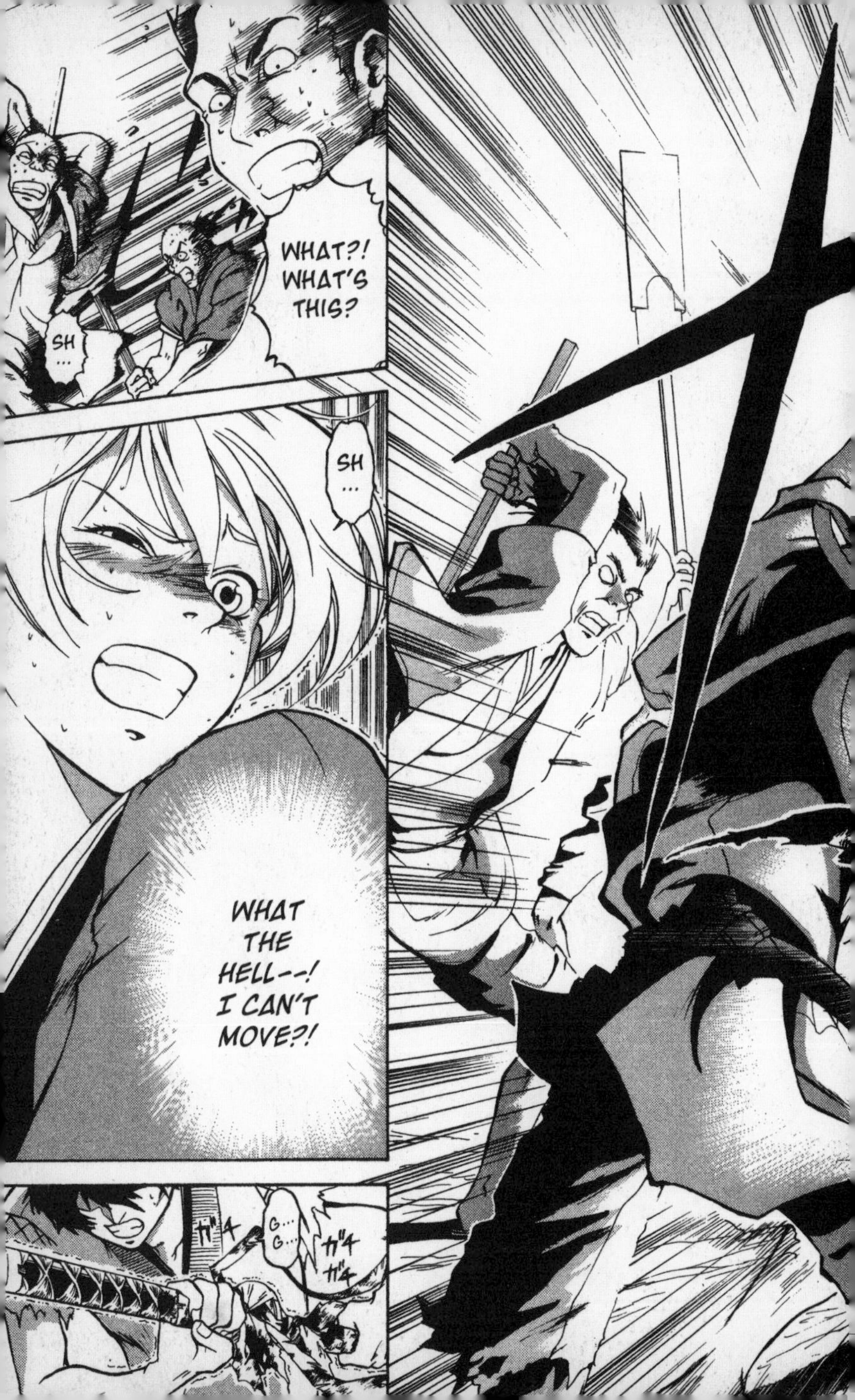
WHAT?! WHAT'S THIS?
SH ...
SH ...
WHAT THE HELL--! I CAN'T MOVE?!
G... G...

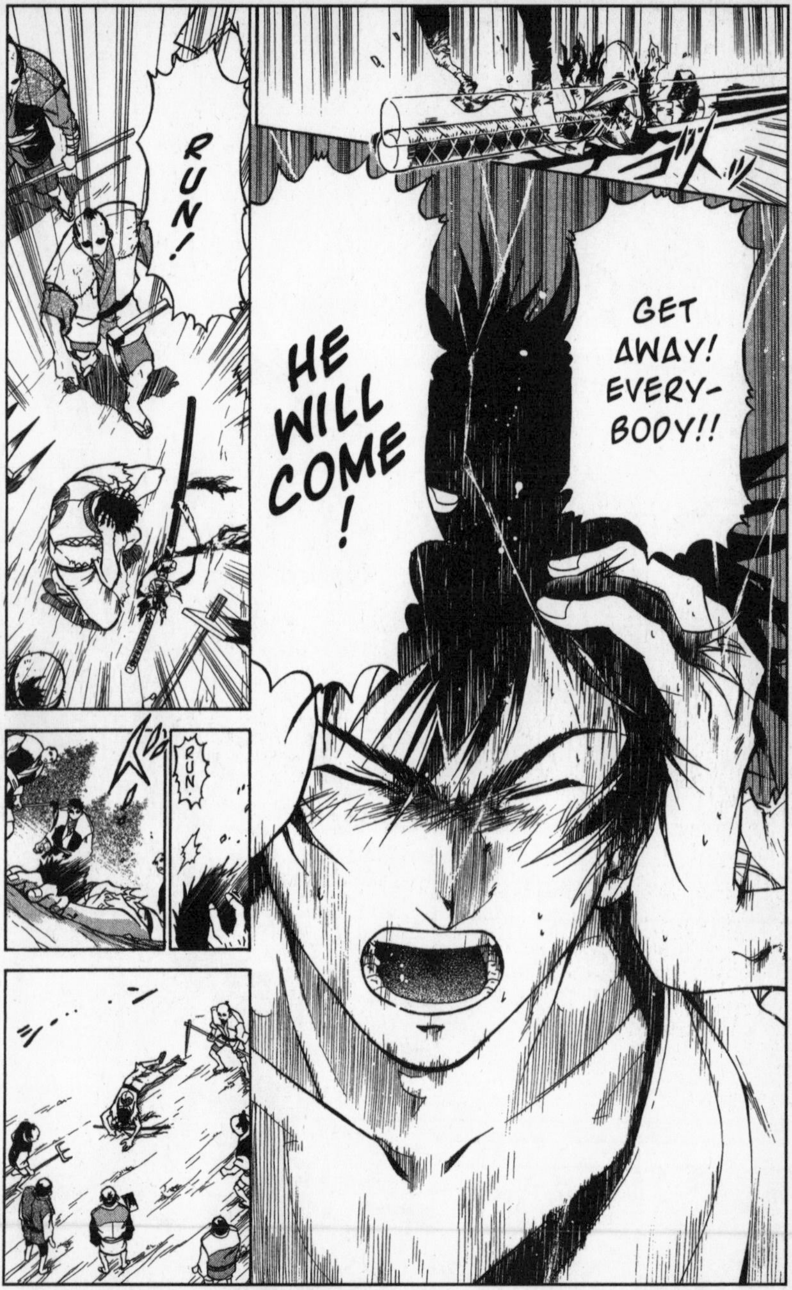
GET AWAY! EVERYBODY!!
HE WILL COME!
RUN!
RUN.

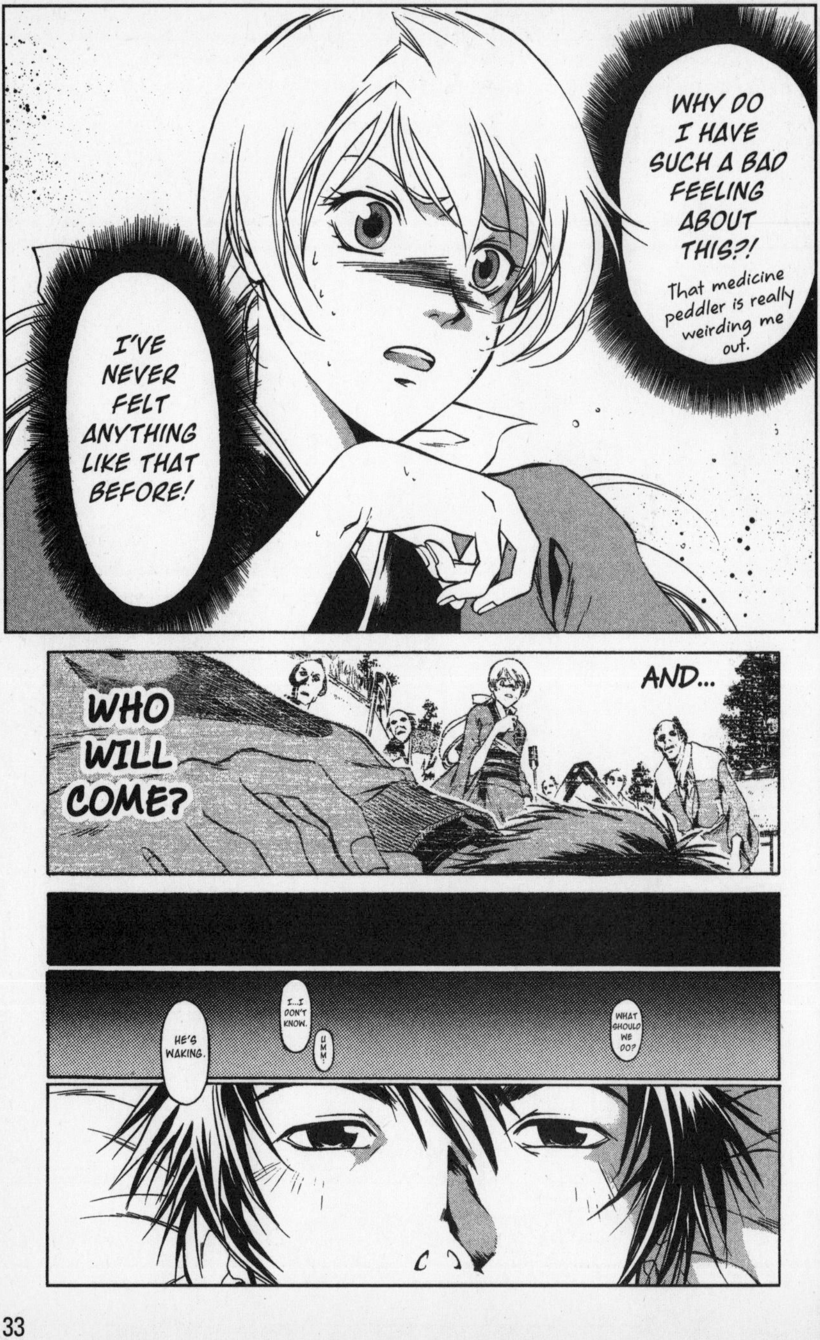
WHY DO I HAVE SUCH A BAD FEELING ABOUT THIS?!
That medicine peddler is really weirding me out.
I'VE NEVER FELT ANYTHING LIKE THAT BEFORE!
AND...
WHO WILL COME?
WHAT SHOULD WE DO?
UMM...
I...I DON'T KNOW.
HE'S WAKING.

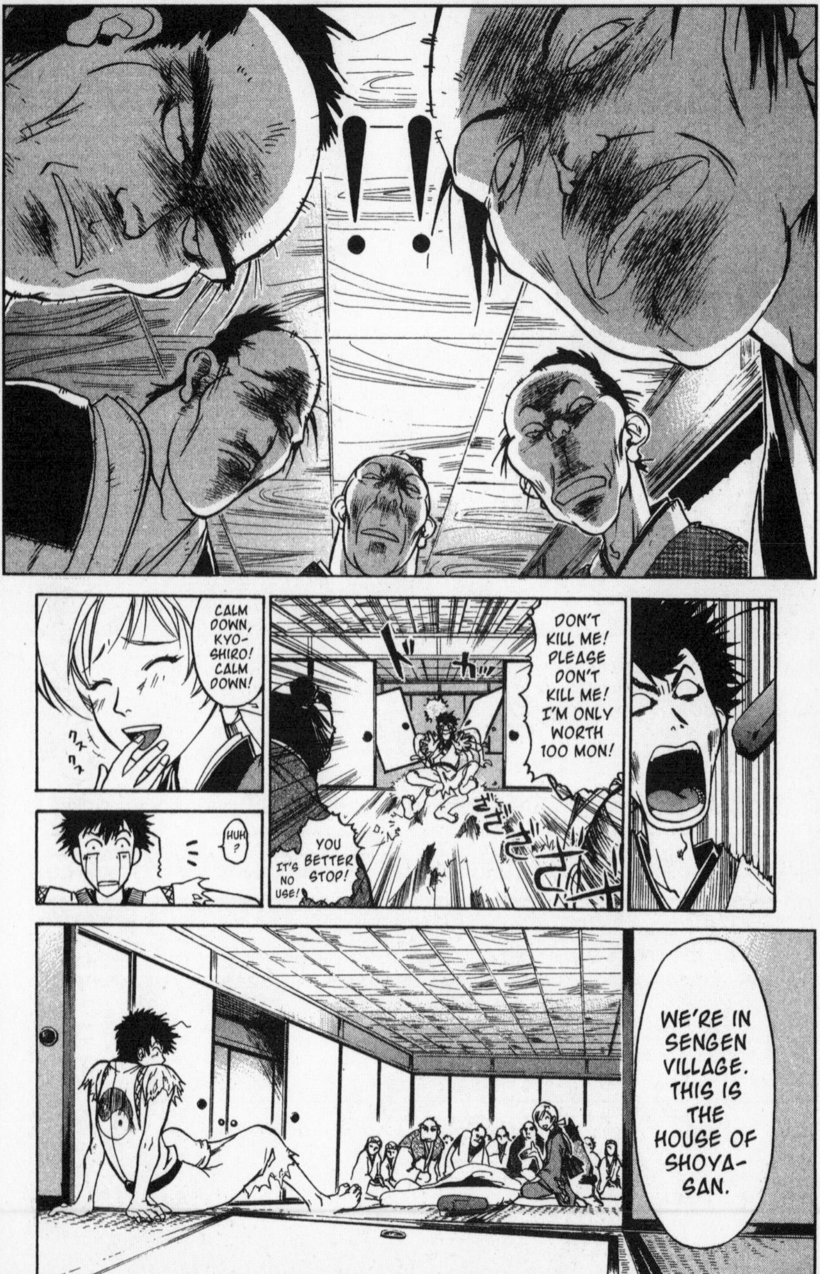
!!
DON'T KILL ME! PLEASE DON'T KILL ME! I'M ONLY WORTH 100 MON!
YOU BETTER STOP!
IT'S NO USE!
CALM DOWN, KYO-SHIRO! CALM DOWN!
HUH?
WE'RE IN SENGEN VILLAGE. THIS IS THE HOUSE OF SHOYA-SAN.

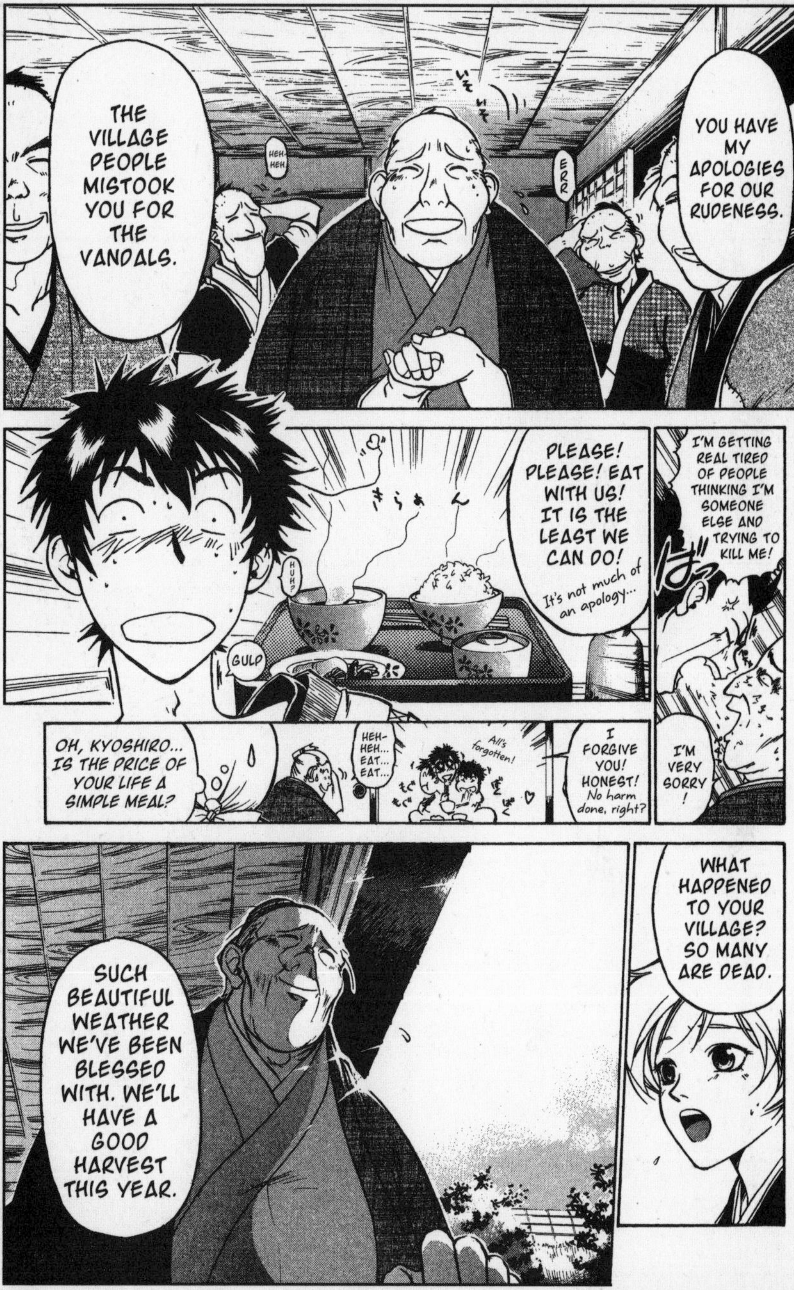
YOU HAVE MY APOLOGIES FOR OUR RUDENESS.
ERR
HEH-HEH
THE VILLAGE PEOPLE MISTOOK YOU FOR THE VANDALS.
I'M GETTING REAL TIRED OF PEOPLE THINKING I'M SOMEONE ELSE AND TRYING TO KILL ME!
I'M VERY SORRY!
PLEASE! PLEASE! EAT WITH US! IT IS THE LEAST WE CAN DO!
It's not much of an apology...
HUH?
GULP
I FORGIVE YOU! HONEST! No harm done, right?
All's forgotten!
HEH-HEH... EAT... EAT...
OH, KYOSHIRO... IS THE PRICE OF YOUR LIFE A SIMPLE MEAL?
WHAT HAPPENED TO YOUR VILLAGE? SO MANY ARE DEAD.
SUCH BEAUTIFUL WEATHER WE'VE BEEN BLESSED WITH. WE'LL HAVE A GOOD HARVEST THIS YEAR.

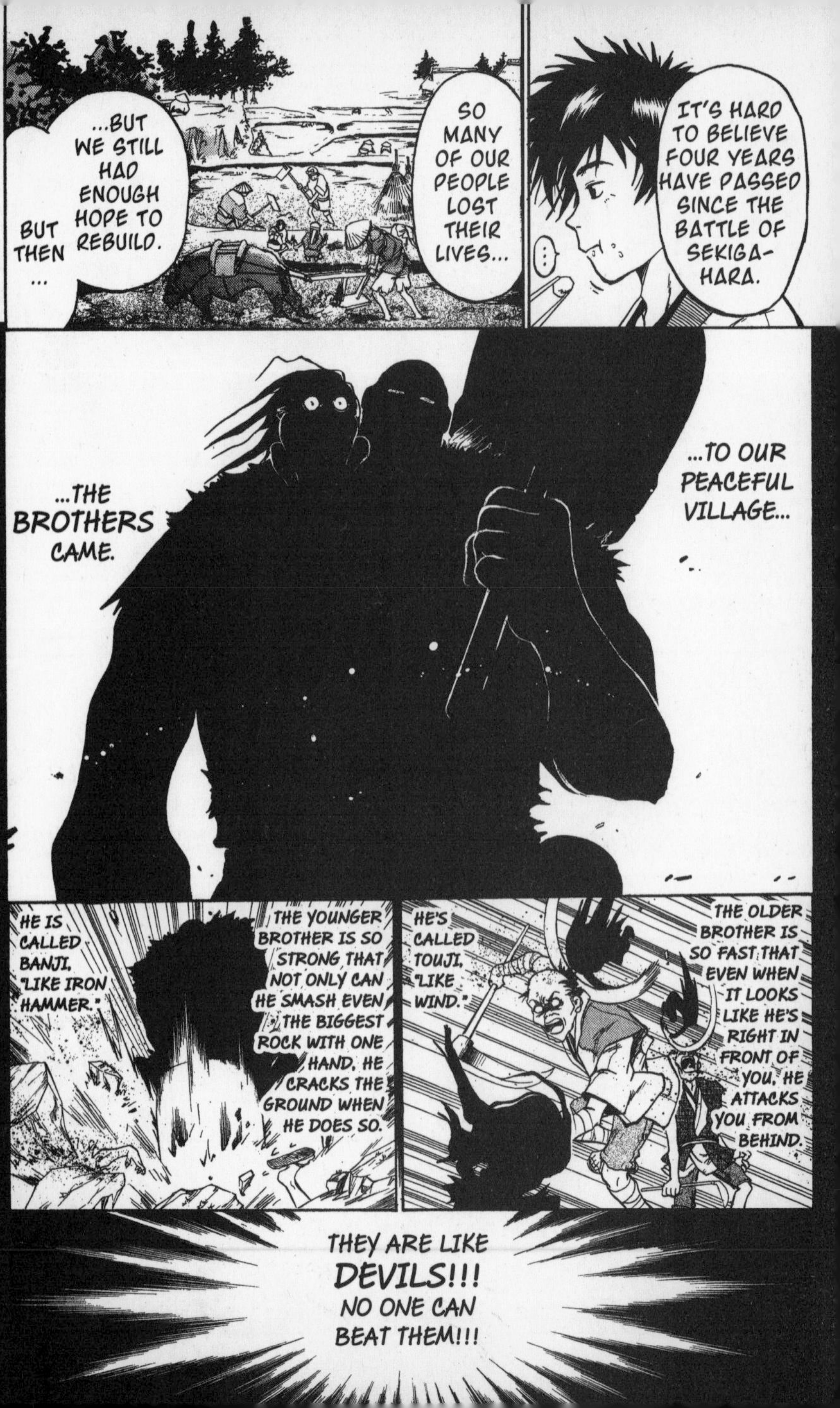
IT'S HARD TO BELIEVE FOUR YEARS HAVE PASSED SINCE THE BATTLE OF SEKIGA-HARA.
...
SO MANY OF OUR PEOPLE LOST THEIR LIVES...
...BUT WE STILL HAD ENOUGH HOPE TO REBUILD.
BUT THEN ...
...TO OUR PEACEFUL VILLAGE...
...THE BROTHERS CAME.
THE OLDER BROTHER IS SO FAST THAT EVEN WHEN IT LOOKS LIKE HE'S RIGHT IN FRONT OF YOU, HE ATTACKS YOU FROM BEHIND.
HE'S CALLED TOUJI, "LIKE WIND."
THE YOUNGER BROTHER IS SO STRONG THAT NOT ONLY CAN HE SMASH EVEN THE BIGGEST ROCK WITH ONE HAND, HE CRACKS THE GROUND WHEN HE DOES SO.
HE IS CALLED BANJI, "LIKE IRON HAMMER."
THEY ARE LIKE DEVILS!!! NO ONE CAN BEAT THEM!!!

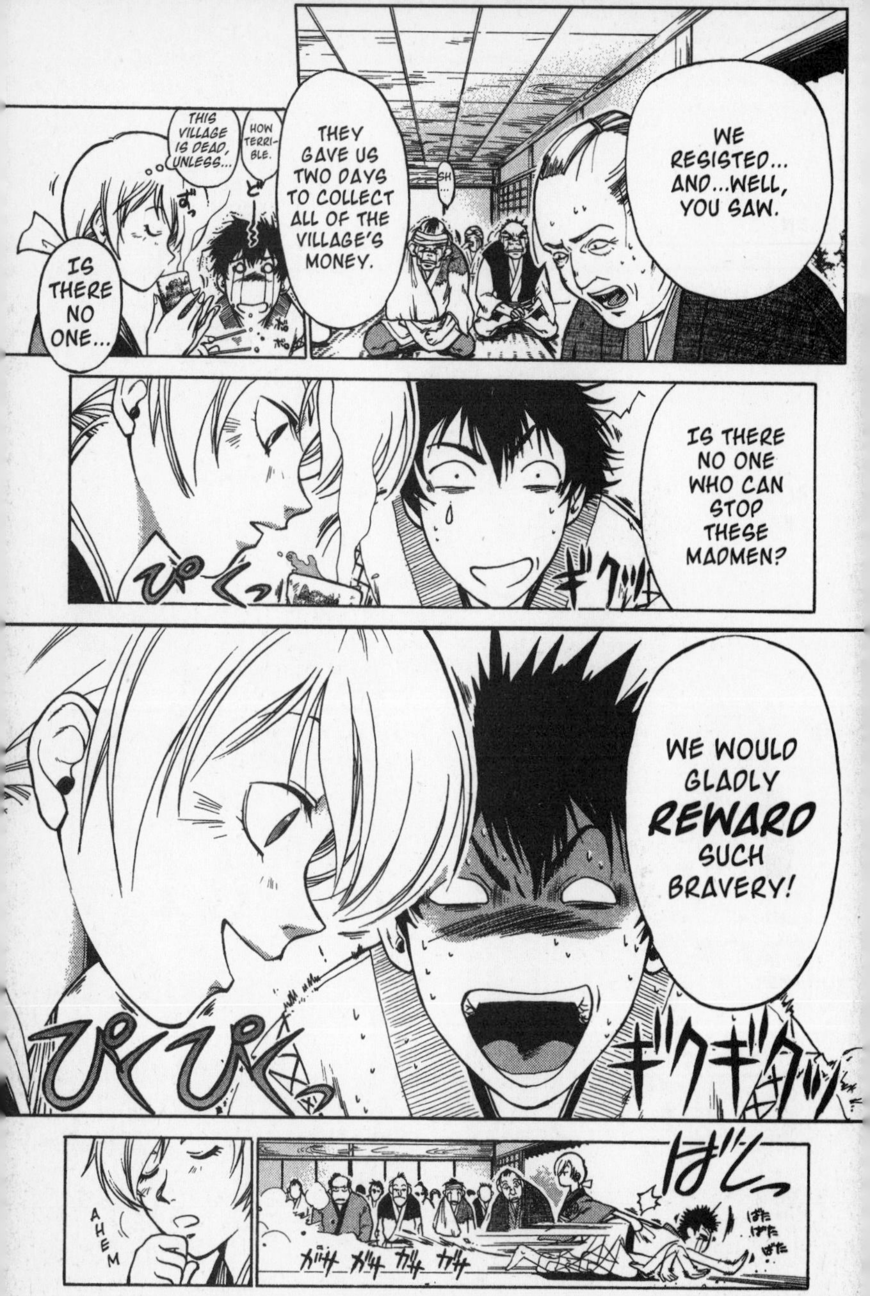
WE RESISTED... AND...WELL, YOU SAW.
SH...
THEY GAVE US TWO DAYS TO COLLECT ALL OF THE VILLAGE'S MONEY.
HOW TERRIBLE.
THIS VILLAGE IS DEAD, UNLESS...
IS THERE NO ONE...
IS THERE NO ONE WHO CAN STOP THESE MADMEN?
WE WOULD GLADLY REWARD SUCH BRAVERY!
AHEM

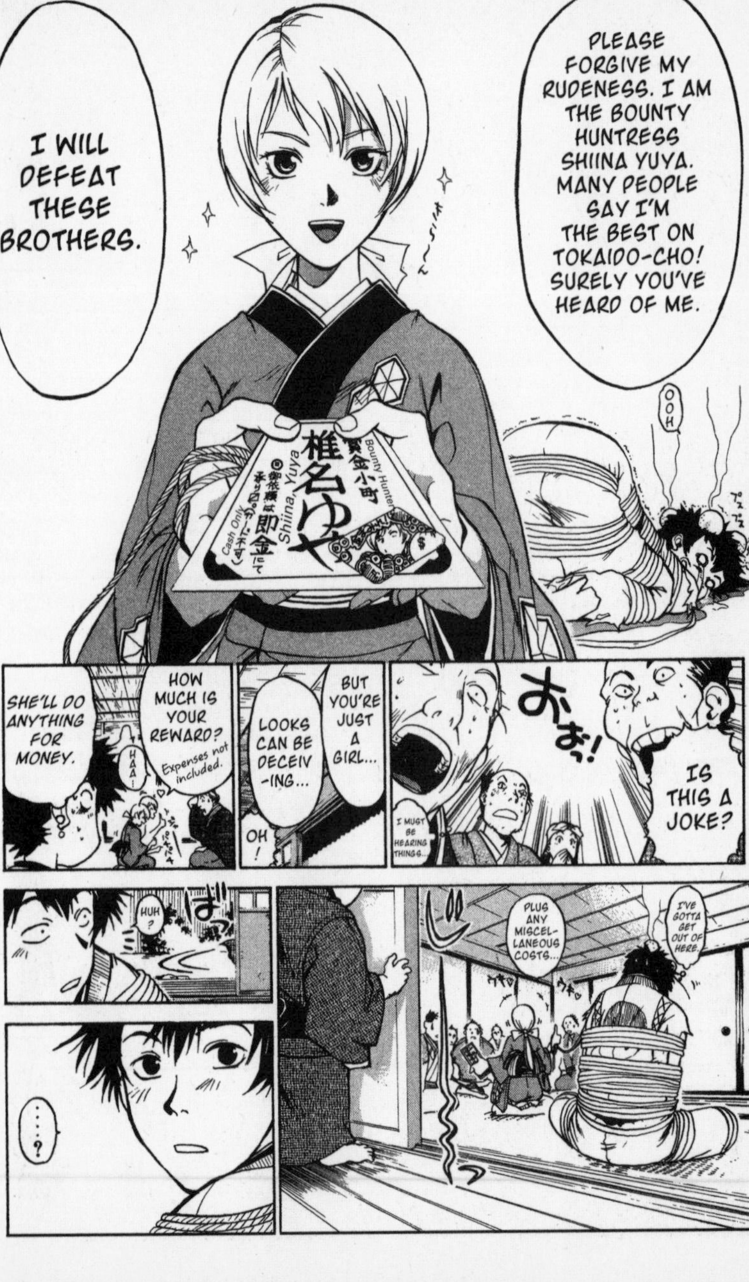
PLEASE FORGIVE MY RUDENESS. I AM THE BOUNTY HUNTRESS SHIINA YUYA. MANY PEOPLE SAY I'M THE BEST ON TOKAIDO-CHO! SURELY YOU'VE HEARD OF ME.
I WILL DEFEAT THESE BROTHERS.
OOH
賞金小町
Bounty Hunter
椎名ゆや
Shiina, Yuya
御依頼は即金にて承ります
Cash Only
おおっ!
IS THIS A JOKE?
I MUST BE HEARING THINGS...
BUT YOU'RE JUST A GIRL...
LOOKS CAN BE DECEIV-ING...
OH!
HOW MUCH IS YOUR REWARD?
Expenses not included.
SHE'LL DO ANYTHING FOR MONEY.
HAA...
I'VE GOTTA GET OUT OF HERE.
PLUS ANY MISCEL-LANEOUS COSTS...
HUH?
....?

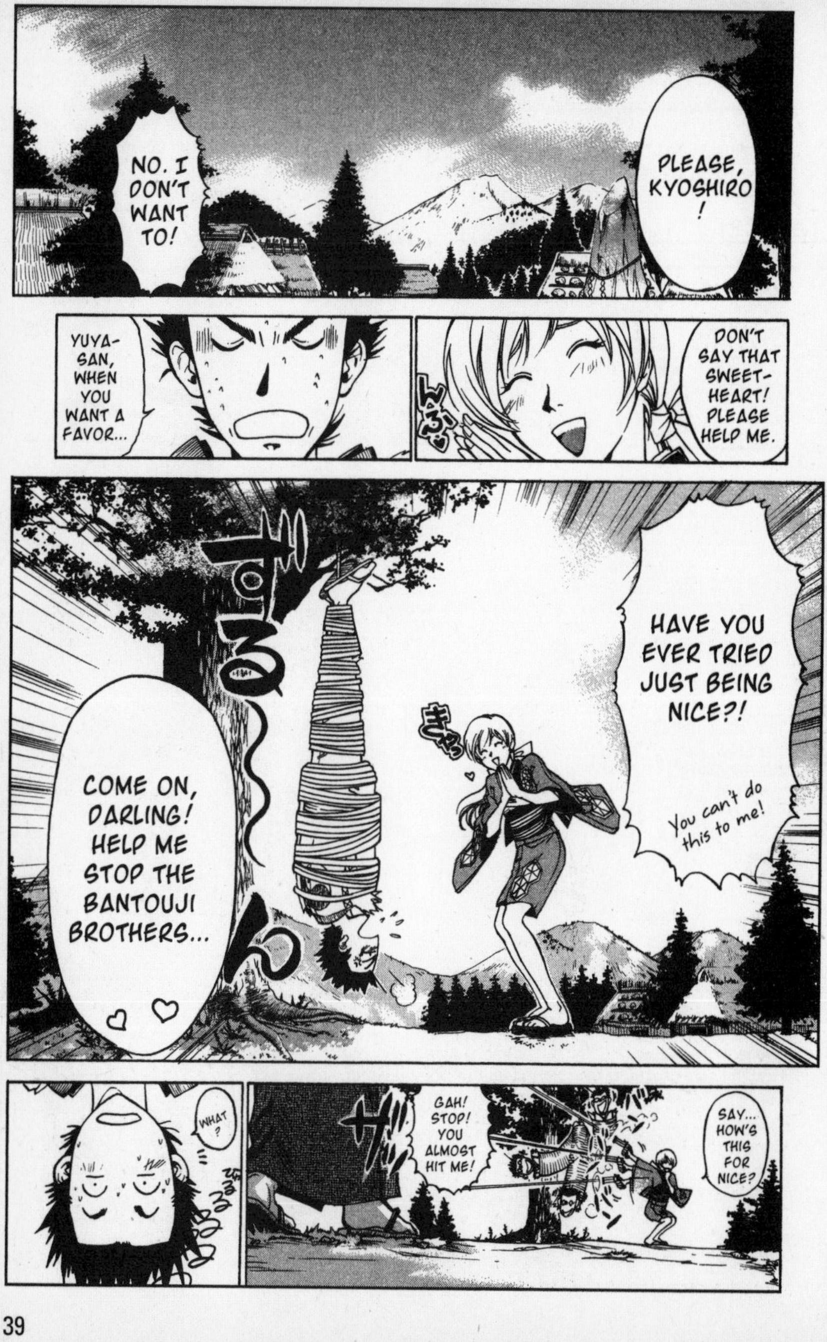
PLEASE, KYOSHIRO!
NO. I DON'T WANT TO!
DON'T SAY THAT SWEET-HEART! PLEASE HELP ME.
YUYA-SAN, WHEN YOU WANT A FAVOR...
HAVE YOU EVER TRIED JUST BEING NICE?!
You can't do this to me!
COME ON, DARLING! HELP ME STOP THE BANTOUJI BROTHERS...
SAY... HOW'S THIS FOR NICE?
GAH! STOP! YOU ALMOST HIT ME!
WHAT?

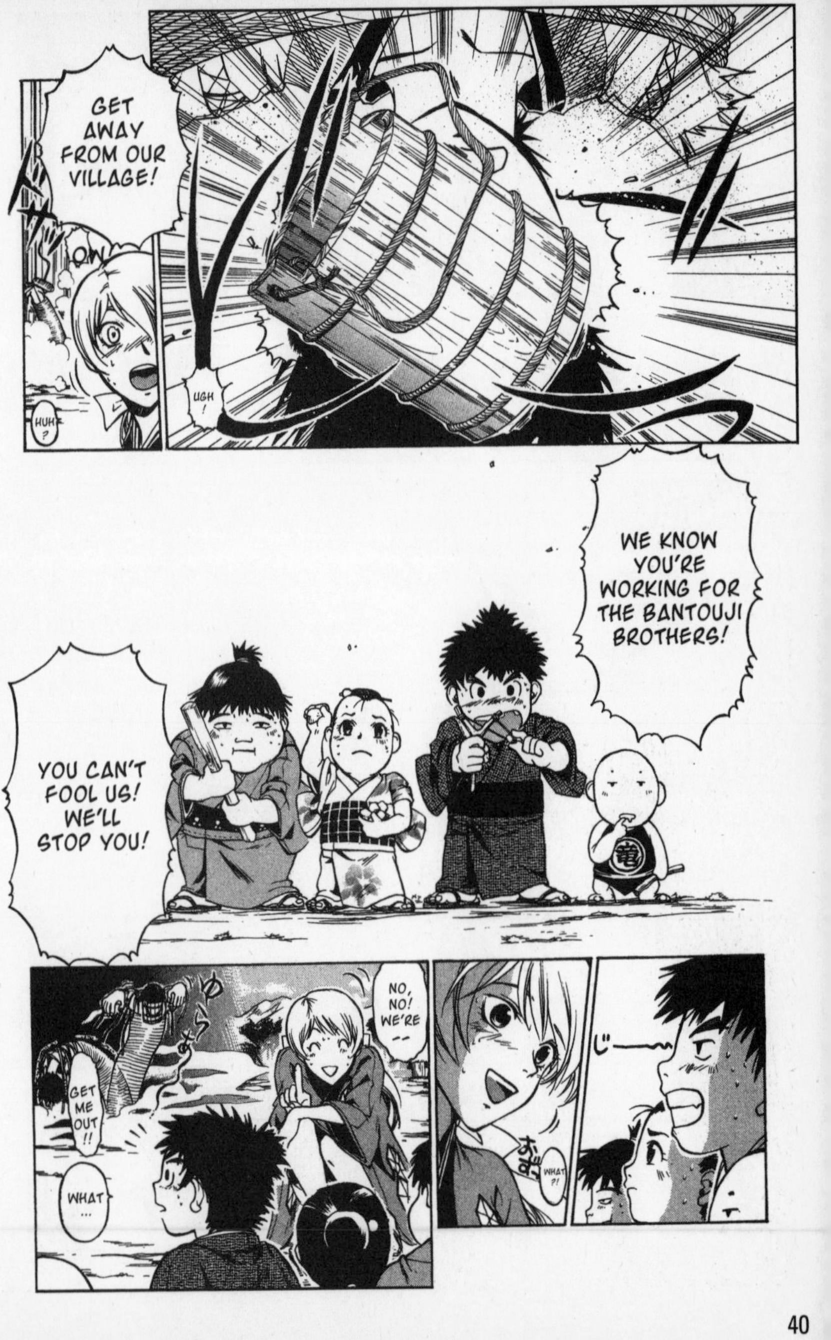
GET AWAY FROM OUR VILLAGE!
OW
UGH!
HUH?
WE KNOW YOU'RE WORKING FOR THE BANTOUJI BROTHERS!
YOU CAN'T FOOL US! WE'LL STOP YOU!
WHAT?!
NO, NO! WE'RE --
GET ME OUT!!
WHAT...

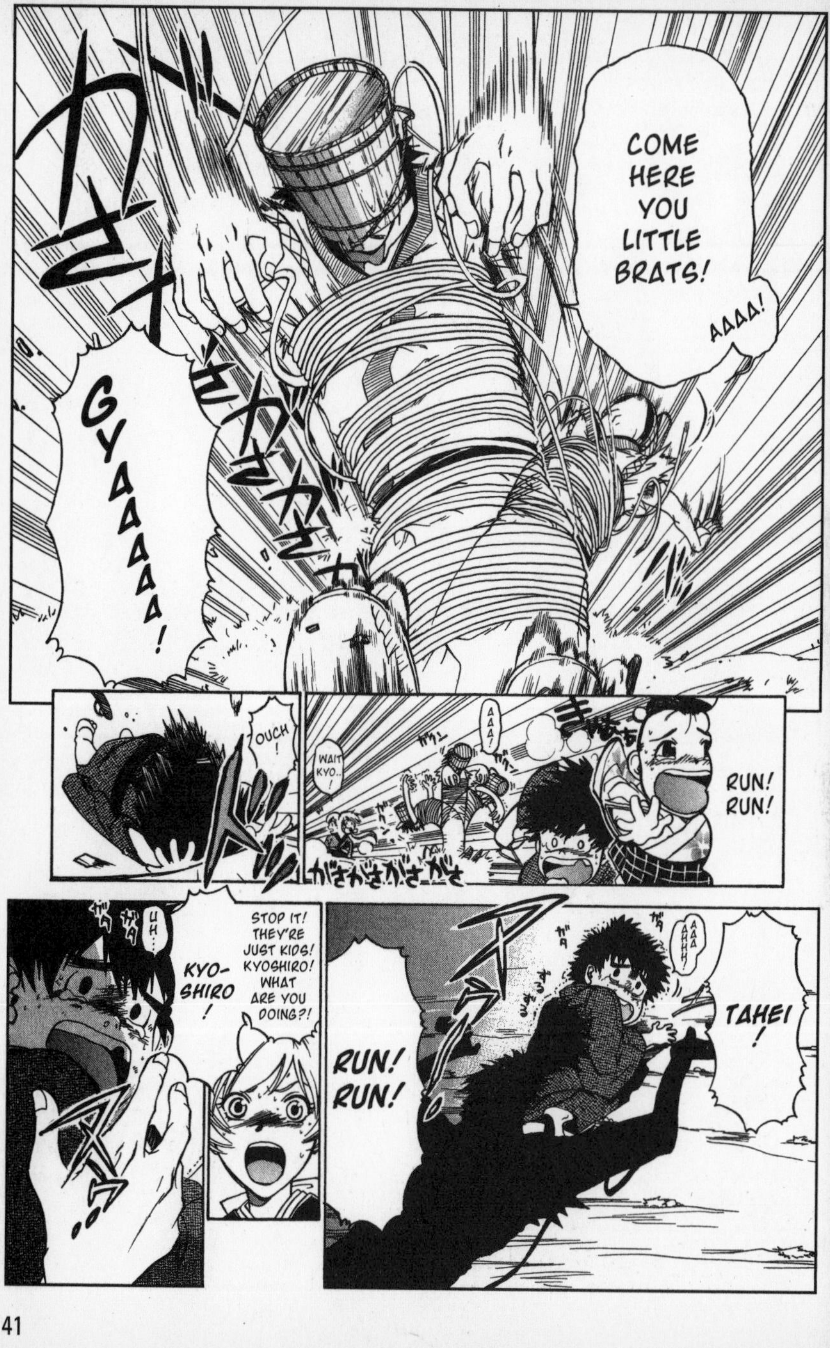
COME HERE YOU LITTLE BRATS!
AAAA!
GYAAAAAA!
RUN! RUN!
AAA!
WAIT KYO...!
OUCH!
TAHEI!
AAA AHHH!
RUN! RUN!
STOP IT! THEY'RE JUST KIDS! KYOSHIRO! WHAT ARE YOU DOING?!
KYO-SHIRO!
UH...

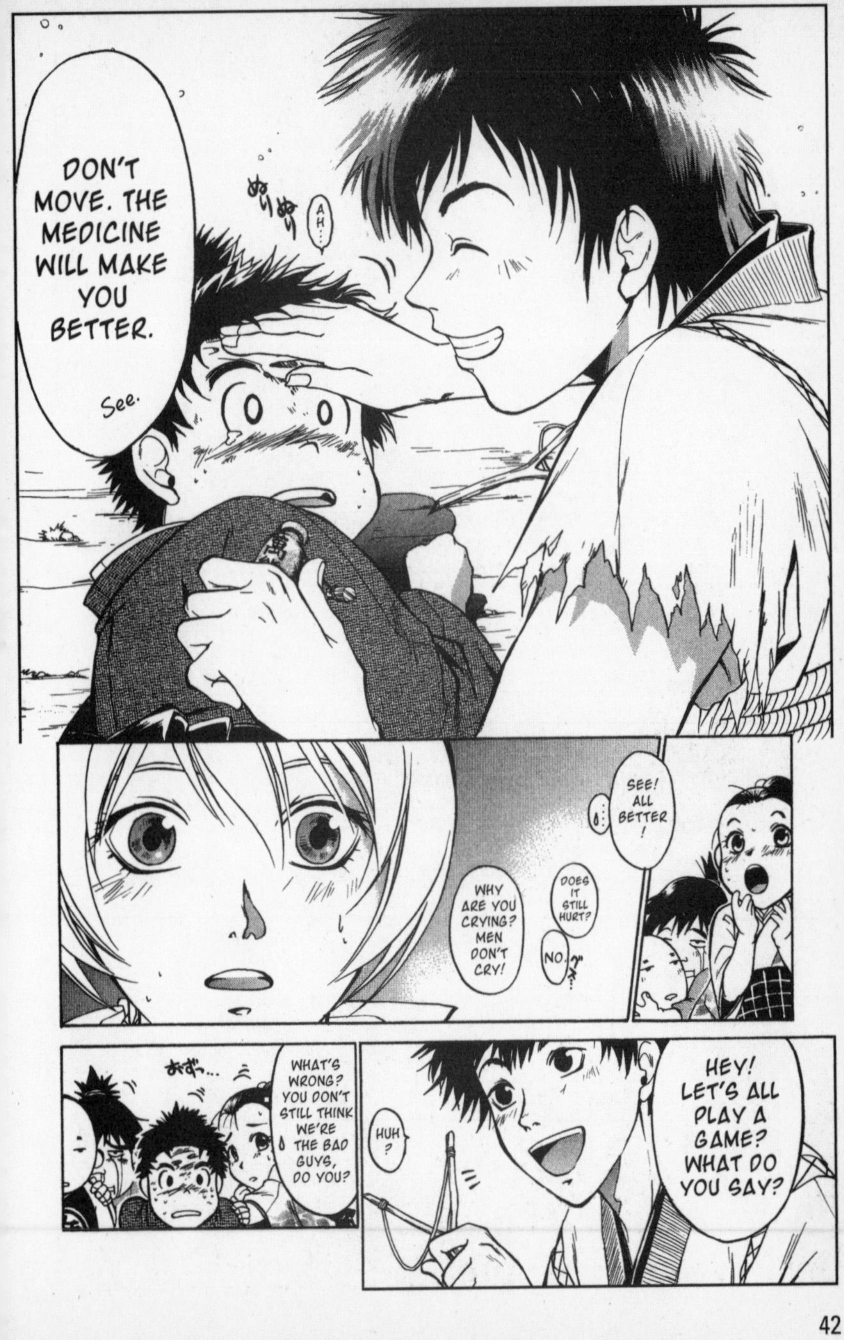
DON'T MOVE. THE MEDICINE WILL MAKE YOU BETTER.
See.
ぬりぬり
AH...
SEE! ALL BETTER!
...
DOES IT STILL HURT?
NO.
WHY ARE YOU CRYING? MEN DON'T CRY!
HEY! LET'S ALL PLAY A GAME? WHAT DO YOU SAY?
HUH?
WHAT'S WRONG? YOU DON'T STILL THINK WE'RE THE BAD GUYS, DO YOU?
おずっ...

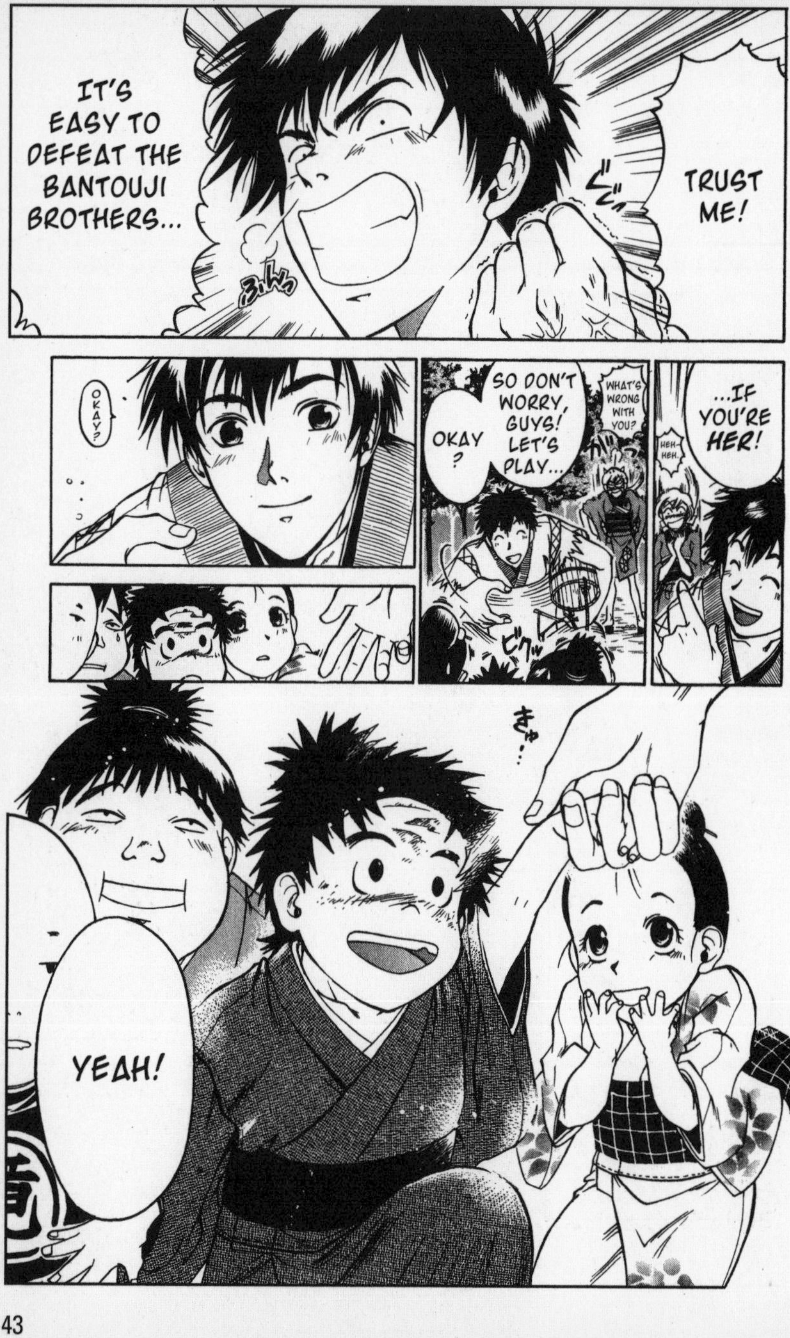
IT'S EASY TO DEFEAT THE BANTOUJI BROTHERS...
TRUST ME!
OKAY?
SO DON'T WORRY, GUYS! LET'S PLAY...
OKAY?
WHAT'S WRONG WITH YOU?
...IF YOU'RE *HER*!
HEH-HEH.
YEAH!

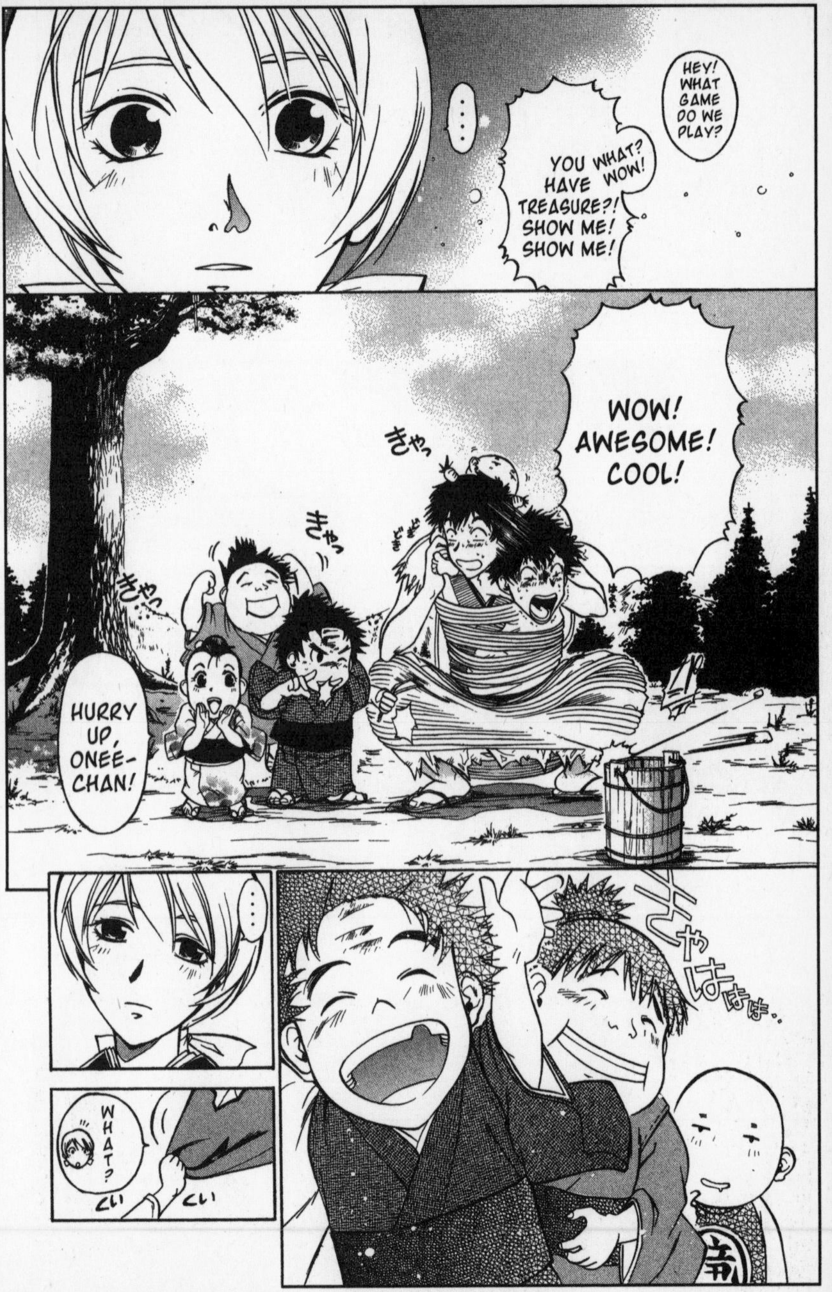
HEY! WHAT GAME DO WE PLAY?
YOU WHAT? HAVE WOW! TREASURE?! SHOW ME! SHOW ME!
....
WOW! AWESOME! COOL!
きゃっ
きゃっ
きゃっ
HURRY UP, ONEÉ-CHAN!
きゃははは..
....
WHAT?
くい くい

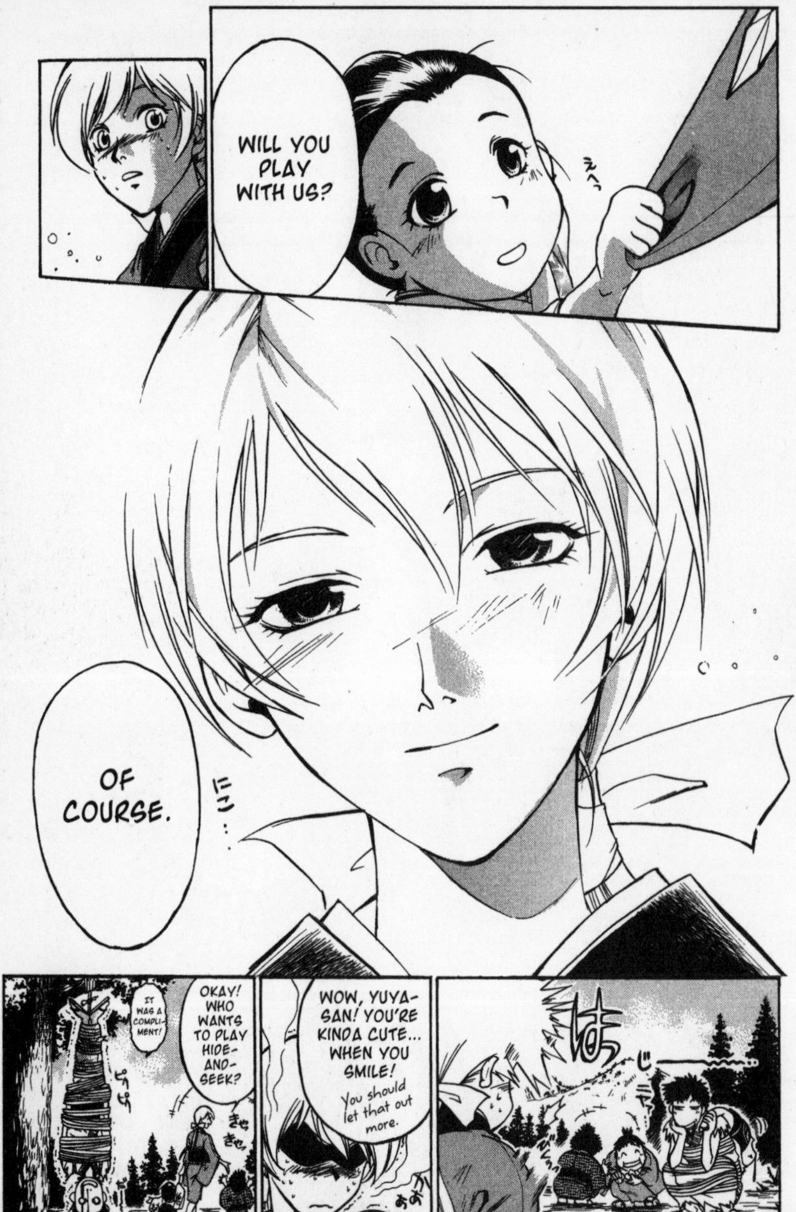
WILL YOU PLAY WITH US?
えへっ
OF COURSE.
にこ…
はっ
WOW, YUYA-SAN! YOU'RE KINDA CUTE... WHEN YOU SMILE!
You should let that out more.
OKAY! WHO WANTS TO PLAY HIDE-AND-SEEK?
IT WAS A COMPLIMENT!

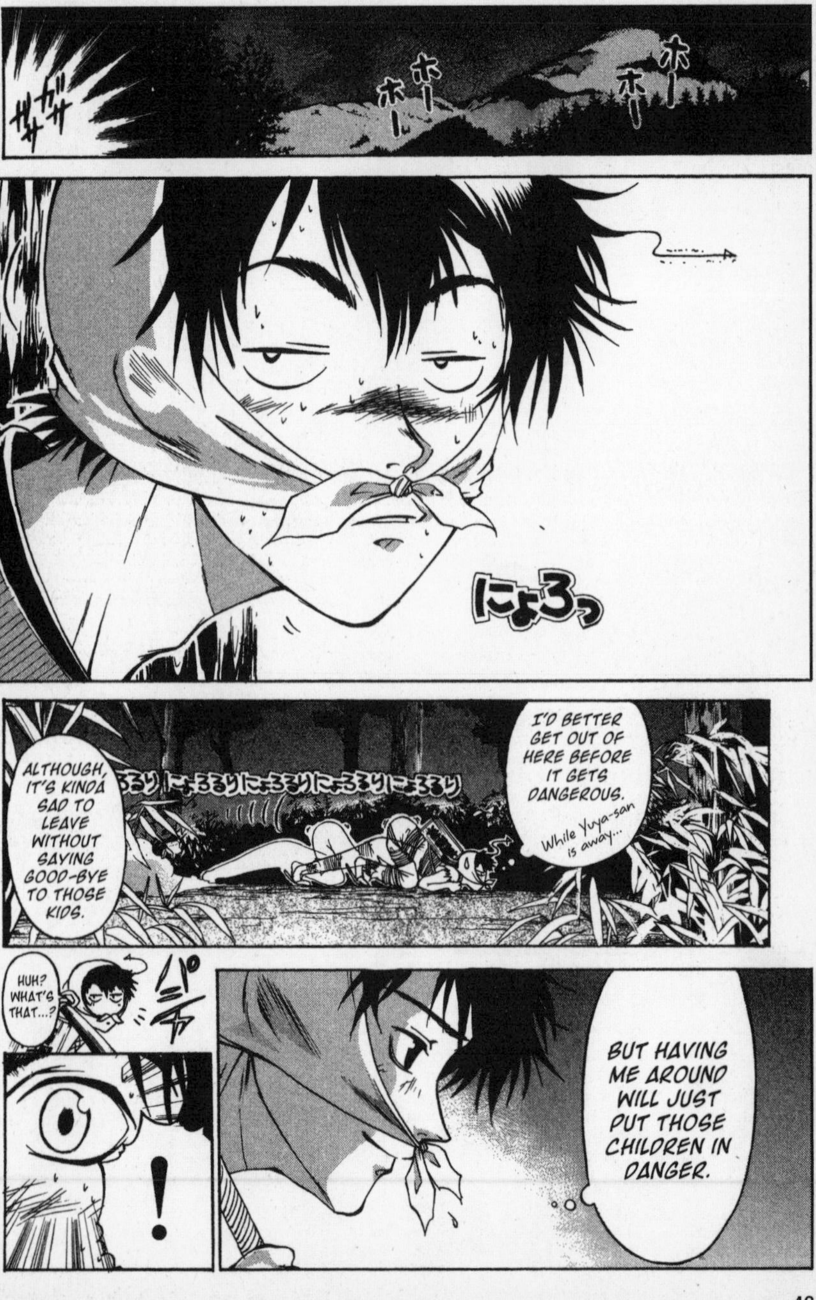
ホー ホー
ホー ホー
にょろっ
I'D BETTER GET OUT OF HERE BEFORE IT GETS DANGEROUS.
While Yuya-san is away...
るり にょろるり にょろるり にょろるり にょろるり
ALTHOUGH, IT'S KINDA SAD TO LEAVE WITHOUT SAYING GOOD-BYE TO THOSE KIDS.
BUT HAVING ME AROUND WILL JUST PUT THOSE CHILDREN IN DANGER.
パ
HUH? WHAT'S THAT...?
!

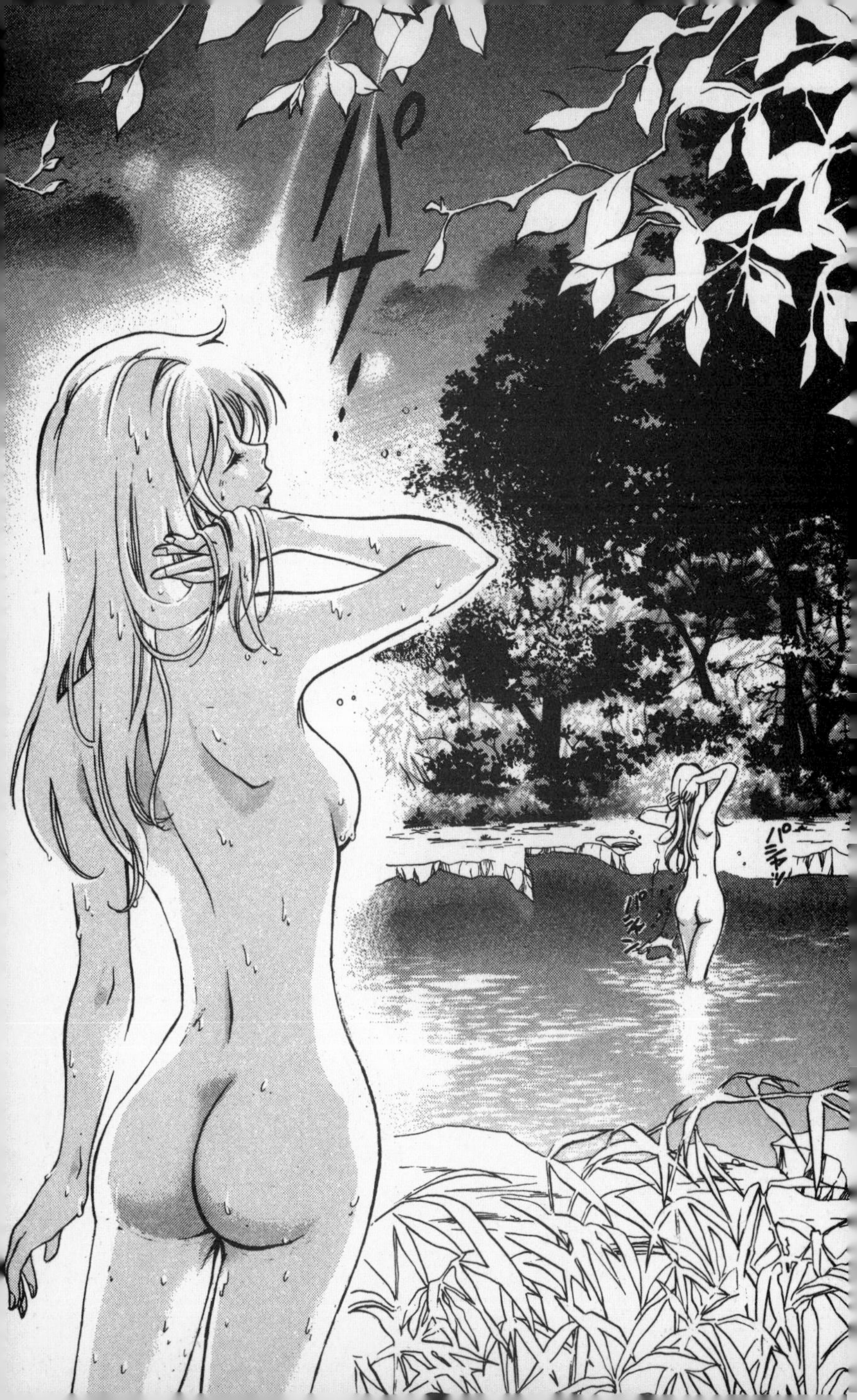
パサ…
パシャッ
パシャー

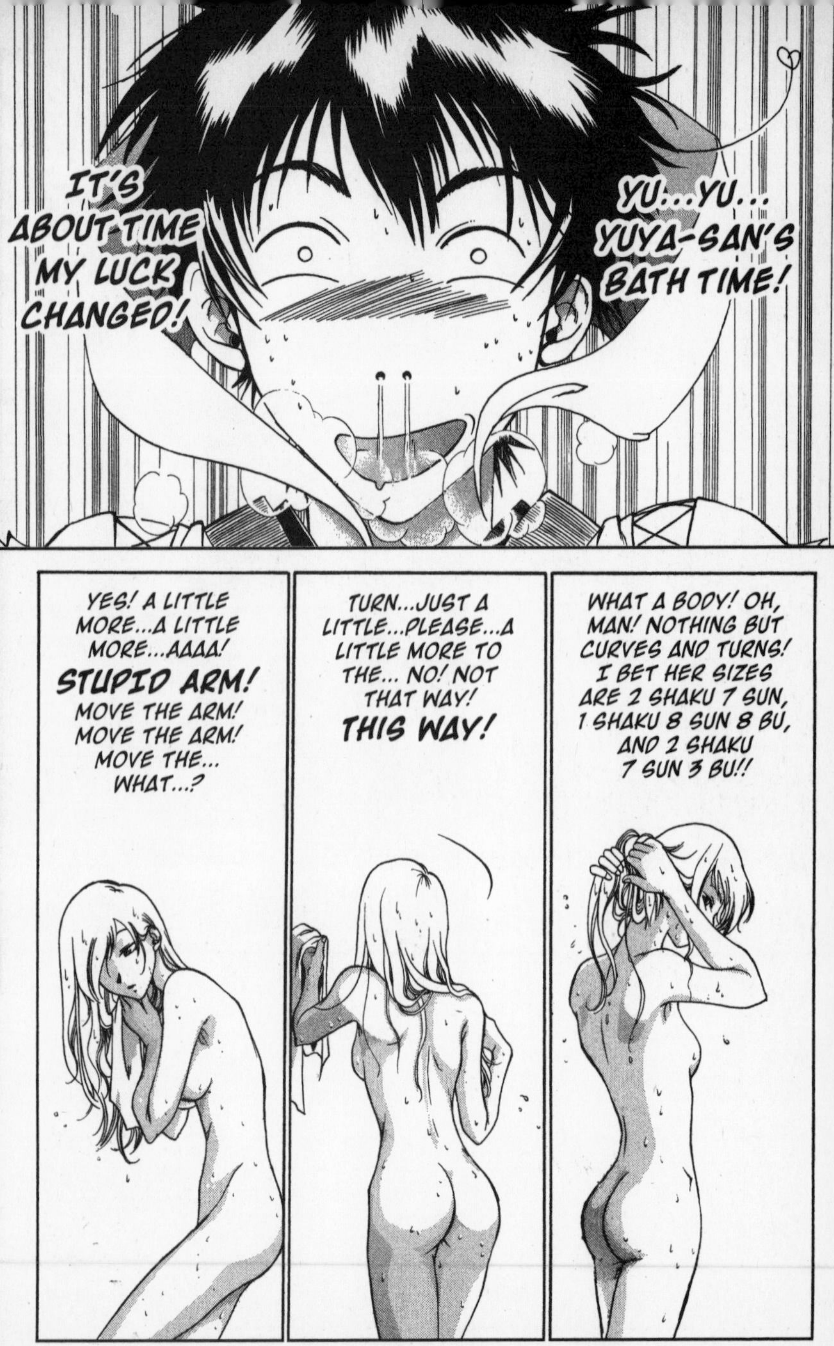
YU...YU... YUYA-SAN'S BATH TIME!
IT'S ABOUT TIME MY LUCK CHANGED!
WHAT A BODY! OH, MAN! NOTHING BUT CURVES AND TURNS! I BET HER SIZES ARE 2 SHAKU 7 SUN, 1 SHAKU 8 SUN 8 BU, AND 2 SHAKU 7 SUN 3 BU!!
TURN...JUST A LITTLE...PLEASE...A LITTLE MORE TO THE... NO! NOT THAT WAY! THIS WAY!
YES! A LITTLE MORE...A LITTLE MORE...AAAA! STUPID ARM! MOVE THE ARM! MOVE THE ARM! MOVE THE... WHAT...?

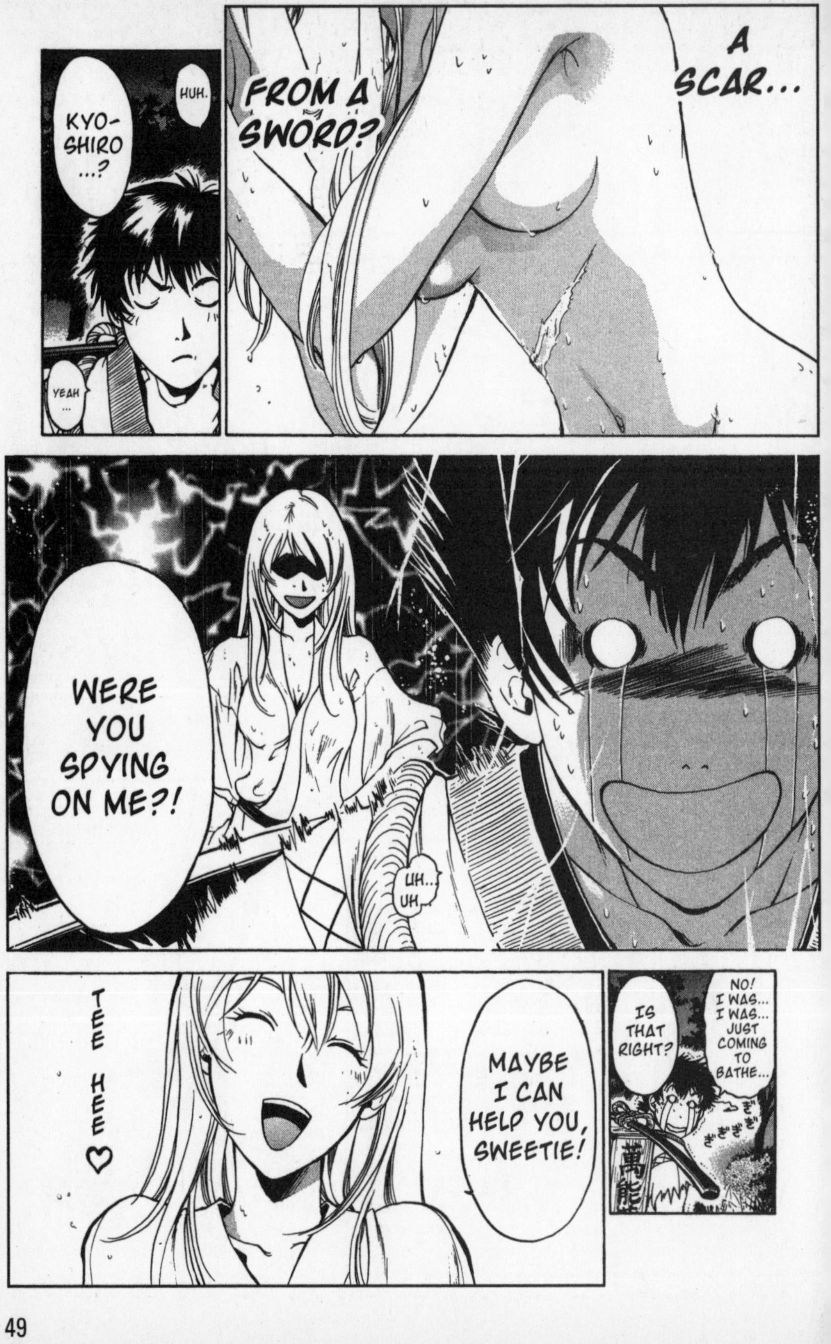
A SCAR...
FROM A SWORD?
HUH.
KYO-SHIRO ...?
YEAH ...
WERE YOU SPYING ON ME?!
UH... UH...
NO! I WAS... I WAS... JUST COMING TO BATHE...
IS THAT RIGHT?
MAYBE I CAN HELP YOU, SWEETIE!
TEE HEE ♡

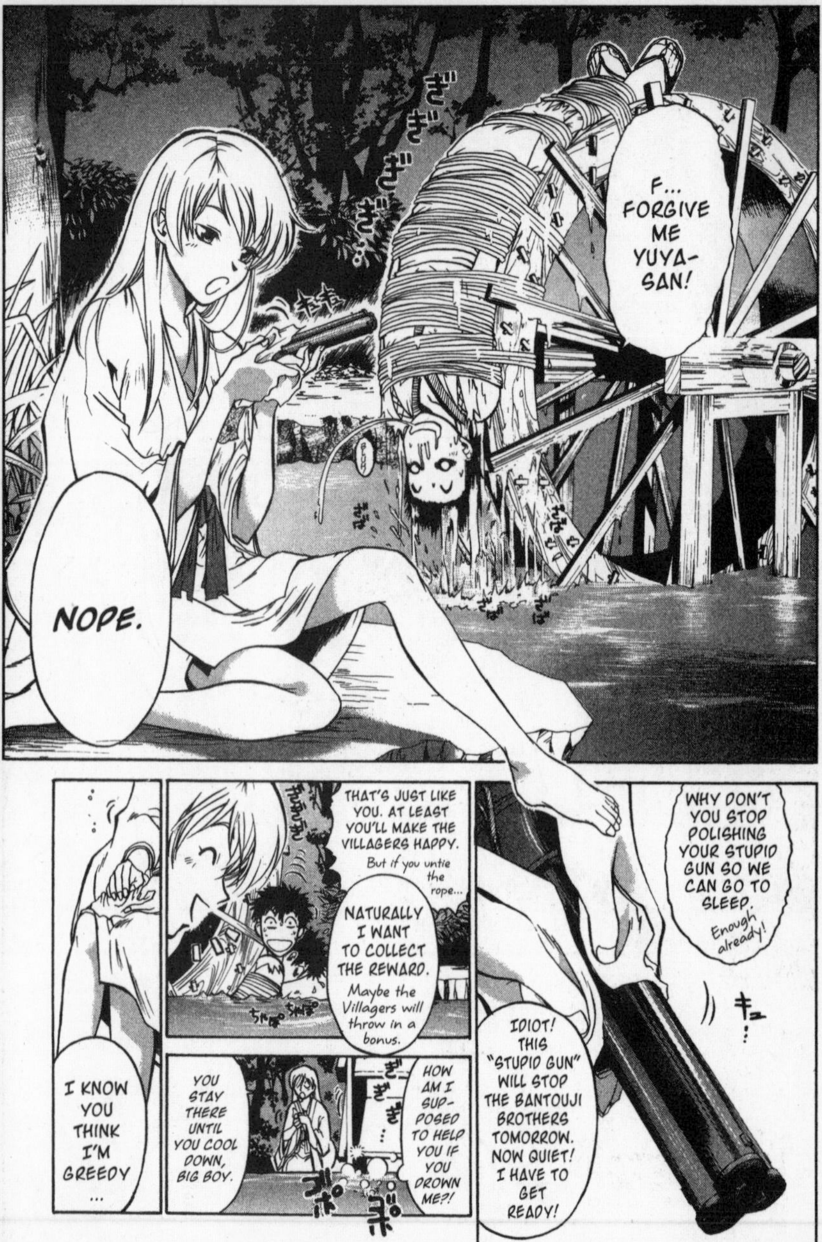
ぎぎぎぎ…
F... FORGIVE ME YUYA-SAN!
NOPE.
WHY DON'T YOU STOP POLISHING YOUR STUPID GUN SO WE CAN GO TO SLEEP.
Enough already!
IDIOT! THIS "STUPID GUN" WILL STOP THE BANTOUJI BROTHERS TOMORROW. NOW QUIET! I HAVE TO GET READY!
THAT'S JUST LIKE YOU. AT LEAST YOU'LL MAKE THE VILLAGERS HAPPY.
But if you untie the rope...
NATURALLY I WANT TO COLLECT THE REWARD.
Maybe the Villagers will throw in a bonus.
HOW AM I SUP-POSED TO HELP YOU IF YOU DROWN ME?!
YOU STAY THERE UNTIL YOU COOL DOWN, BIG BOY.
I KNOW YOU THINK I'M GREEDY ...

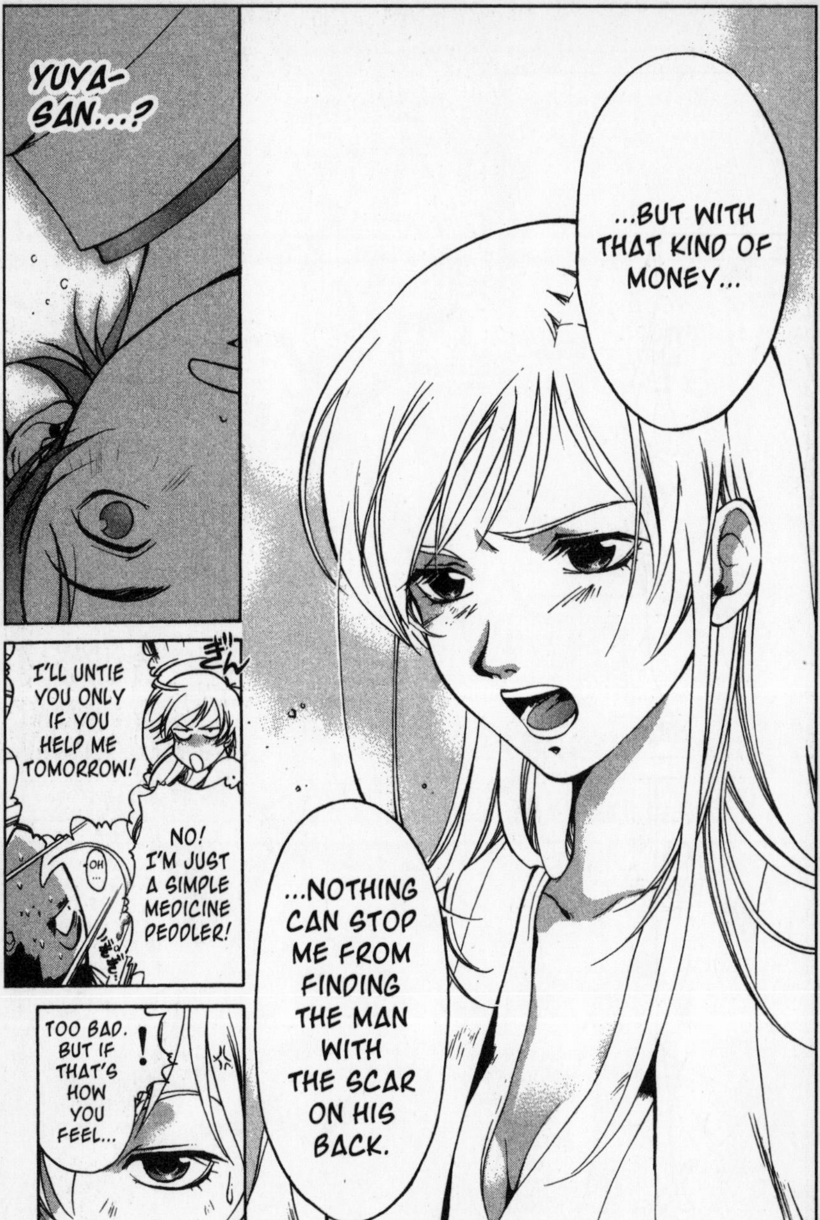
...BUT WITH THAT KIND OF MONEY...
...NOTHING CAN STOP ME FROM FINDING THE MAN WITH THE SCAR ON HIS BACK.
YUYA-SAN...?
I'LL UNTIE YOU ONLY IF YOU HELP ME TOMORROW!
NO! I'M JUST A SIMPLE MEDICINE PEDDLER!
OH...
TOO BAD. BUT IF THAT'S HOW YOU FEEL...
!

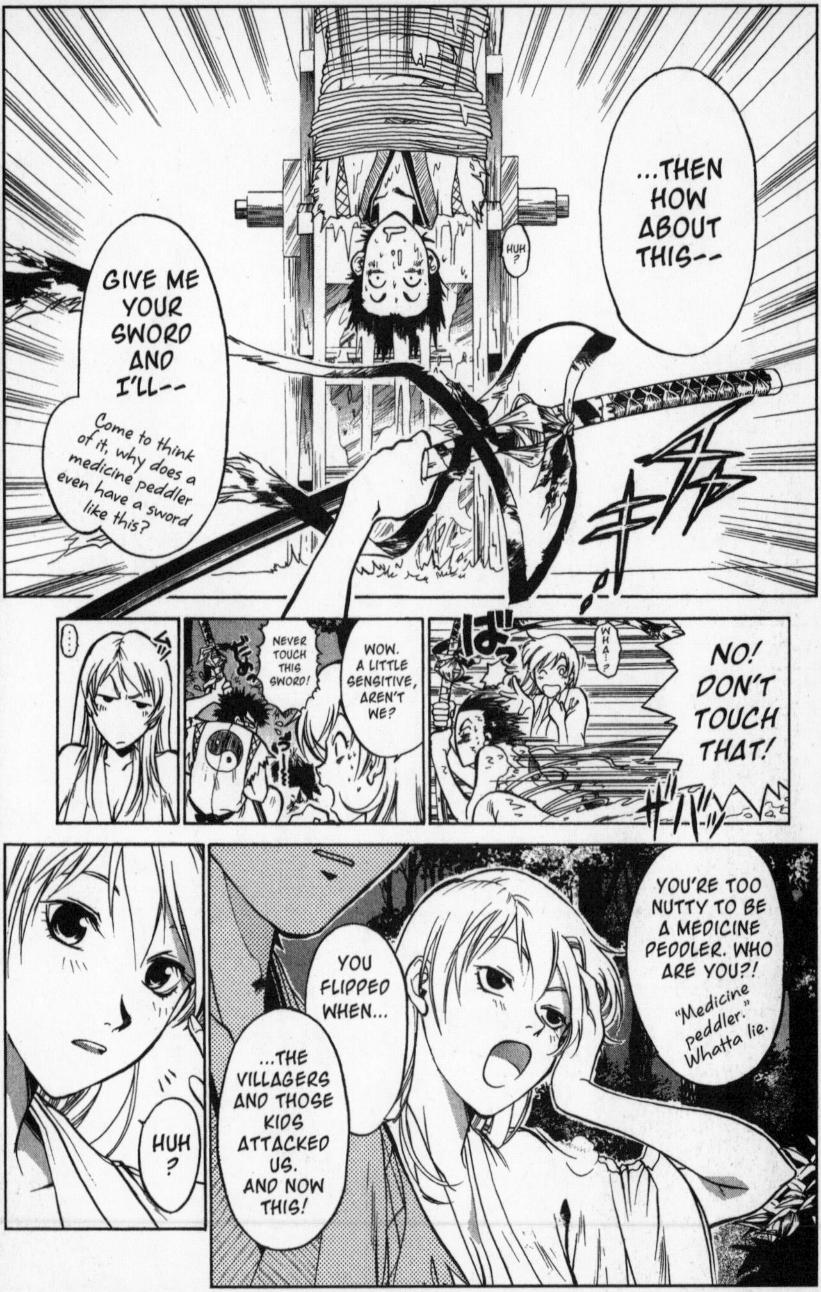
...THEN HOW ABOUT THIS--
HUH?
GIVE ME YOUR SWORD AND I'LL--
Come to think of it, why does a medicine peddler even have a sword like this?
NO! DON'T TOUCH THAT!
WHA...?
NEVER TOUCH THIS SWORD!
WOW. A LITTLE SENSITIVE, AREN'T WE?
...
YOU'RE TOO NUTTY TO BE A MEDICINE PEDDLER. WHO ARE YOU?!
"Medicine peddler." Whatta lie.
YOU FLIPPED WHEN...
...THE VILLAGERS AND THOSE KIDS ATTACKED US. AND NOW THIS!
HUH?

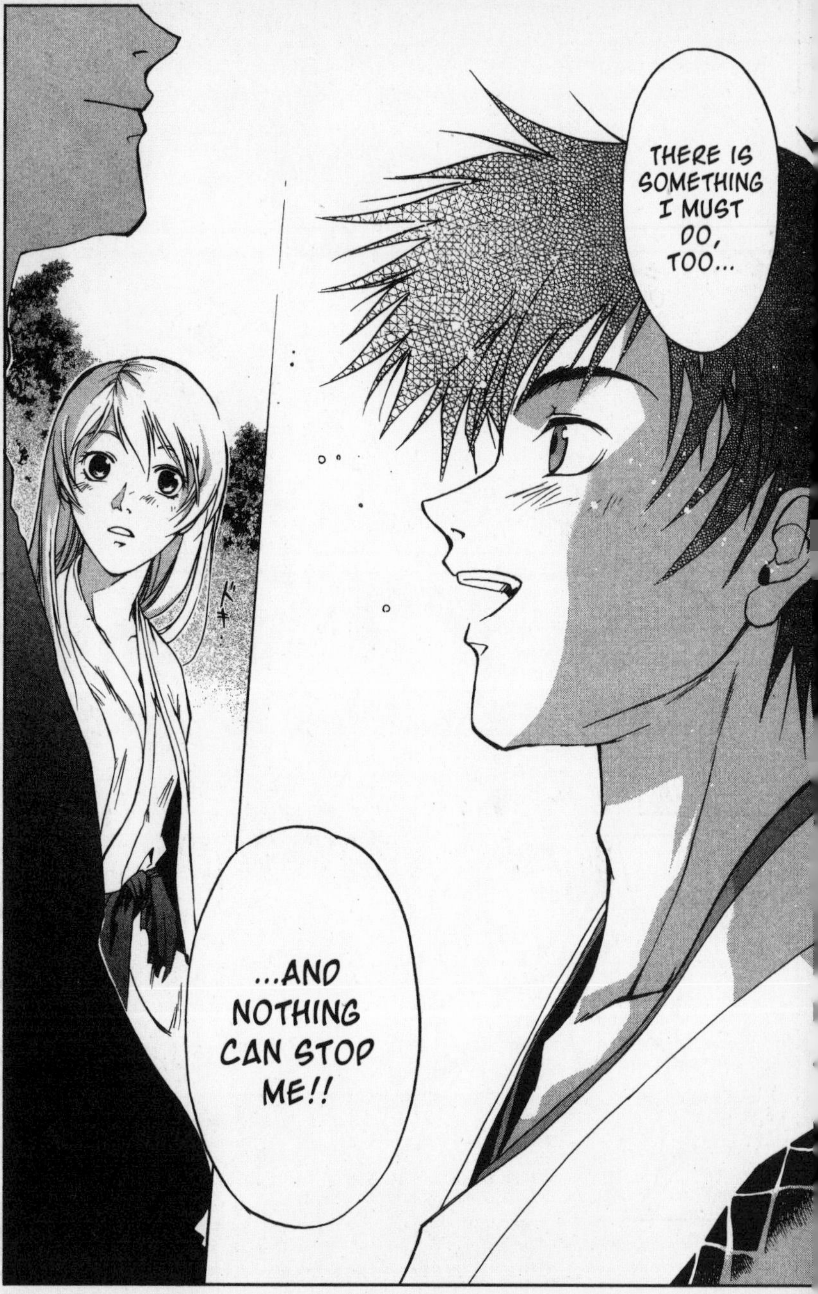
THERE IS SOMETHING I MUST DO, TOO...
ドキ
...AND NOTHING CAN STOP ME!!

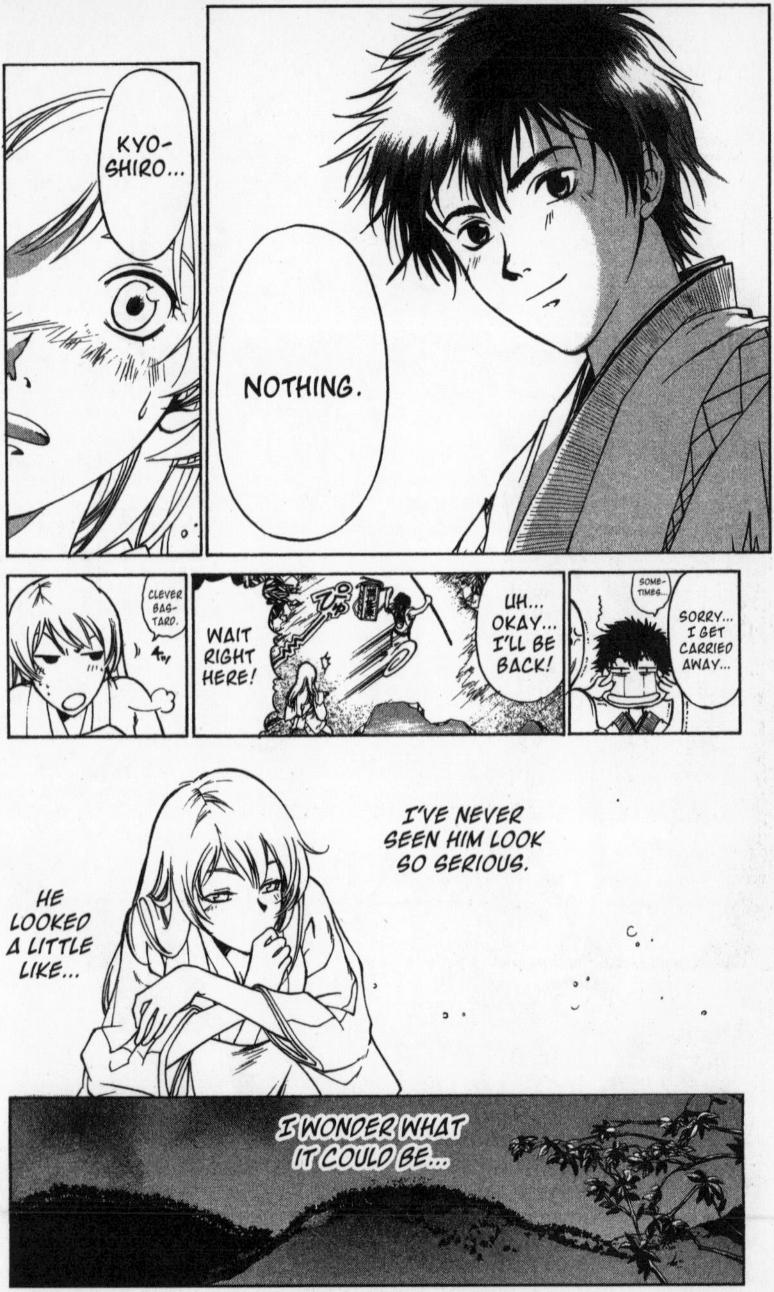
NOTHING.
KYO-SHIRO...
SORRY... I GET CARRIED AWAY...
SOME-TIMES...
UH... OKAY... I'LL BE BACK!
WAIT RIGHT HERE!
CLEVER BAS-TARD.
I'VE NEVER SEEN HIM LOOK SO SERIOUS.
HE LOOKED A LITTLE LIKE...
I WONDER WHAT IT COULD BE...

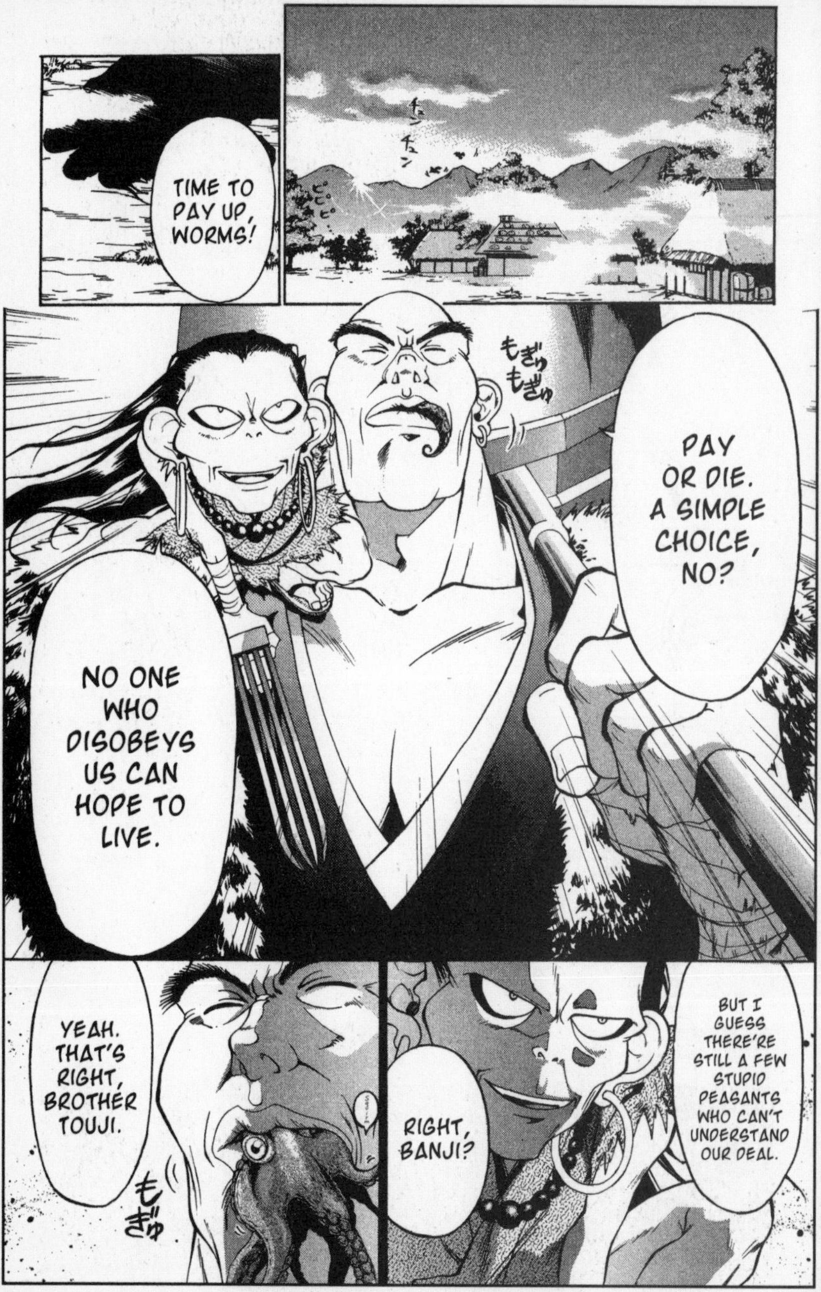
TIME TO PAY UP, WORMS!
PAY OR DIE. A SIMPLE CHOICE, NO?
もぎゅ もぎゅ
NO ONE WHO DISOBEYS US CAN HOPE TO LIVE.
BUT I GUESS THERE'RE STILL A FEW STUPID PEASANTS WHO CAN'T UNDERSTAND OUR DEAL.
RIGHT, BANJI?
YEAH. THAT'S RIGHT, BROTHER TOUJI.
もぎゅ

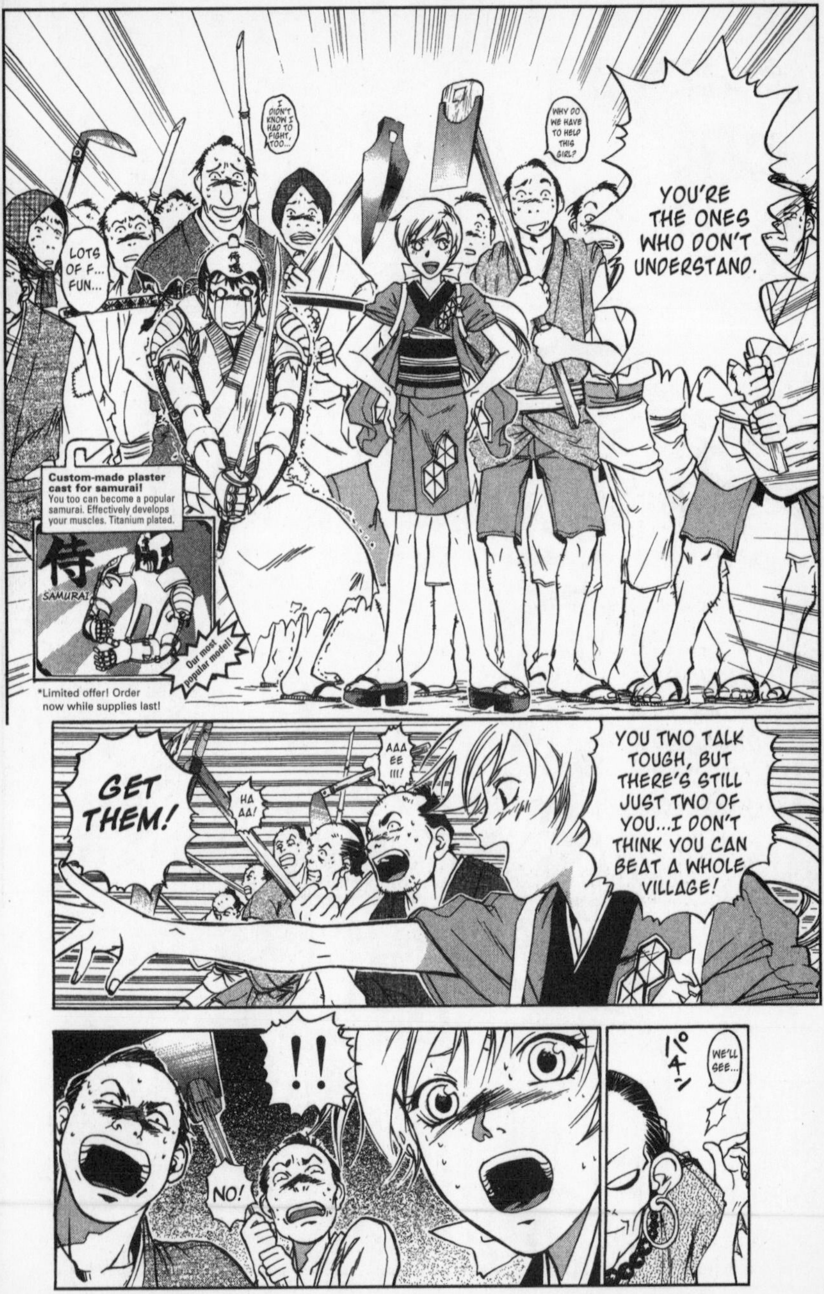
YOU'RE THE ONES WHO DON'T UNDERSTAND.
WHY DO WE HAVE TO HELP THIS GIRL?
I DIDN'T KNOW I HAD TO FIGHT, TOO...
LOTS OF F... FUN...
Custom-made plaster cast for samurai!
You too can become a popular samurai. Effectively develops your muscles. Titanium plated.
侍
SAMURAI
Our most popular model!
*Limited offer! Order now while supplies last!
YOU TWO TALK TOUGH, BUT THERE'S STILL JUST TWO OF YOU...I DON'T THINK YOU CAN BEAT A WHOLE VILLAGE!
AAA EE !!!!
HA AA!
GET THEM!
パチン
WE'LL SEE...
!!
NO!

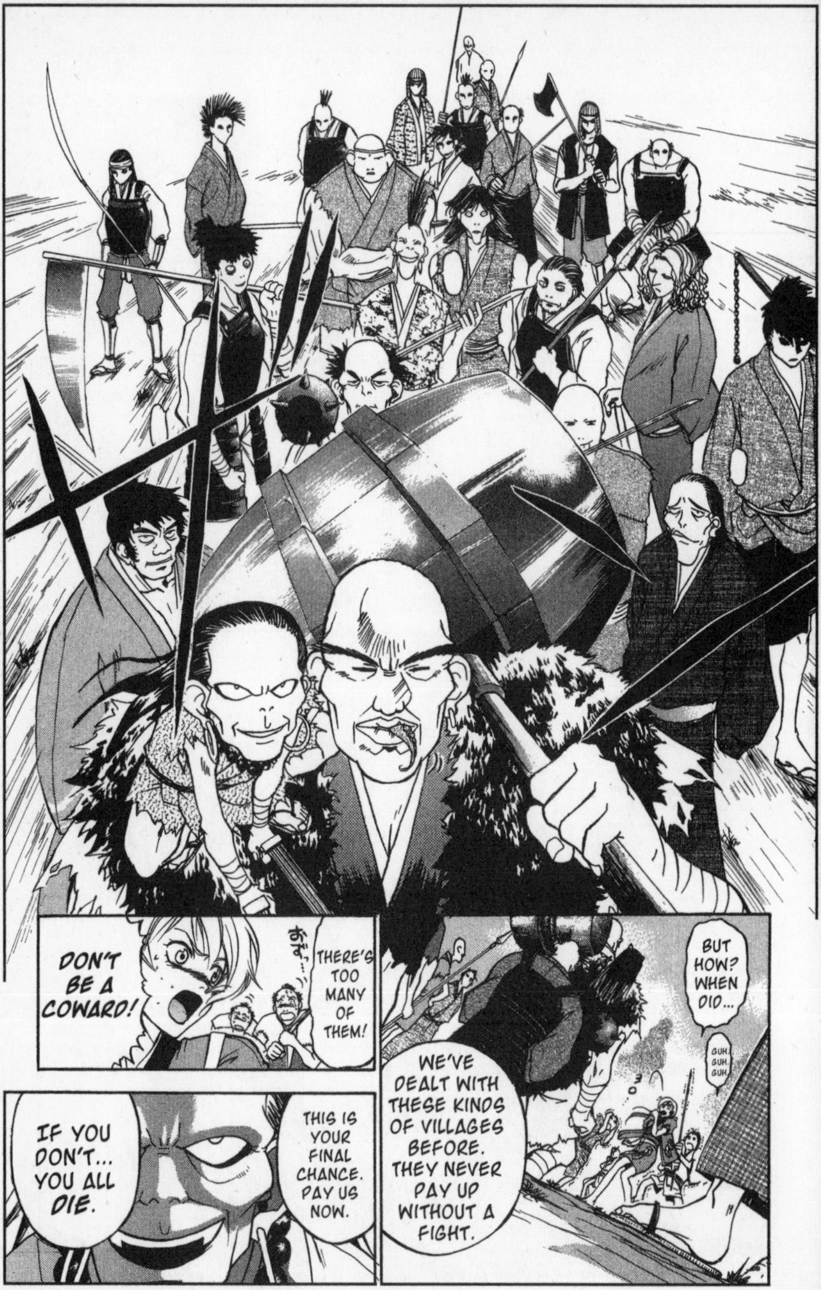
BUT HOW? WHEN DIO...
GUH. GUH. GUH.
WE'VE DEALT WITH THESE KINDS OF VILLAGES BEFORE. THEY NEVER PAY UP WITHOUT A FIGHT.
おず…
THERE'S TOO MANY OF THEM!
DON'T BE A COWARD!
THIS IS YOUR FINAL CHANCE. PAY US NOW.
IF YOU DON'T... YOU ALL DIE.

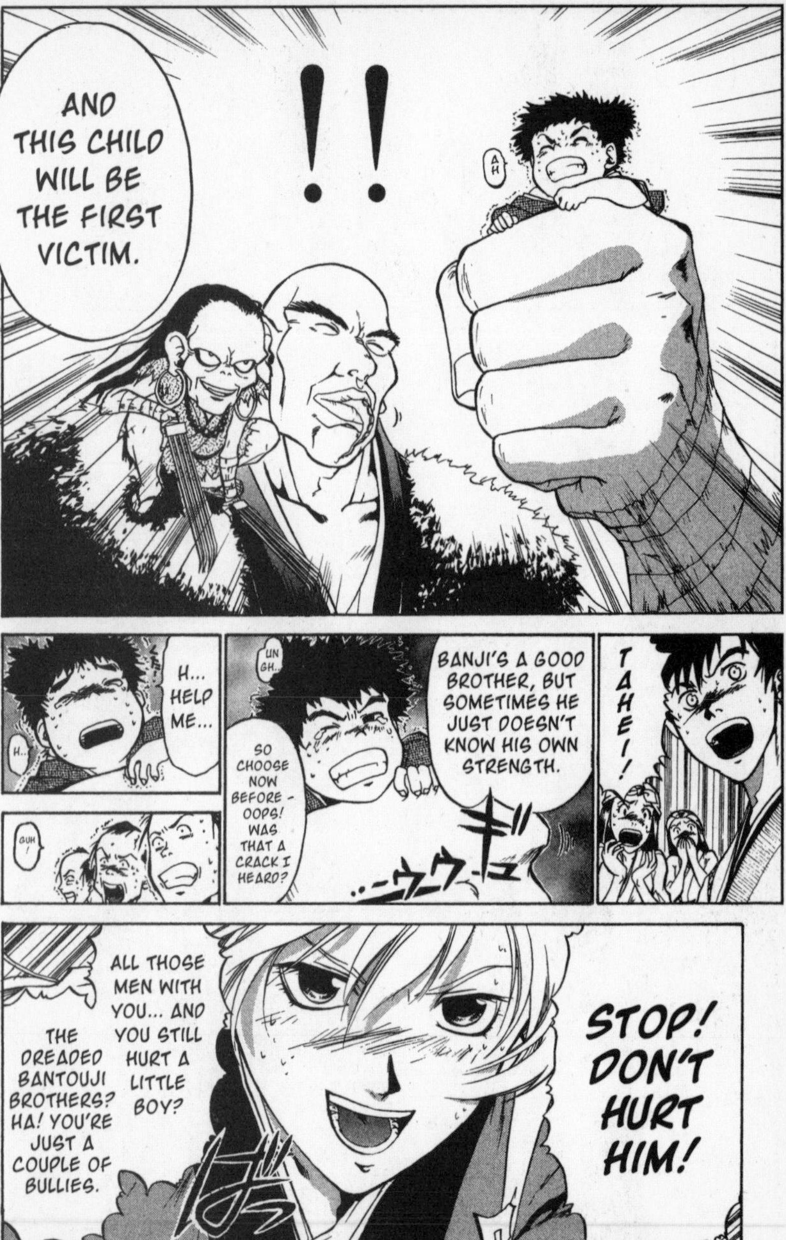
AH
!!
AND THIS CHILD WILL BE THE FIRST VICTIM.
TAHEI!!
BANJI'S A GOOD BROTHER, BUT SOMETIMES HE JUST DOESN'T KNOW HIS OWN STRENGTH.
UNGH...
SO CHOOSE NOW BEFORE - OOPS! WAS THAT A CRACK I HEARD?
H... HELP ME...
H...
GUH!
STOP! DON'T HURT HIM!
ALL THOSE MEN WITH YOU... AND YOU STILL HURT A LITTLE BOY?
THE DREADED BANTOUJI BROTHERS? HA! YOU'RE JUST A COUPLE OF BULLIES.

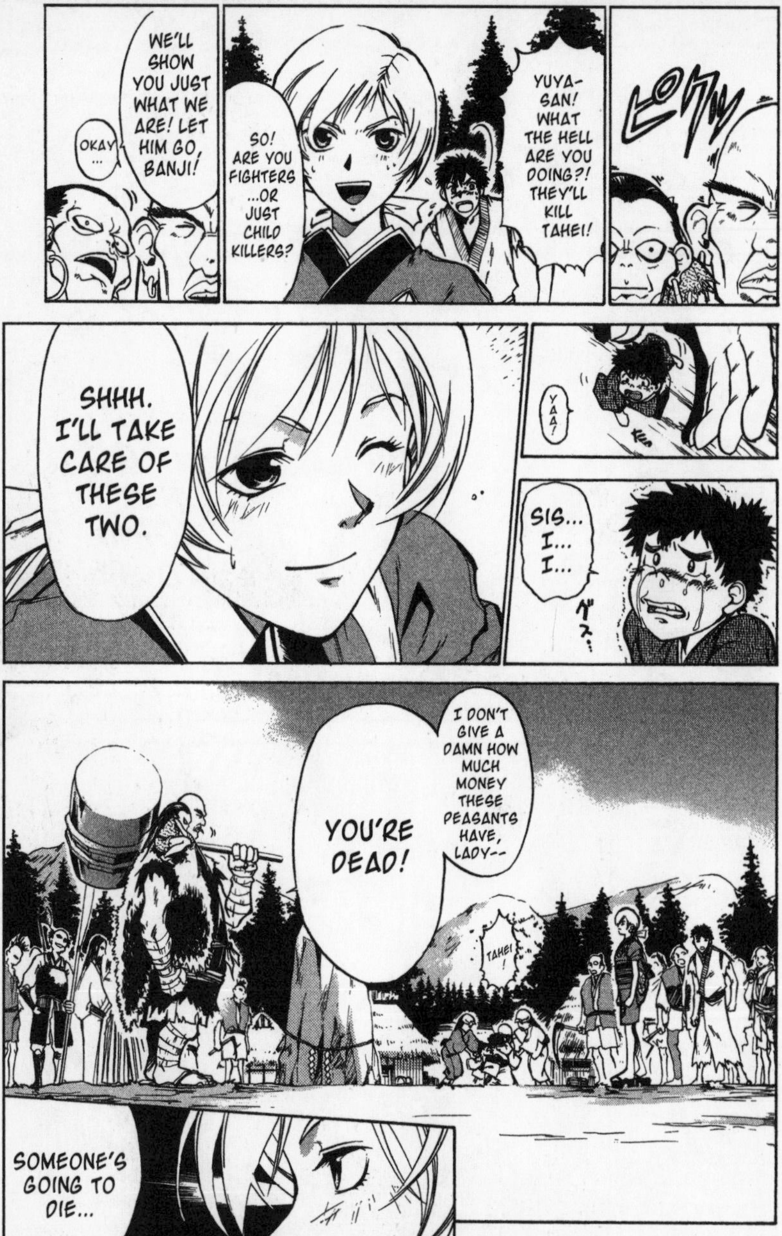
YUYA-SAN! WHAT THE HELL ARE YOU DOING?! THEY'LL KILL TAHEI!
SO! ARE YOU FIGHTERS ...OR JUST CHILD KILLERS?
WE'LL SHOW YOU JUST WHAT WE ARE! LET HIM GO, BANJI!
OKAY ...
YAAA!
SIS... I... I...
SHHH. I'LL TAKE CARE OF THESE TWO.
I DON'T GIVE A DAMN HOW MUCH MONEY THESE PEASANTS HAVE, LADY--
YOU'RE DEAD!
TAHEI!
SOMEONE'S GOING TO DIE...

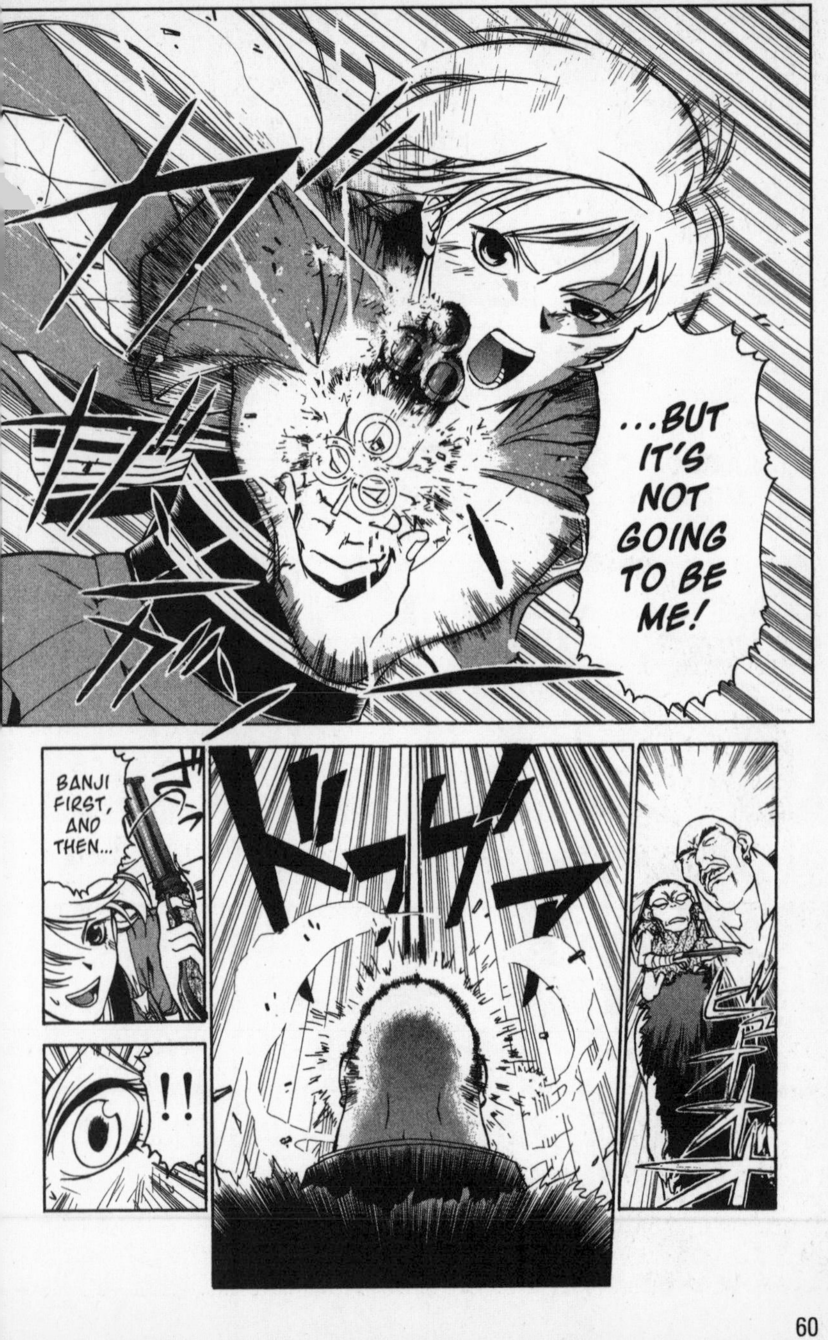
...BUT IT'S NOT GOING TO BE ME!
BANJI FIRST, AND THEN...
!!

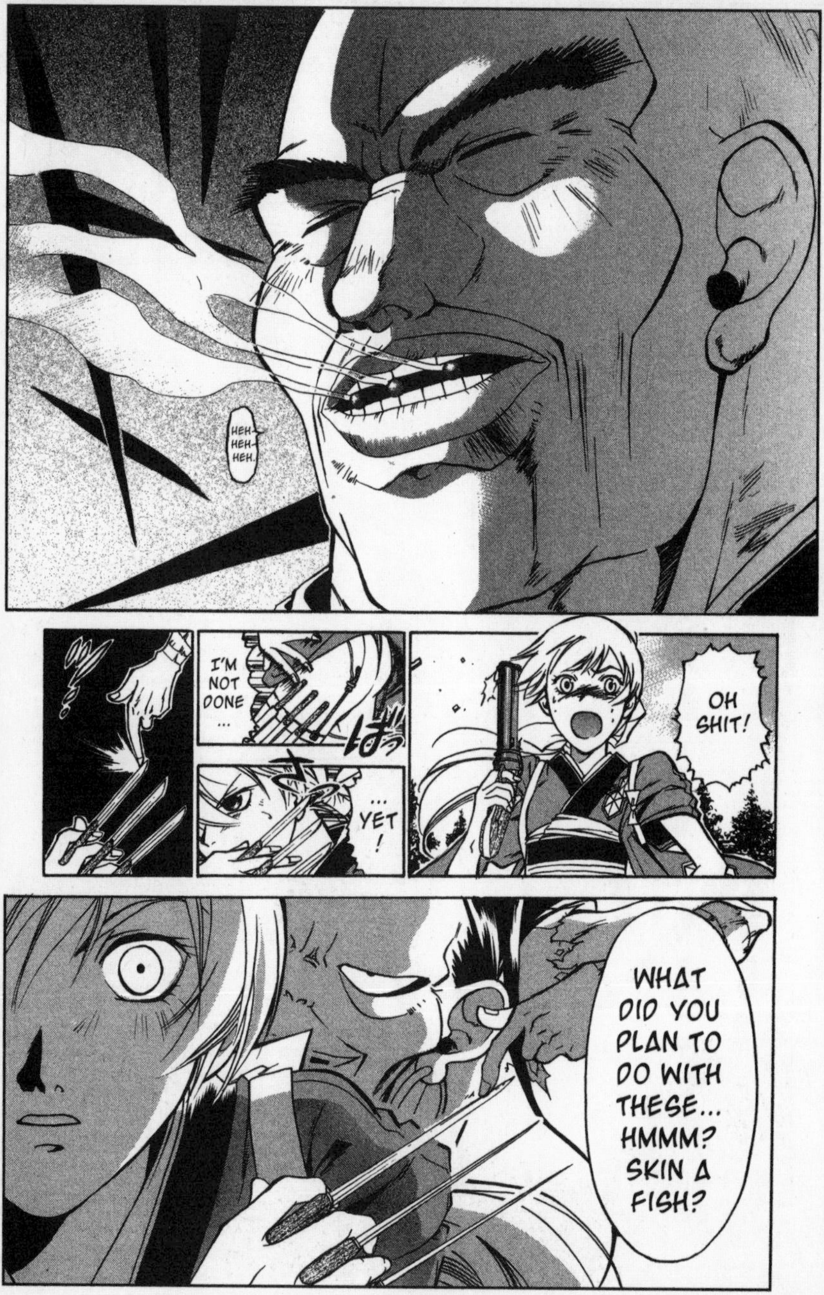
HEH-HEH-HEH.
OH SHIT!
I'M NOT DONE ...
... YET!
WHAT DID YOU PLAN TO DO WITH THESE... HMMM? SKIN A FISH?

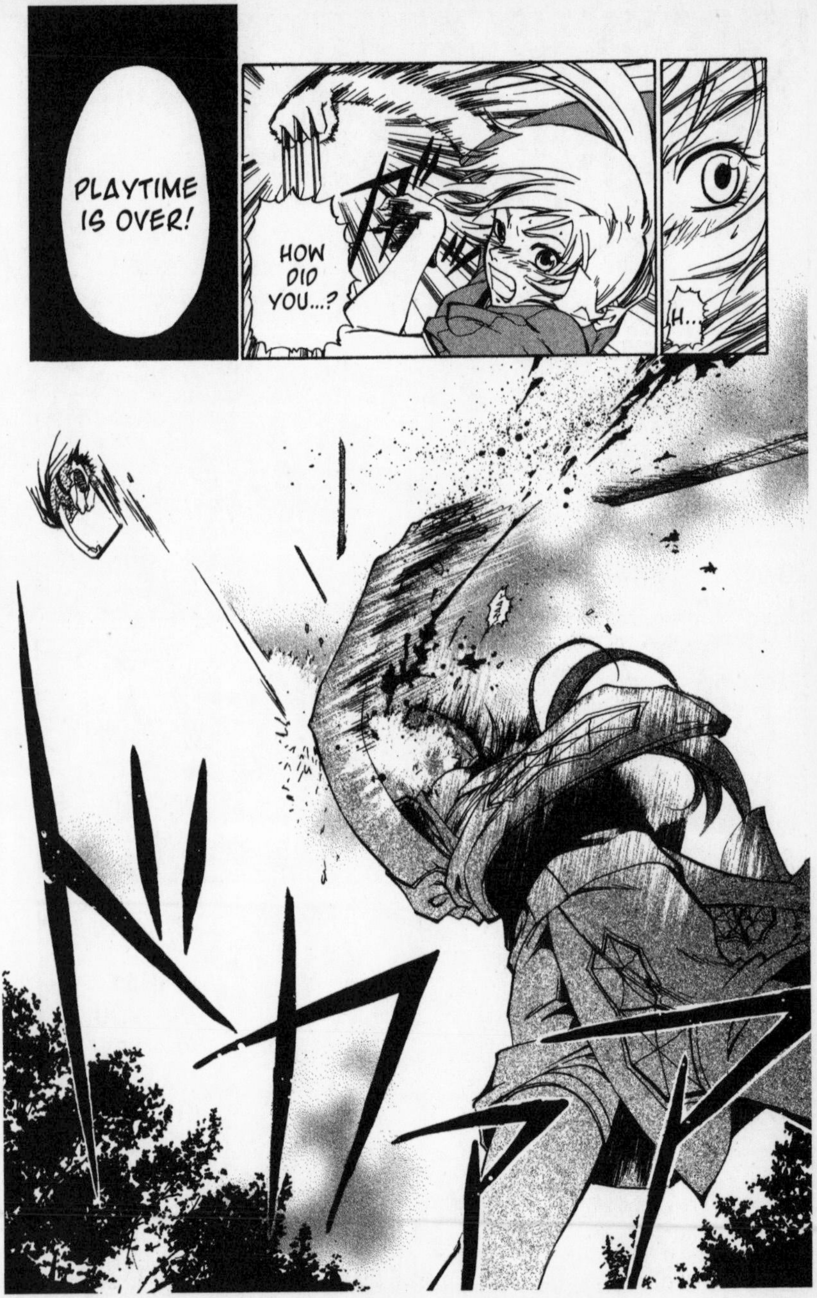
H...
HOW DID YOU...?
PLAYTIME IS OVER!

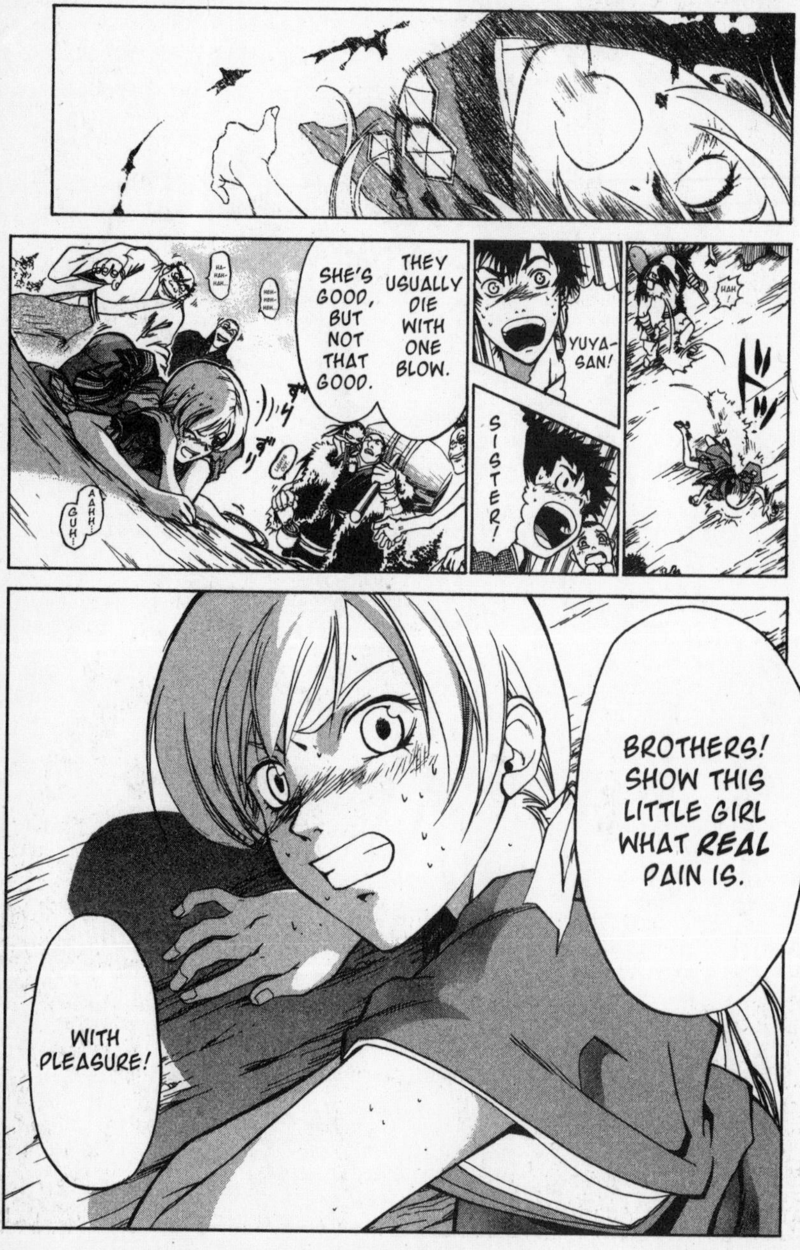
HAH!
YUYA-SAN!
SISTER!
THEY USUALLY DIE WITH ONE BLOW.
SHE'S GOOD, BUT NOT THAT GOOD.
HA-HAH-HAH...
HEH-HEH-HEH...
LIGHTS OUT.
GUH! AAHH...
BROTHERS! SHOW THIS LITTLE GIRL WHAT REAL PAIN IS.
WITH PLEASURE!

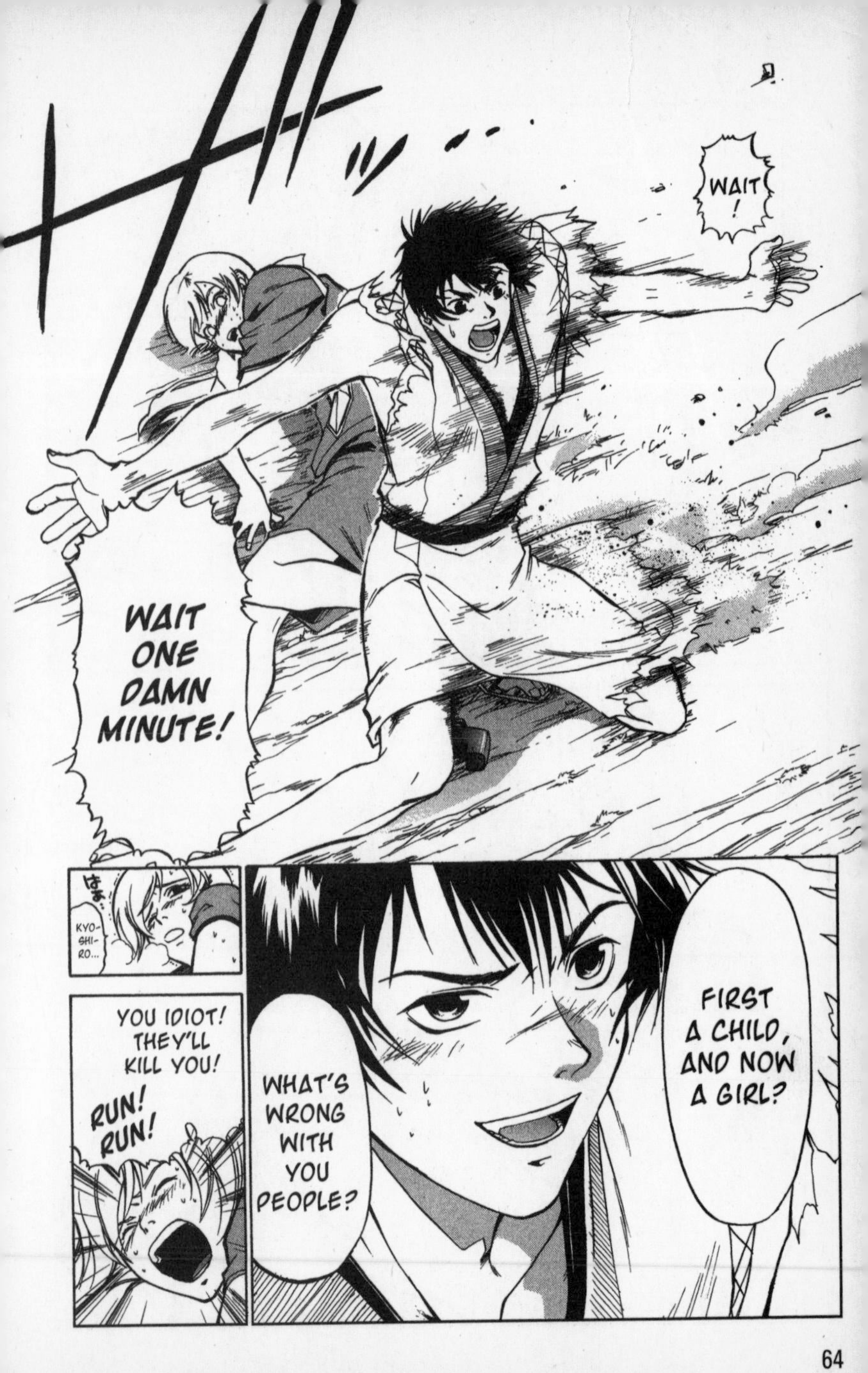
WAIT!
WAIT ONE DAMN MINUTE!
FIRST A CHILD, AND NOW A GIRL?
WHAT'S WRONG WITH YOU PEOPLE?
はぁ
KYO-SHI-RO...
YOU IDIOT! THEY'LL KILL YOU!
RUN! RUN!

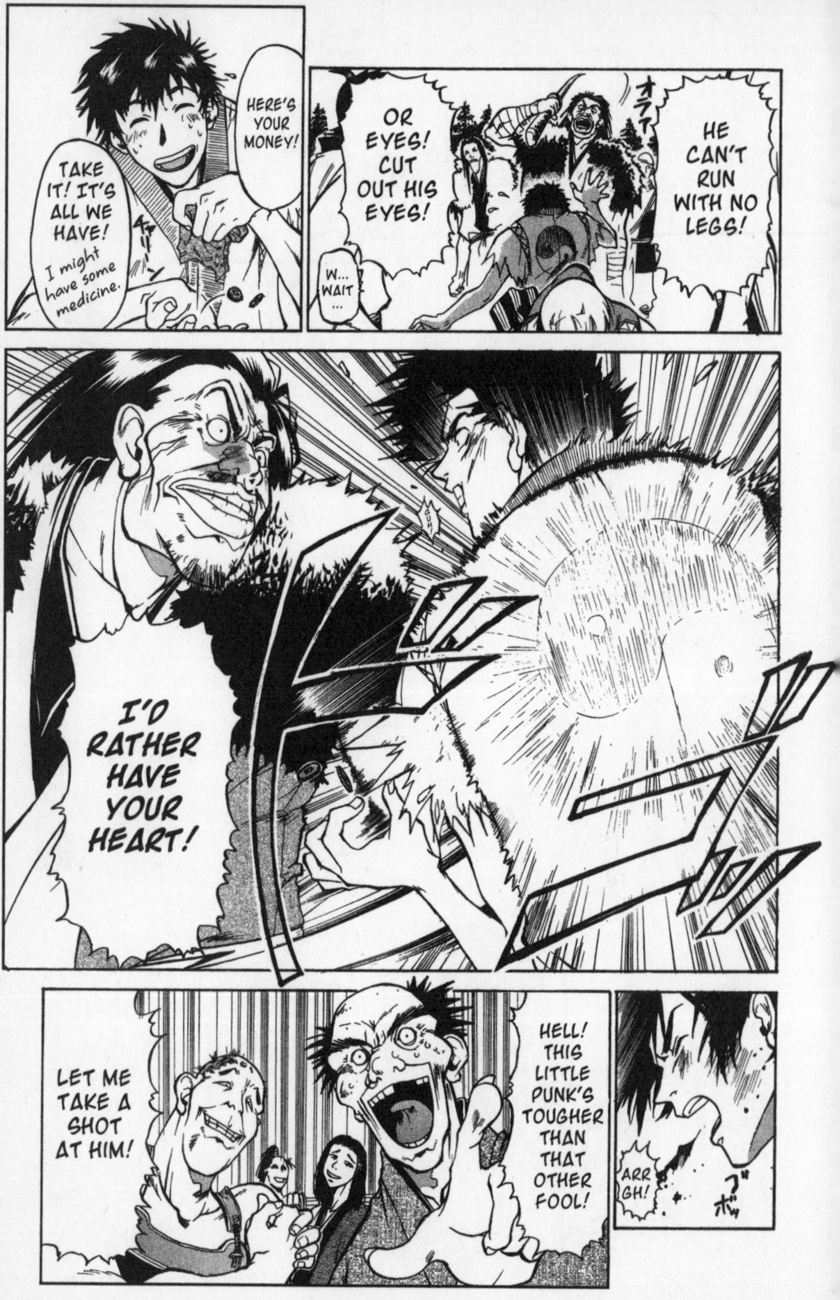
HE CAN'T RUN WITH NO LEGS!
オラァ
OR EYES! CUT OUT HIS EYES!
W... WAIT ...
HERE'S YOUR MONEY!
TAKE IT! IT'S ALL WE HAVE!
I might have some medicine.
GUH!
I'D RATHER HAVE YOUR HEART!
ARRGH!
HELL! THIS LITTLE PUNK'S TOUGHER THAN THAT OTHER FOOL!
LET ME TAKE A SHOT AT HIM!

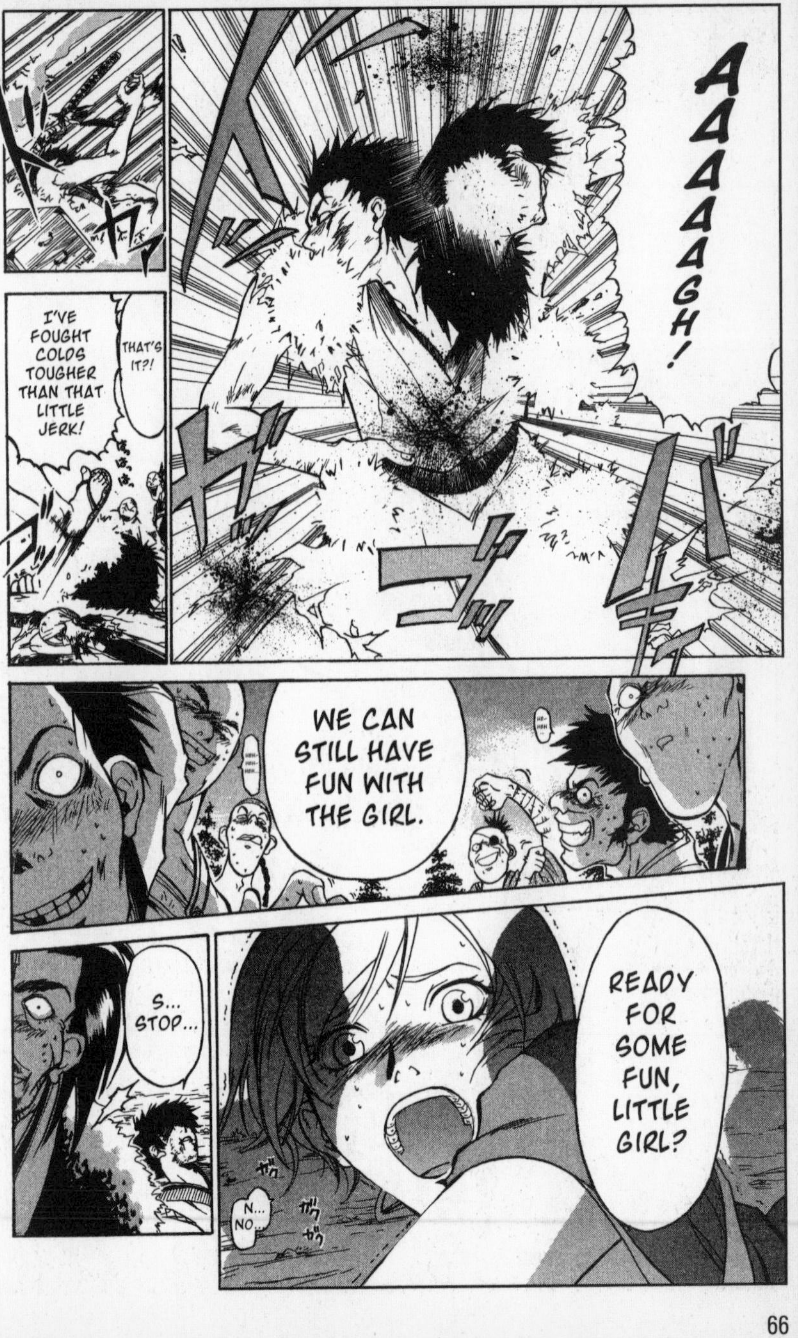
AAAAAAAGH!
THAT'S IT?!
I'VE FOUGHT COLDS TOUGHER THAN THAT LITTLE JERK!
WE CAN STILL HAVE FUN WITH THE GIRL.
READY FOR SOME FUN, LITTLE GIRL?
N... NO...
S... STOP...

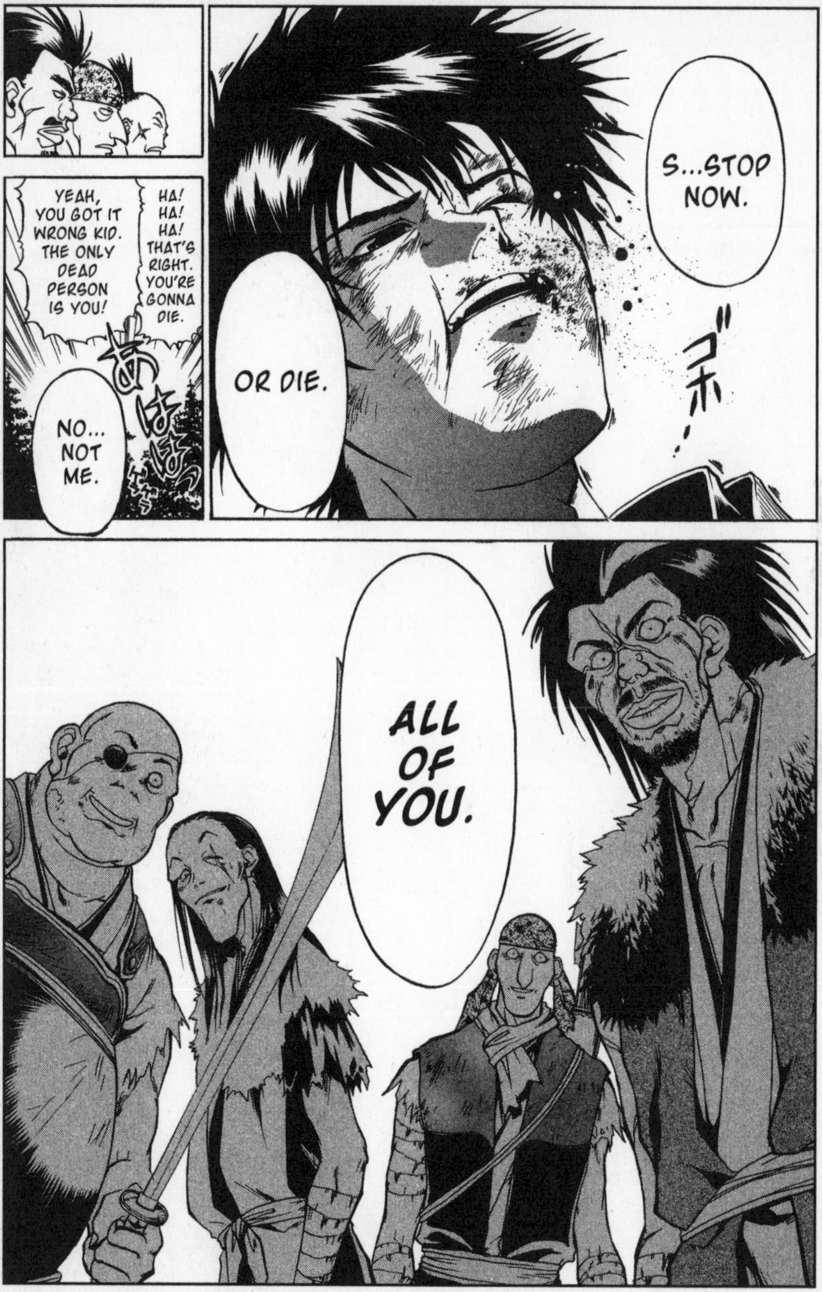
S...STOP NOW.
ゴボ
OR DIE.
HA! HA! HA! THAT'S RIGHT. YOU'RE GONNA DIE.
YEAH, YOU GOT IT WRONG KID. THE ONLY DEAD PERSON IS YOU!
NO... NOT ME.
ALL OF YOU.

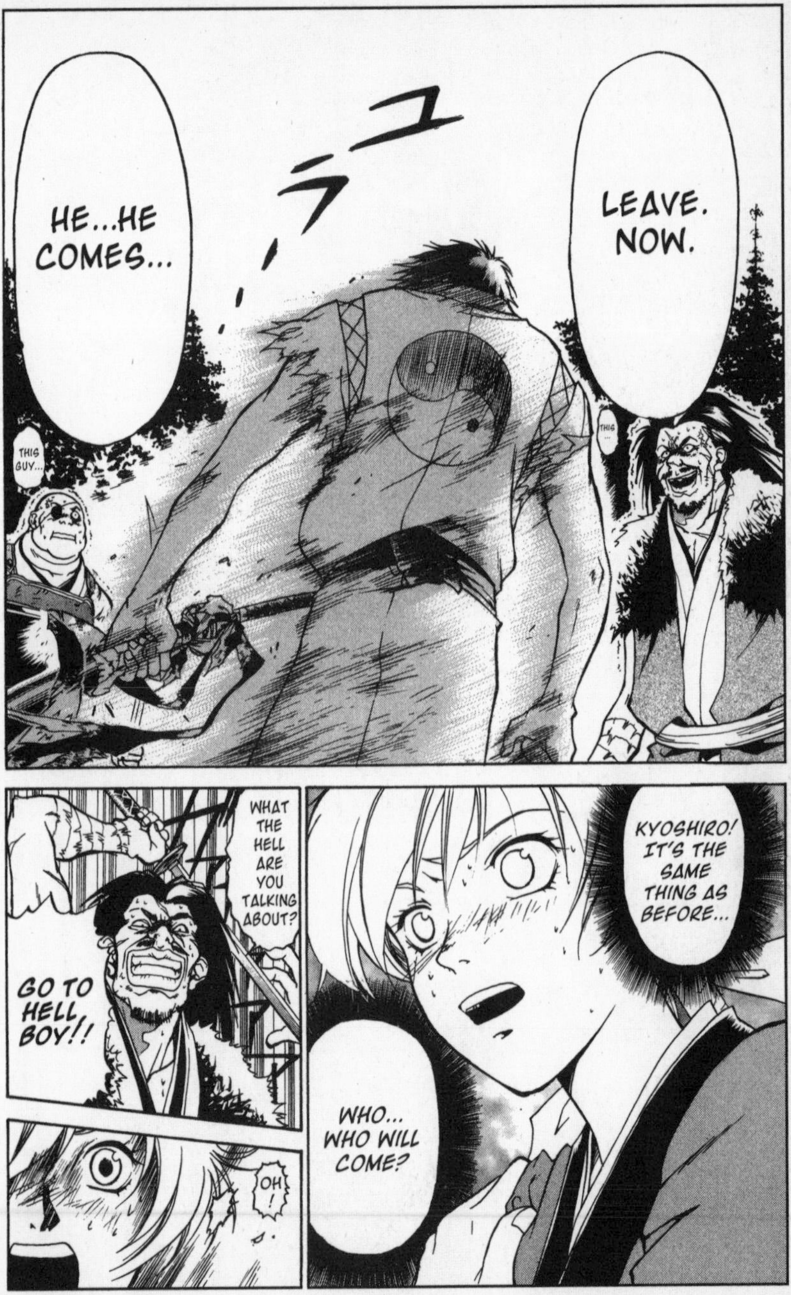
LEAVE. NOW.
THIS...
ユラ
HE...HE COMES...
THIS GUY...
KYOSHIRO! IT'S THE SAME THING AS BEFORE...
WHO... WHO WILL COME?
WHAT THE HELL ARE YOU TALKING ABOUT?
GO TO HELL BOY!!
OH!

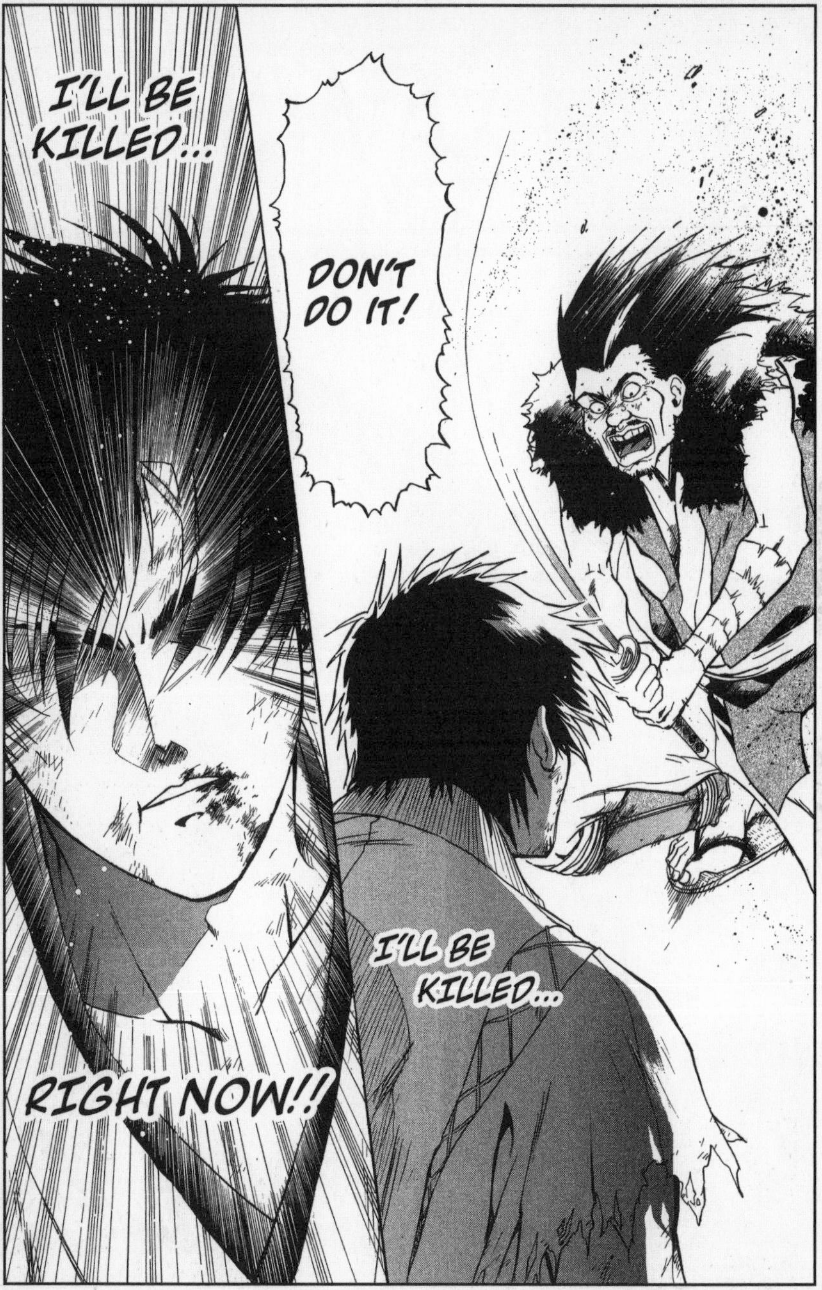
DON'T DO IT!
I'LL BE KILLED...
I'LL BE KILLED...
RIGHT NOW!!

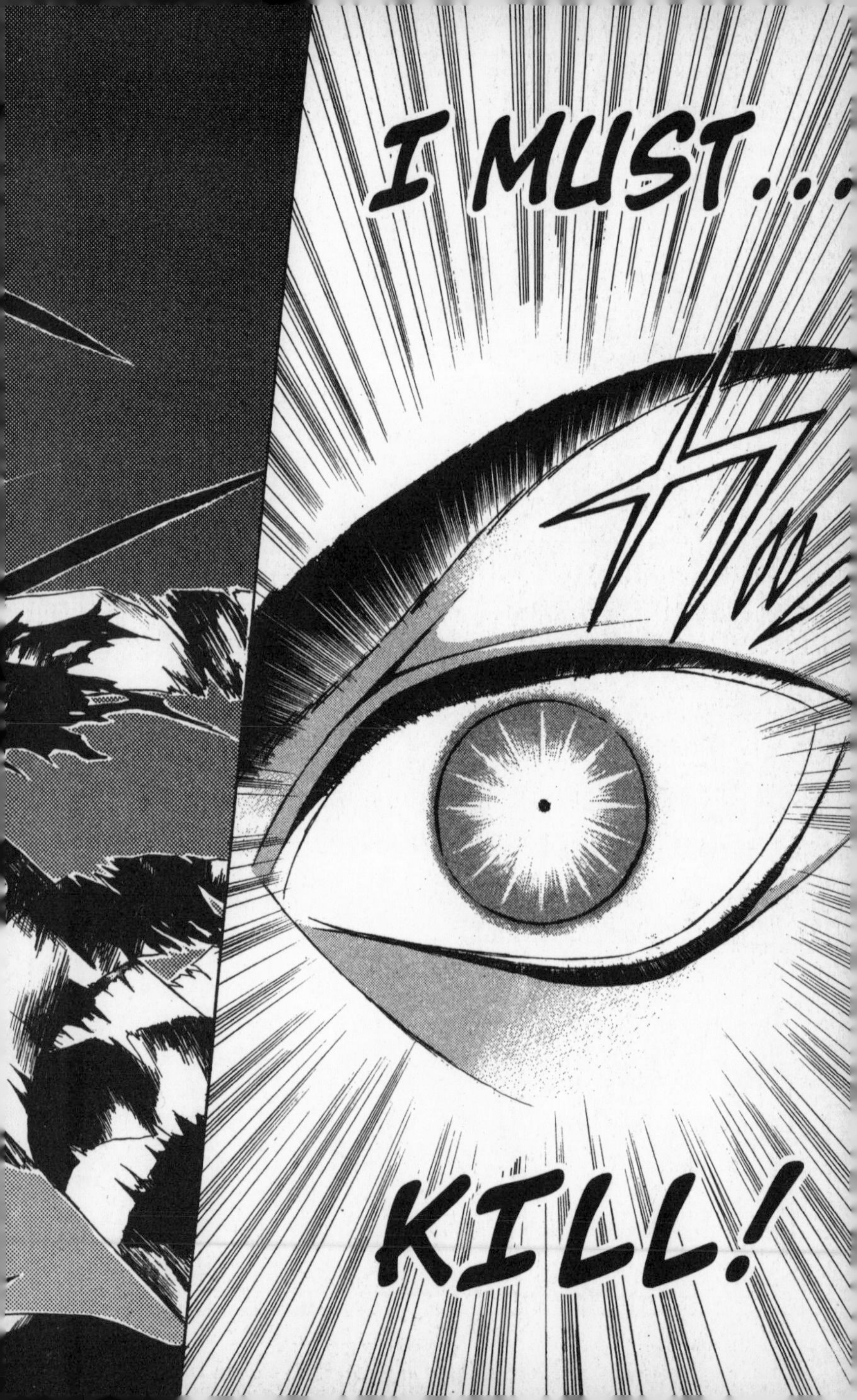
I MUST...
KILL!

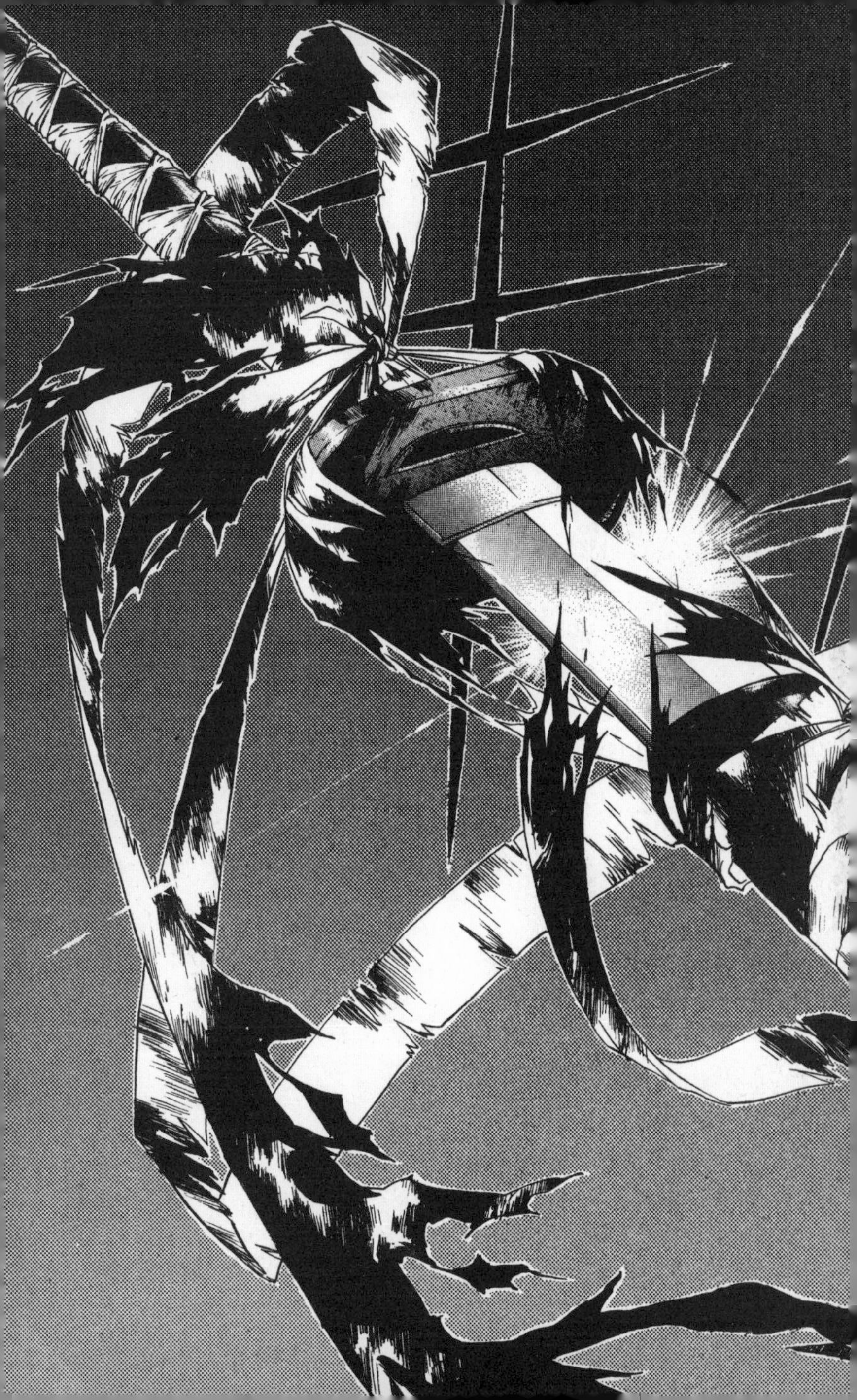

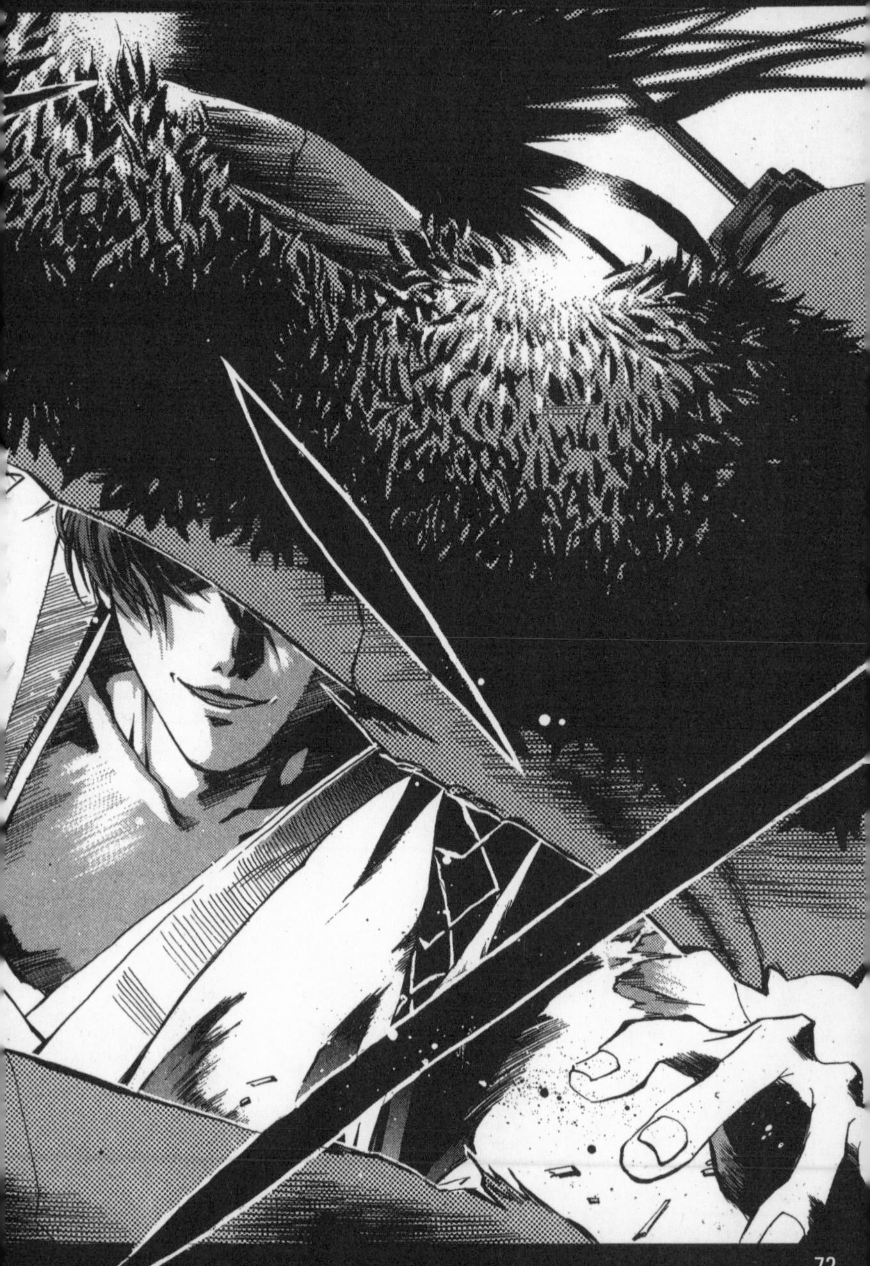

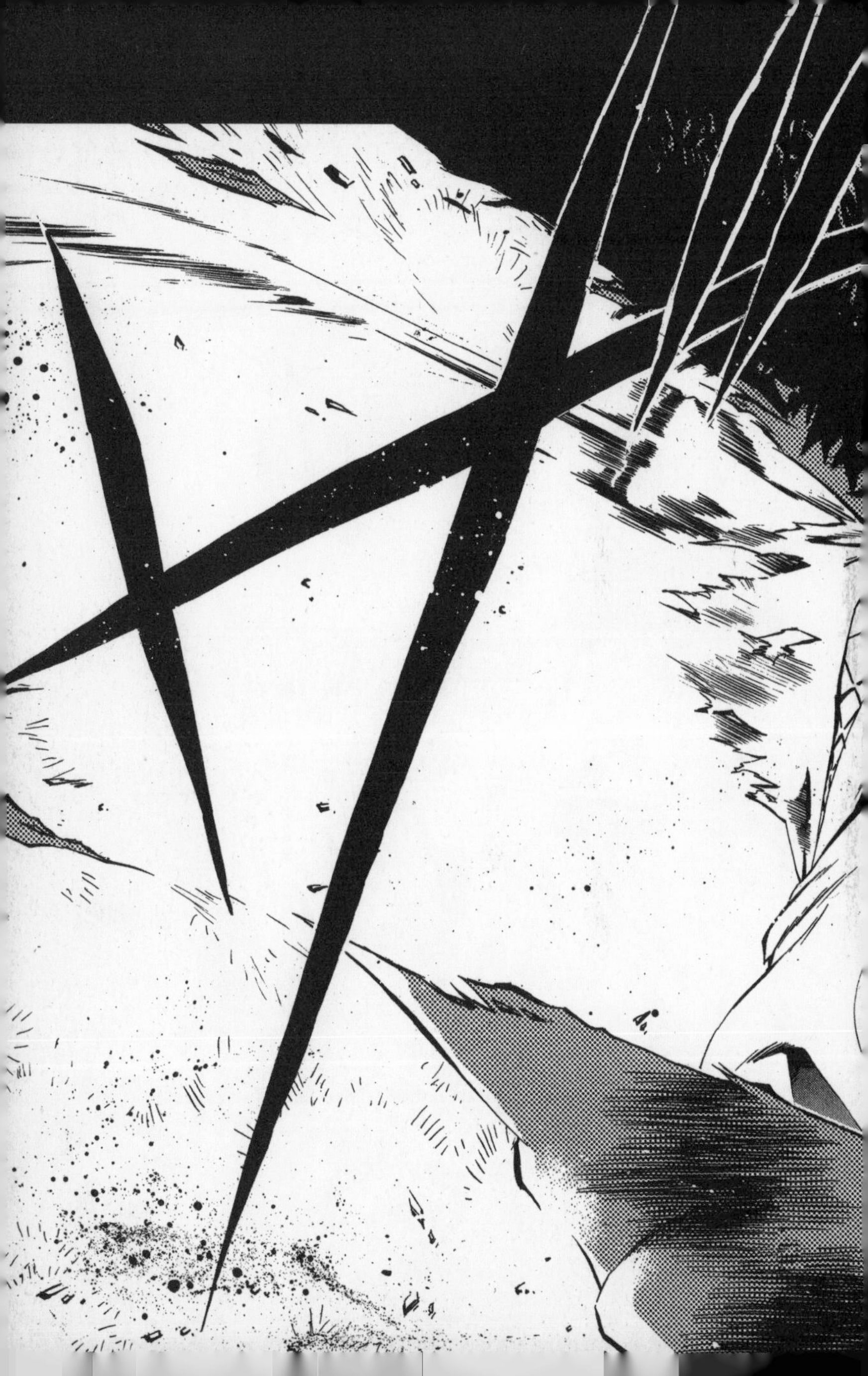

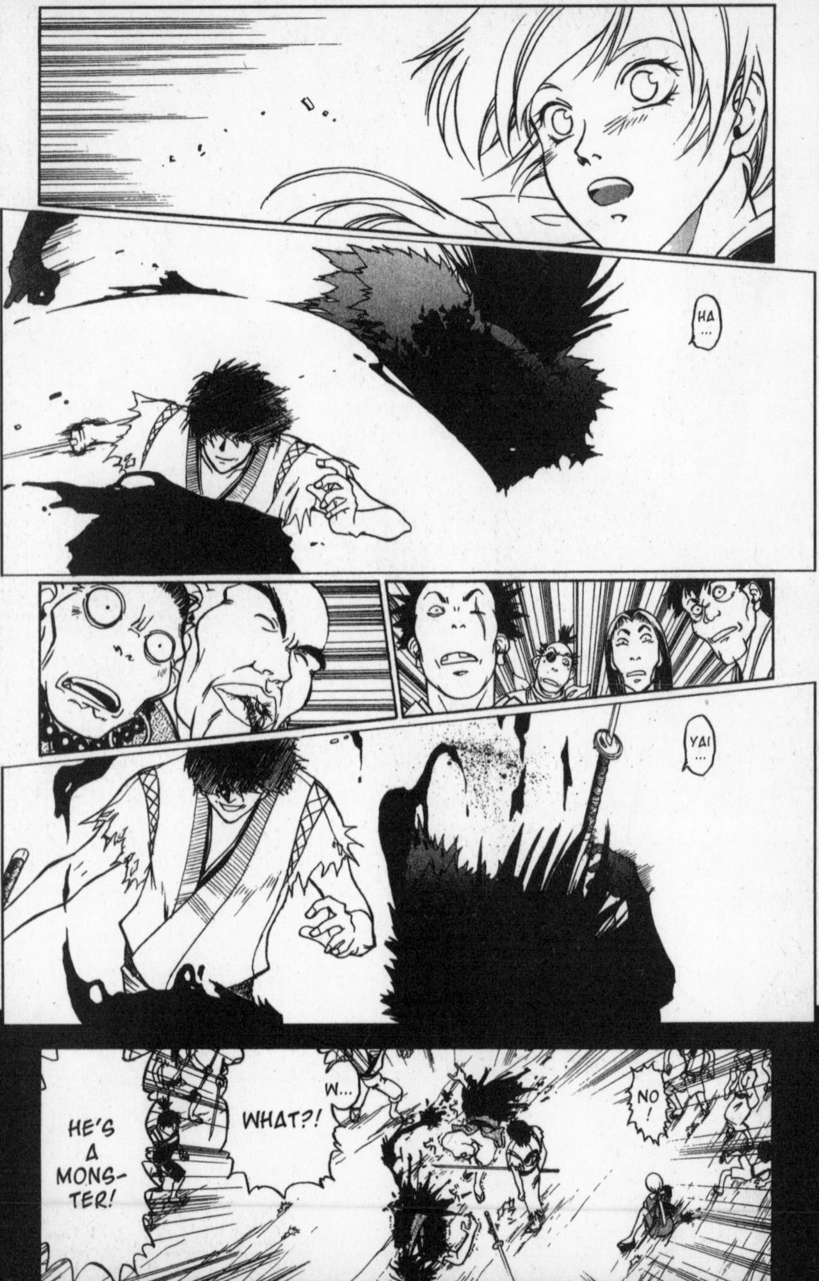
HA ...
YAI ...
NO!
W...
WHAT?!
HE'S A MONSTER!

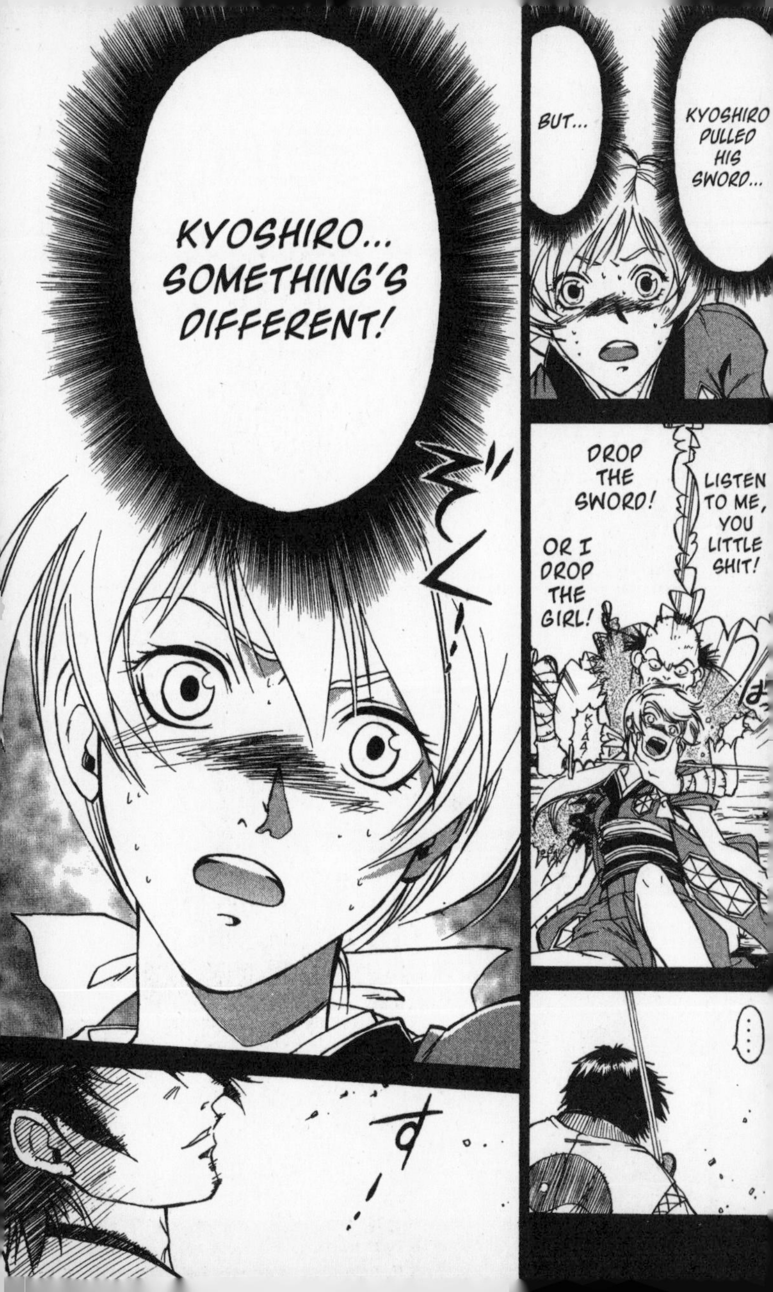
KYOSHIRO PULLED HIS SWORD...
BUT...
LISTEN TO ME, YOU LITTLE SHIT!
DROP THE SWORD!
OR I DROP THE GIRL!
...
KYOSHIRO... SOMETHING'S DIFFERENT!

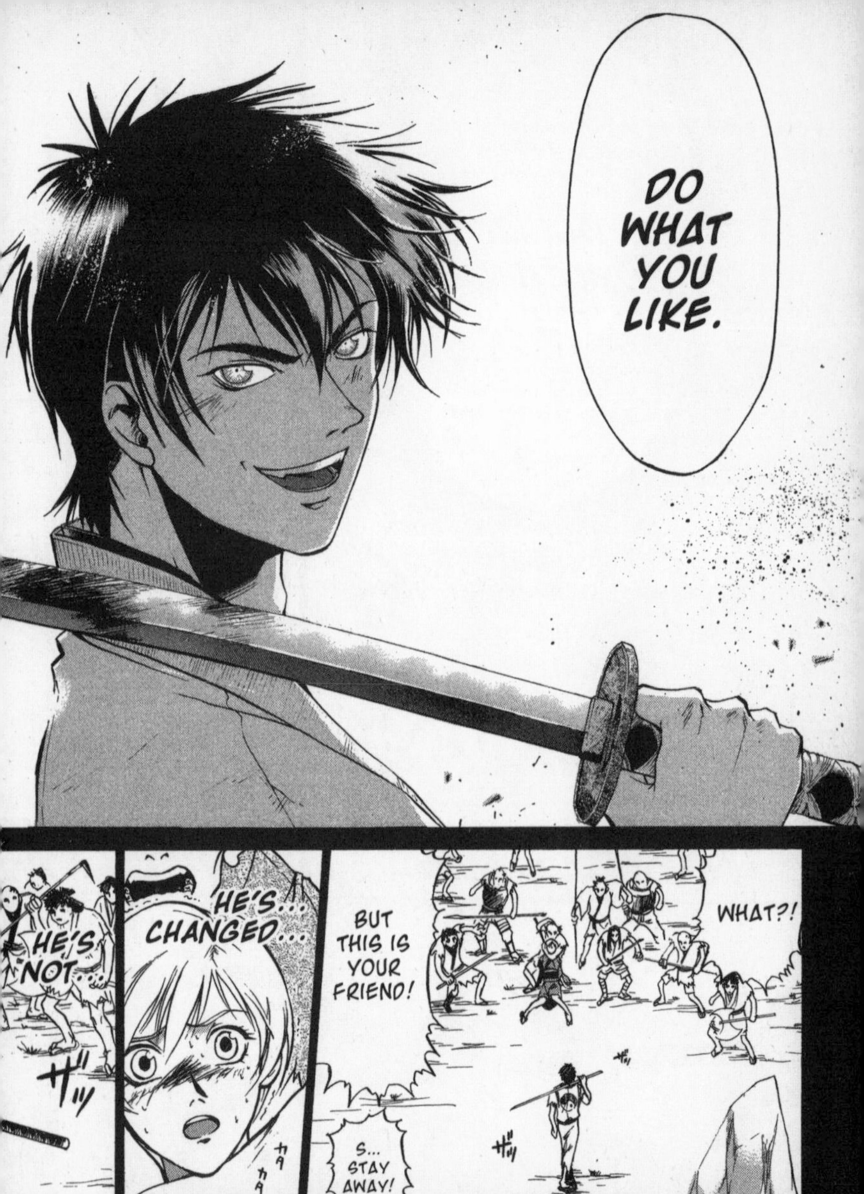
DO WHAT YOU LIKE.
WHAT?!
BUT THIS IS YOUR FRIEND!
S... STAY AWAY!
HE'S... CHANGED...
HE'S NOT...

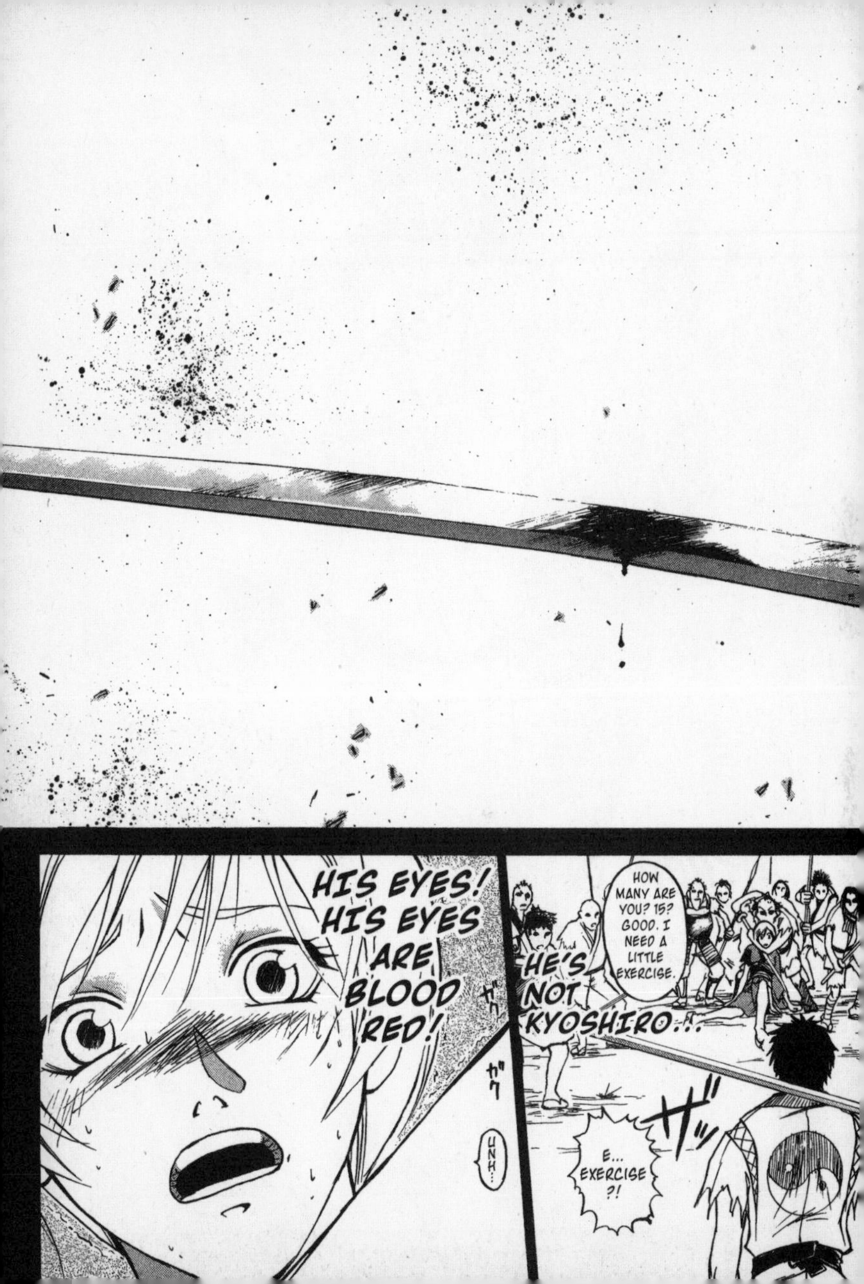
HOW MANY ARE YOU? 15? GOOD. I NEED A LITTLE EXERCISE.
HE'S NOT KYOSHIRO...!!
ザッ
E... EXERCISE?!
HIS EYES! HIS EYES ARE BLOOD RED!
ガク
ガク
UNH...

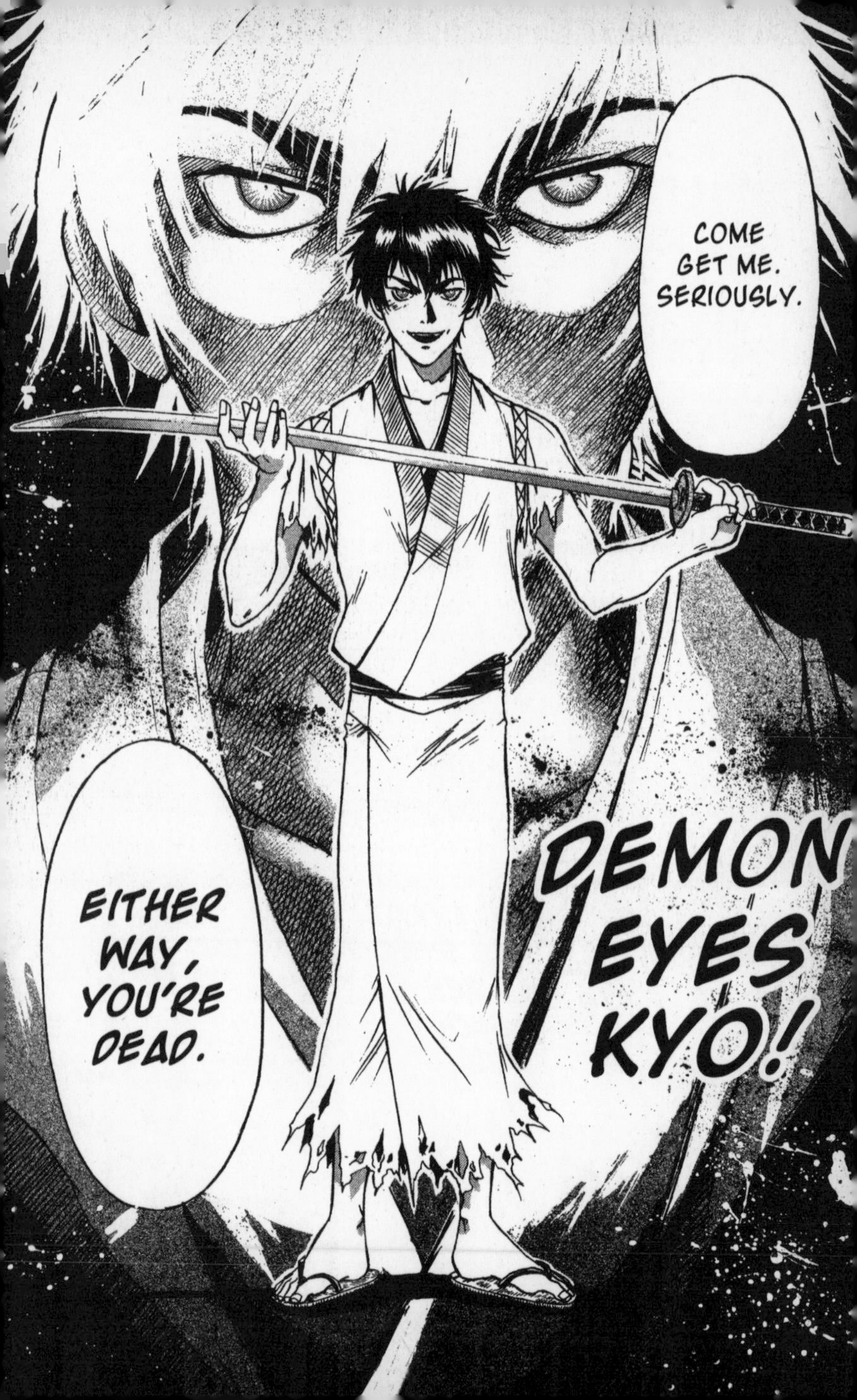
COME GET ME. SERIOUSLY.
EITHER WAY, YOU'RE DEAD.
DEMON EYES KYO!

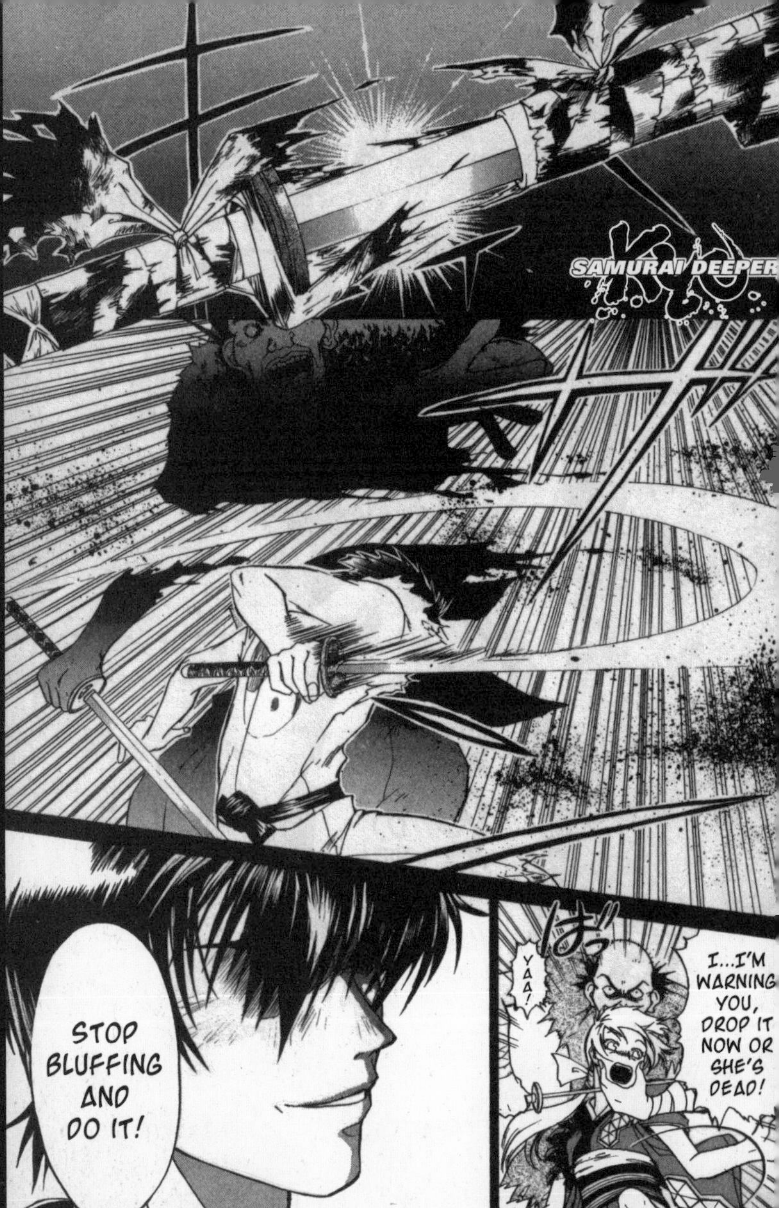
SAMURAI DEEPER KYO
ばっ
YAAA!
I...I'M WARNING YOU, DROP IT NOW OR SHE'S DEAD!
STOP BLUFFING AND DO IT!

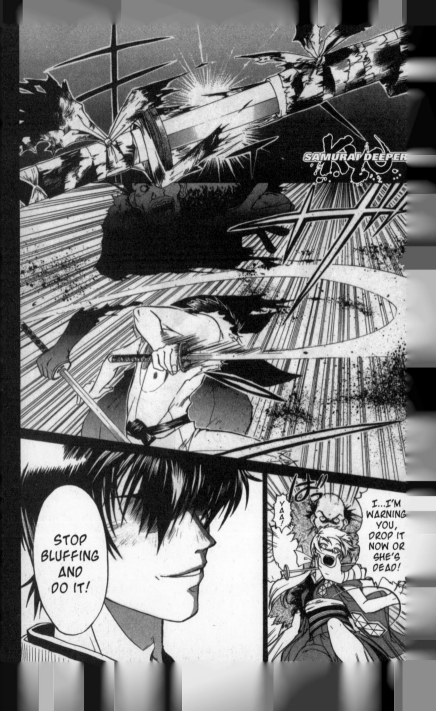

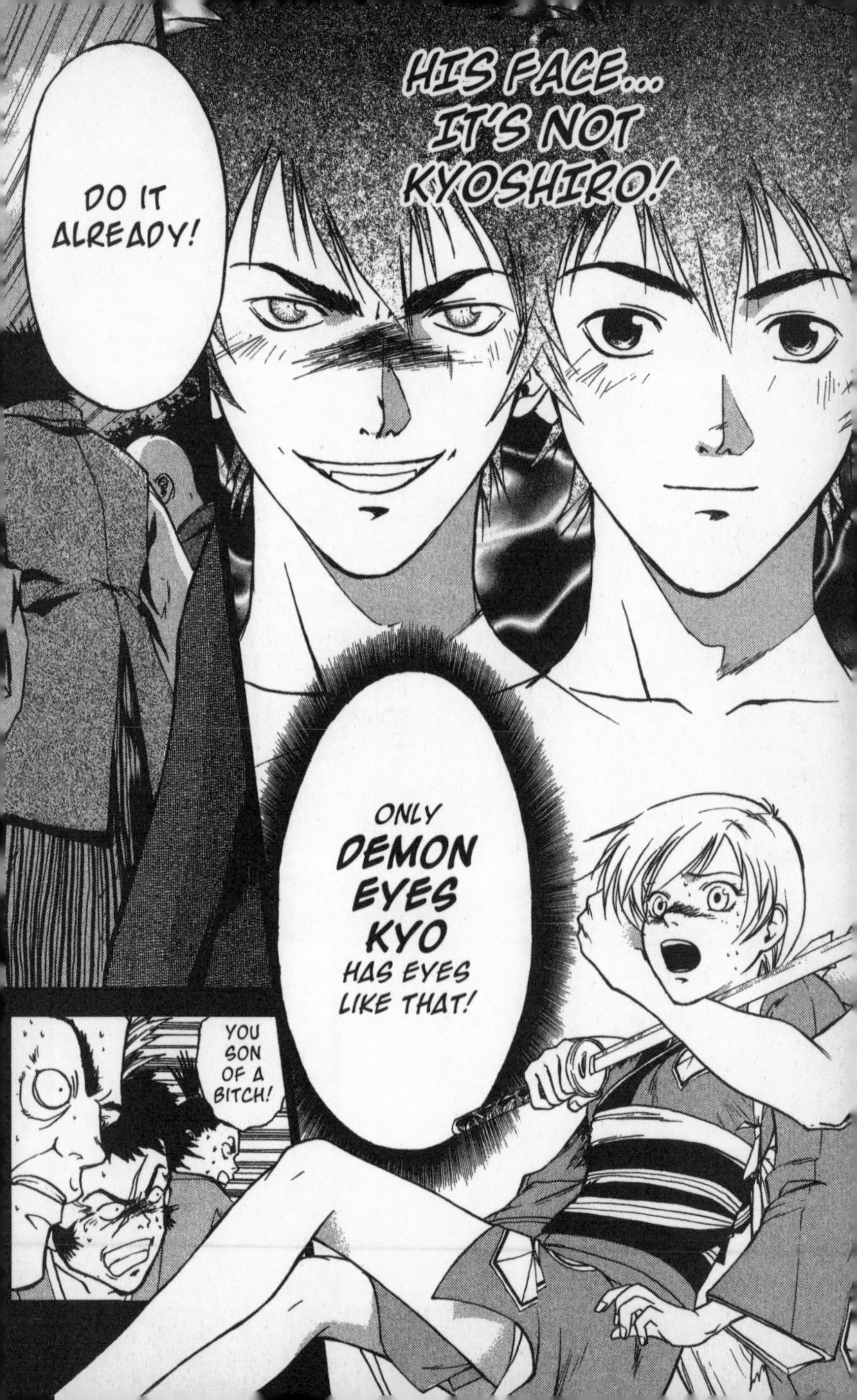
HIS FACE... IT'S NOT KYOSHIRO!
DO IT ALREADY!
ONLY DEMON EYES KYO HAS EYES LIKE THAT!
YOU SON OF A BITCH!

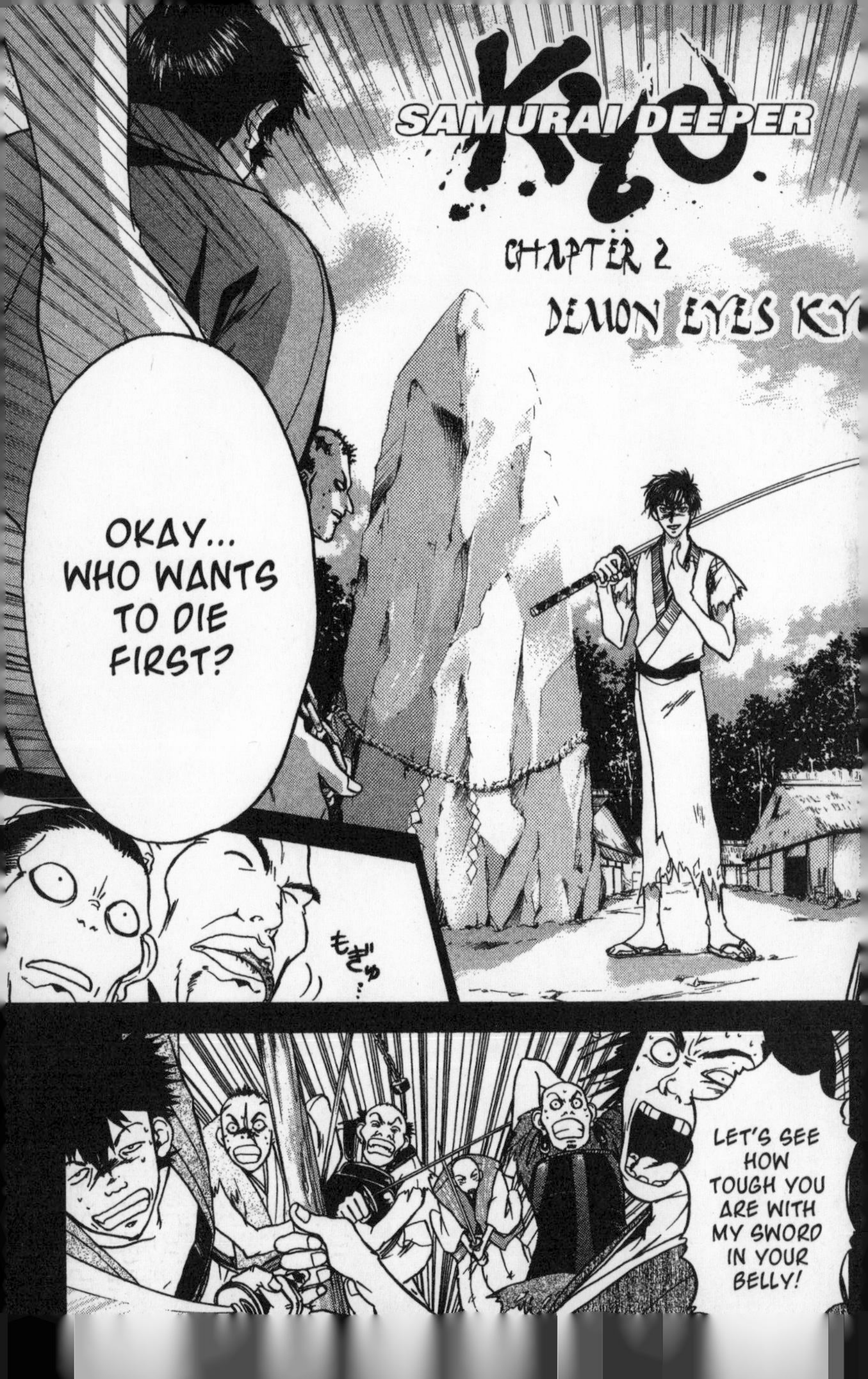
SAMURAI DEEPER KYO
CHAPTER 2
DEMON EYES KY
OKAY... WHO WANTS TO DIE FIRST?
もぎゅ…
LET'S SEE HOW TOUGH YOU ARE WITH MY SWORD IN YOUR BELLY!

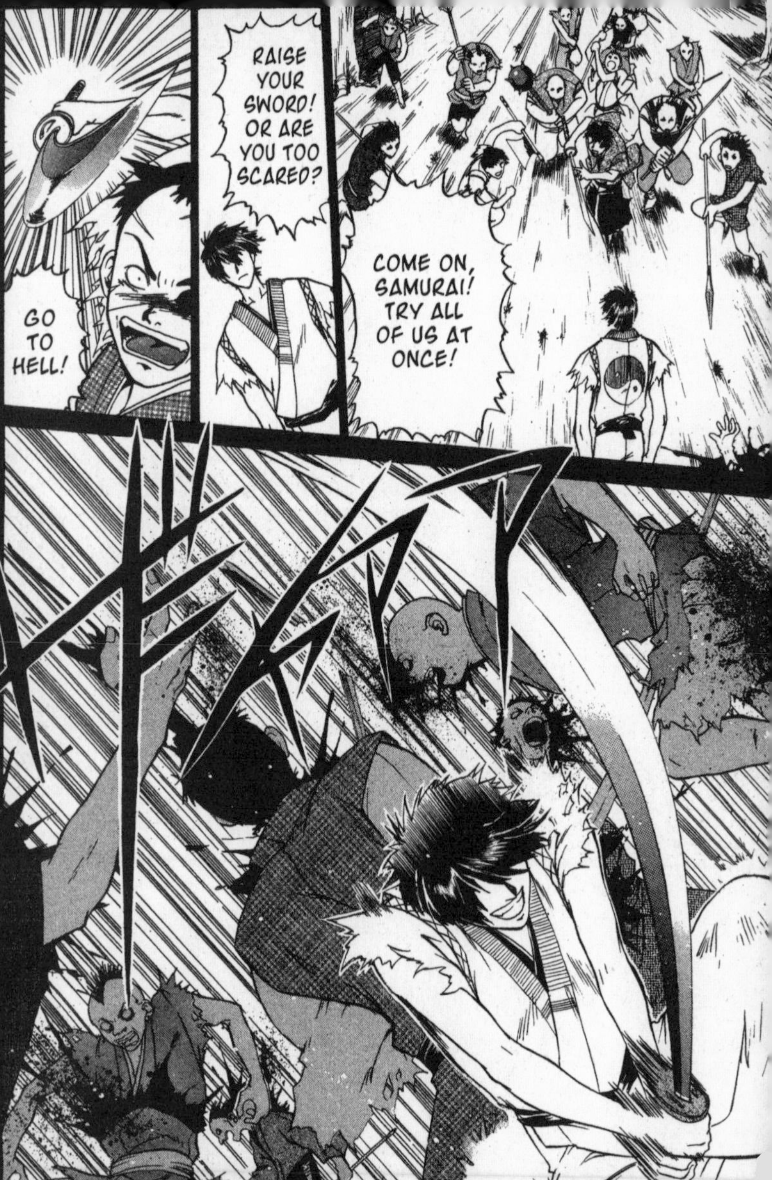
COME ON, SAMURAI! TRY ALL OF US AT ONCE!
RAISE YOUR SWORD! OR ARE YOU TOO SCARED?
GO TO HELL!

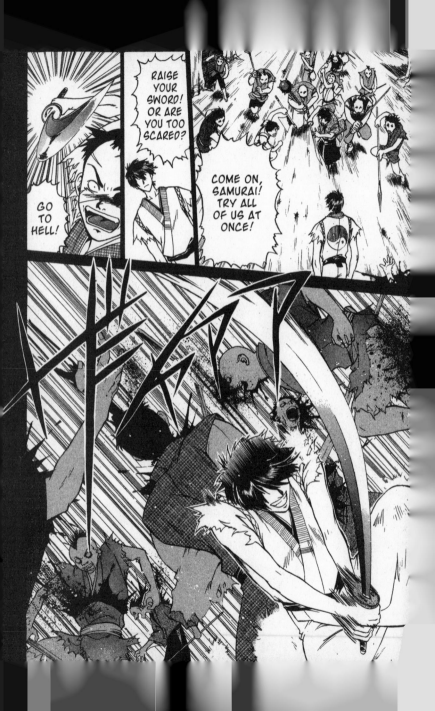

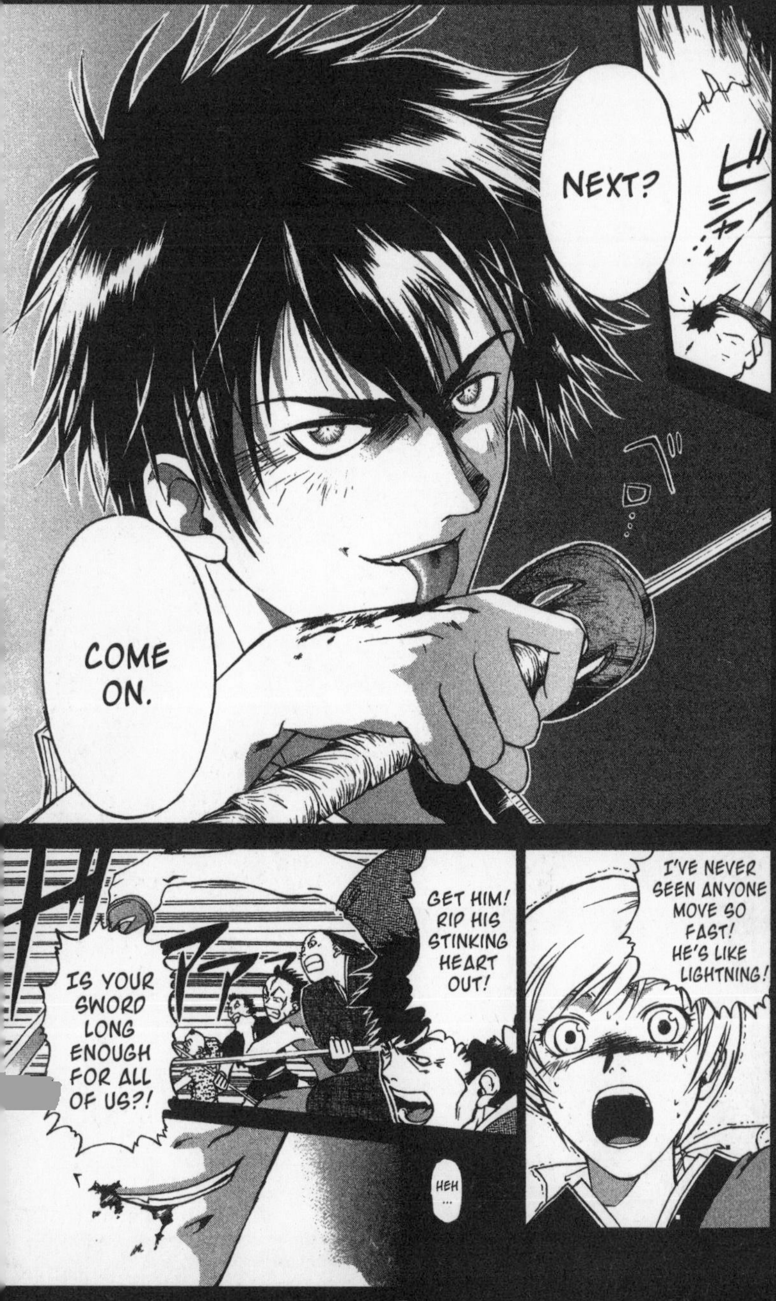
NEXT?
COME ON.
I'VE NEVER SEEN ANYONE MOVE SO FAST! HE'S LIKE LIGHTNING!
GET HIM! RIP HIS STINKING HEART OUT!
IS YOUR SWORD LONG ENOUGH FOR ALL OF US?!
HEH ...

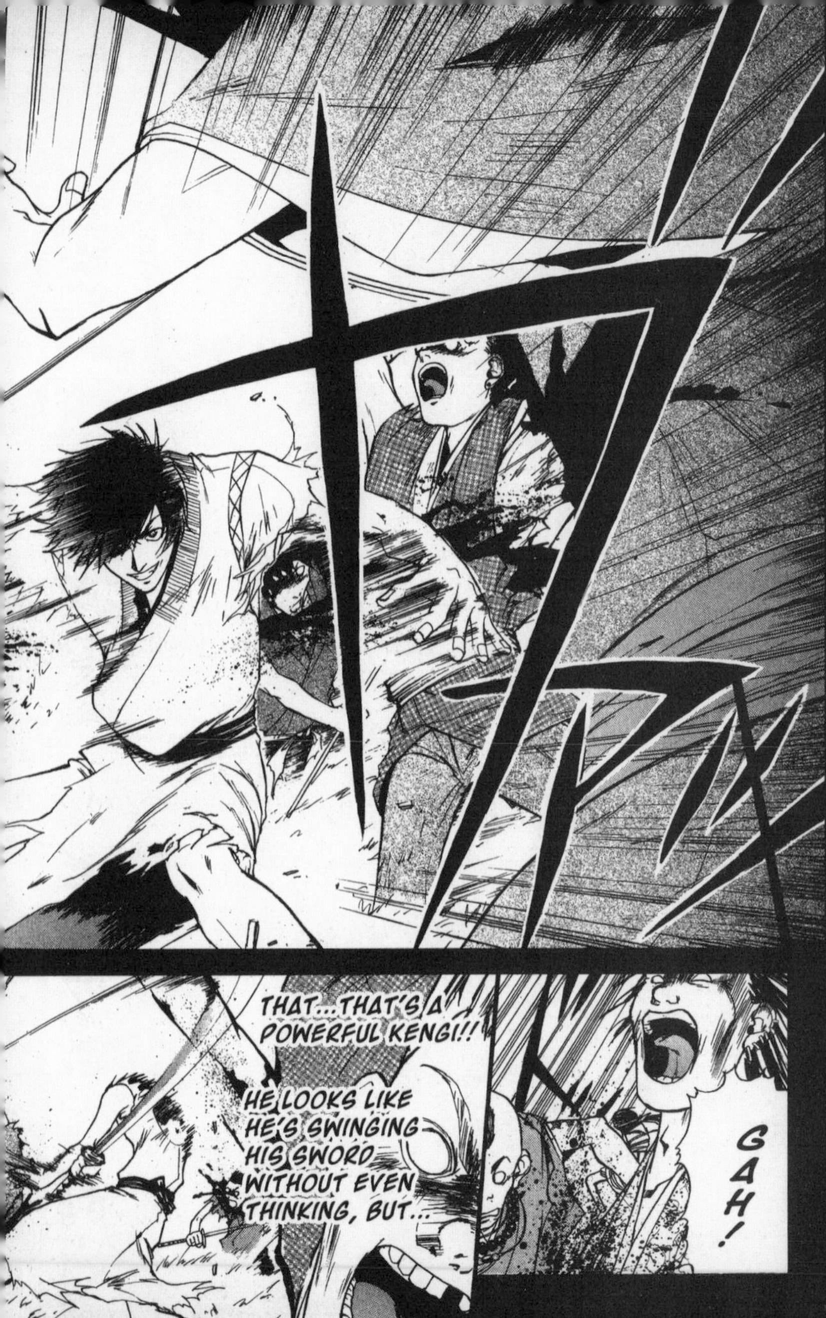
GAH!
THAT...THAT'S A POWERFUL KENGI!!
HE LOOKS LIKE HE'S SWINGING HIS SWORD WITHOUT EVEN THINKING, BUT...

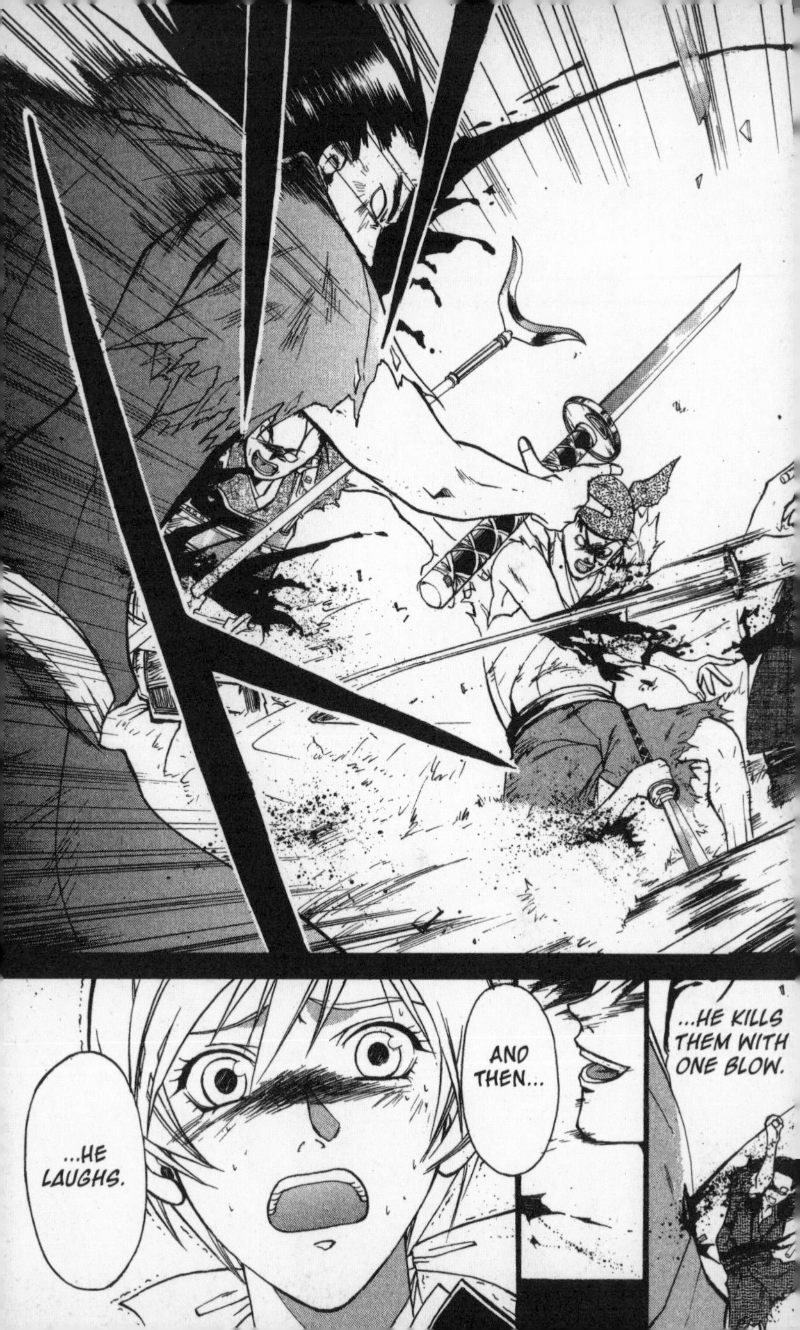
...HE KILLS THEM WITH ONE BLOW.
AND THEN...
...HE LAUGHS.

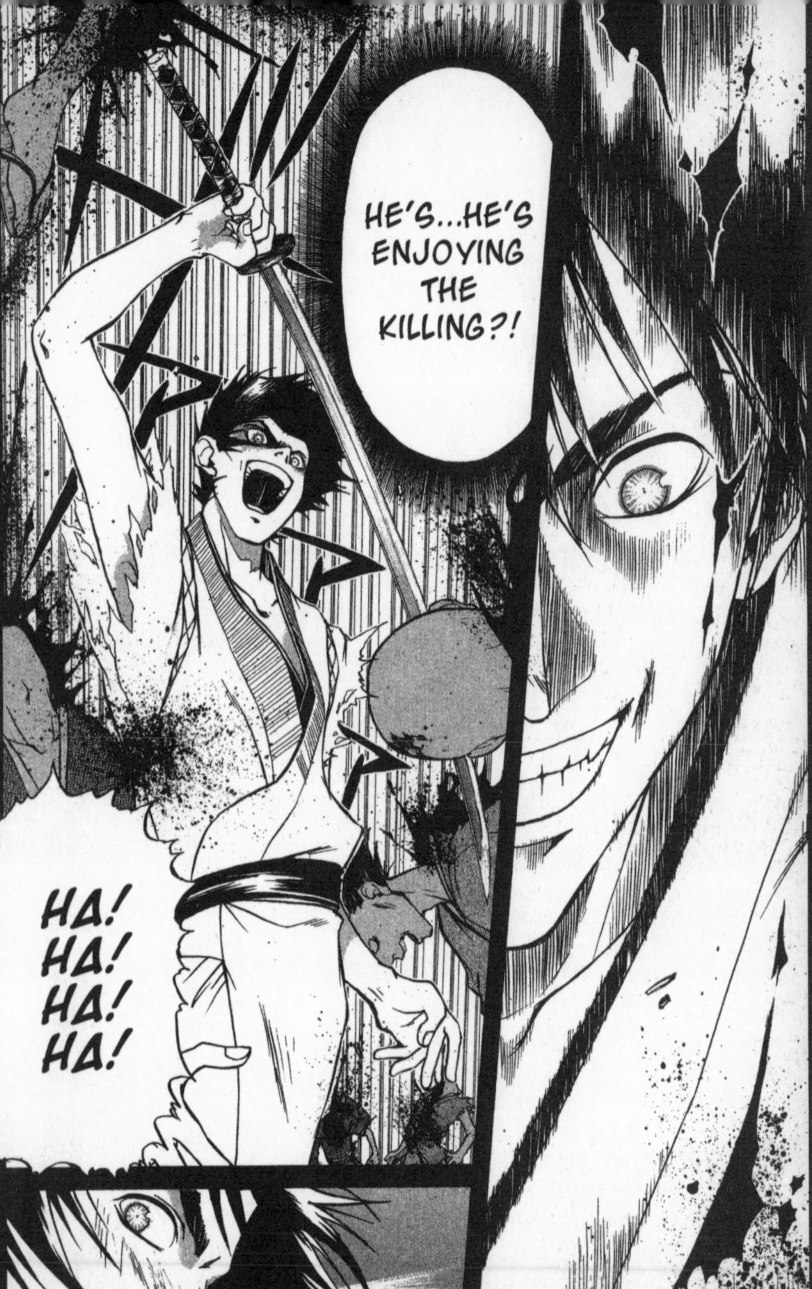
HE'S...HE'S ENJOYING THE KILLING?!
HA! HA! HA! HA!

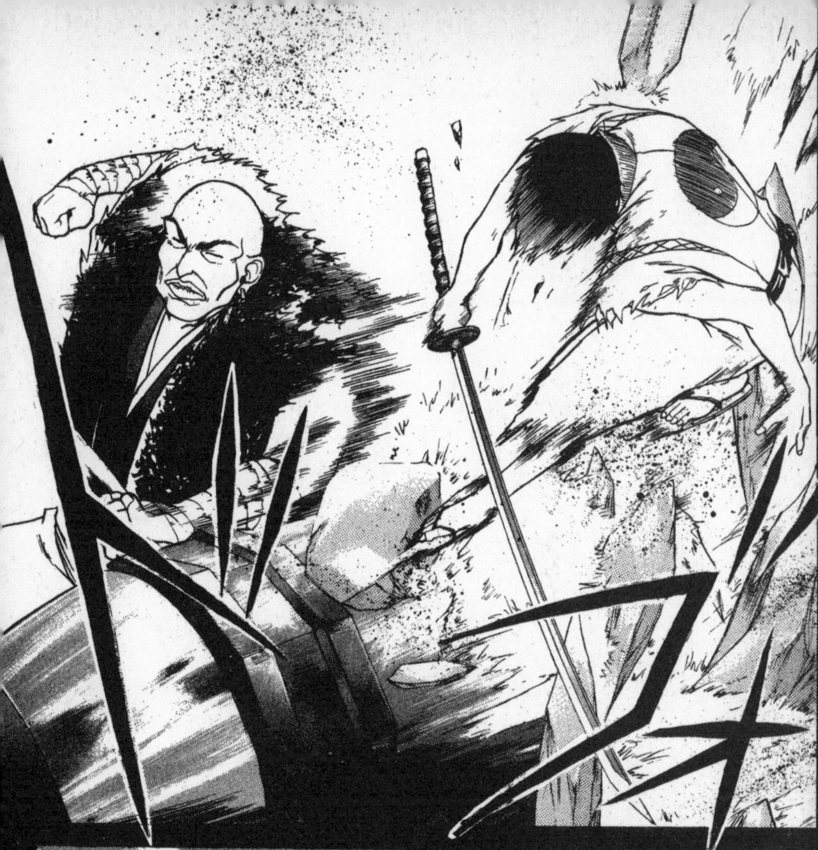
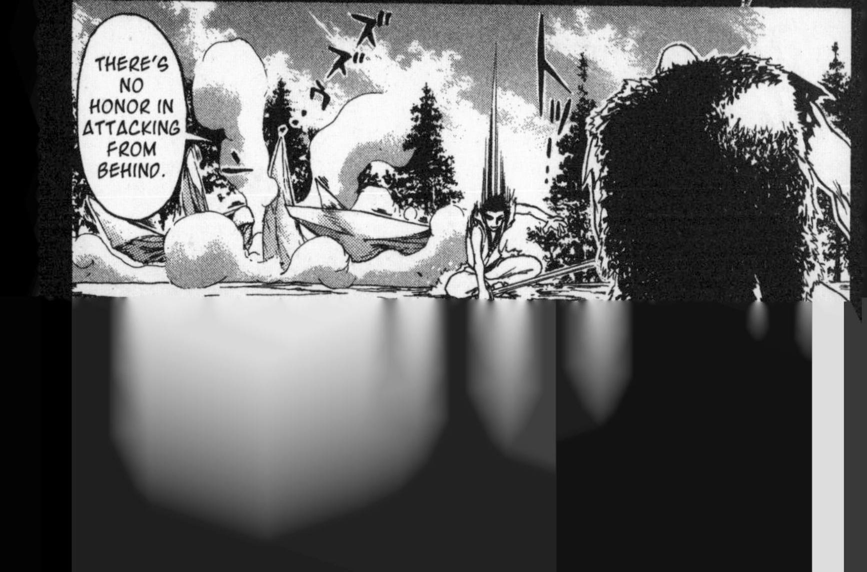
THERE'S NO HONOR IN ATTACKING FROM BEHIND.

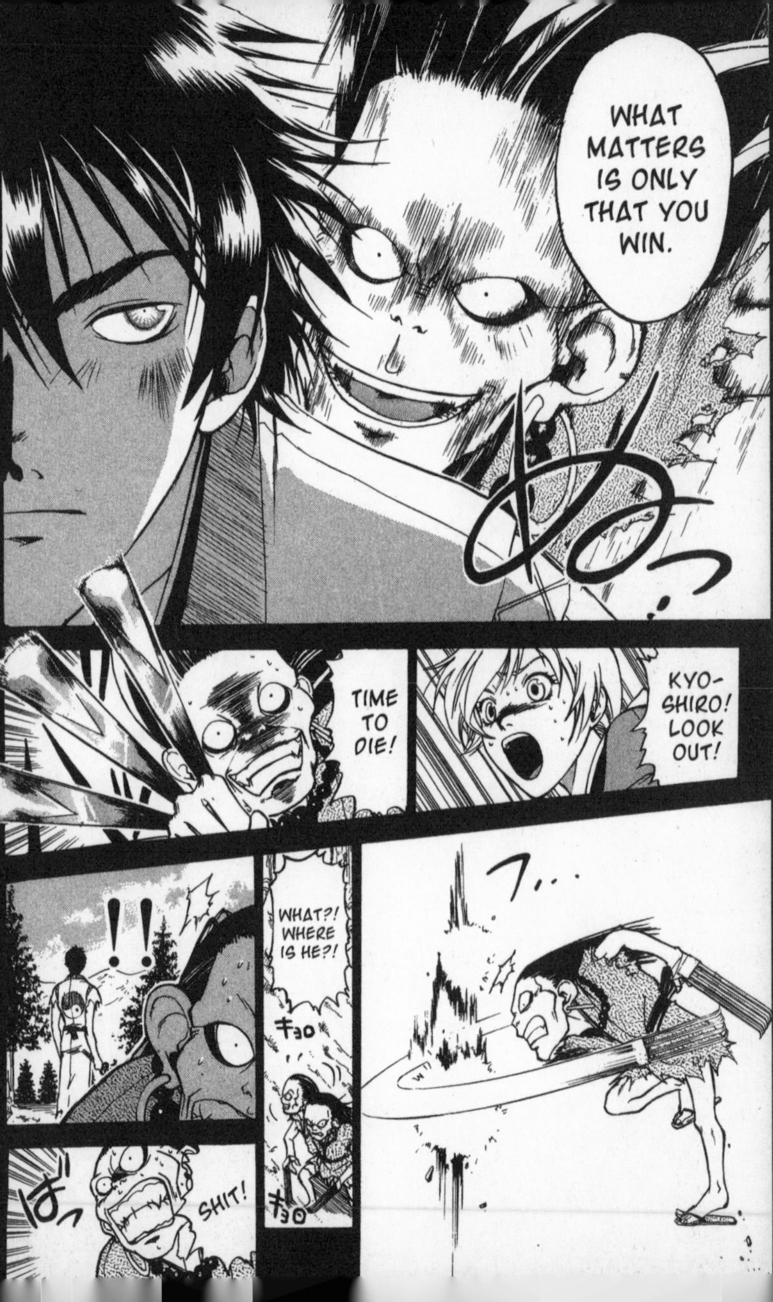
WHAT MATTERS IS ONLY THAT YOU WIN.
KYO-SHIRO! LOOK OUT!
TIME TO DIE!
WHAT?! WHERE IS HE?!
!!
SHIT!

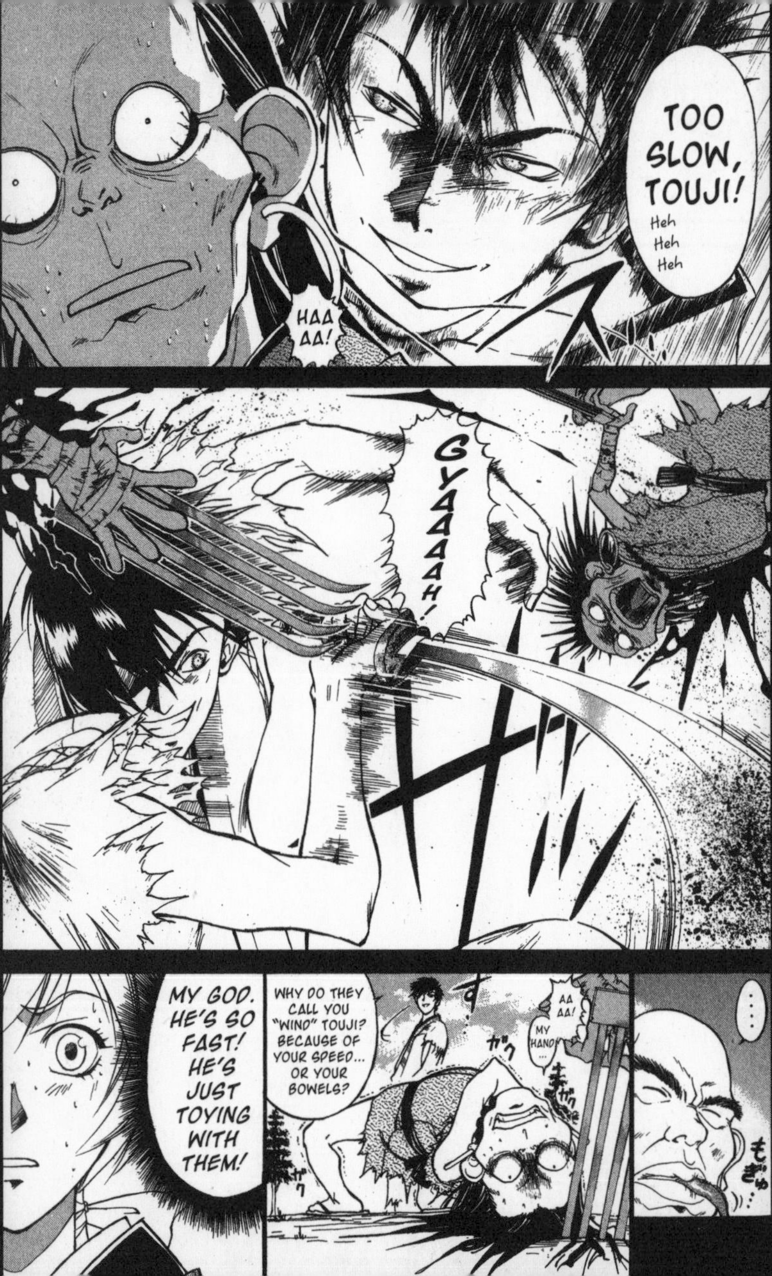
TOO SLOW, TOUJI!
Heh Heh Heh
HAAAA!
GYAAAAAH!
....
AA AA!
MY HAND! ...
WHY DO THEY CALL YOU "WIND" TOUJI? BECAUSE OF YOUR SPEED... OR YOUR BOWELS?
MY GOD. HE'S SO FAST! HE'S JUST TOYING WITH THEM!

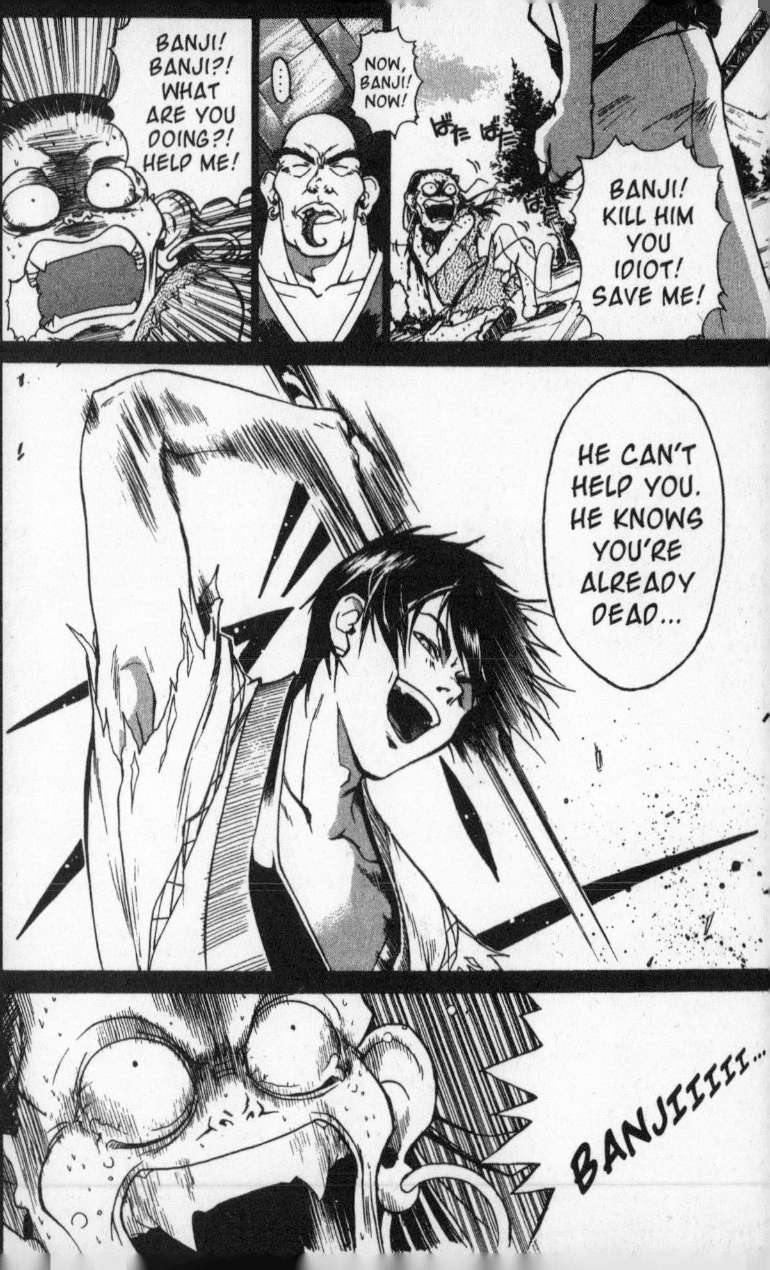

ばた ばた
BANJI! KILL HIM YOU IDIOT! SAVE ME!
NOW, BANJI! NOW!
...
BANJI! BANJI?! WHAT ARE YOU DOING?! HELP ME!
HE CAN'T HELP YOU. HE KNOWS YOU'RE ALREADY DEAD...
BANJIIIII...

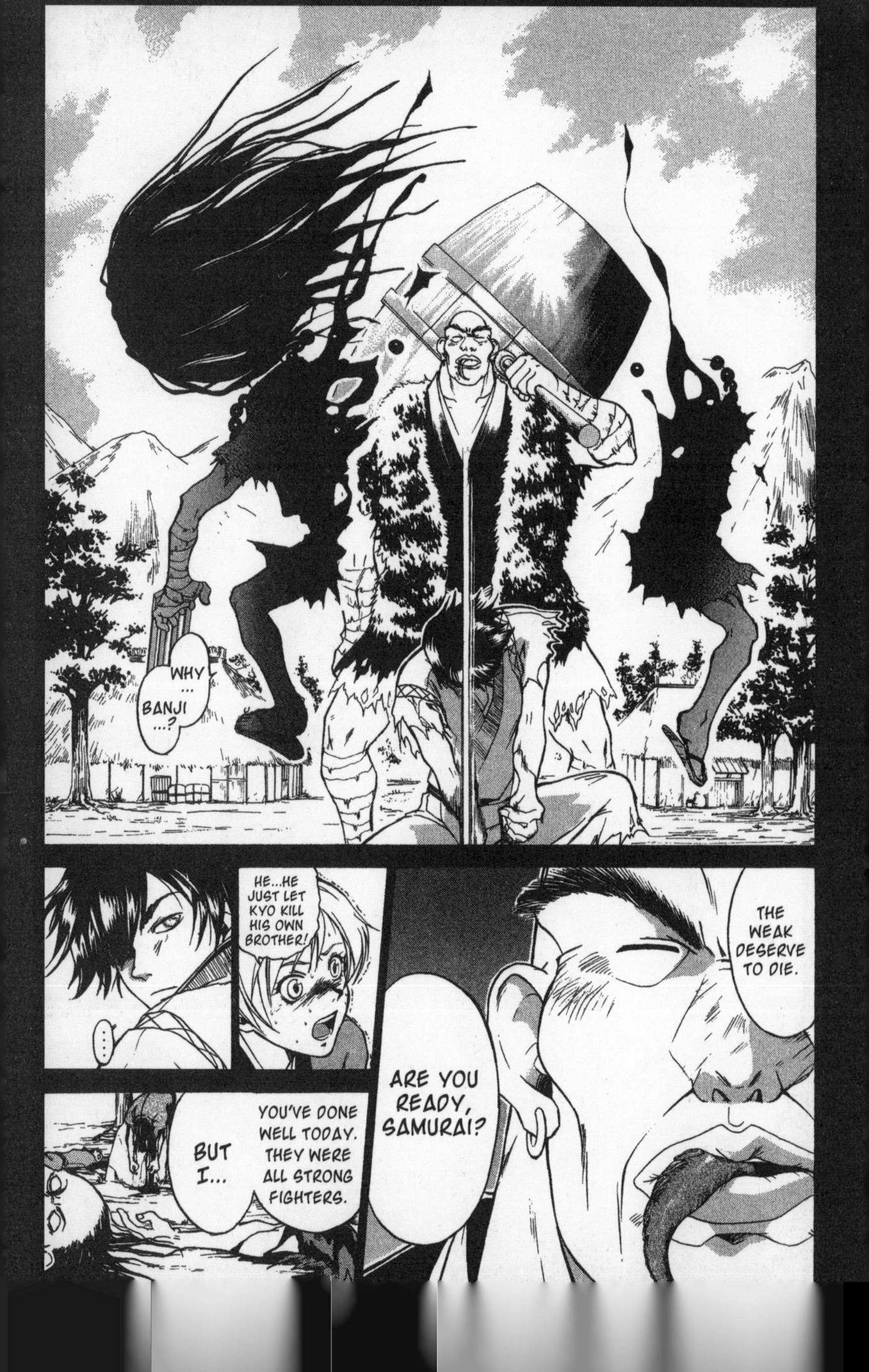
WHY ... BANJI ...?
THE WEAK DESERVE TO DIE.
ARE YOU READY, SAMURAI?
HE...HE JUST LET KYO KILL HIS OWN BROTHER!
....
YOU'VE DONE WELL TODAY. THEY WERE ALL STRONG FIGHTERS.
BUT I...

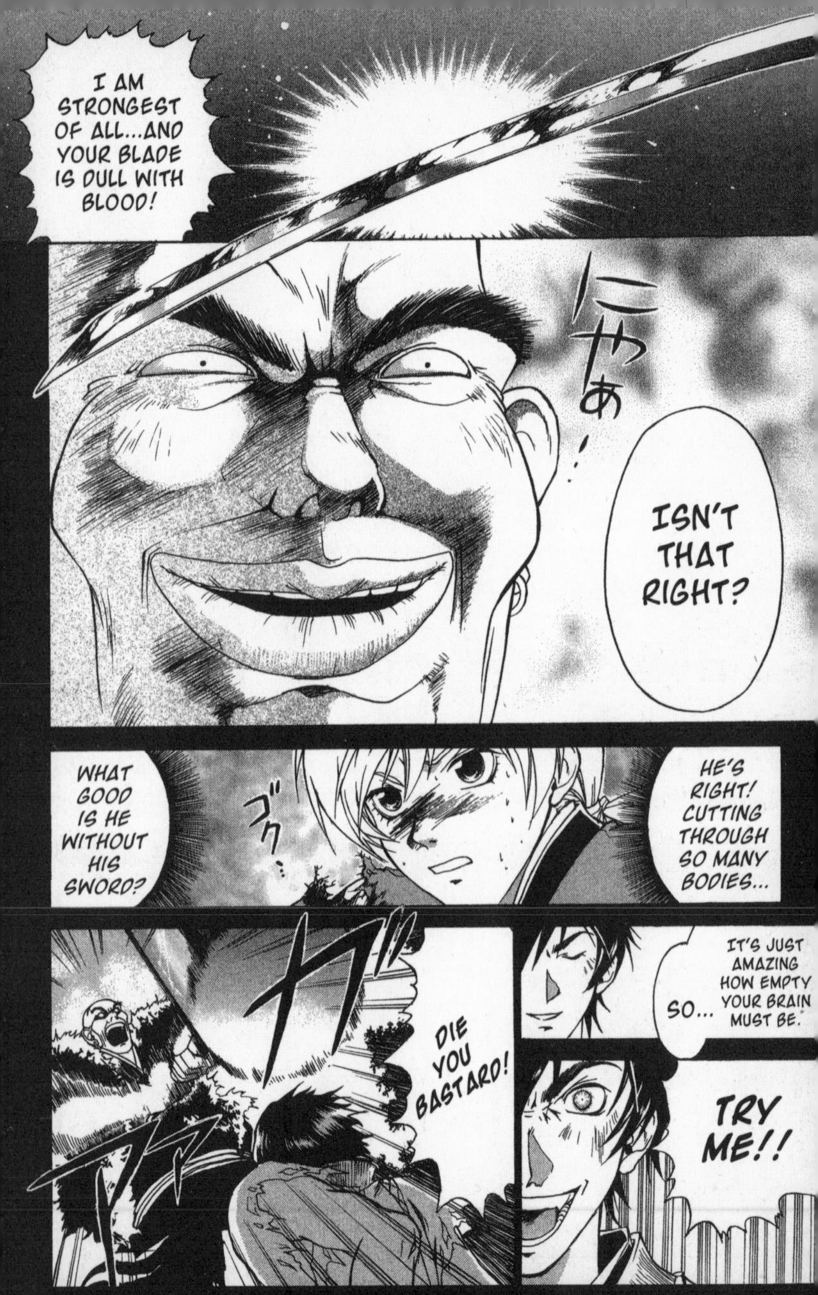
I AM STRONGEST OF ALL...AND YOUR BLADE IS DULL WITH BLOOD!
にやぁ
ISN'T THAT RIGHT?
HE'S RIGHT! CUTTING THROUGH SO MANY BODIES...
ゴク...
WHAT GOOD IS HE WITHOUT HIS SWORD?
SO...
IT'S JUST AMAZING HOW EMPTY YOUR BRAIN MUST BE.
TRY ME!!
DIE YOU BASTARD!

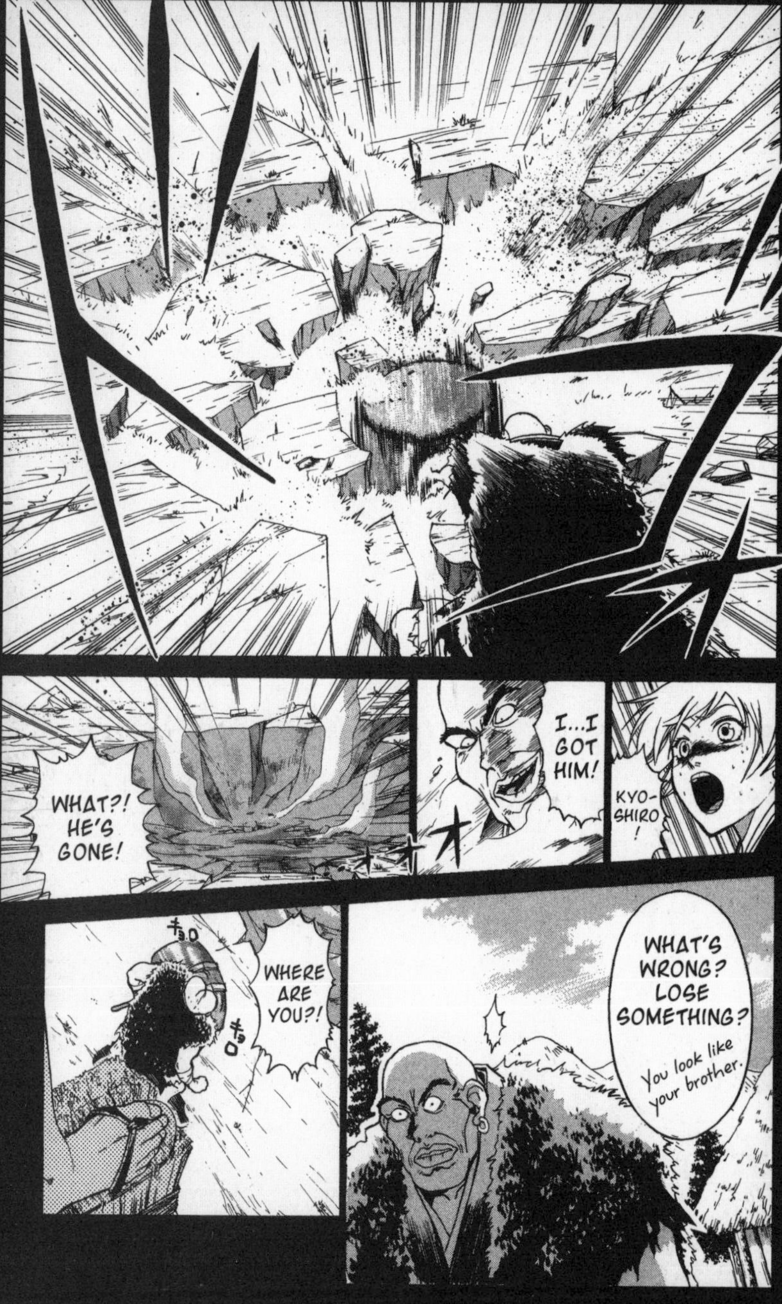
KYO-SHIRO!
I...I GOT HIM!
WHAT?! HE'S GONE!
WHAT'S WRONG? LOSE SOMETHING?
You look like your brother.
WHERE ARE YOU?!

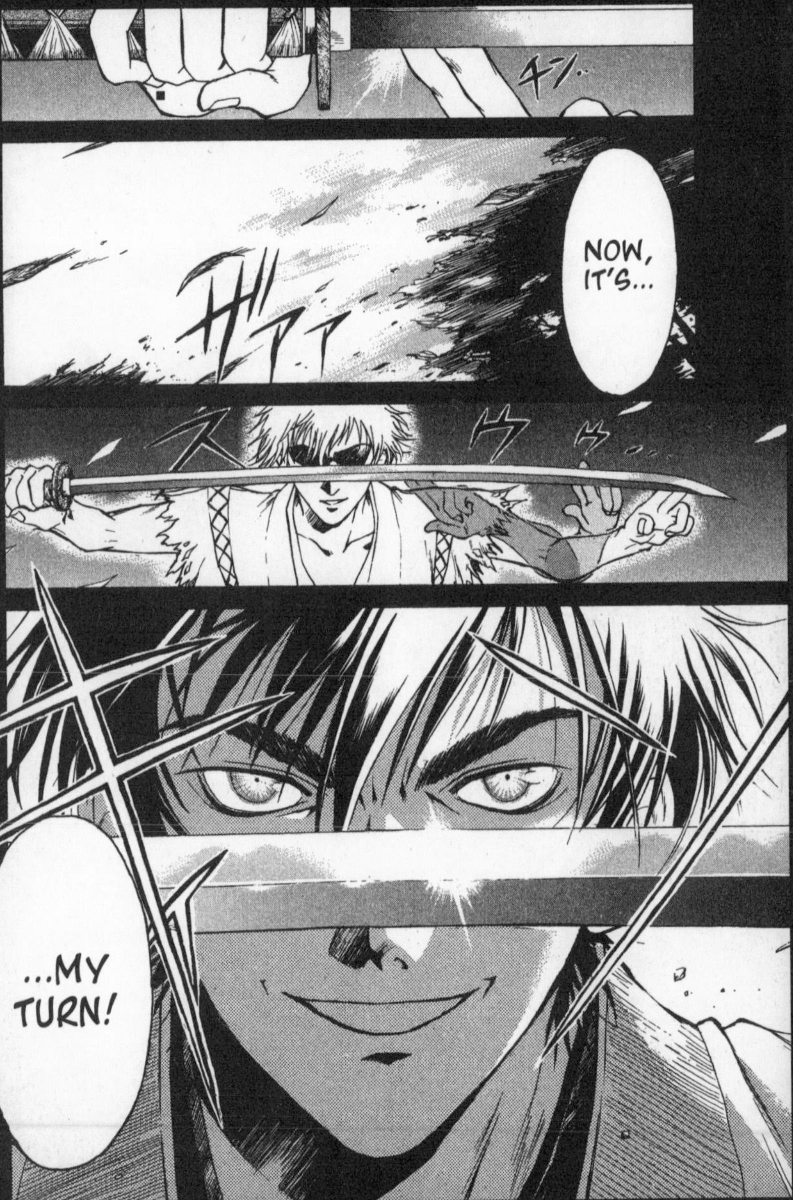
チン..
NOW, IT'S...
ザァァ
スウゥ...
...MY TURN!

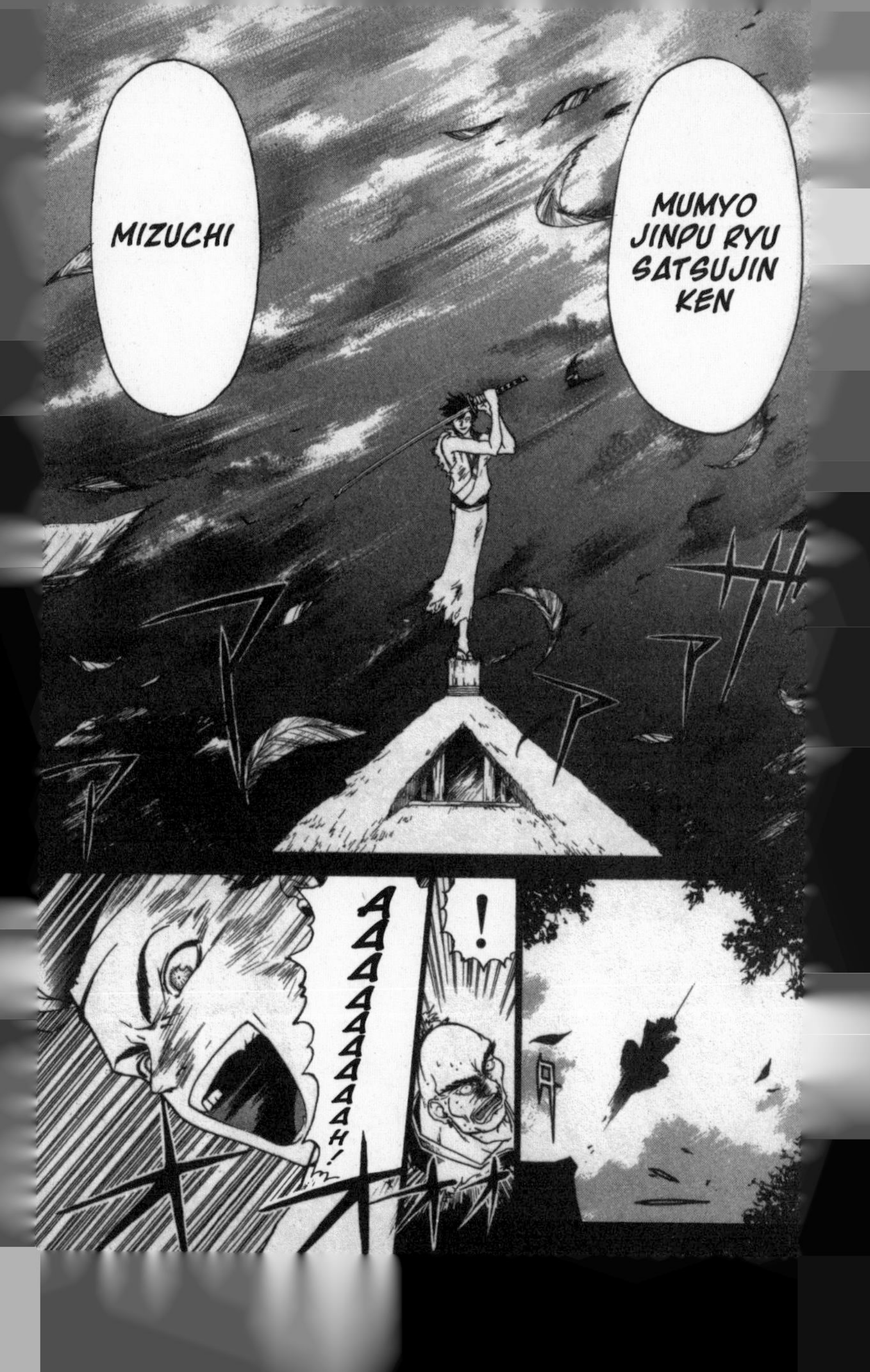
MUMYO JINPU RYU SATSUJIN KEN
MIZUCHI
!
AAAAAAAAAH!

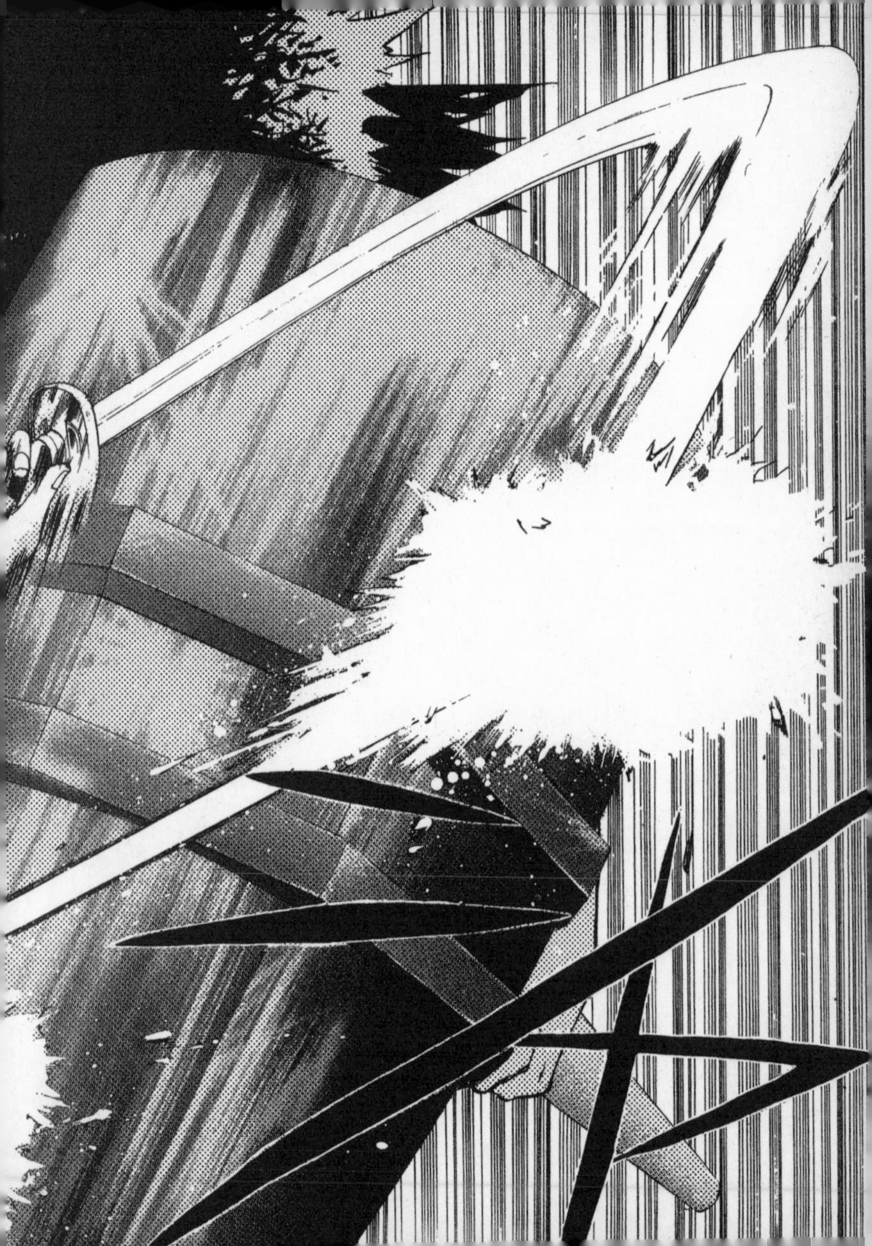

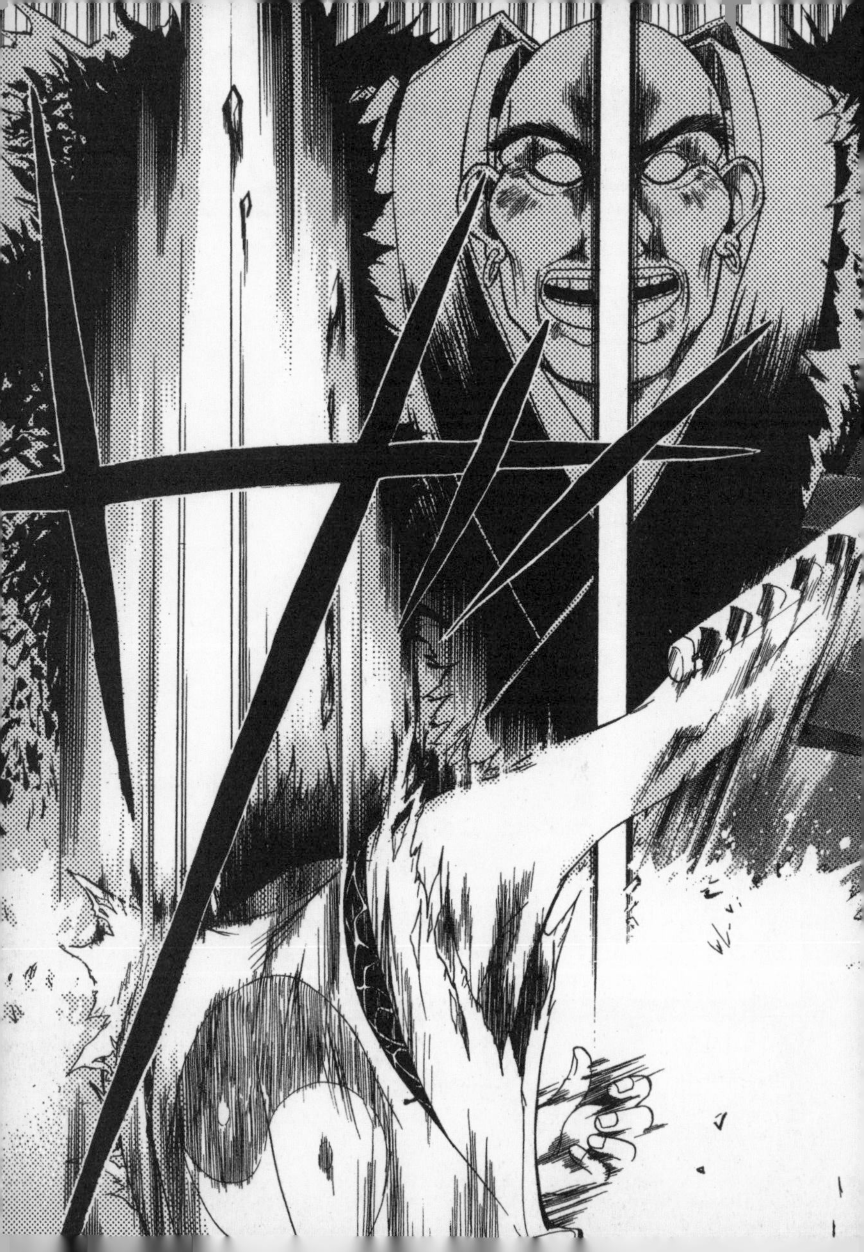

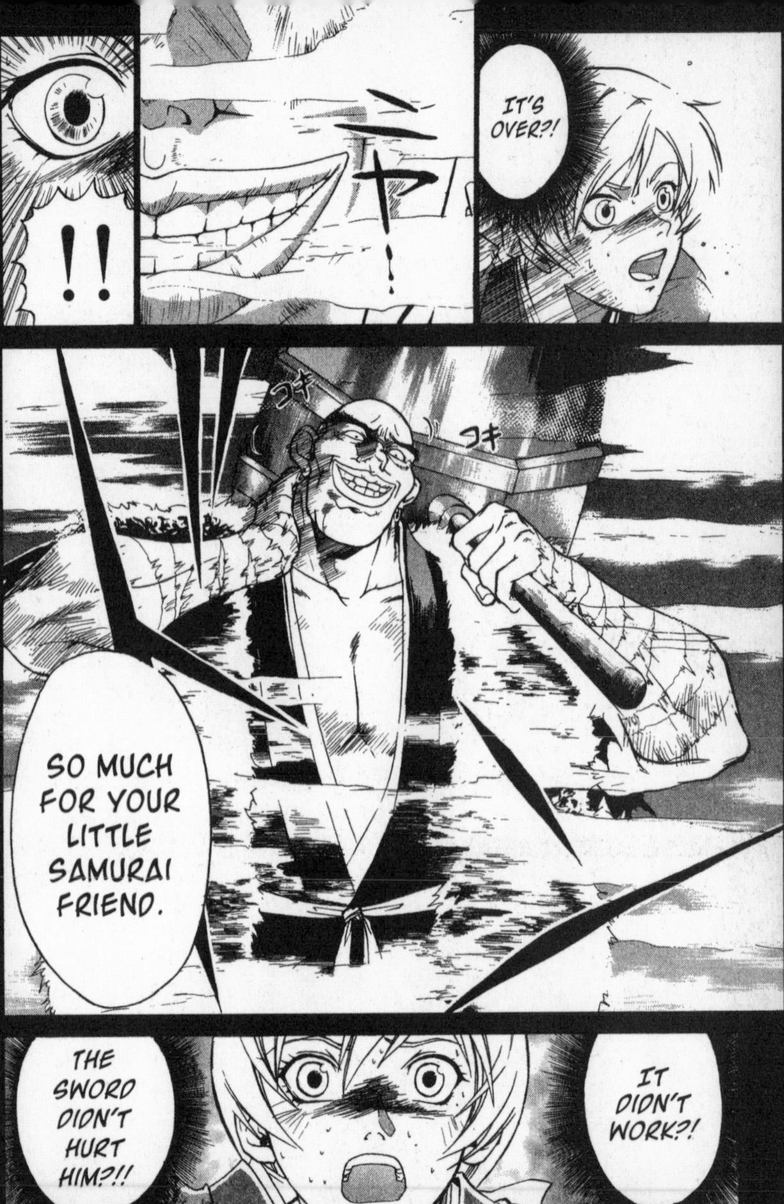
IT'S OVER?!
ニヤ
!!
コキ
コキ
SO MUCH FOR YOUR LITTLE SAMURAI FRIEND.
IT DIDN'T WORK?!
THE SWORD DIDN'T HURT HIM?!!

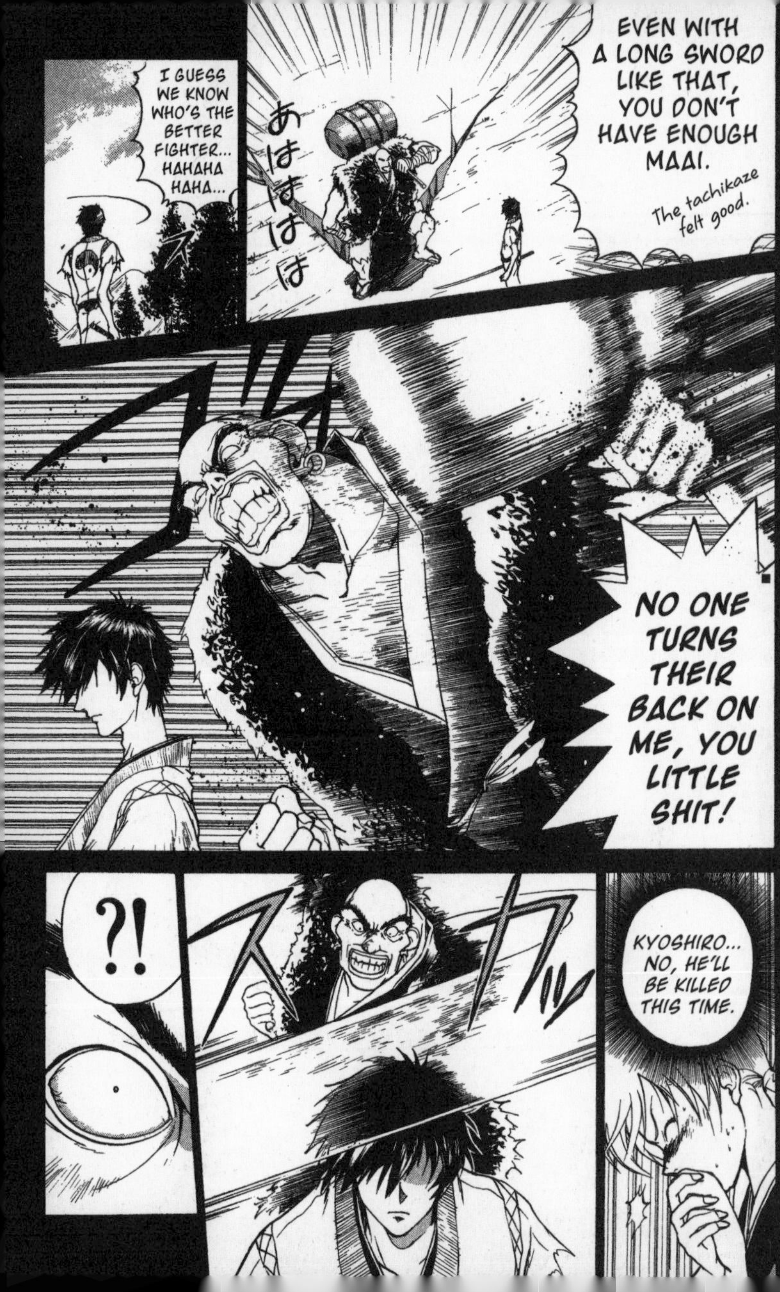
EVEN WITH A LONG SWORD LIKE THAT, YOU DON'T HAVE ENOUGH MAAI.
The tachikaze felt good.
あはすははは
I GUESS WE KNOW WHO'S THE BETTER FIGHTER... HAHAHA HAHA...
NO ONE TURNS THEIR BACK ON ME, YOU LITTLE SHIT!
KYOSHIRO... NO, HE'LL BE KILLED THIS TIME.
?!

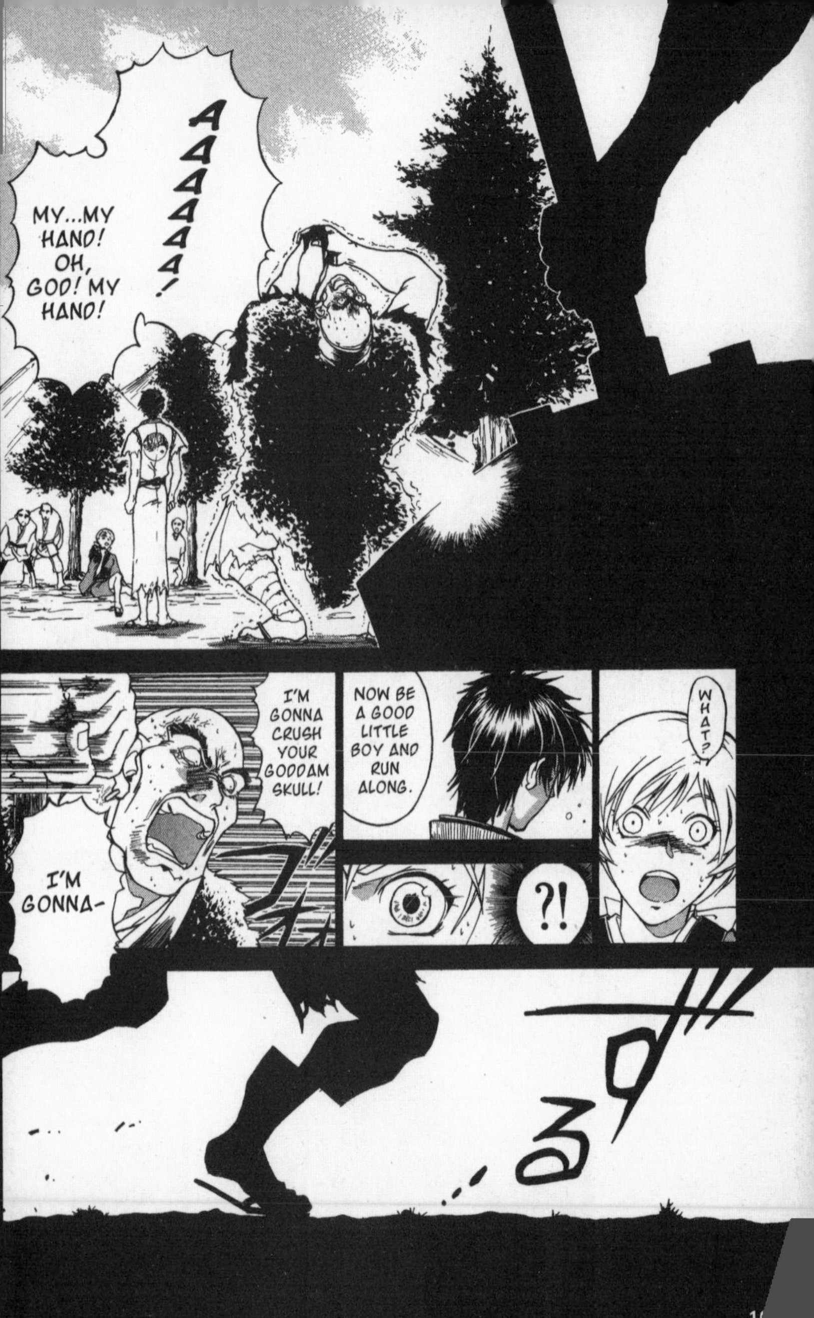
AAAAAAA!
MY...MY HAND! OH, GOD! MY HAND!
WHAT?
NOW BE A GOOD LITTLE BOY AND RUN ALONG.
?!
I'M GONNA CRUSH YOUR GODDAM SKULL!
I'M GONNA-

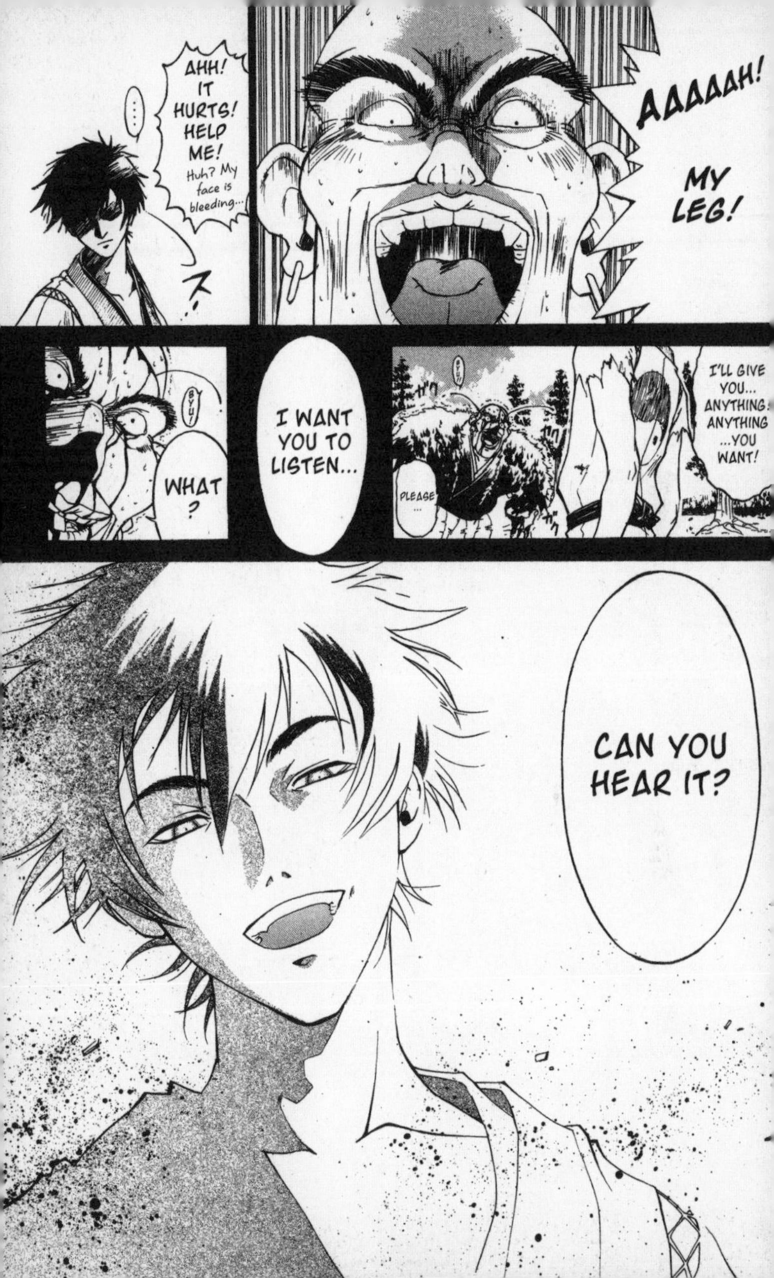
AAAAAH!
MY LEG!
AHH! IT HURTS! HELP ME! Huh? My face is bleeding...
...
I'LL GIVE YOU... ANYTHING! ANYTHING ...YOU WANT!
BYU!
PLEASE ...
I WANT YOU TO LISTEN...
BYU!
WHAT ?
CAN YOU HEAR IT?

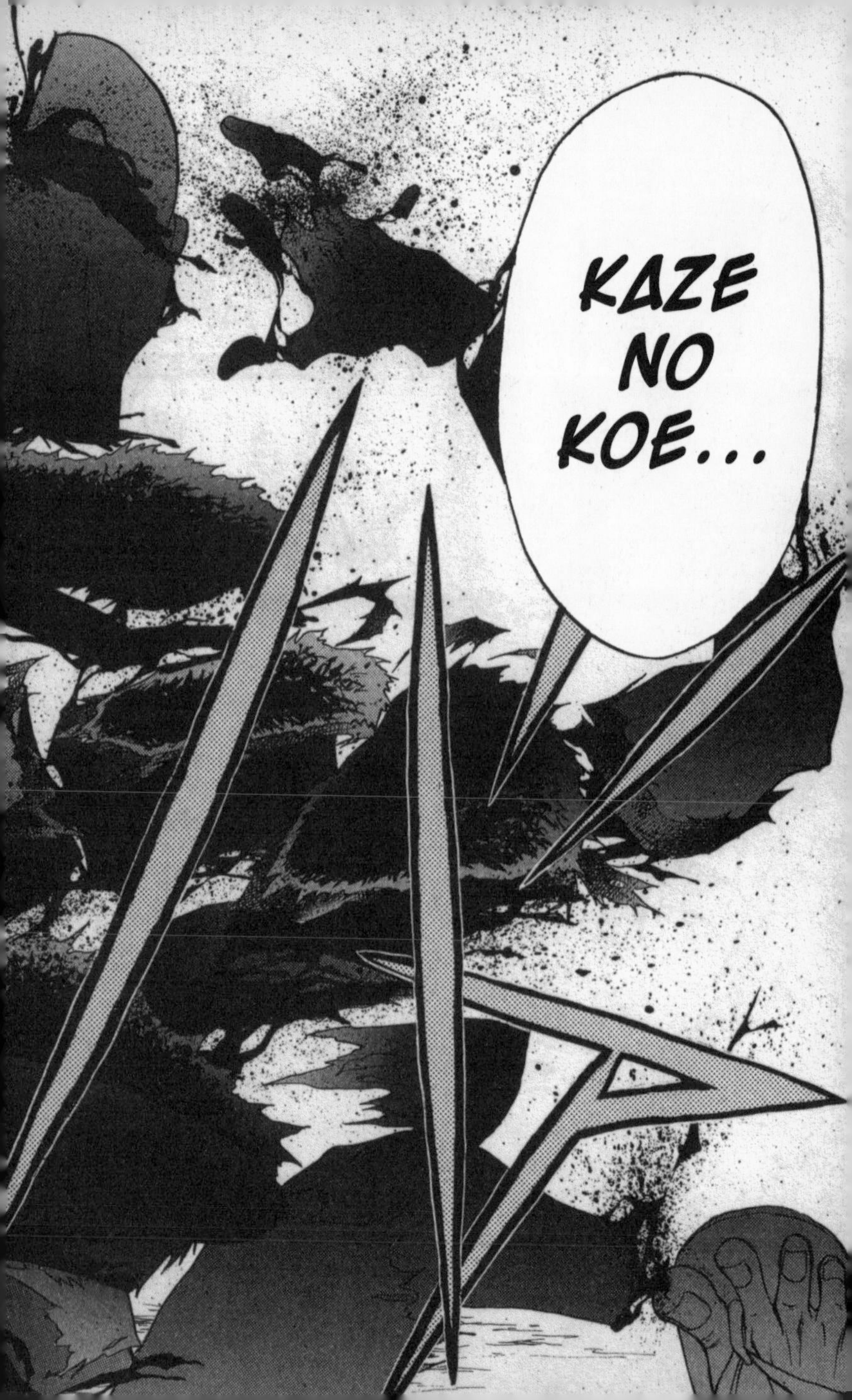
KAZE NO KOE...

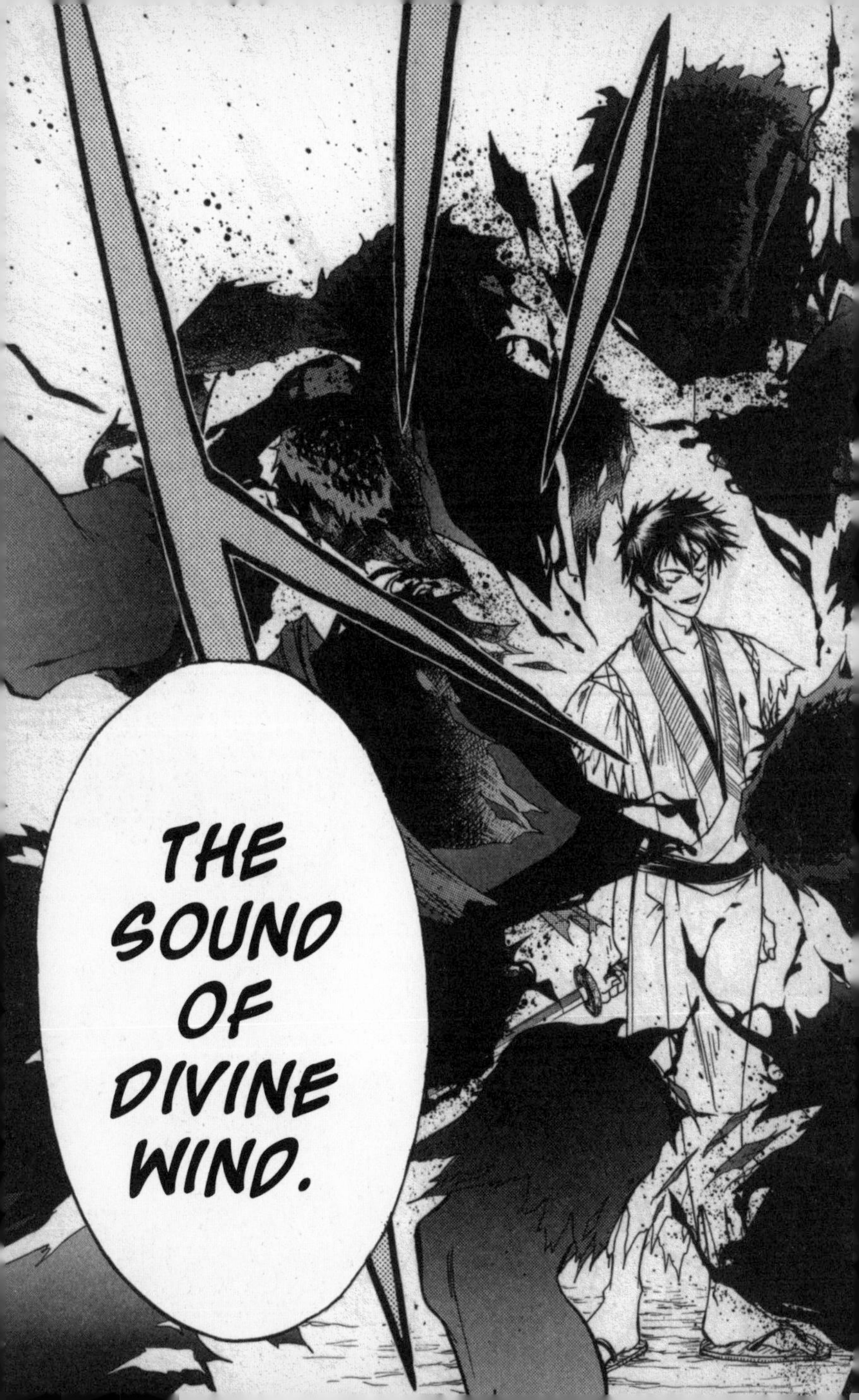
THE SOUND OF DIVINE WIND.

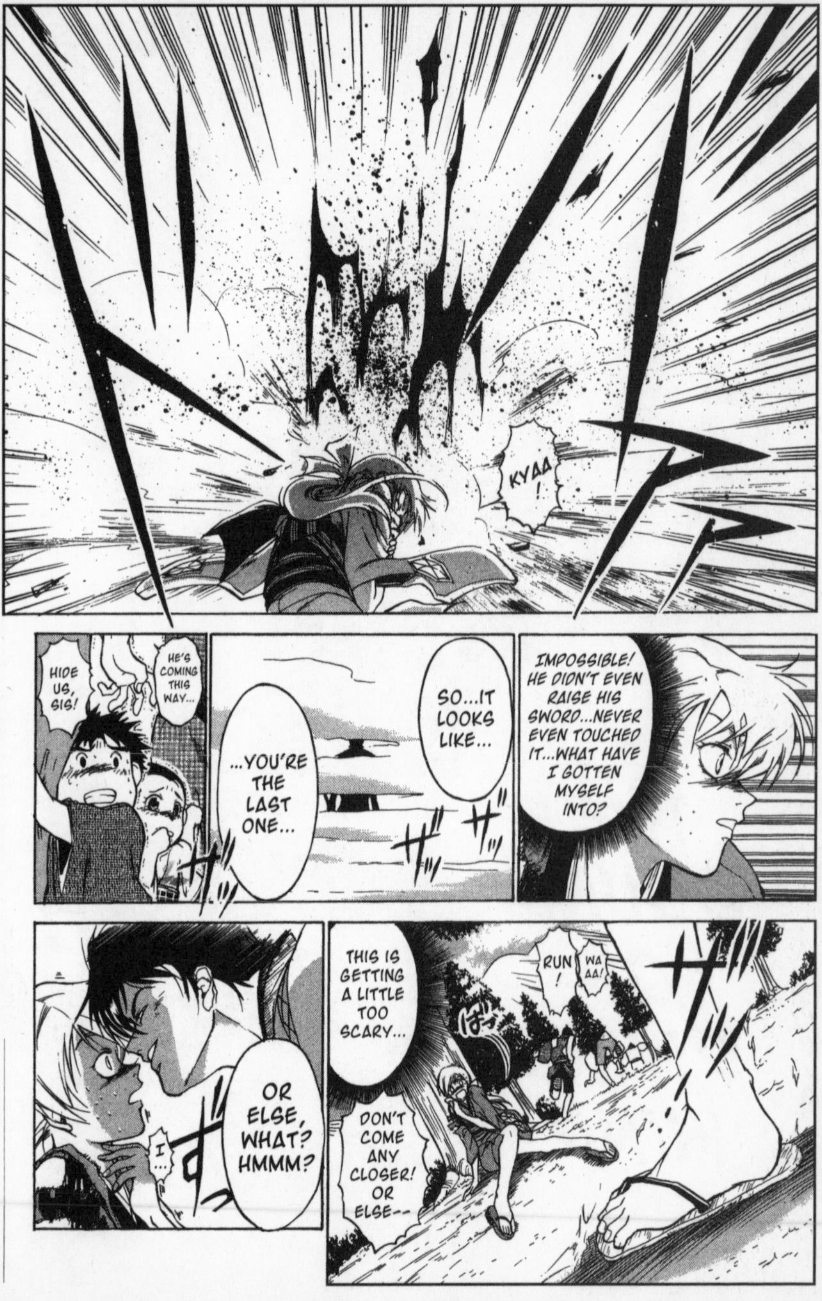
KYAA!
IMPOSSIBLE! HE DIDN'T EVEN RAISE HIS SWORD...NEVER EVEN TOUCHED IT...WHAT HAVE I GOTTEN MYSELF INTO?
SO...IT LOOKS LIKE...
...YOU'RE THE LAST ONE...
HE'S COMING THIS WAY...
HIDE US, SIS!
RUN!
WAAA!
THIS IS GETTING A LITTLE TOO SCARY...
DON'T COME ANY CLOSER! OR ELSE--
OR ELSE, WHAT? HMMM?
I...

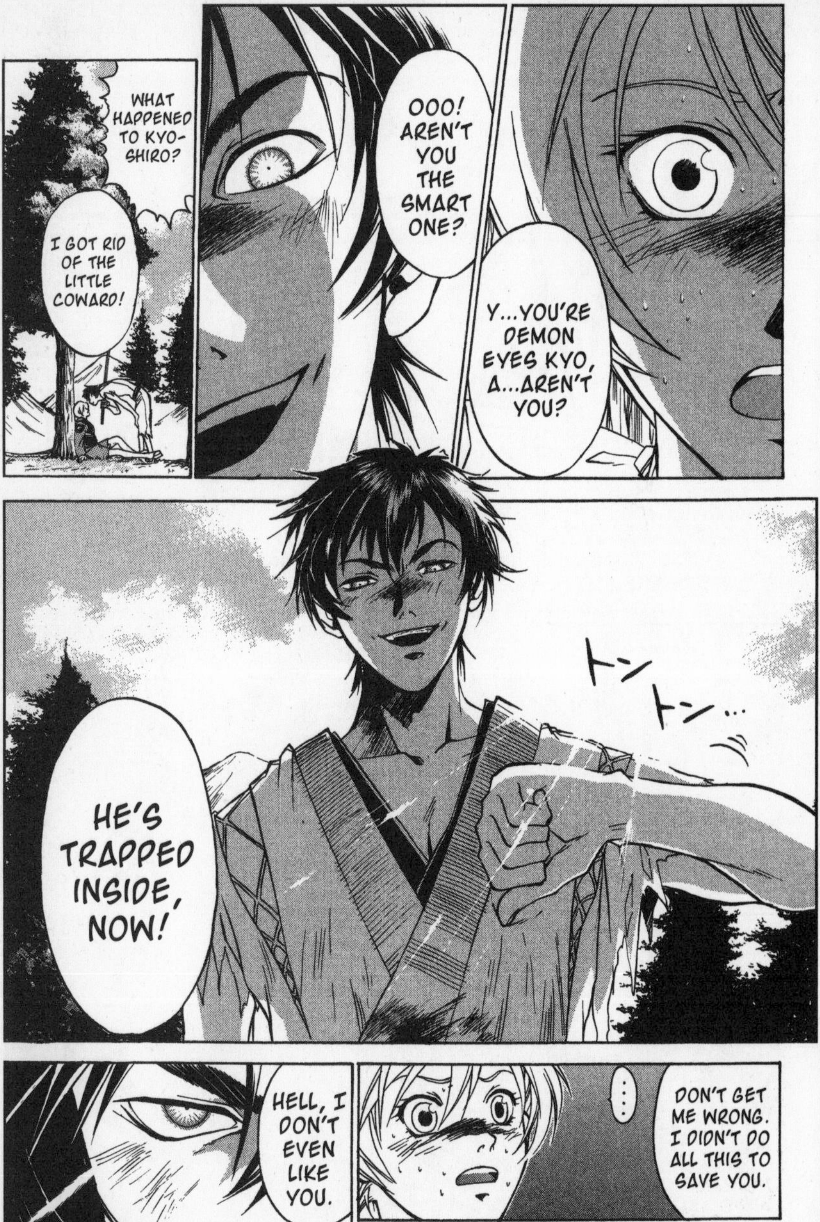
Y...YOU'RE DEMON EYES KYO, A...AREN'T YOU?
OOO! AREN'T YOU THE SMART ONE?
WHAT HAPPENED TO KYO-SHIRO?
I GOT RID OF THE LITTLE COWARD!
トン トン…
HE'S TRAPPED INSIDE, NOW!
DON'T GET ME WRONG. I DIDN'T DO ALL THIS TO SAVE YOU.
…
HELL, I DON'T EVEN LIKE YOU.

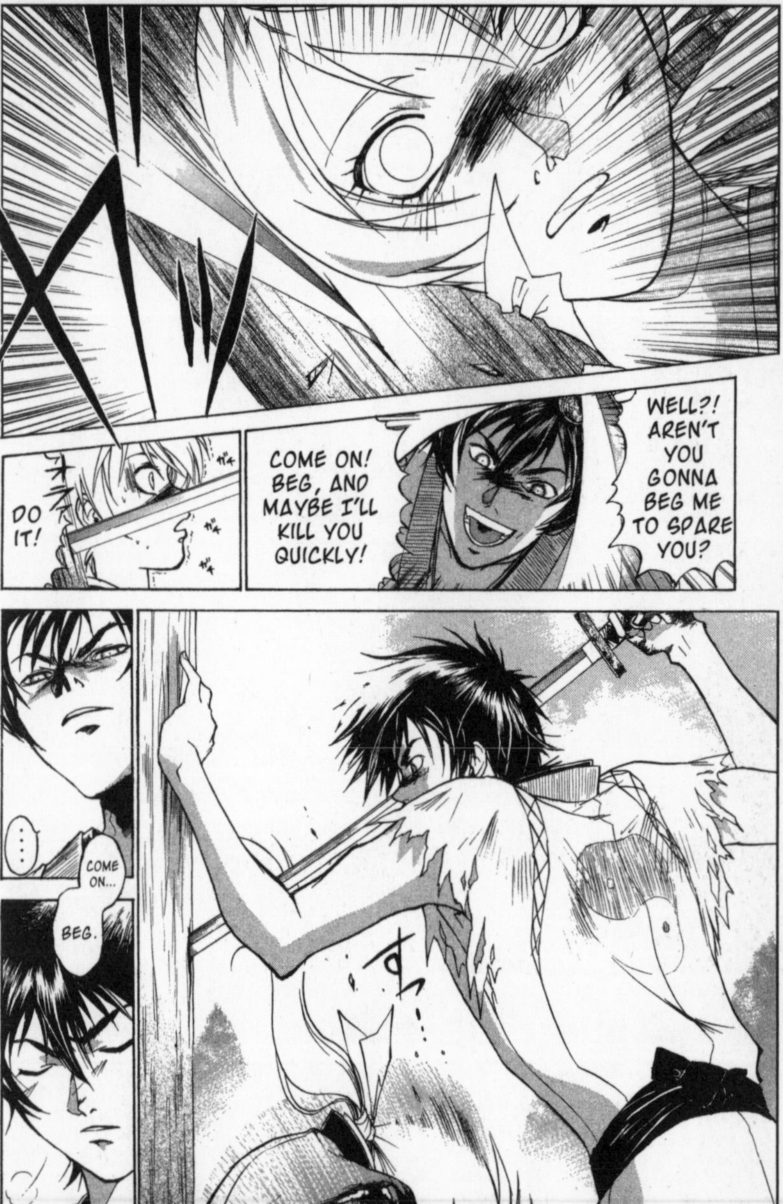
WELL?! AREN'T YOU GONNA BEG ME TO SPARE YOU?
COME ON! BEG, AND MAYBE I'LL KILL YOU QUICKLY!
DO IT!
...
COME ON...
BEG.

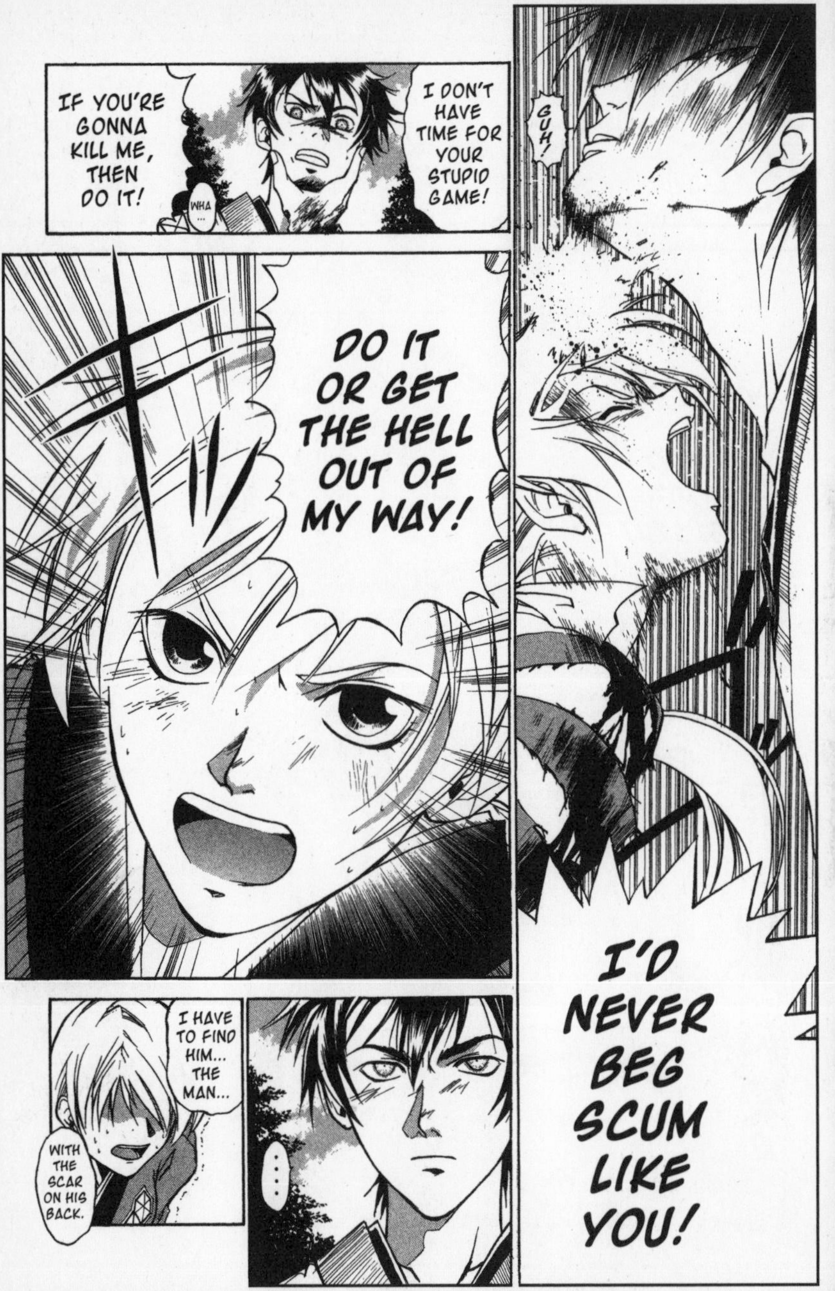
I DON'T HAVE TIME FOR YOUR STUPID GAME!
IF YOU'RE GONNA KILL ME, THEN DO IT!
WHA...
DO IT OR GET THE HELL OUT OF MY WAY!
GUH!
I'D NEVER BEG SCUM LIKE YOU!
...
I HAVE TO FIND HIM... THE MAN...
WITH THE SCAR ON HIS BACK.

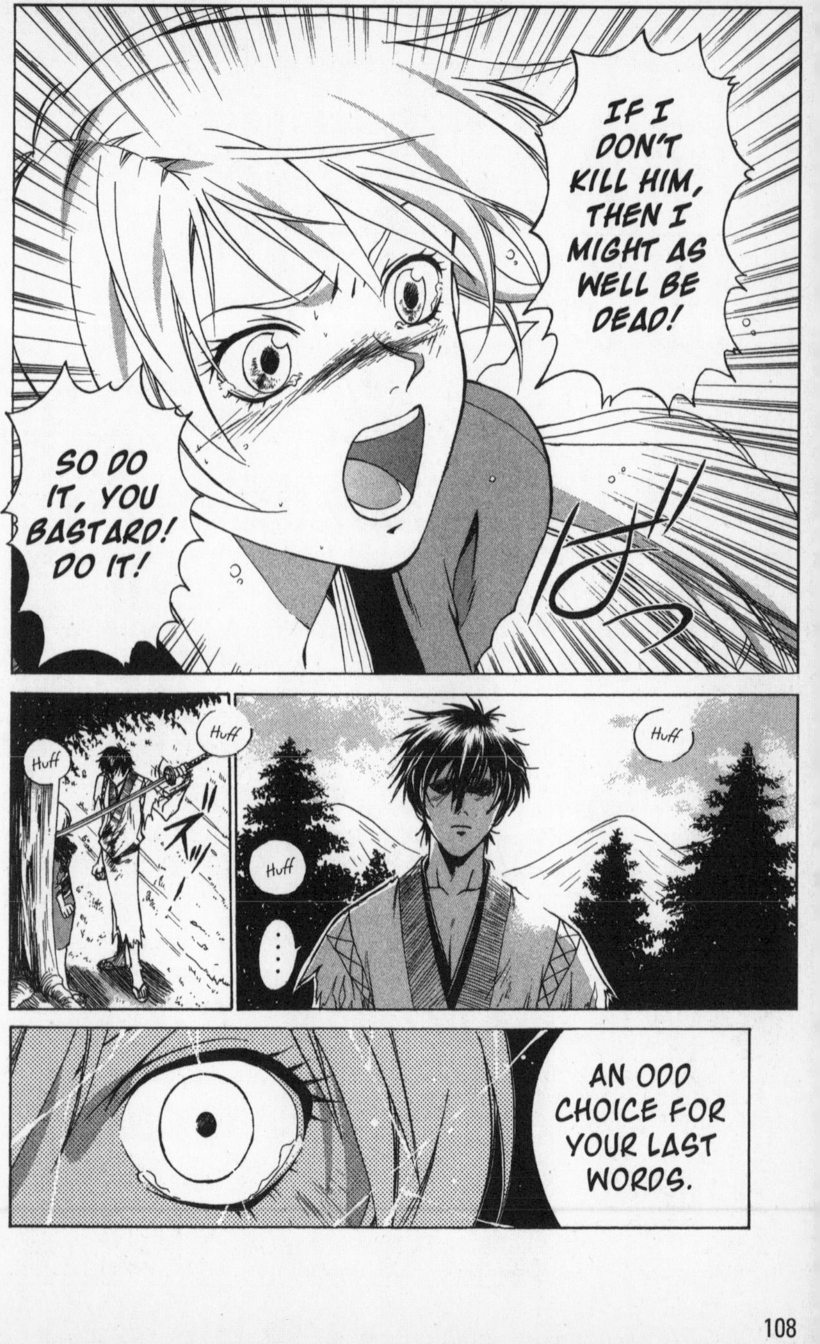
IF I DON'T KILL HIM, THEN I MIGHT AS WELL BE DEAD!
SO DO IT, YOU BASTARD! DO IT!
ばっ
Huff
Huff
...
Huff
Huff
AN ODD CHOICE FOR YOUR LAST WORDS.

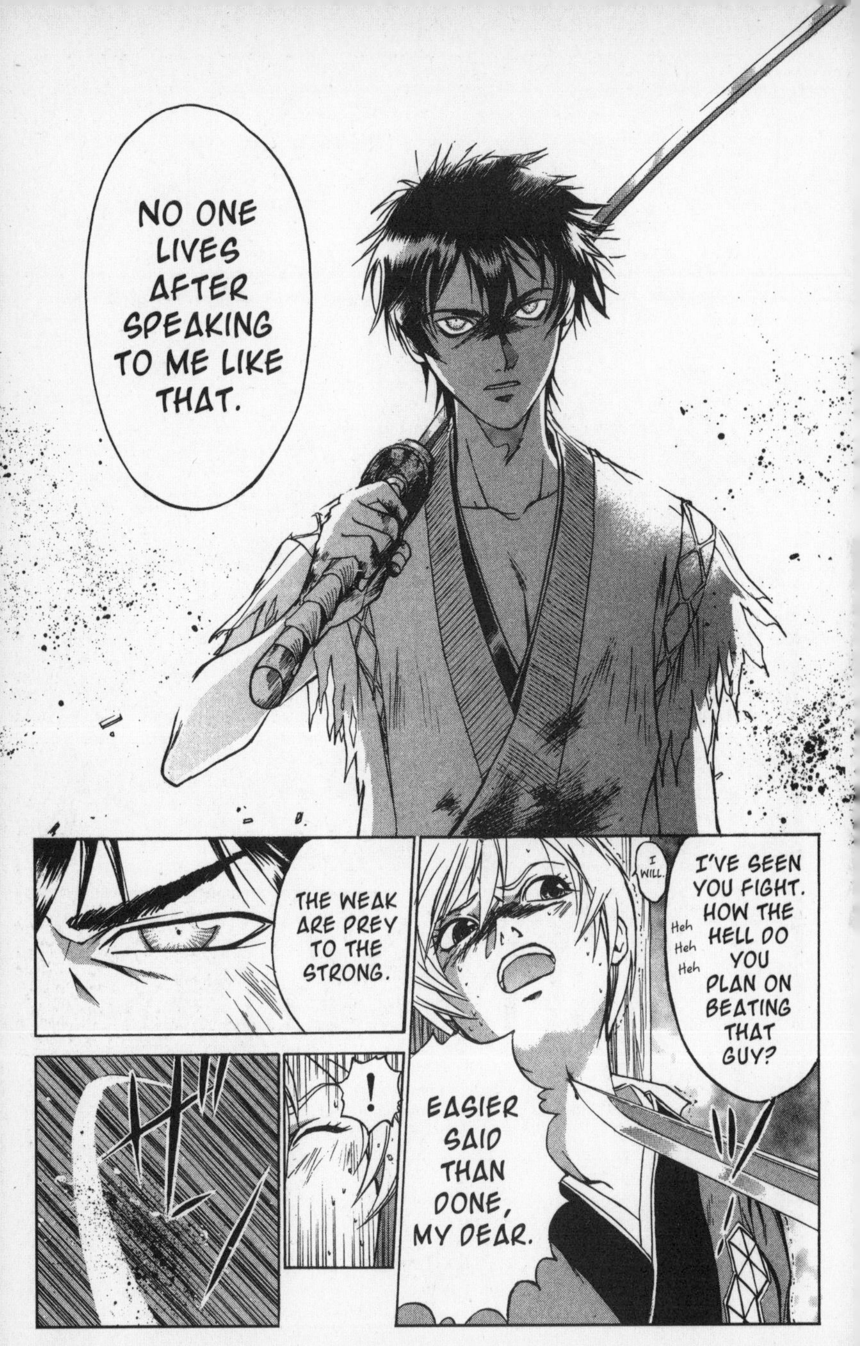
NO ONE LIVES AFTER SPEAKING TO ME LIKE THAT.
THE WEAK ARE PREY TO THE STRONG.
I'VE SEEN YOU FIGHT. HOW THE HELL DO YOU PLAN ON BEATING THAT GUY?
Heh Heh Heh
I WILL.
EASIER SAID THAN DONE, MY DEAR.
!

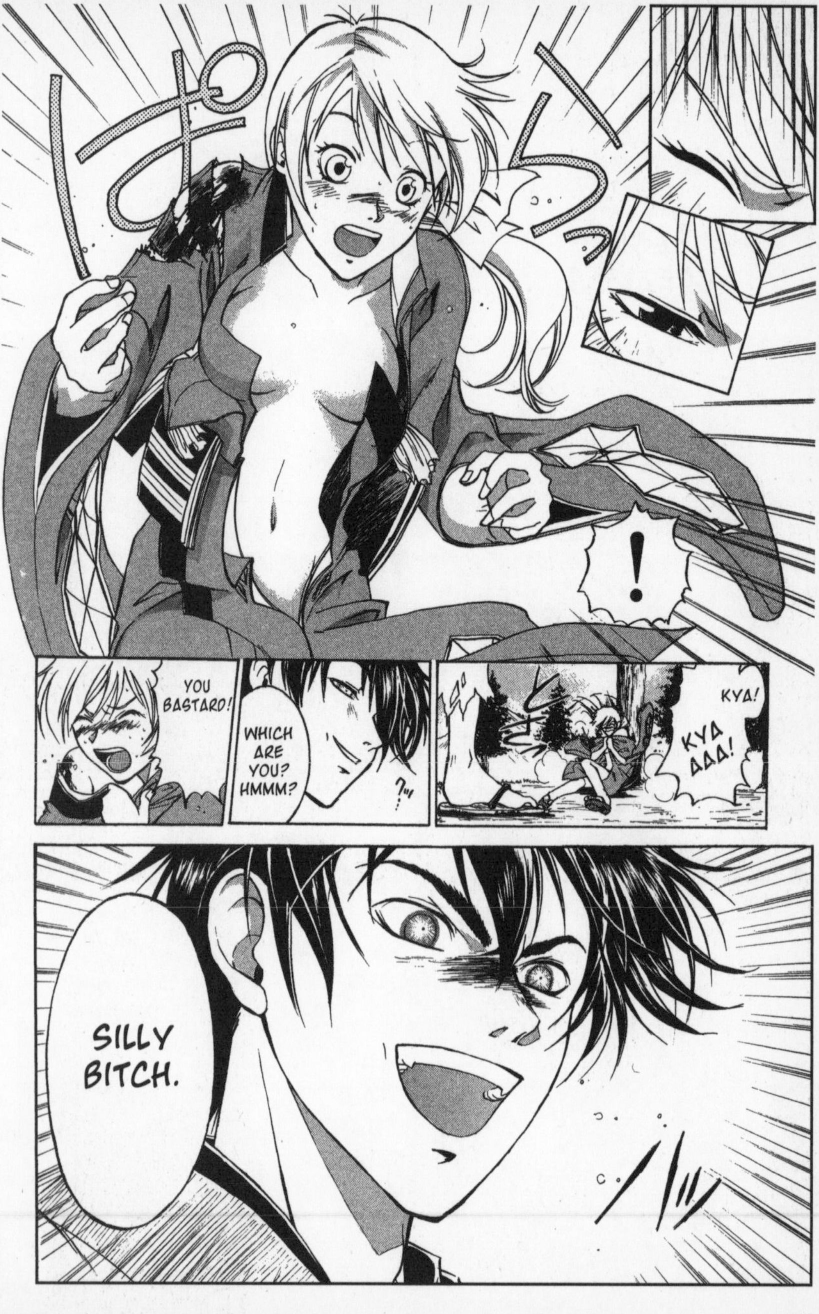
!
KYA!
KYA AAA!
WHICH ARE YOU? HMMM?
YOU BASTARD!
SILLY BITCH.

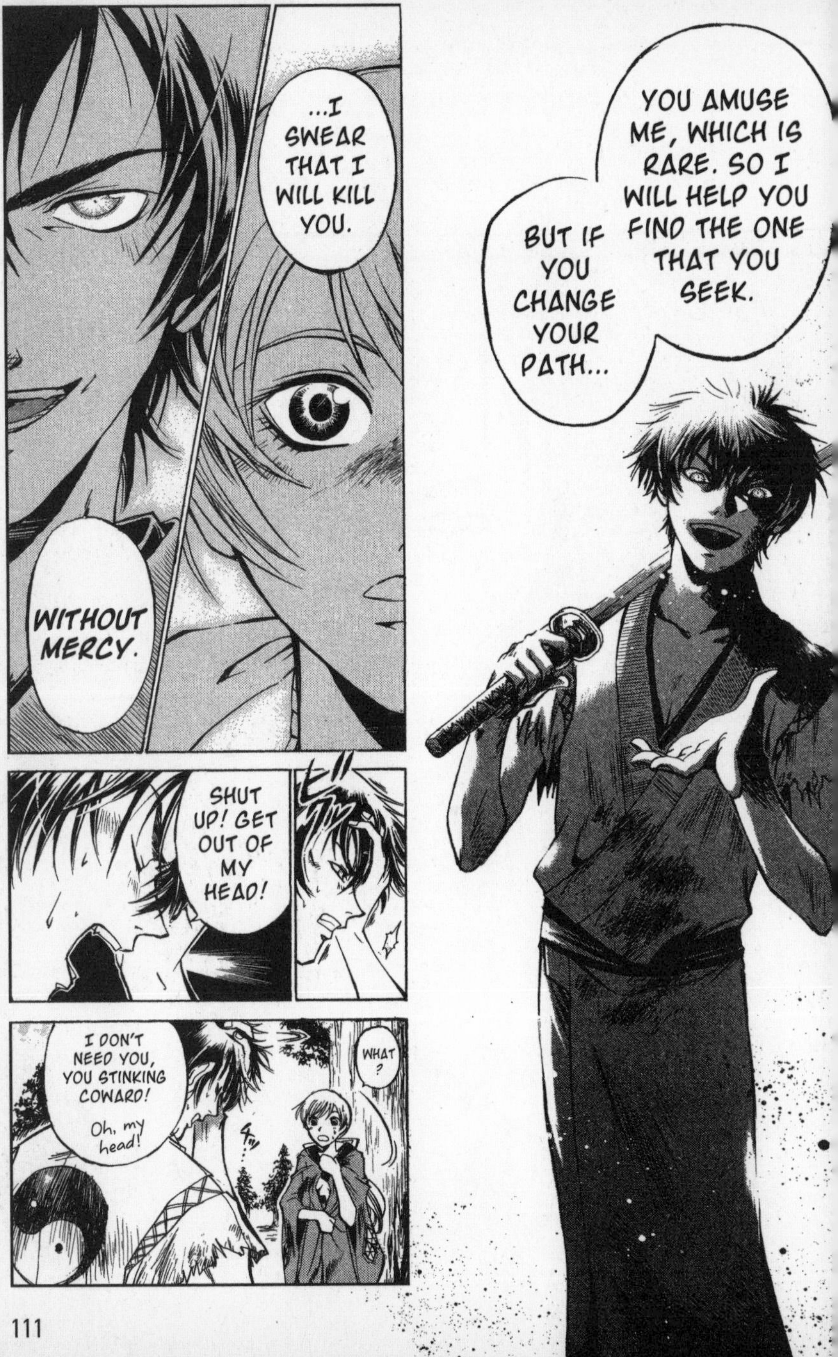
YOU AMUSE ME, WHICH IS RARE. SO I WILL HELP YOU FIND THE ONE THAT YOU SEEK.
BUT IF YOU CHANGE YOUR PATH...
...I SWEAR THAT I WILL KILL YOU.
WITHOUT MERCY.
SHUT UP! GET OUT OF MY HEAD!
I DON'T NEED YOU, YOU STINKING COWARD!
Oh, my head!
WHAT?

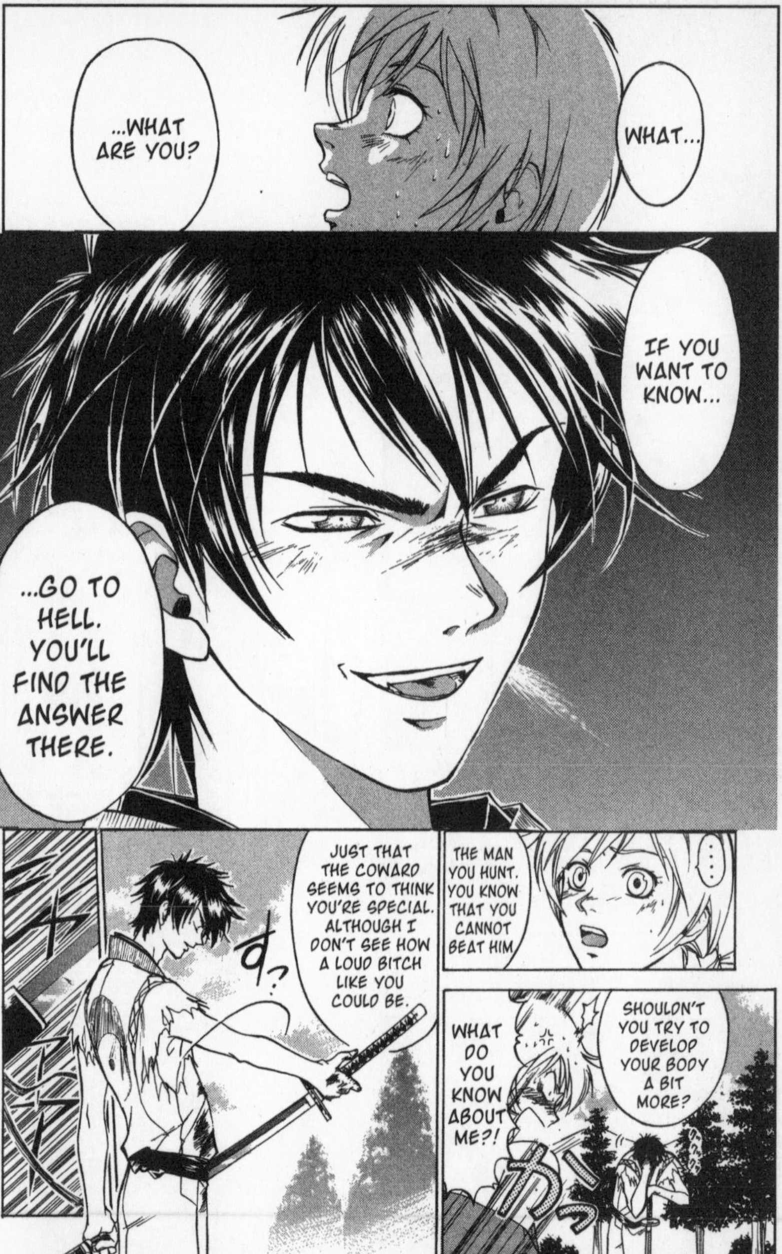
WHAT...
...WHAT ARE YOU?
IF YOU WANT TO KNOW...
...GO TO HELL. YOU'LL FIND THE ANSWER THERE.
...
THE MAN YOU HUNT. YOU KNOW THAT YOU CANNOT BEAT HIM
SHOULDN'T YOU TRY TO DEVELOP YOUR BODY A BIT MORE?
WHAT DO YOU KNOW ABOUT ME?!
JUST THAT THE COWARD SEEMS TO THINK YOU'RE SPECIAL. ALTHOUGH I DON'T SEE HOW A LOUD BITCH LIKE YOU COULD BE.

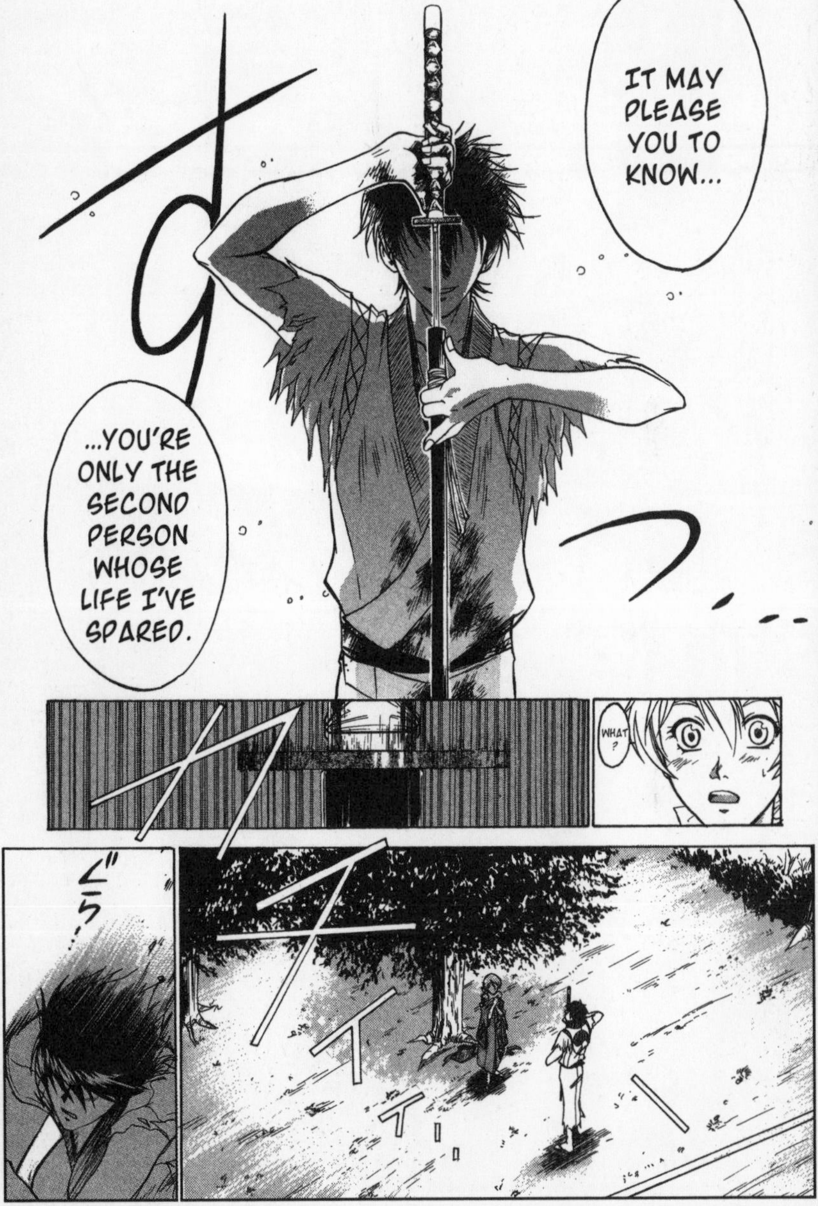
IT MAY PLEASE YOU TO KNOW...
...YOU'RE ONLY THE SECOND PERSON WHOSE LIFE I'VE SPARED.
WHAT ?
ぐら

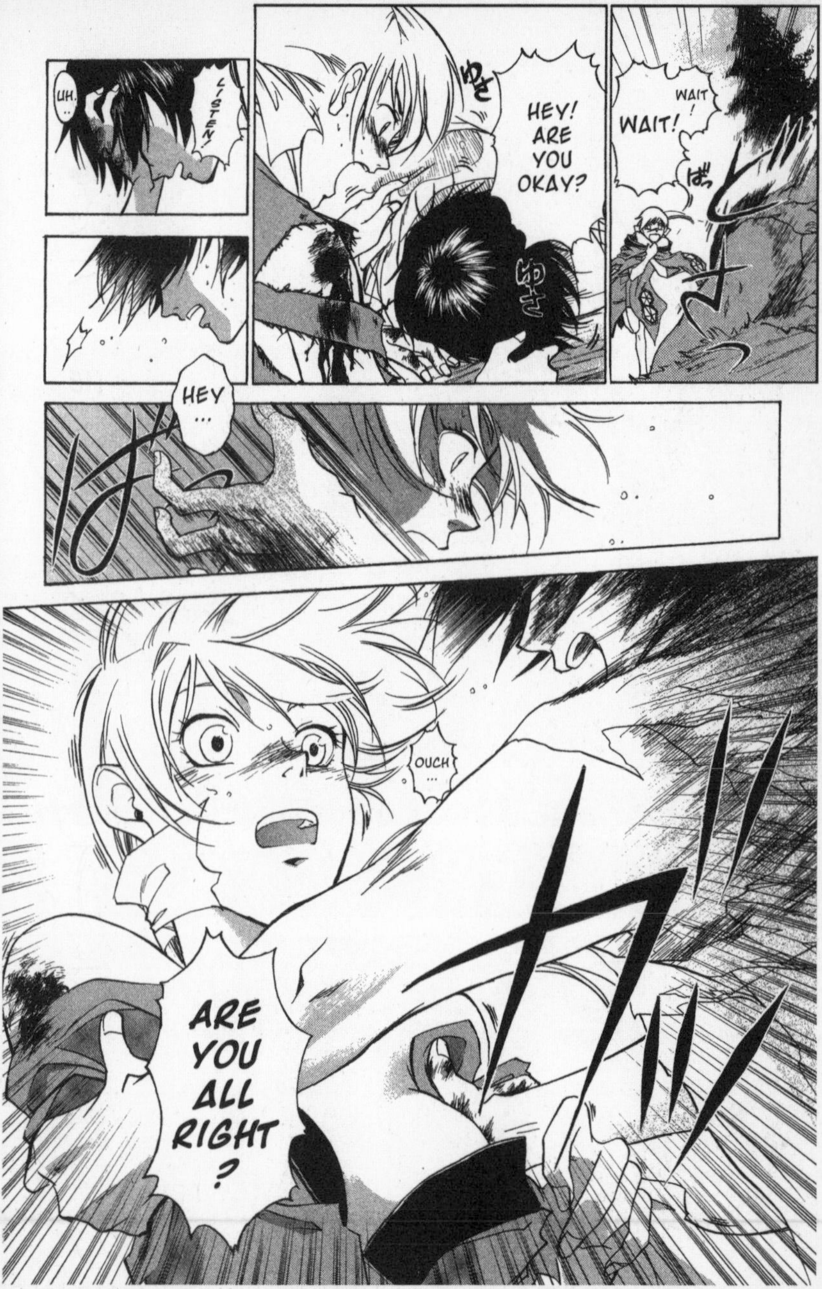
WAIT!
WAIT!
ばっ
HEY! ARE YOU OKAY?
ゆさ
ゆさ
UH..
LISTEN!
HEY ...
OUCH ...
ARE YOU ALL RIGHT?

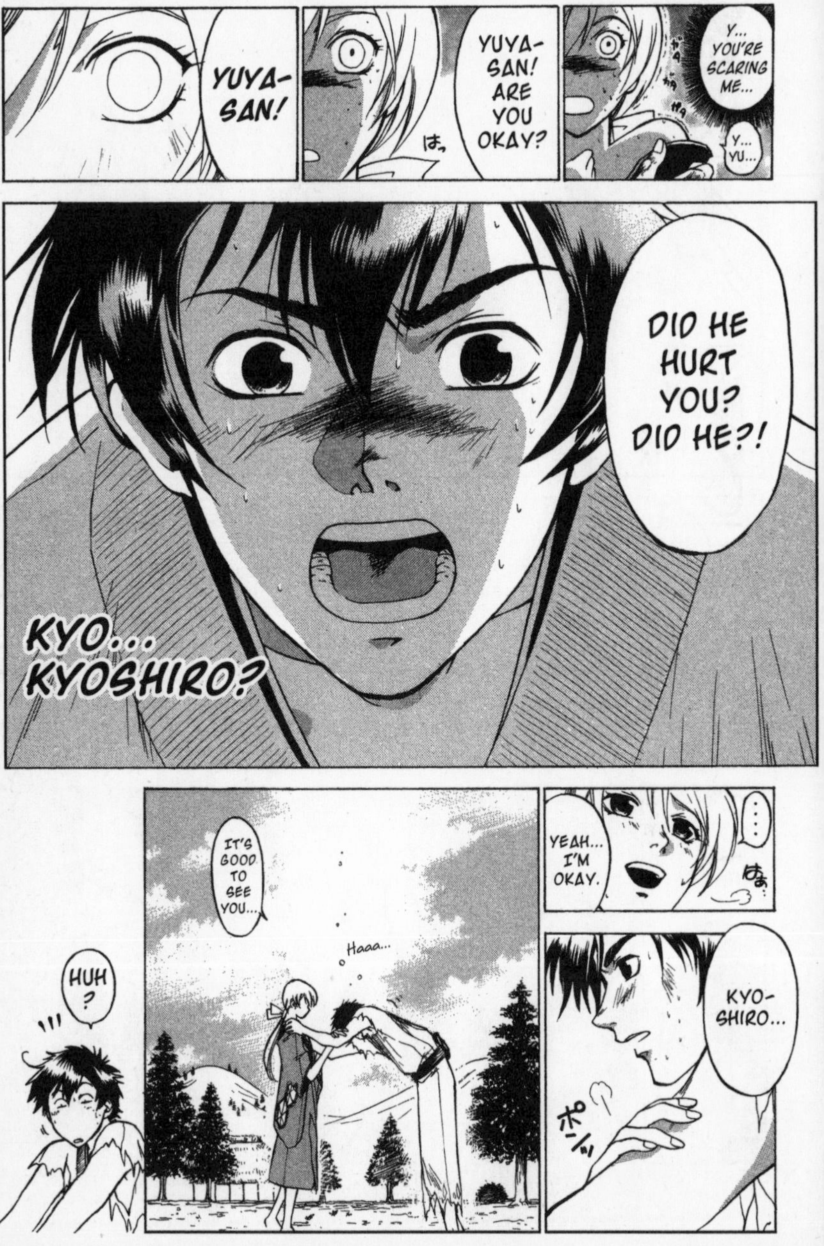
Y... YOU'RE SCARING ME...
Y... YU...
YUYA-SAN! ARE YOU OKAY?
はっ
YUYA-SAN!
DID HE HURT YOU? DID HE?!
KYO... KYOSHIRO?
....
YEAH... I'M OKAY.
KYO-SHIRO...
IT'S GOOD TO SEE YOU...
Haaa...
HUH?

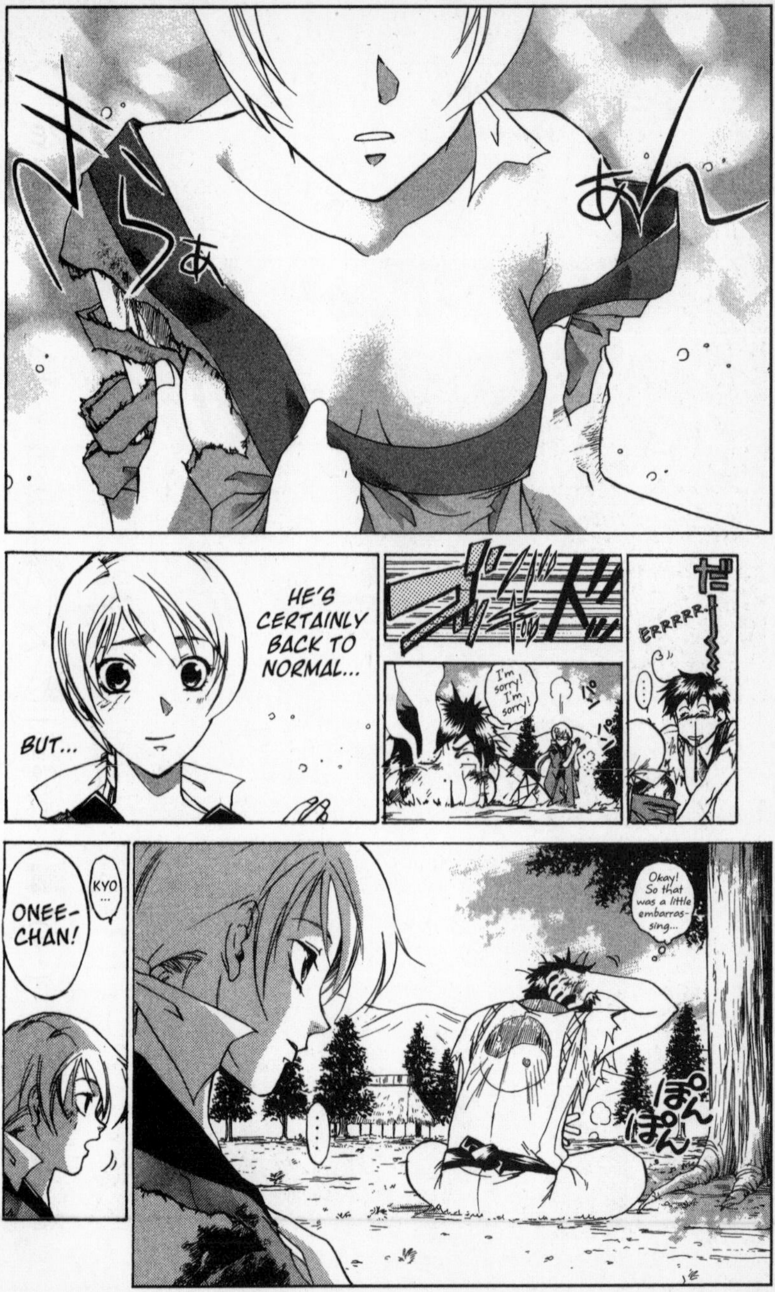
ERRRRR...
...
I'm sorry! I'm sorry!
HE'S CERTAINLY BACK TO NORMAL...
BUT...
Okay! So that was a little embarras-sing...
...
ぽんぽん
KYO...
ONEE-CHAN!

YOU HAVE OUR GRATITUDE, SHIINA-SAN. THE VILLAGE IS SAVED!

YOU'RE ALIVE!

YAY! IT'S ONEE-CHAN!

YOU'RE SAFE! YOU'RE ALL SAFE!

I...I'M SORRY, KIDS. I'M NOT THE ONE WHO STOPPED THE BANTOUJI BROTHERS.

YEAH! 'CAUSE ONEE-CHAN! KICKED THOSE GUYS' BUTTS!

AND TAHEI! HE'S OKAY, TOO!

No one's hurt...

WHAT?

I...

...

?

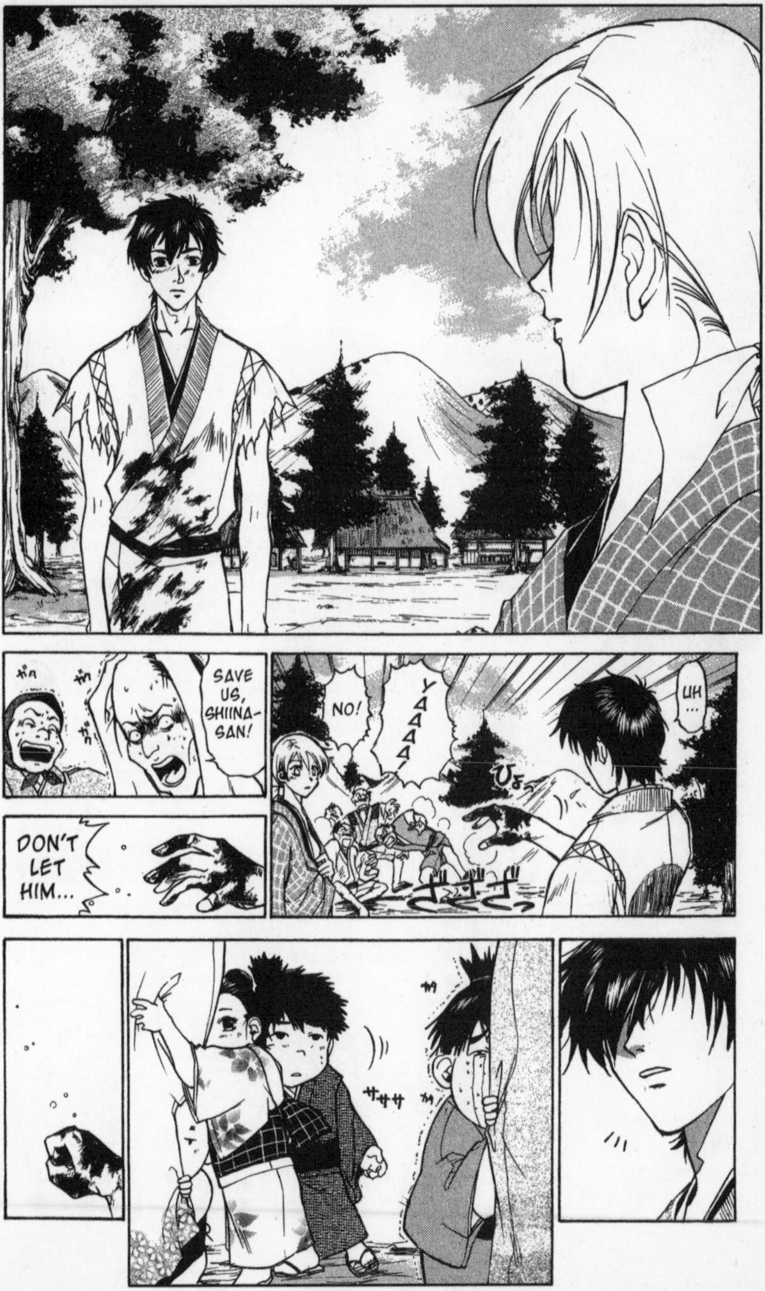
UH ...
NO!
YAAAA!
SAVE US, SHIINA-SAN!
DON'T LET HIM...

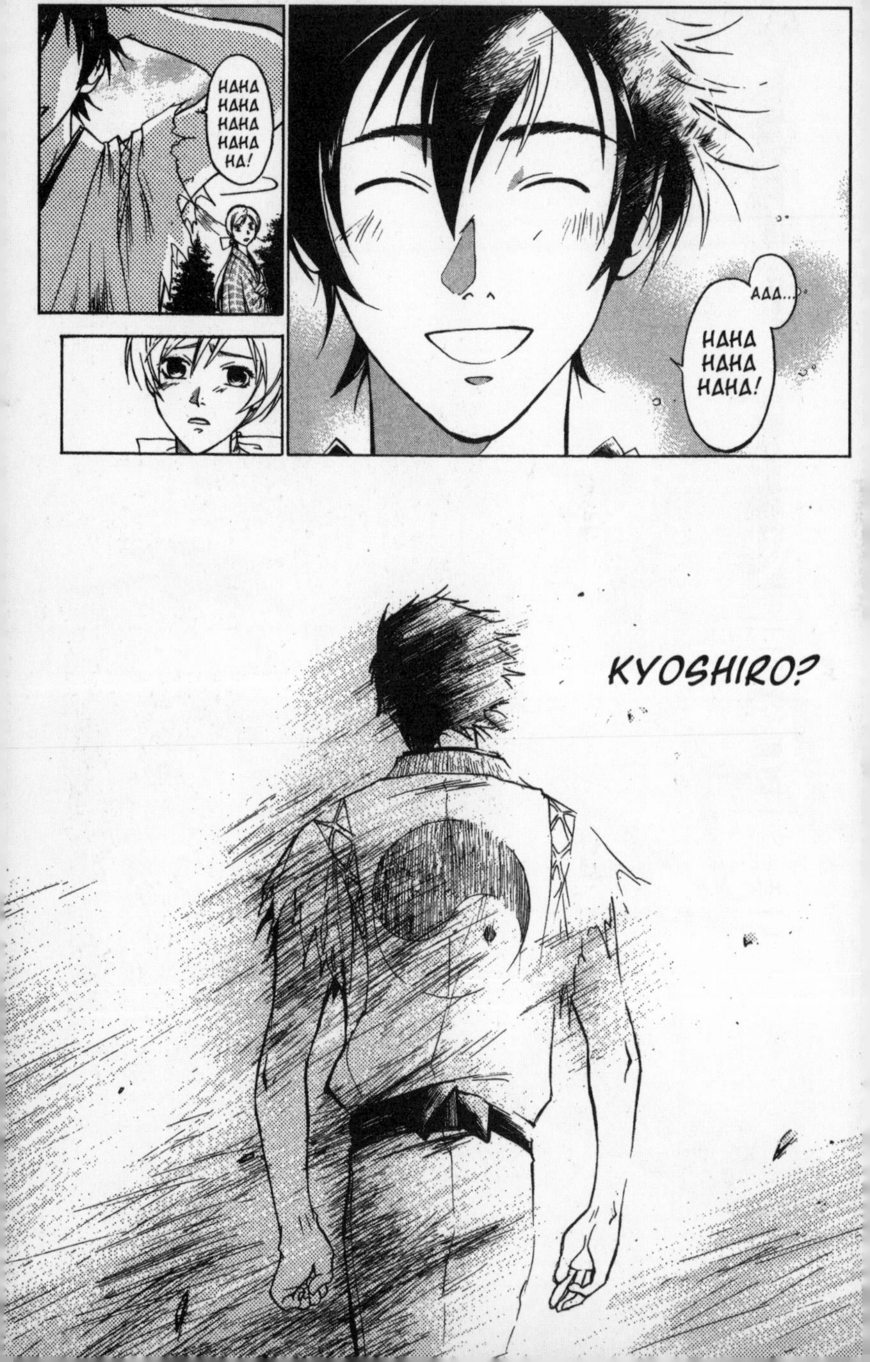
AAA...
HAHA HAHA HAHA!
HAHA HAHA HAHA HAHA HA!
KYOSHIRO?

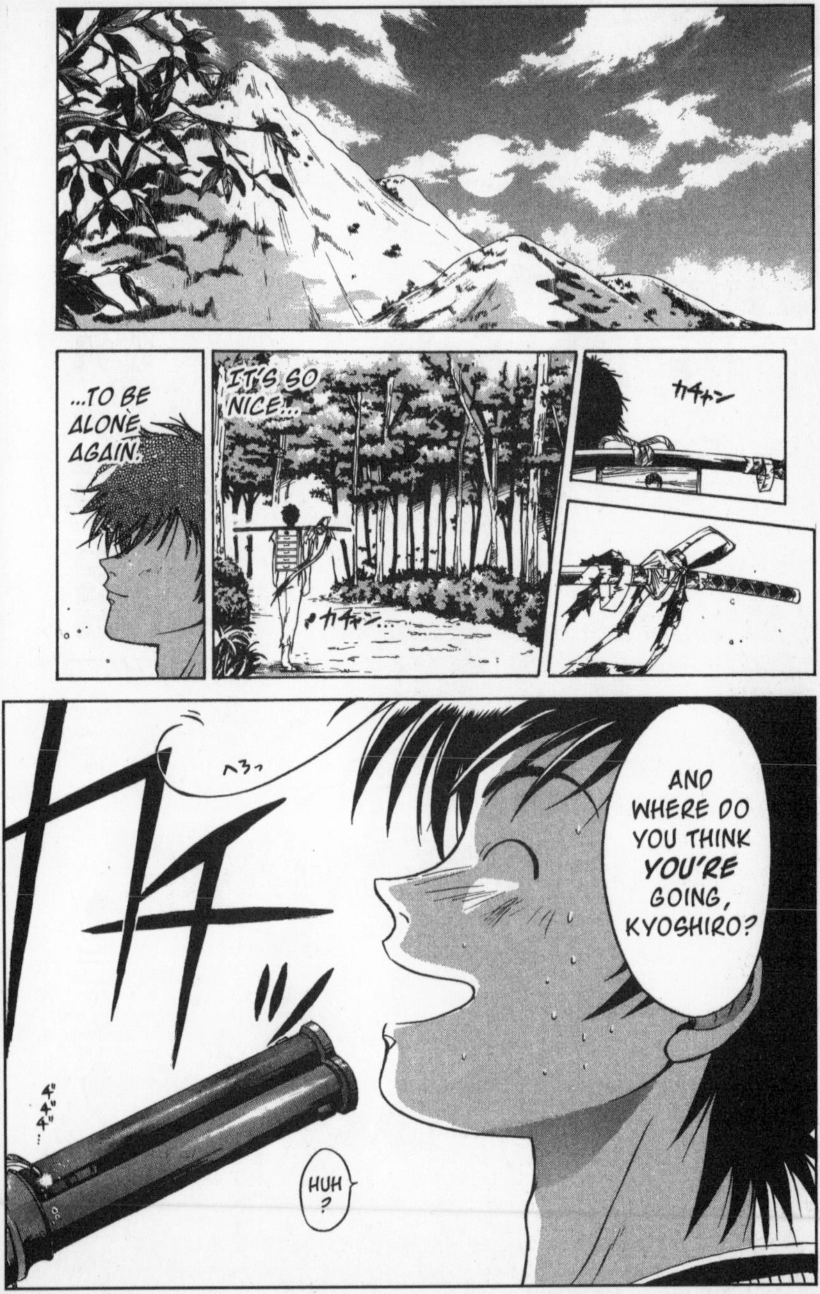
カチャン
IT'S SO NICE...
カチャン...
...TO BE ALONE AGAIN.
AND WHERE DO YOU THINK YOU'RE GOING, KYOSHIRO?
HUH?

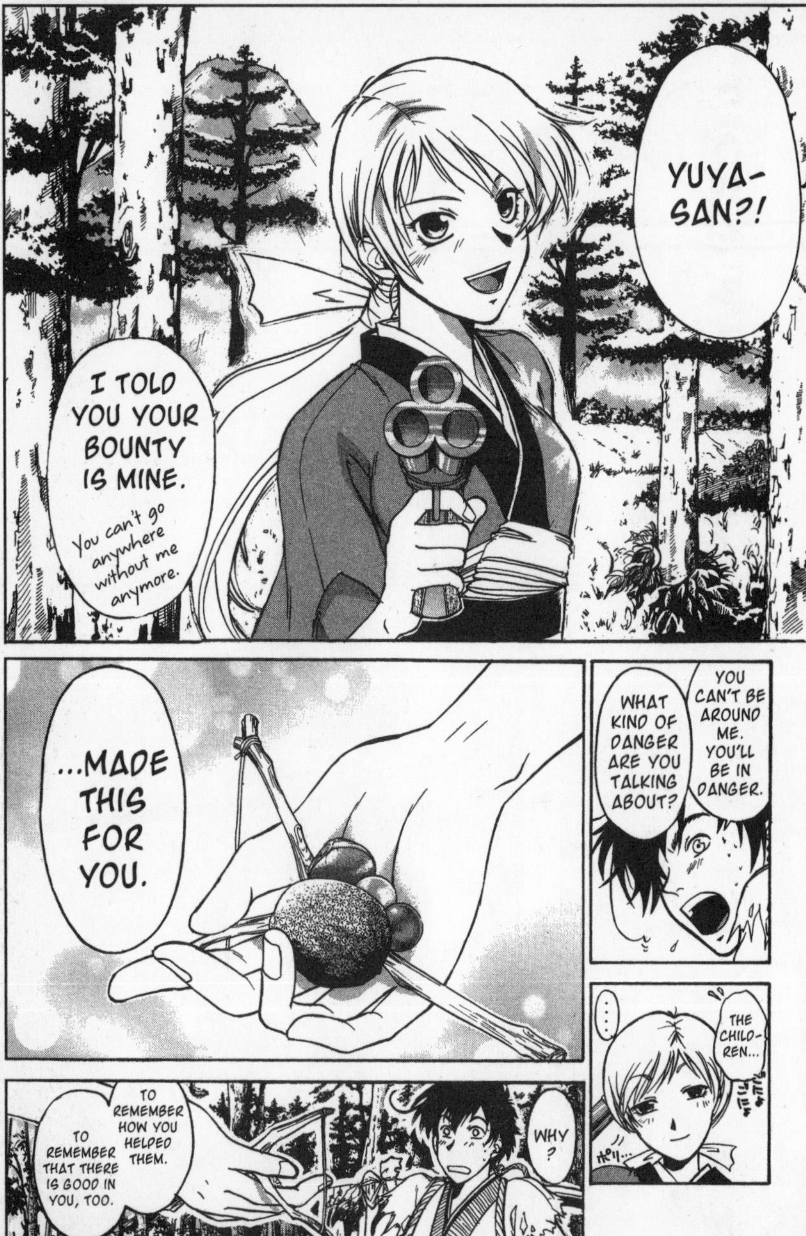
YUYA-SAN?!
I TOLD YOU YOUR BOUNTY IS MINE.
You can't go anywhere without me anymore.
YOU CAN'T BE AROUND ME. YOU'LL BE IN DANGER.
WHAT KIND OF DANGER ARE YOU TALKING ABOUT?
THE CHILDREN...
....
...MADE THIS FOR YOU.
WHY?
TO REMEMBER HOW YOU HELPED THEM.
TO REMEMBER THAT THERE IS GOOD IN YOU, TOO.

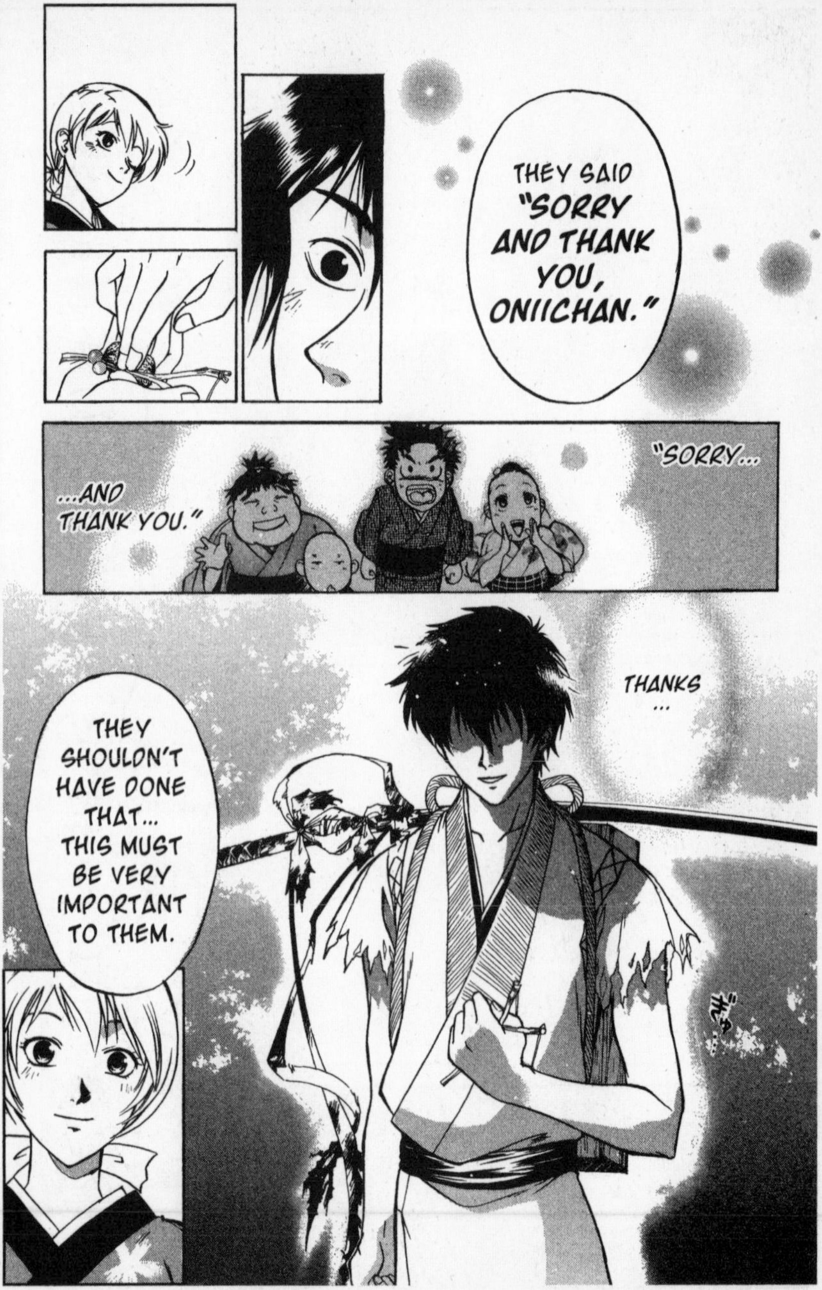
THEY SAID "SORRY AND THANK YOU, ONIICHAN."
"SORRY...
...AND THANK YOU."
THANKS...
THEY SHOULDN'T HAVE DONE THAT... THIS MUST BE VERY IMPORTANT TO THEM.

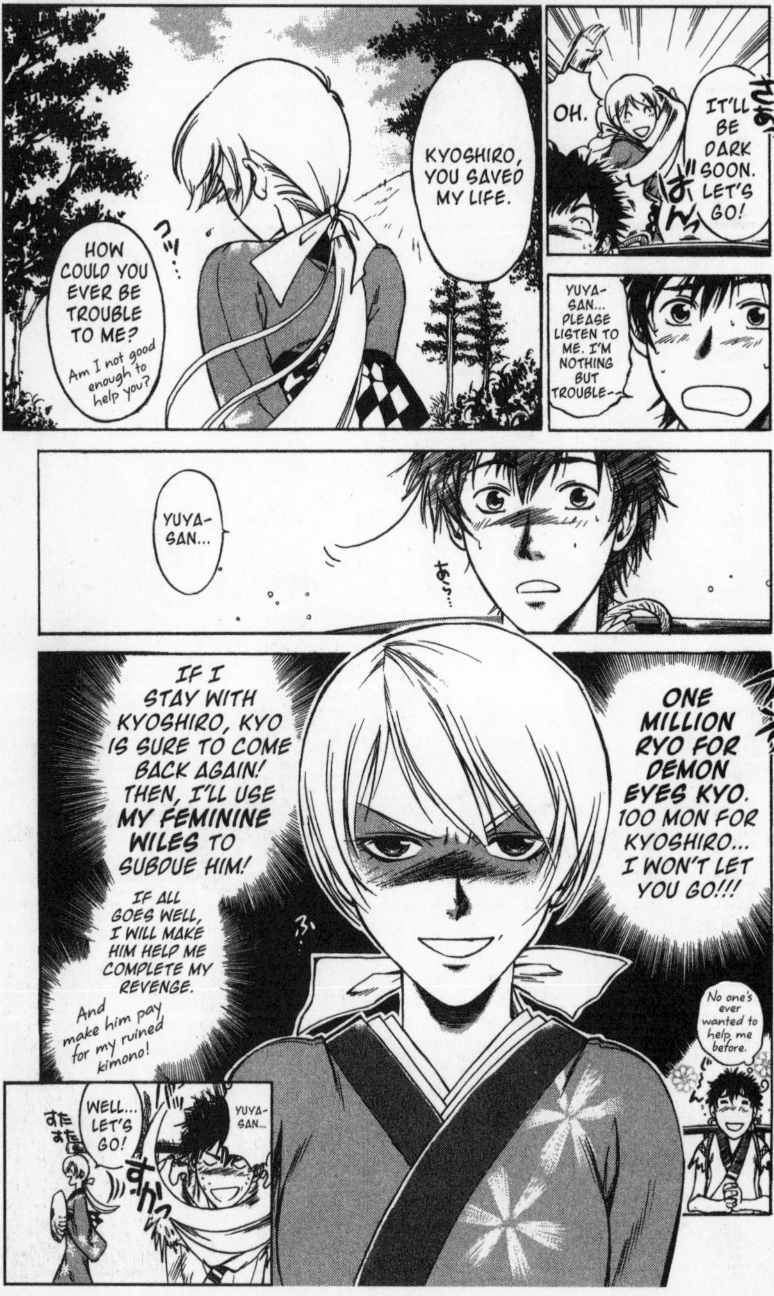
さあっ
IT'LL BE DARK SOON. LET'S GO!
OH.
ばんっ
YUYA-SAN... PLEASE LISTEN TO ME. I'M NOTHING BUT TROUBLE--
KYOSHIRO, YOU SAVED MY LIFE.
コツ...
HOW COULD YOU EVER BE TROUBLE TO ME?
Am I not good enough to help you?
YUYA-SAN...
あっ...
ONE MILLION RYO FOR DEMON EYES KYO. 100 MON FOR KYOSHIRO... I WON'T LET YOU GO!!!
IF I STAY WITH KYOSHIRO, KYO IS SURE TO COME BACK AGAIN! THEN, I'LL USE MY FEMININE WILES TO SUBDUE HIM!
IF ALL GOES WELL, I WILL MAKE HIM HELP ME COMPLETE MY REVENGE.
And make him pay for my ruined kimono!
ふ
No one's ever wanted to help me before.
じ～ん
YUYA-SAN...
WELL... LET'S GO!
すたすた
すかっ

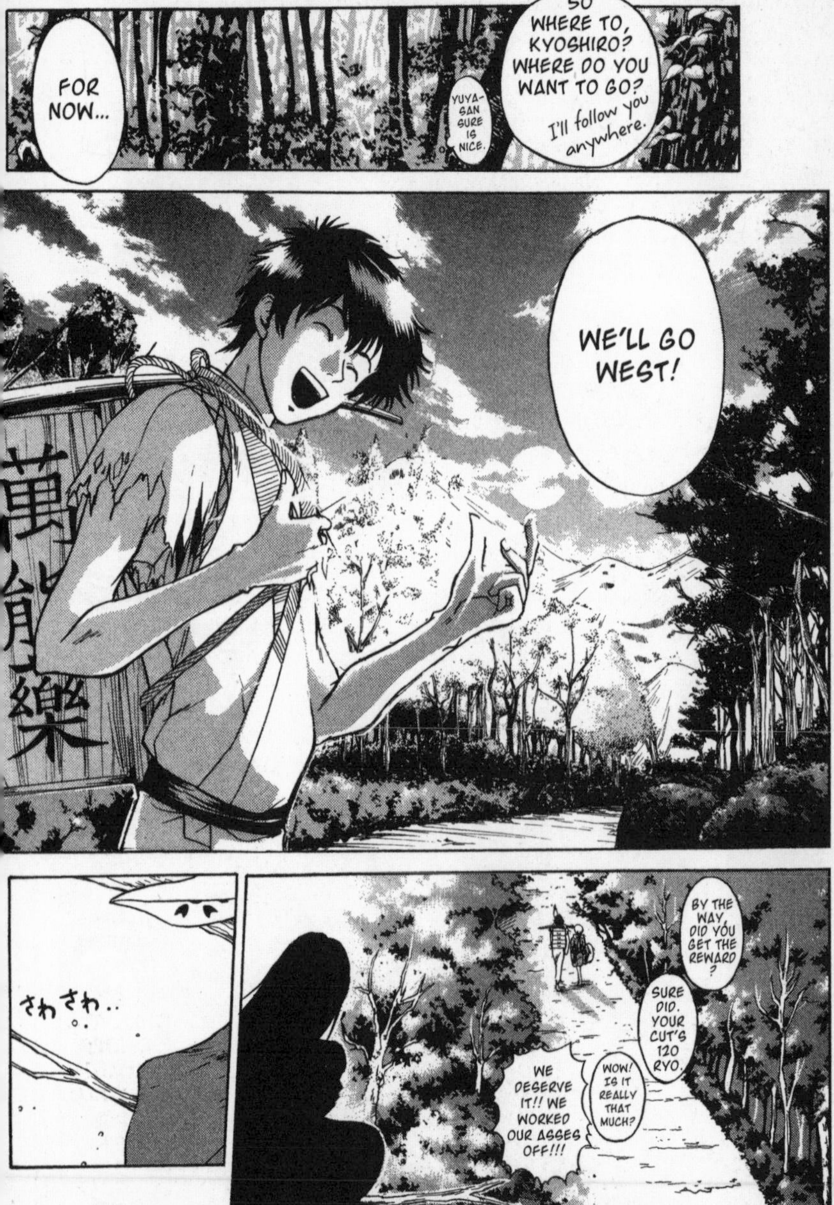
SO WHERE TO, KYOSHIRO? WHERE DO YOU WANT TO GO? I'll follow you anywhere.
YUYA-SAN SURE IS NICE.
FOR NOW...
WE'LL GO WEST!
BY THE WAY, DID YOU GET THE REWARD?
SURE DID. YOUR CUT'S 120 RYO.
WOW! IS IT REALLY THAT MUCH?
WE DESERVE IT!! WE WORKED OUR ASSES OFF!!!
さわさわ..

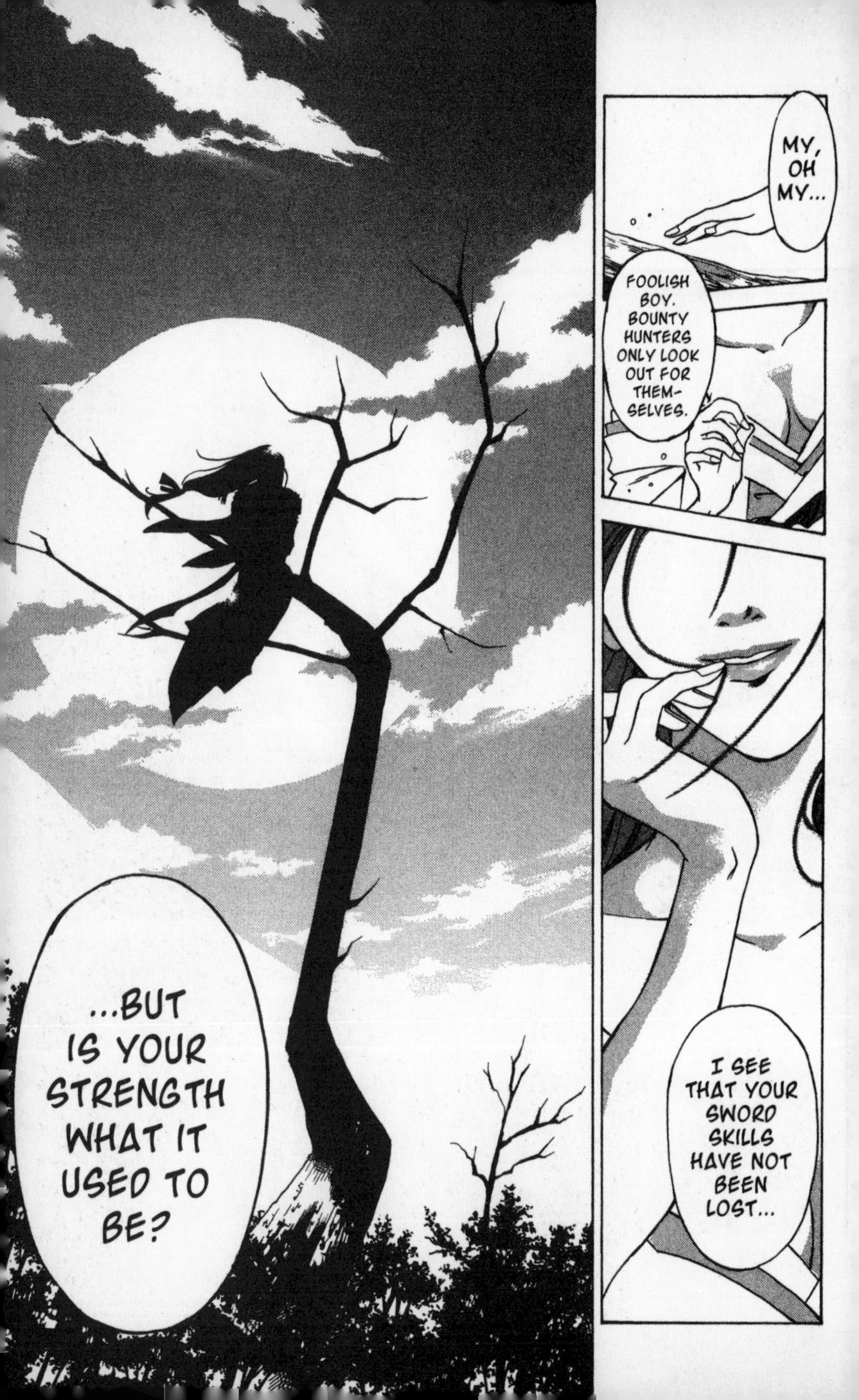
MY, OH MY...
FOOLISH BOY. BOUNTY HUNTERS ONLY LOOK OUT FOR THEM-SELVES.
I SEE THAT YOUR SWORD SKILLS HAVE NOT BEEN LOST...
...BUT IS YOUR STRENGTH WHAT IT USED TO BE?

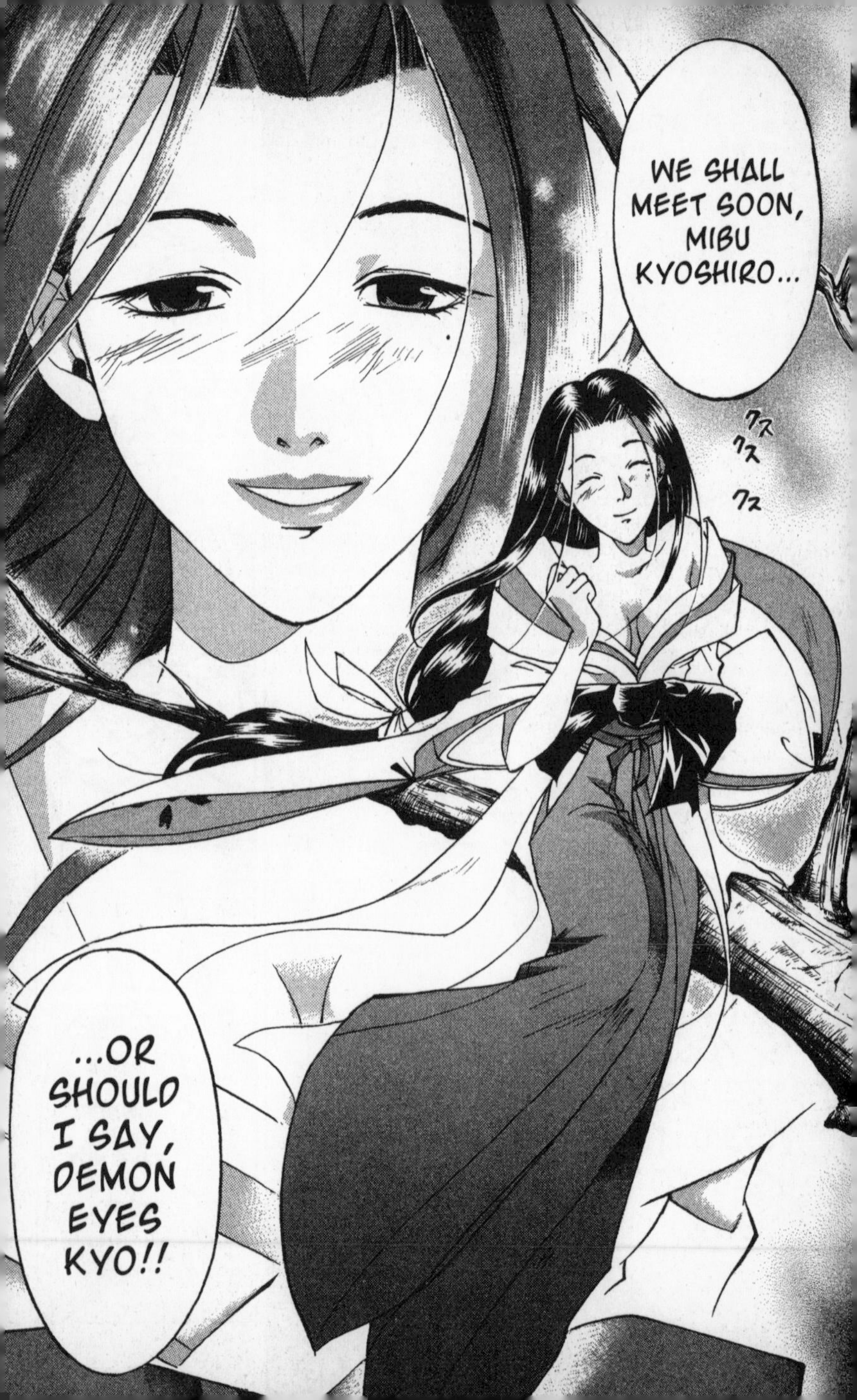
WE SHALL MEET SOON, MIBU KYOSHIRO...
...OR SHOULD I SAY, DEMON EYES KYO!!

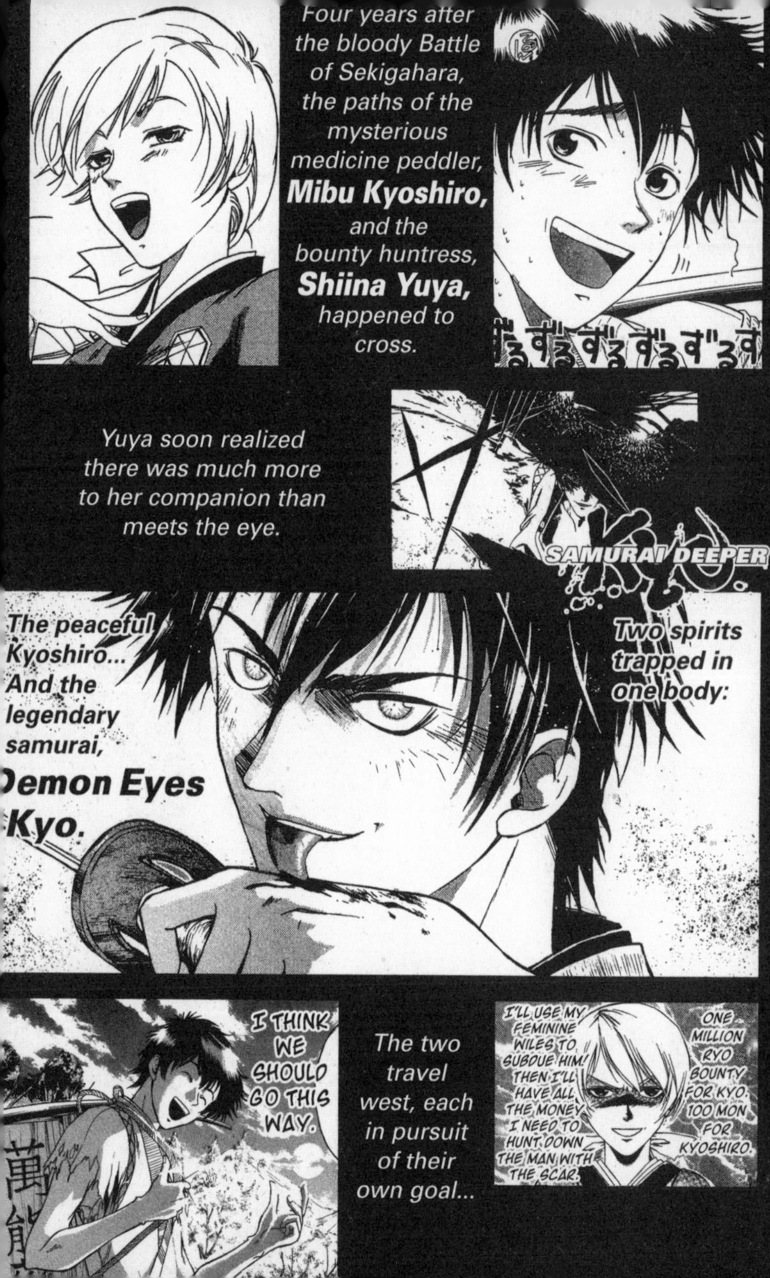

Four years after the bloody Battle of Sekigahara, the paths of the mysterious medicine peddler, **Mibu Kyoshiro,** and the bounty huntress, **Shiina Yuya,** happened to cross.
Yuya soon realized there was much more to her companion than meets the eye.
SAMURAI DEEPER KYO
Two spirits trapped in one body:
The peaceful Kyoshiro... And the legendary samurai, **Demon Eyes Kyo.**
The two travel west, each in pursuit of their own goal...
ONE MILLION RYO BOUNTY FOR KYO. 100 MON FOR KYOSHIRO.
I'LL USE MY FEMININE WILES TO SUBDUE HIM! THEN I'LL HAVE ALL THE MONEY I NEED TO HUNT DOWN THE MAN WITH THE SCAR.
I THINK WE SHOULD GO THIS WAY.

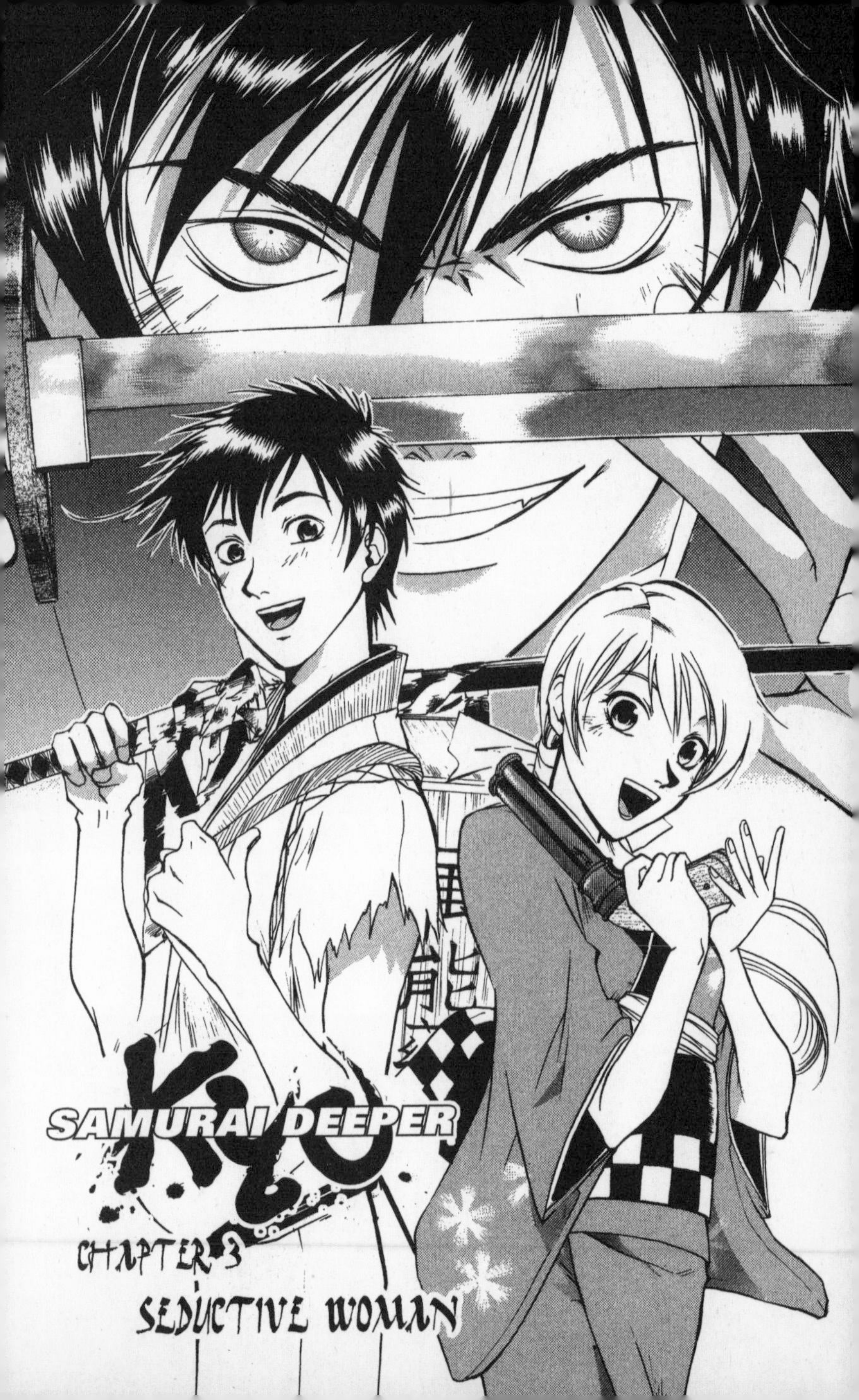
SAMURAI DEEPER
KYO
CHAPTER 3
SEDUCTIVE WOMAN

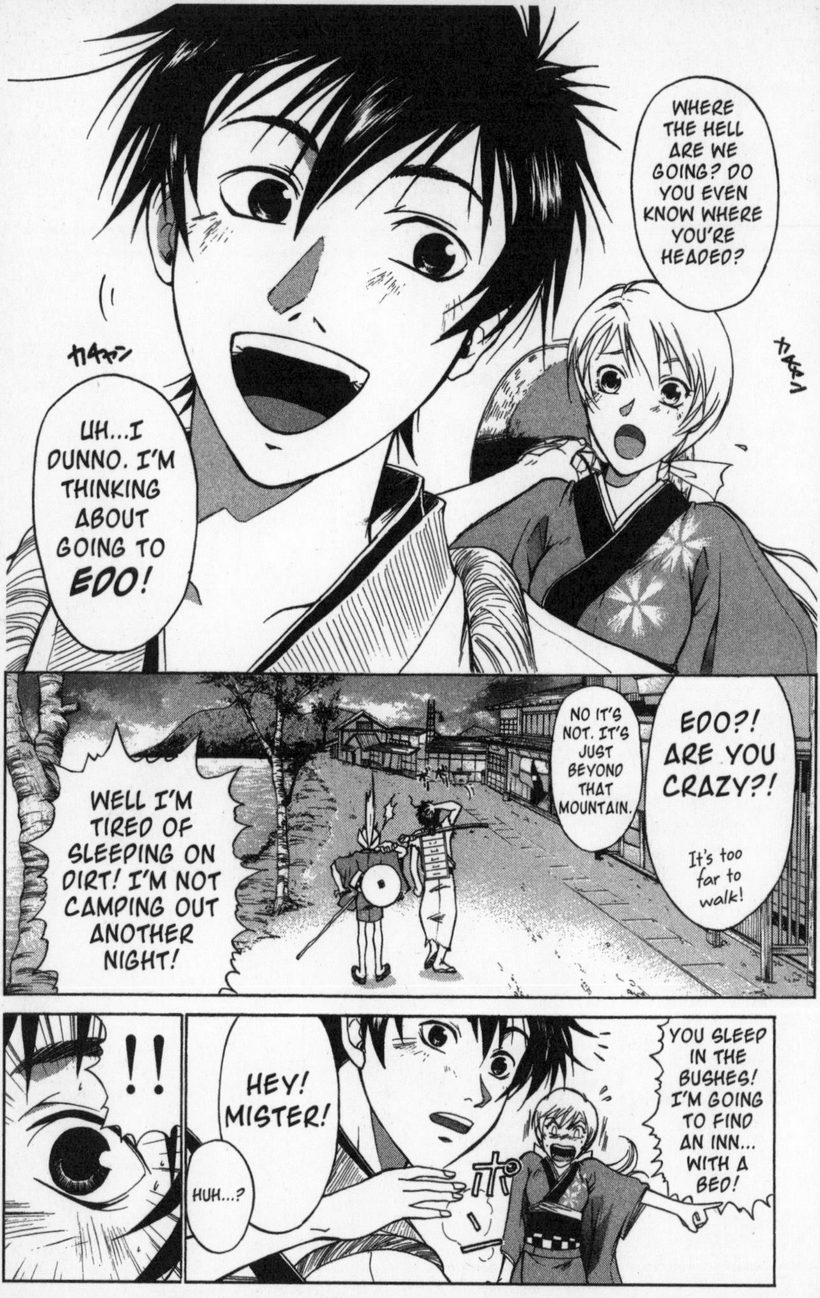
WHERE THE HELL ARE WE GOING? DO YOU EVEN KNOW WHERE YOU'RE HEADED?
UH...I DUNNO. I'M THINKING ABOUT GOING TO EDO!
EDO?! ARE YOU CRAZY?!
It's too far to walk!
NO IT'S NOT. IT'S JUST BEYOND THAT MOUNTAIN.
WELL I'M TIRED OF SLEEPING ON DIRT! I'M NOT CAMPING OUT ANOTHER NIGHT!
YOU SLEEP IN THE BUSHES! I'M GOING TO FIND AN INN... WITH A BED!
HEY! MISTER!
HUH...?
!!

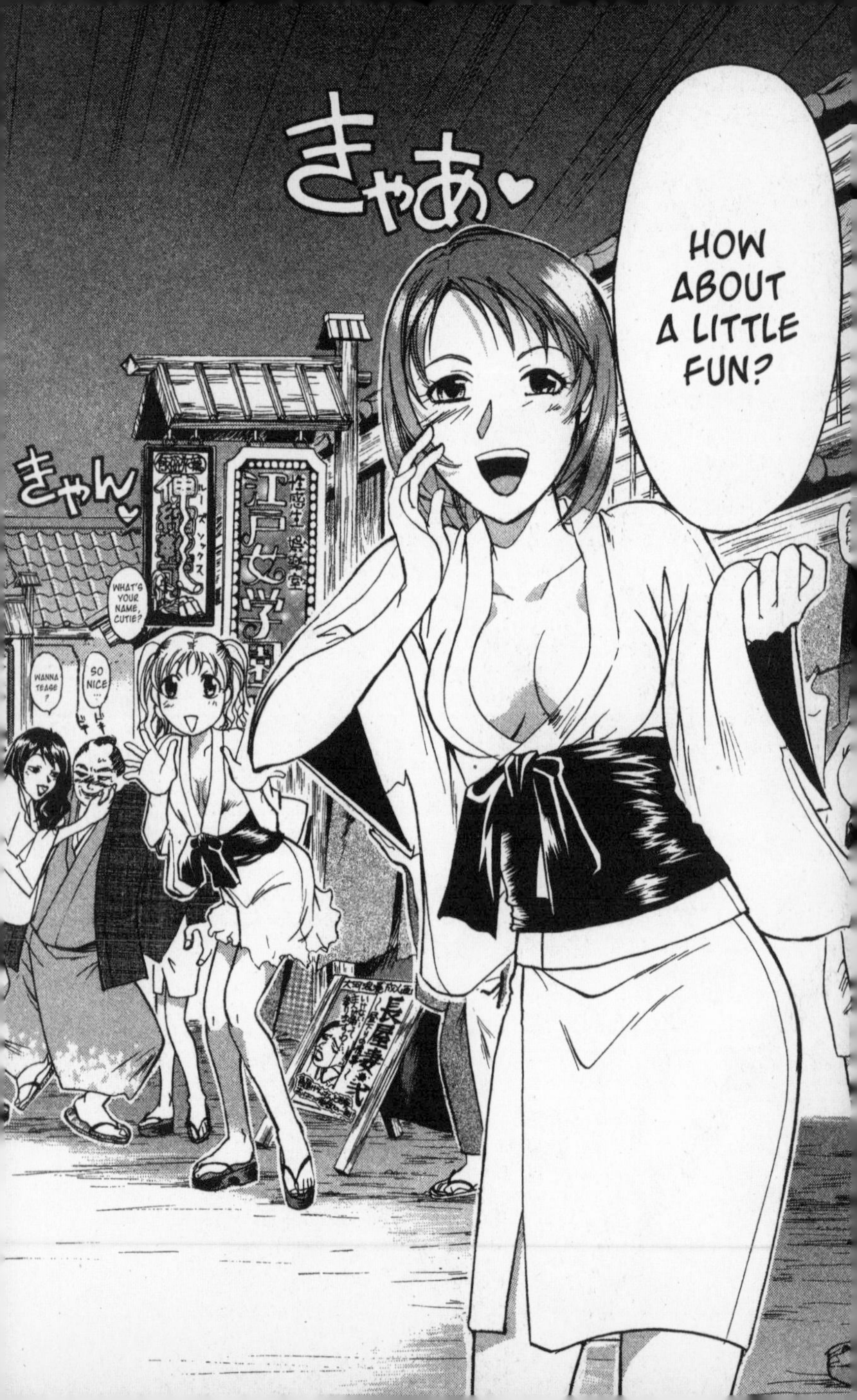
HOW ABOUT A LITTLE FUN?
きゃあ♥
きゃん♥
WHAT'S YOUR NAME, CUTIE?
SO NICE...
WANNA TEASE?

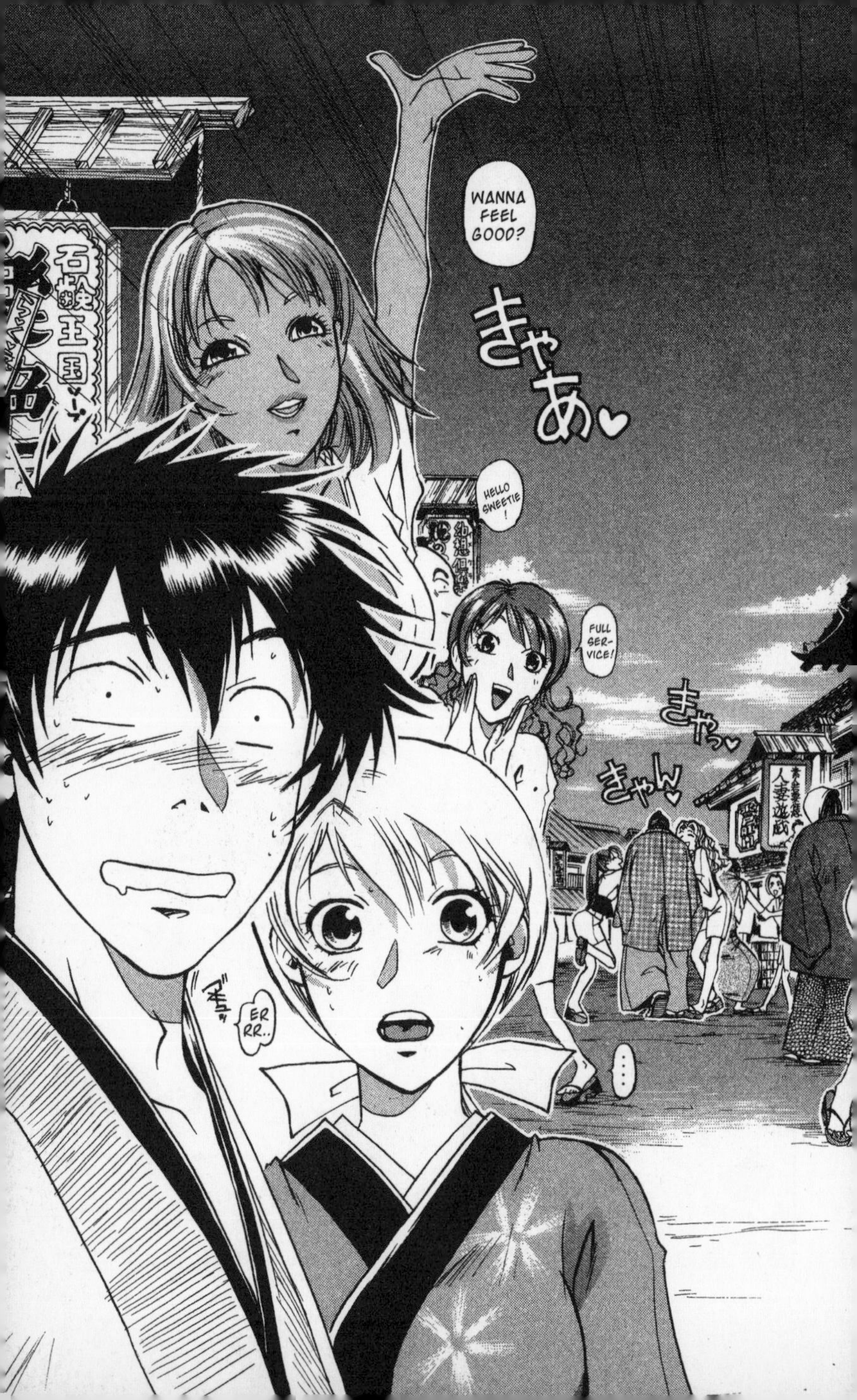
WANNA FEEL GOOD?
きゃあ♥
HELLO SWEETIE!
FULL SER-VICE!
きゃっ♥
きゃん♥
人妻遊戯
石鹸王国
...
ERR RR..

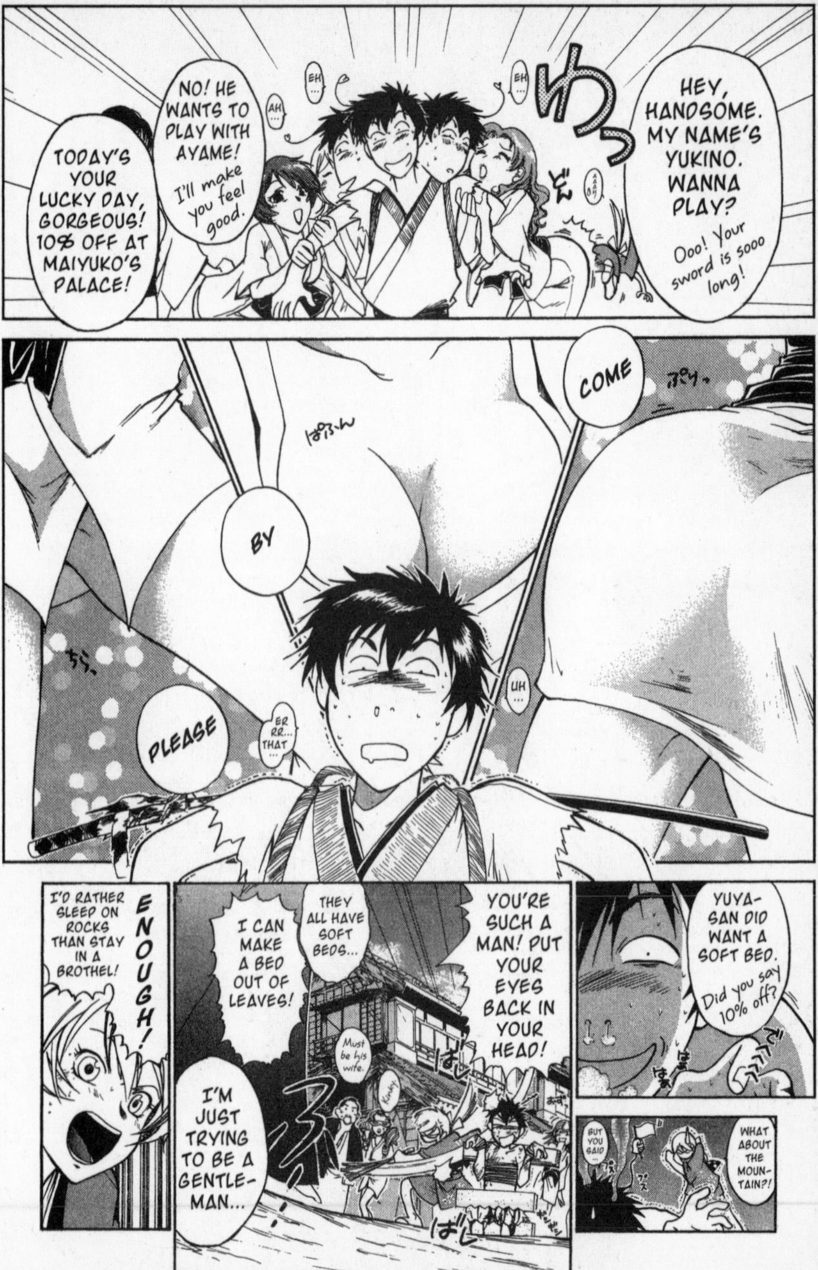
HEY, HANDSOME. MY NAME'S YUKINO. WANNA PLAY?
Ooo! Your sword is sooo long!
EH...
EH...
AH...
NO! HE WANTS TO PLAY WITH AYAME!
I'll make you feel good.
TODAY'S YOUR LUCKY DAY, GORGEOUS! 10% OFF AT MAIYUKO'S PALACE!
COME
BY
UH...
ERRR... THAT...
PLEASE
YUYA-SAN DID WANT A SOFT BED.
Did you say 10% off?
WHAT ABOUT THE MOUNTAIN?!
BUT YOU SAID...
YOU'RE SUCH A MAN! PUT YOUR EYES BACK IN YOUR HEAD!
THEY ALL HAVE SOFT BEDS...
I CAN MAKE A BED OUT OF LEAVES!
Must be his wife.
Kinky.
I'M JUST TRYING TO BE A GENTLEMAN...
ENOUGH!
I'D RATHER SLEEP ON ROCKS THAN STAY IN A BROTHEL!

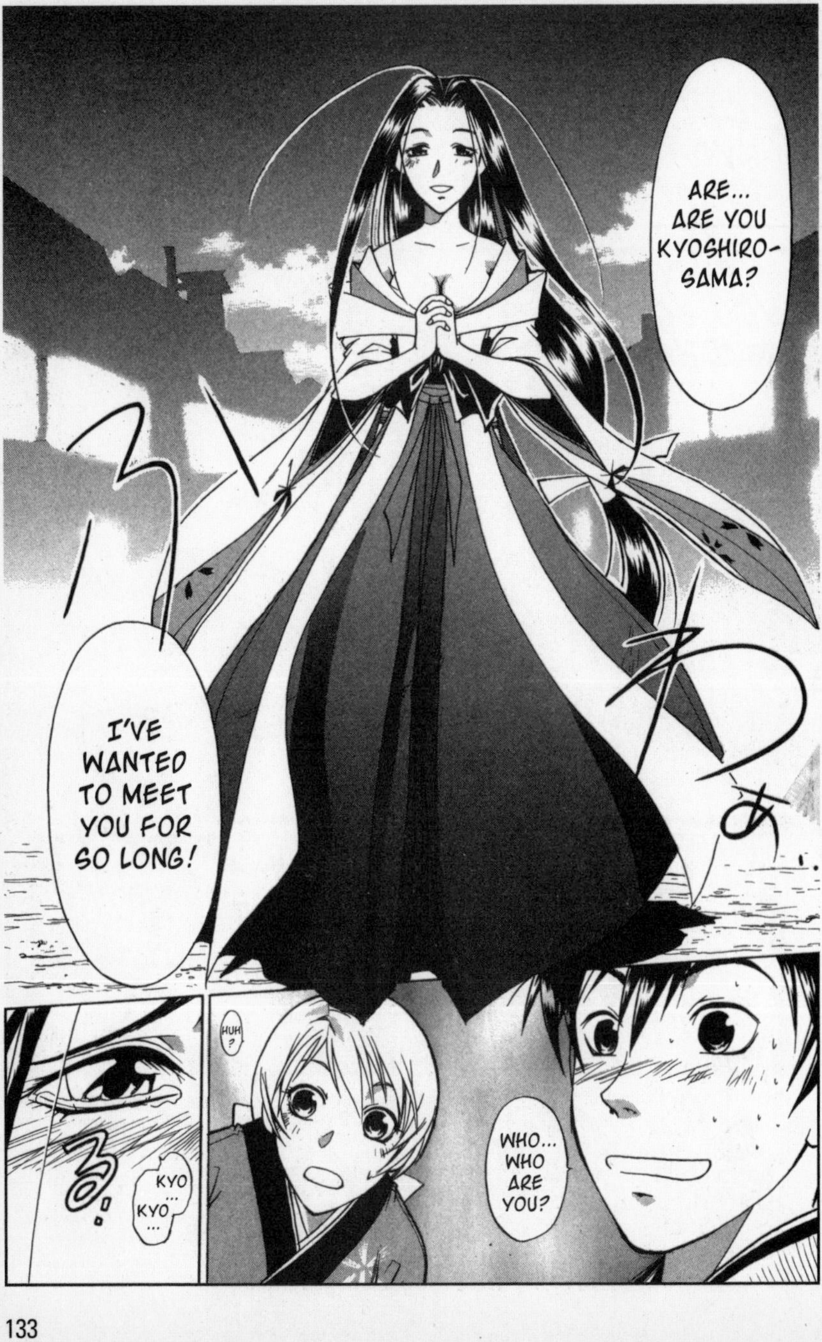
ARE... ARE YOU KYOSHIRO-SAMA?
I'VE WANTED TO MEET YOU FOR SO LONG!
WHO... WHO ARE YOU?
HUH?
KYO... KYO...

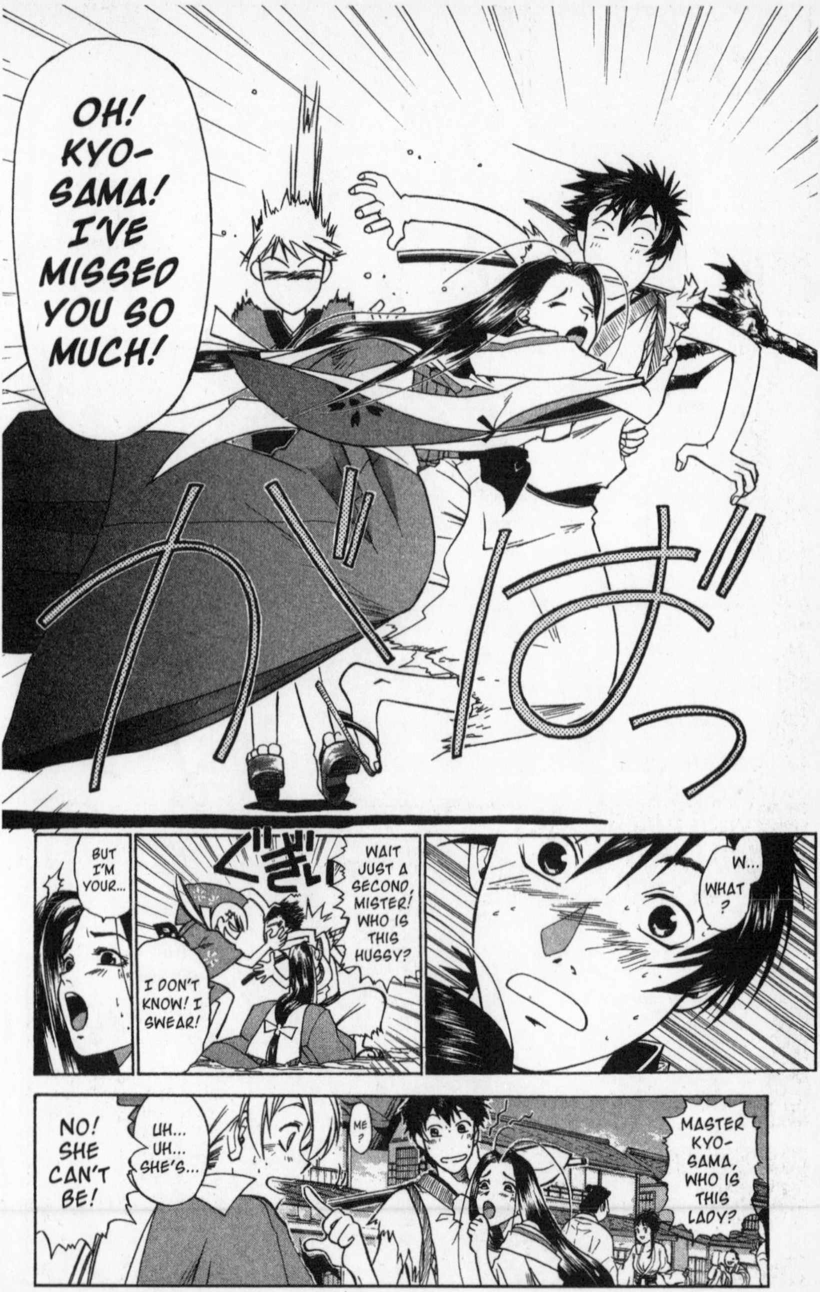
OH! KYO-SAMA! I'VE MISSED YOU SO MUCH!
がばっ
W... WHAT?
WAIT JUST A SECOND, MISTER! WHO IS THIS HUSSY?
I DON'T KNOW! I SWEAR!
BUT I'M YOUR...
MASTER KYO-SAMA, WHO IS THIS LADY?
ME?
UH... UH... SHE'S...
NO! SHE CAN'T BE!

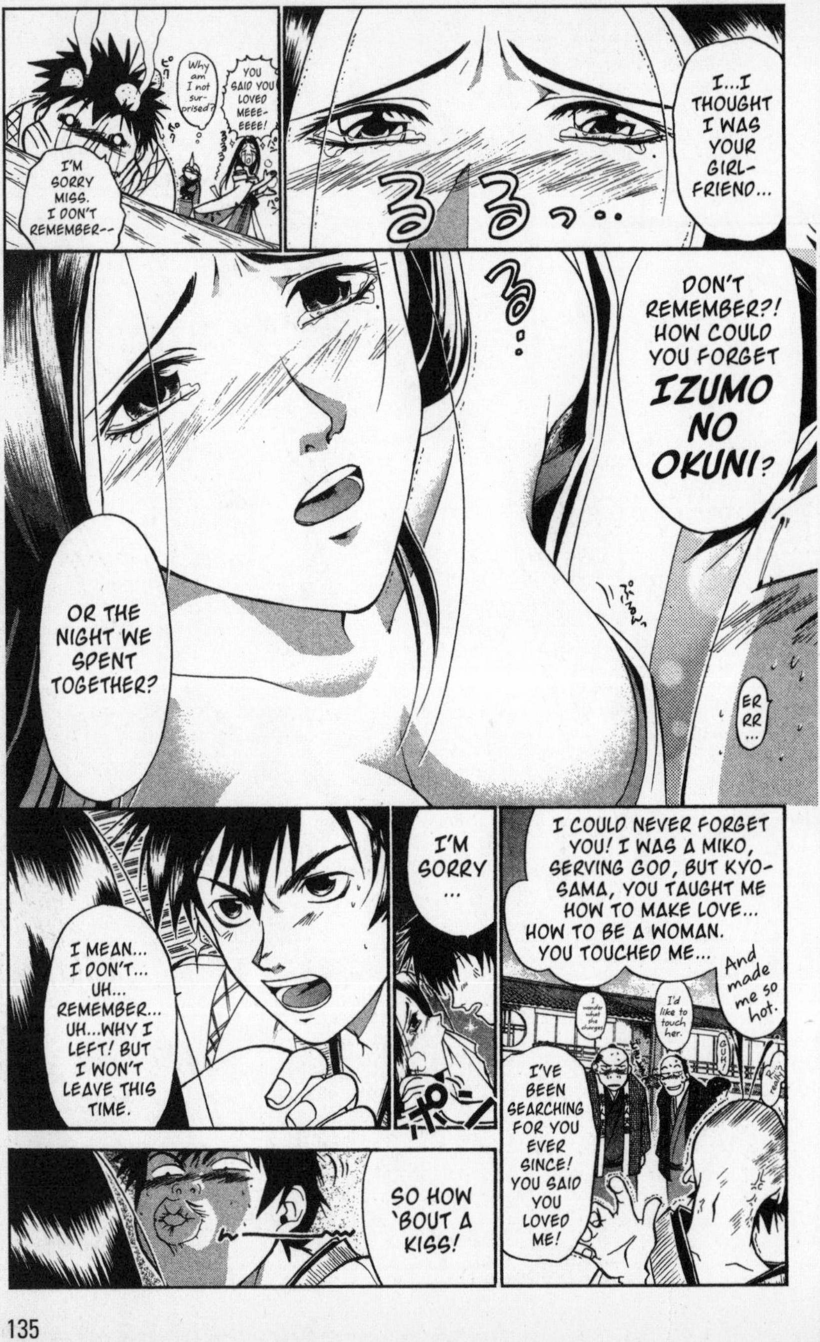
I...I THOUGHT I WAS YOUR GIRL-FRIEND...
るるっ..
YOU SAID YOU LOVED MEEE-EEEE!
Why am I not sur-prised?
I'M SORRY MISS. I DON'T REMEMBER--
るっ..
DON'T REMEMBER?! HOW COULD YOU FORGET IZUMO NO OKUNI?
ERR RR ...
OR THE NIGHT WE SPENT TOGETHER?
I COULD NEVER FORGET YOU! I WAS A MIKO, SERVING GOD, BUT KYO-SAMA, YOU TAUGHT ME HOW TO MAKE LOVE... HOW TO BE A WOMAN. YOU TOUCHED ME...
And made me so hot.
I'd like to touch her.
I wonder what she charges
GUH!
I'VE BEEN SEARCHING FOR YOU EVER SINCE! YOU SAID YOU LOVED ME!
I'M SORRY ...
I MEAN... I DON'T... UH... REMEMBER... UH...WHY I LEFT! BUT I WON'T LEAVE THIS TIME.
SO HOW 'BOUT A KISS!

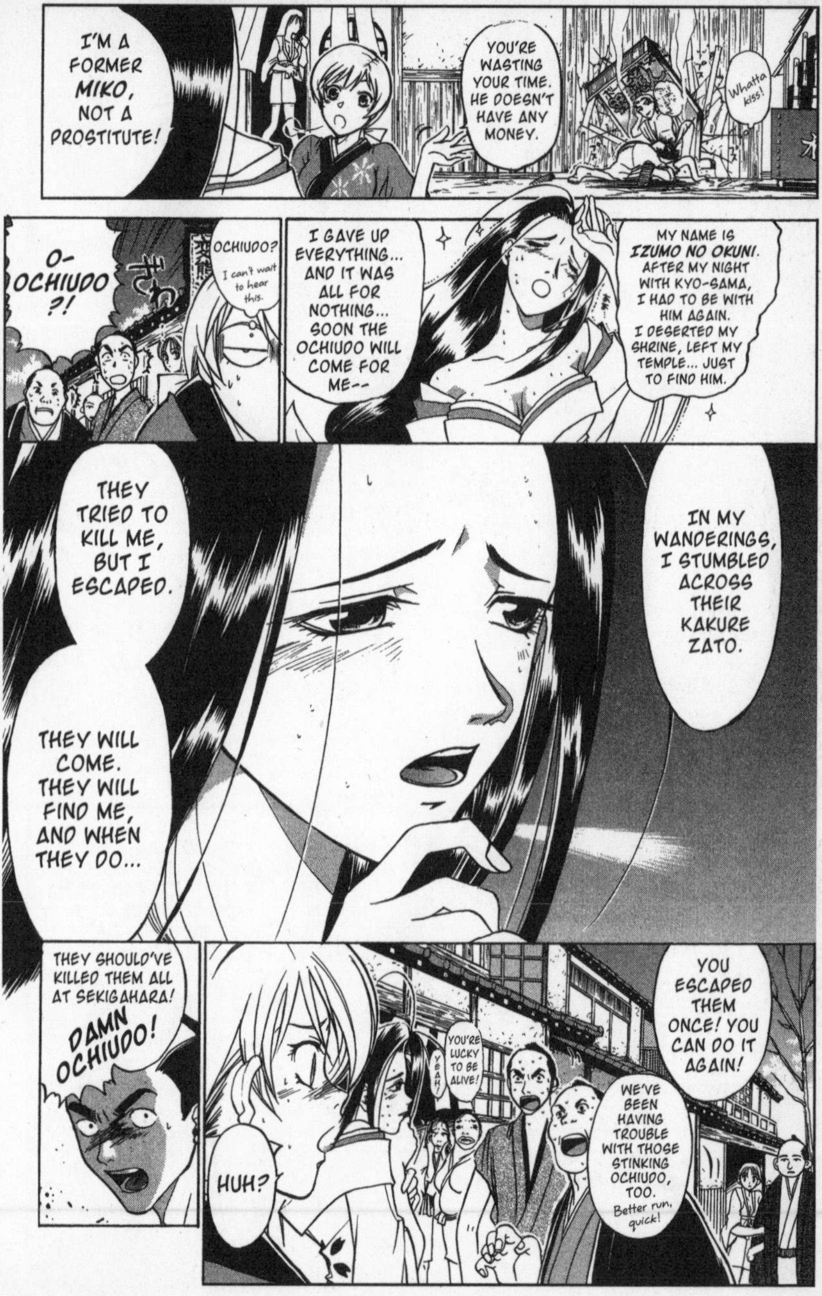
Whatta kiss!
YOU'RE WASTING YOUR TIME. HE DOESN'T HAVE ANY MONEY.
I'M A FORMER MIKO, NOT A PROSTITUTE!
MY NAME IS IZUMO NO OKUNI. AFTER MY NIGHT WITH KYO-SAMA, I HAD TO BE WITH HIM AGAIN. I DESERTED MY SHRINE, LEFT MY TEMPLE... JUST TO FIND HIM.
I GAVE UP EVERYTHING... AND IT WAS ALL FOR NOTHING... SOON THE OCHIUDO WILL COME FOR ME--
OCHIUDO?
I can't wait to hear this.
ざわ
O-OCHIUDO?!
IN MY WANDERINGS, I STUMBLED ACROSS THEIR KAKURE ZATO.
THEY TRIED TO KILL ME, BUT I ESCAPED.
THEY WILL COME. THEY WILL FIND ME, AND WHEN THEY DO...
YOU ESCAPED THEM ONCE! YOU CAN DO IT AGAIN!
WE'VE BEEN HAVING TROUBLE WITH THOSE STINKING OCHIUDO, TOO.
Better run, quick!
YOU'RE LUCKY TO BE ALIVE!
YEAH!
HUH?
THEY SHOULD'VE KILLED THEM ALL AT SEKIGAHARA!
DAMN OCHIUDO!

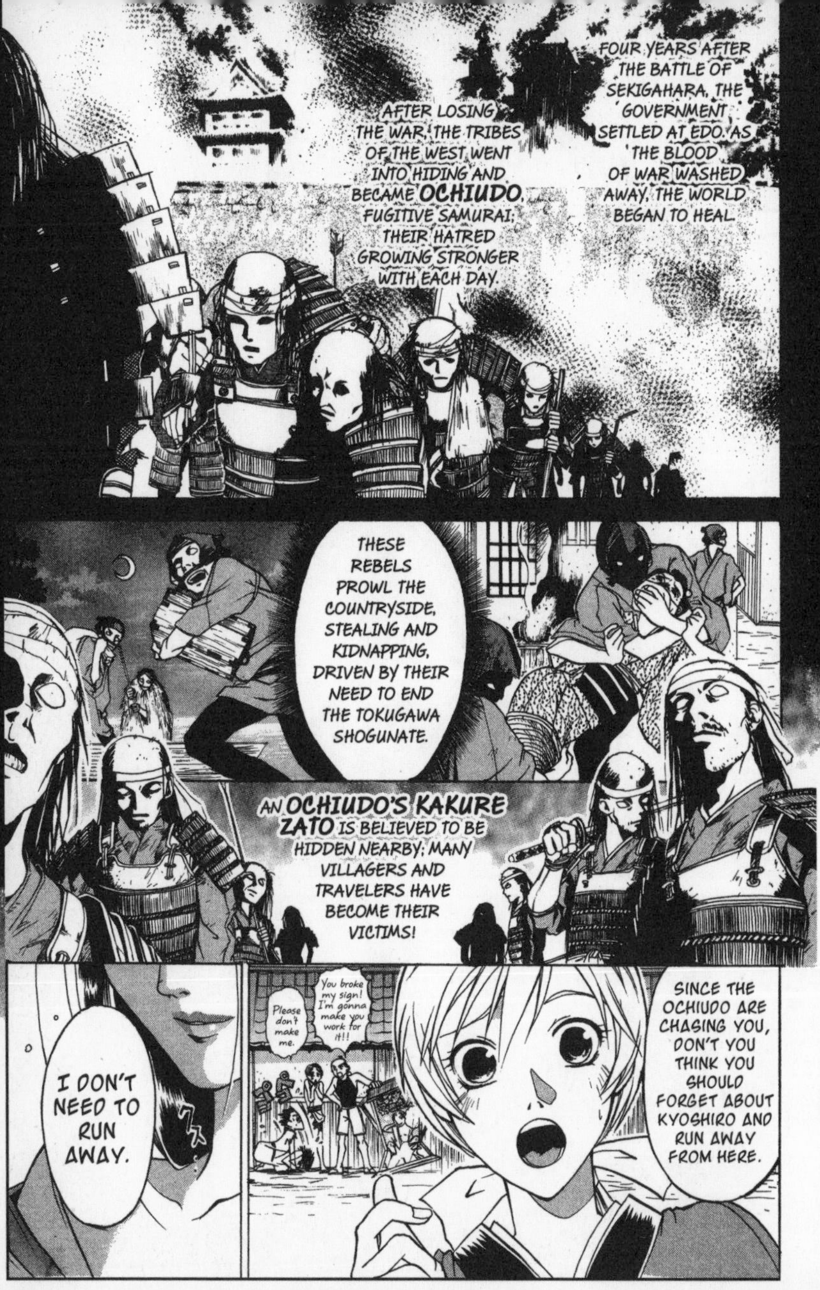
FOUR YEARS AFTER THE BATTLE OF SEKIGAHARA, THE GOVERNMENT SETTLED AT EDO. AS THE BLOOD OF WAR WASHED AWAY, THE WORLD BEGAN TO HEAL.
AFTER LOSING THE WAR, THE TRIBES OF THE WEST WENT INTO HIDING AND BECAME OCHIUDO, FUGITIVE SAMURAI; THEIR HATRED GROWING STRONGER WITH EACH DAY.
THESE REBELS PROWL THE COUNTRYSIDE, STEALING AND KIDNAPPING, DRIVEN BY THEIR NEED TO END THE TOKUGAWA SHOGUNATE.
AN OCHIUDO'S KAKURE ZATO IS BELIEVED TO BE HIDDEN NEARBY; MANY VILLAGERS AND TRAVELERS HAVE BECOME THEIR VICTIMS!
SINCE THE OCHIUDO ARE CHASING YOU, DON'T YOU THINK YOU SHOULD FORGET ABOUT KYOSHIRO AND RUN AWAY FROM HERE.
You broke my sign! I'm gonna make you work for it!!
Please don't make me.
I DON'T NEED TO RUN AWAY.

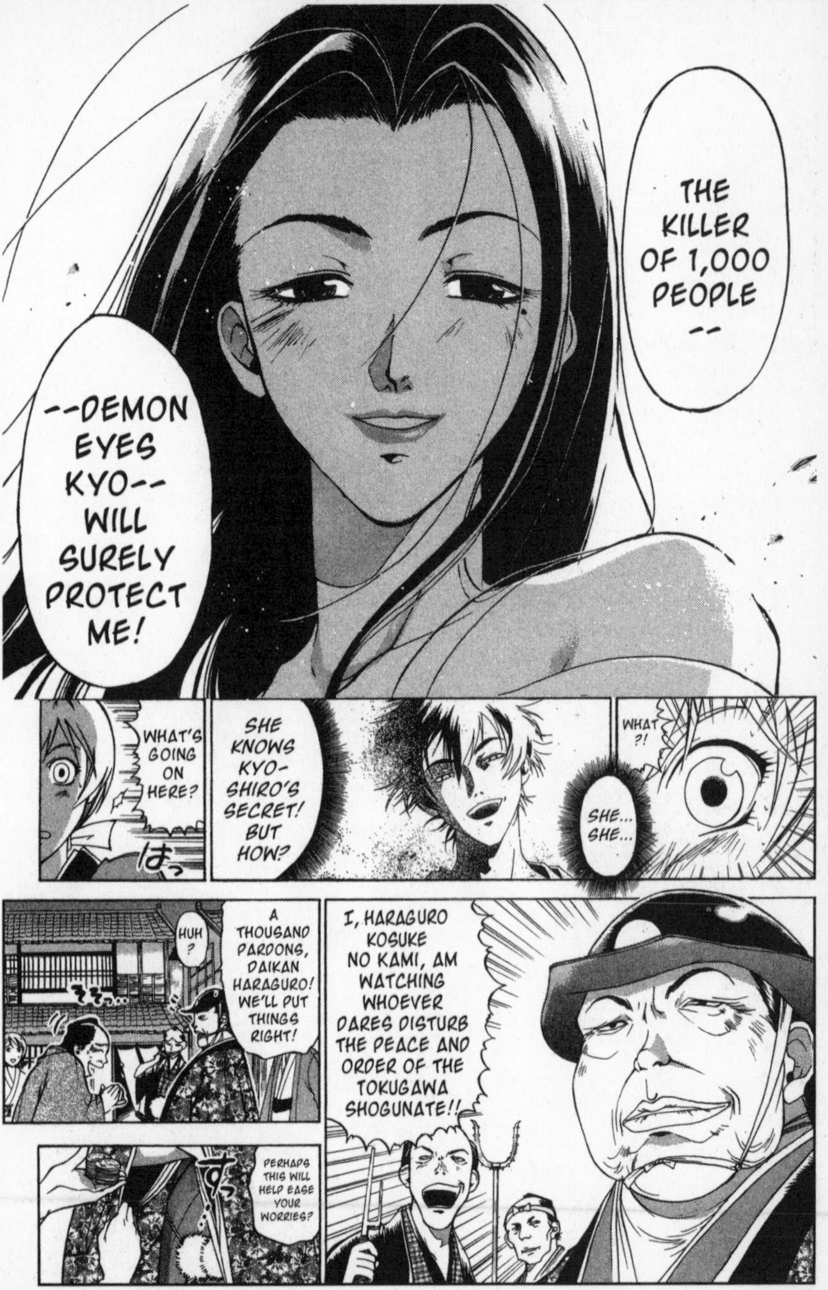
THE KILLER OF 1,000 PEOPLE --
--DEMON EYES KYO--WILL SURELY PROTECT ME!
WHAT?!
SHE... SHE...
SHE KNOWS KYO-SHIRO'S SECRET! BUT HOW?
WHAT'S GOING ON HERE?
はっ
I, HARAGURO KOSUKE NO KAMI, AM WATCHING WHOEVER DARES DISTURB THE PEACE AND ORDER OF THE TOKUGAWA SHOGUNATE!!
A THOUSAND PARDONS, DAIKAN HARAGURO! WE'LL PUT THINGS RIGHT!
HUH?
PERHAPS THIS WILL HELP EASE YOUR WORRIES?
すっ

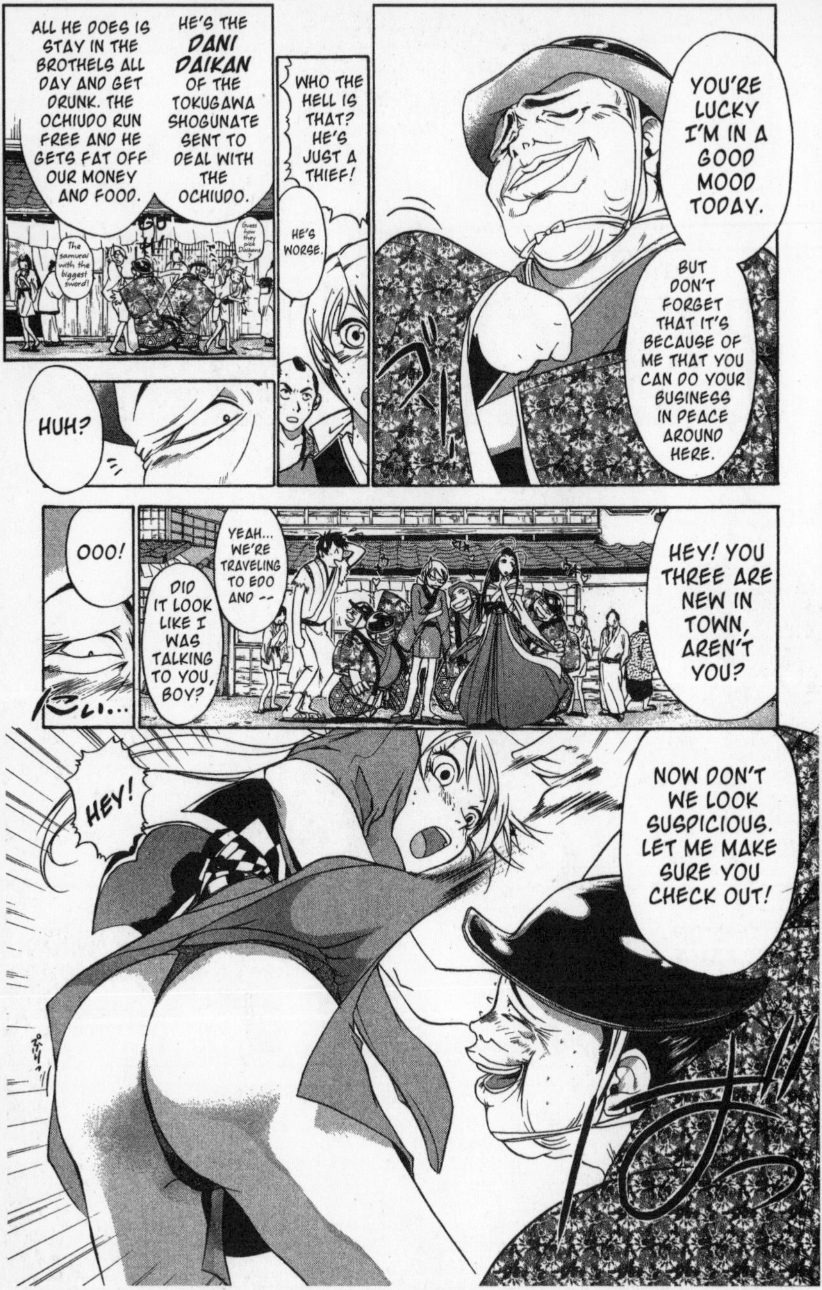
YOU'RE LUCKY I'M IN A GOOD MOOD TODAY.
BUT DON'T FORGET THAT IT'S BECAUSE OF ME THAT YOU CAN DO YOUR BUSINESS IN PEACE AROUND HERE.
WHO THE HELL IS THAT? HE'S JUST A THIEF!
HE'S WORSE.
HE'S THE DANI DAIKAN OF THE TOKUGAWA SHOGUNATE SENT TO DEAL WITH THE OCHIUDO.
ALL HE DOES IS STAY IN THE BROTHELS ALL DAY AND GET DRUNK. THE OCHIUDO RUN FREE AND HE GETS FAT OFF OUR MONEY AND FOOD.
Guess how they pick Daikans?
The samurai with the biggest sword!
HUH?
HEY! YOU THREE ARE NEW IN TOWN, AREN'T YOU?
YEAH... WE'RE TRAVELING TO EDO AND --
DID IT LOOK LIKE I WAS TALKING TO YOU, BOY?
OOO!
NOW DON'T WE LOOK SUSPICIOUS. LET ME MAKE SURE YOU CHECK OUT!
HEY!

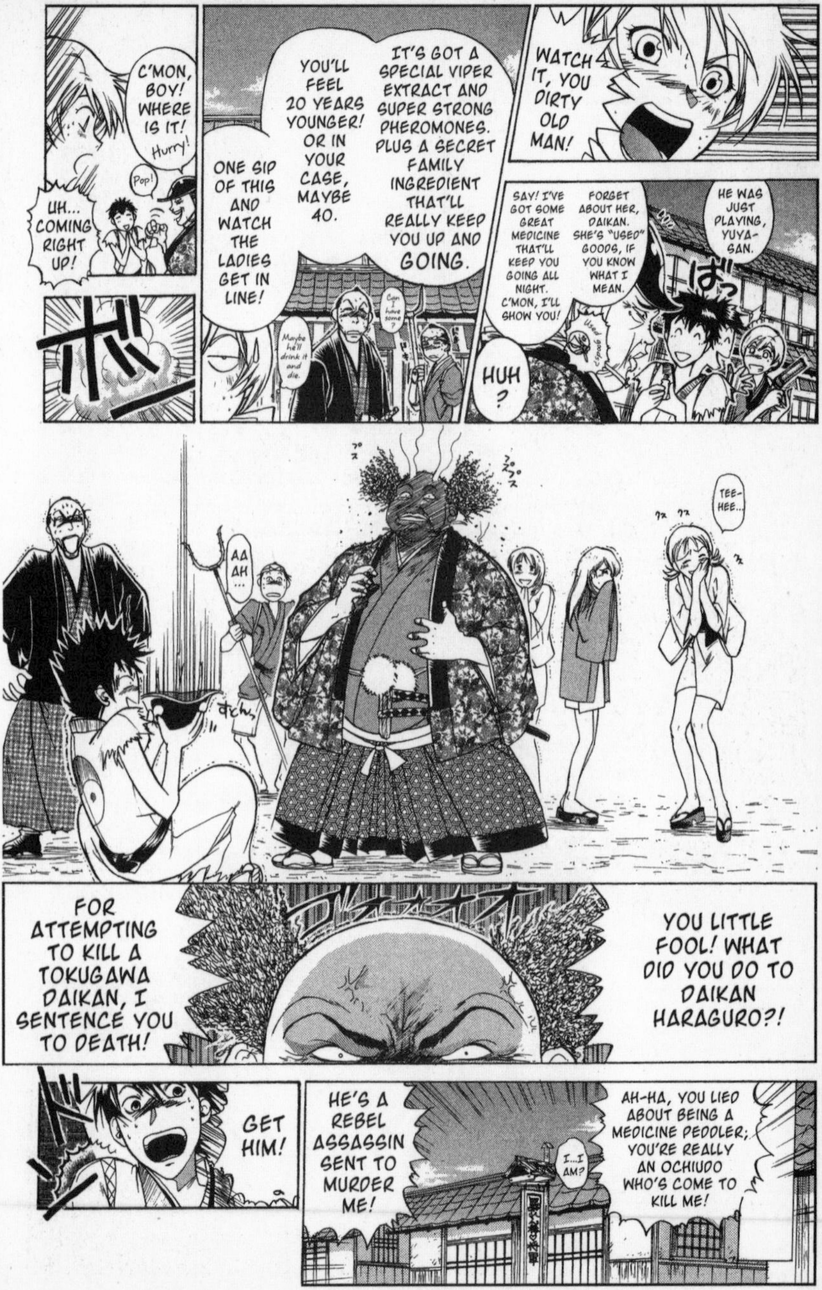
WATCH IT, YOU DIRTY OLD MAN!
HE WAS JUST PLAYING, YUYA-SAN.
FORGET ABOUT HER, DAIKAN. SHE'S "USED" GOODS, IF YOU KNOW WHAT I MEAN.
SAY! I'VE GOT SOME GREAT MEDICINE THAT'LL KEEP YOU GOING ALL NIGHT. C'MON, I'LL SHOW YOU!
HUH?
IT'S GOT A SPECIAL VIPER EXTRACT AND SUPER STRONG PHEROMONES. PLUS A SECRET FAMILY INGREDIENT THAT'LL REALLY KEEP YOU UP AND GOING.
YOU'LL FEEL 20 YEARS YOUNGER! OR IN YOUR CASE, MAYBE 40.
ONE SIP OF THIS AND WATCH THE LADIES GET IN LINE!
Can I have some?
Maybe he'll drink it and die.
C'MON, BOY! WHERE IS IT!
Hurry!
Pop!
UH... COMING RIGHT UP!
TEE-HEE...
AA AH...
YOU LITTLE FOOL! WHAT DID YOU DO TO DAIKAN HARAGURO?!
FOR ATTEMPTING TO KILL A TOKUGAWA DAIKAN, I SENTENCE YOU TO DEATH!
AH-HA, YOU LIED ABOUT BEING A MEDICINE PEDDLER; YOU'RE REALLY AN OCHIUDO WHO'S COME TO KILL ME!
I...I AM?
HE'S A REBEL ASSASSIN SENT TO MURDER ME!
GET HIM!

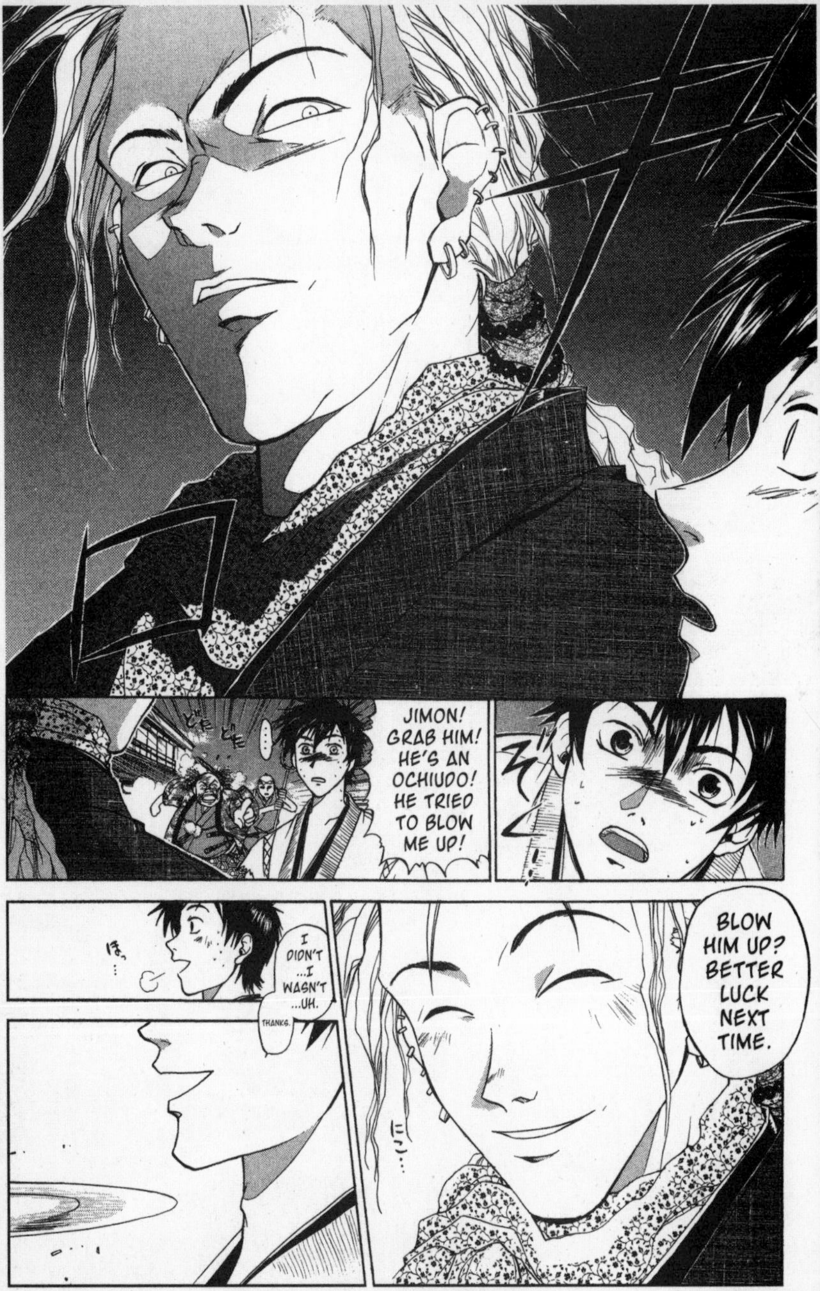
JIMON! GRAB HIM! HE'S AN OCHIUDO! HE TRIED TO BLOW ME UP!
BLOW HIM UP? BETTER LUCK NEXT TIME.
I DIDN'T ...I WASN'T ...UH.
THANKS.

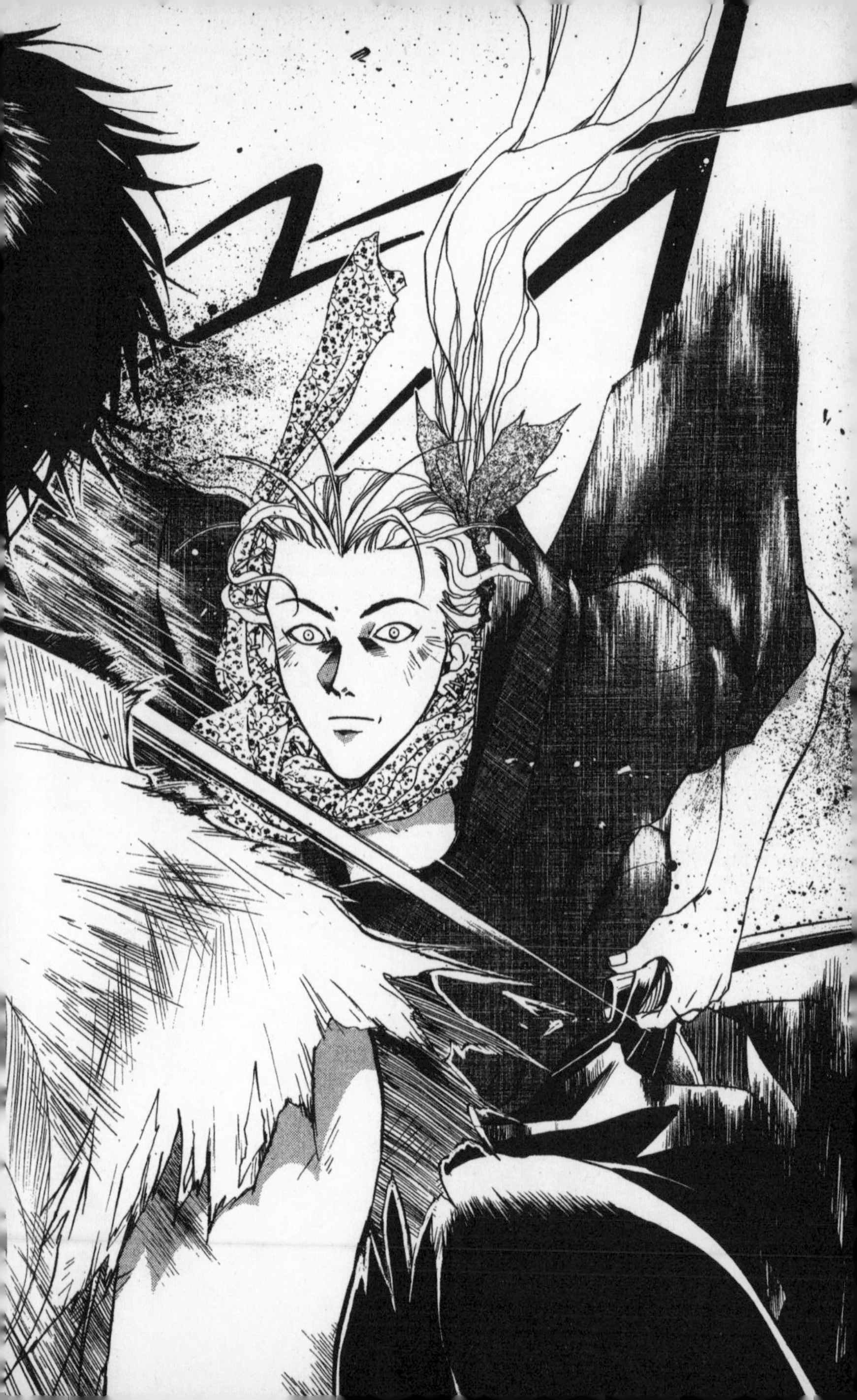

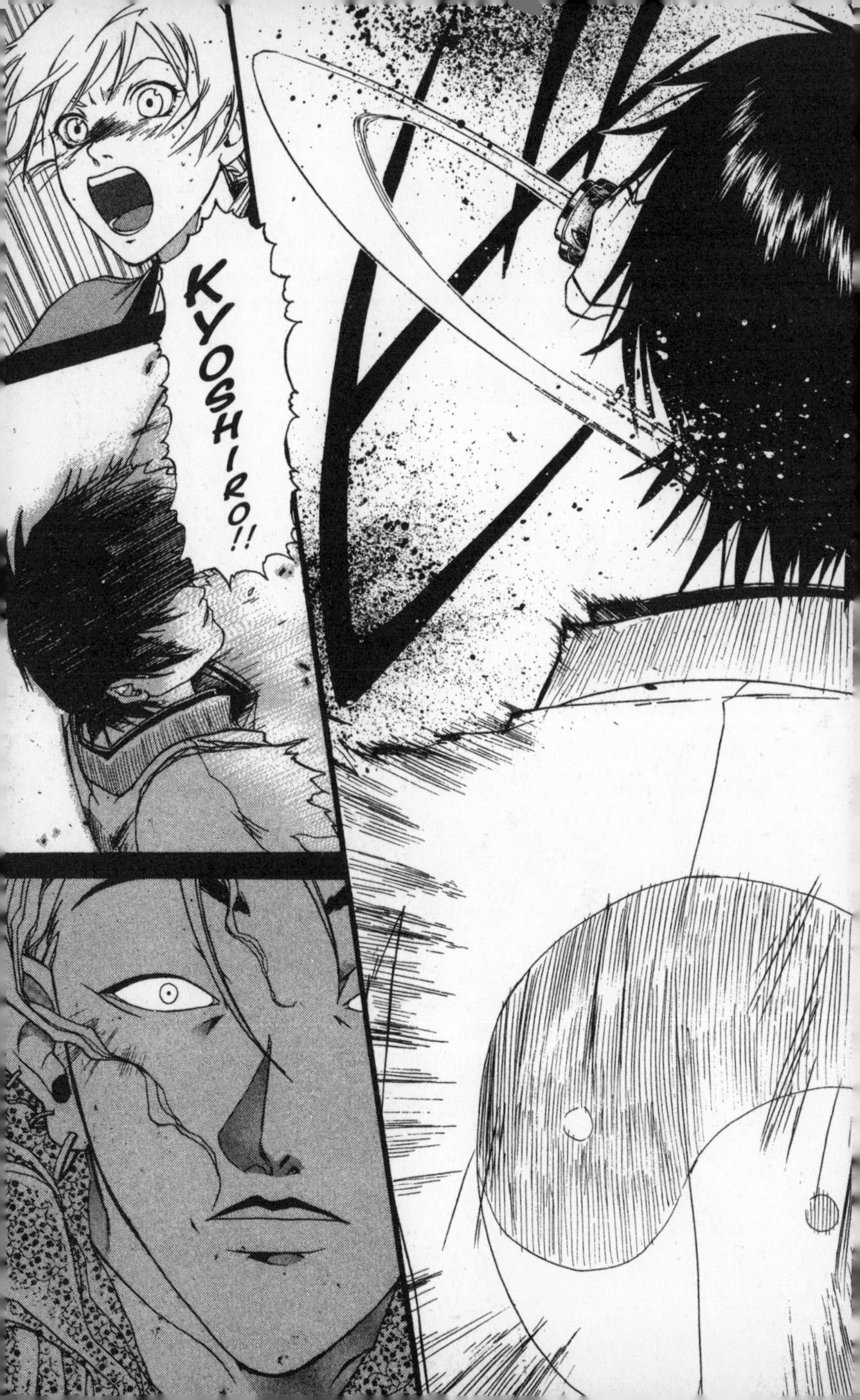
KYOSHIRO!!

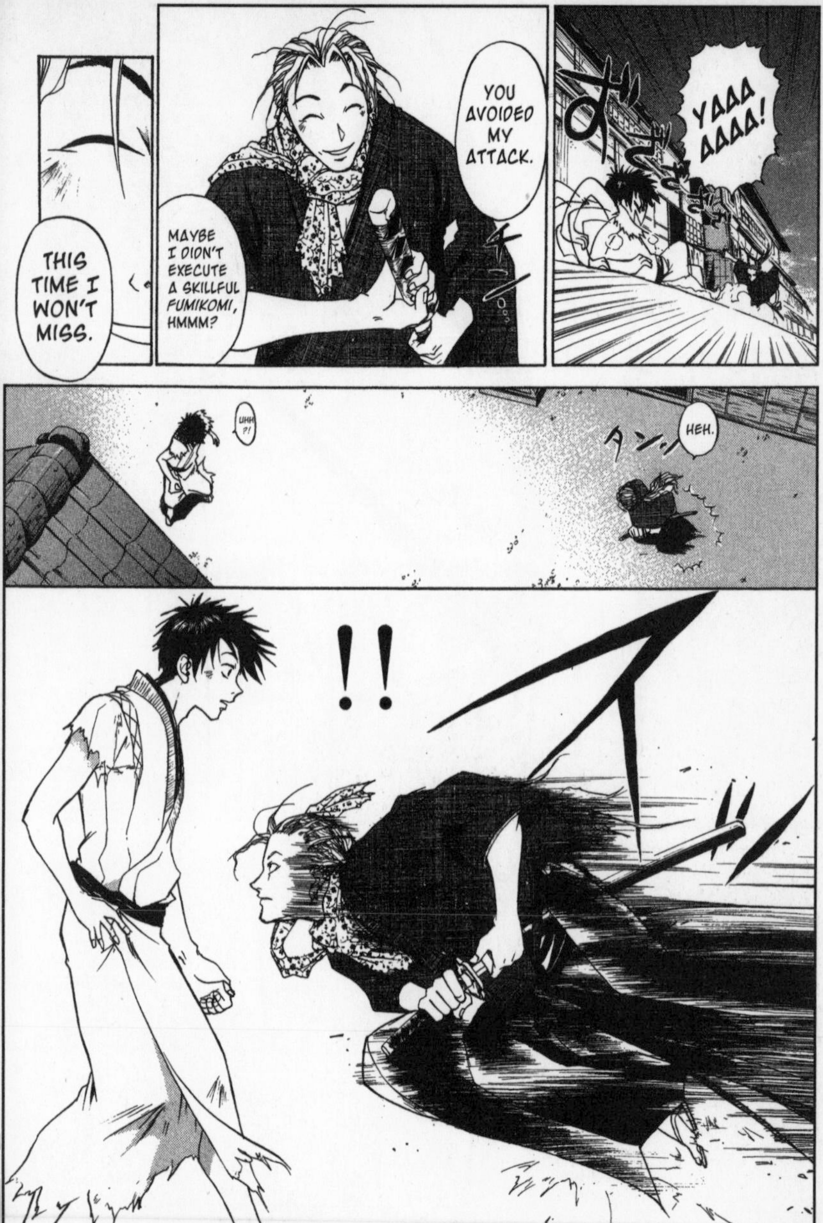
YAAA AAAA!
YOU AVOIDED MY ATTACK.
MAYBE I DIDN'T EXECUTE A SKILLFUL FUMIKOMI, HMMM?
THIS TIME I WON'T MISS.
HEH.
UHH ?!
!!

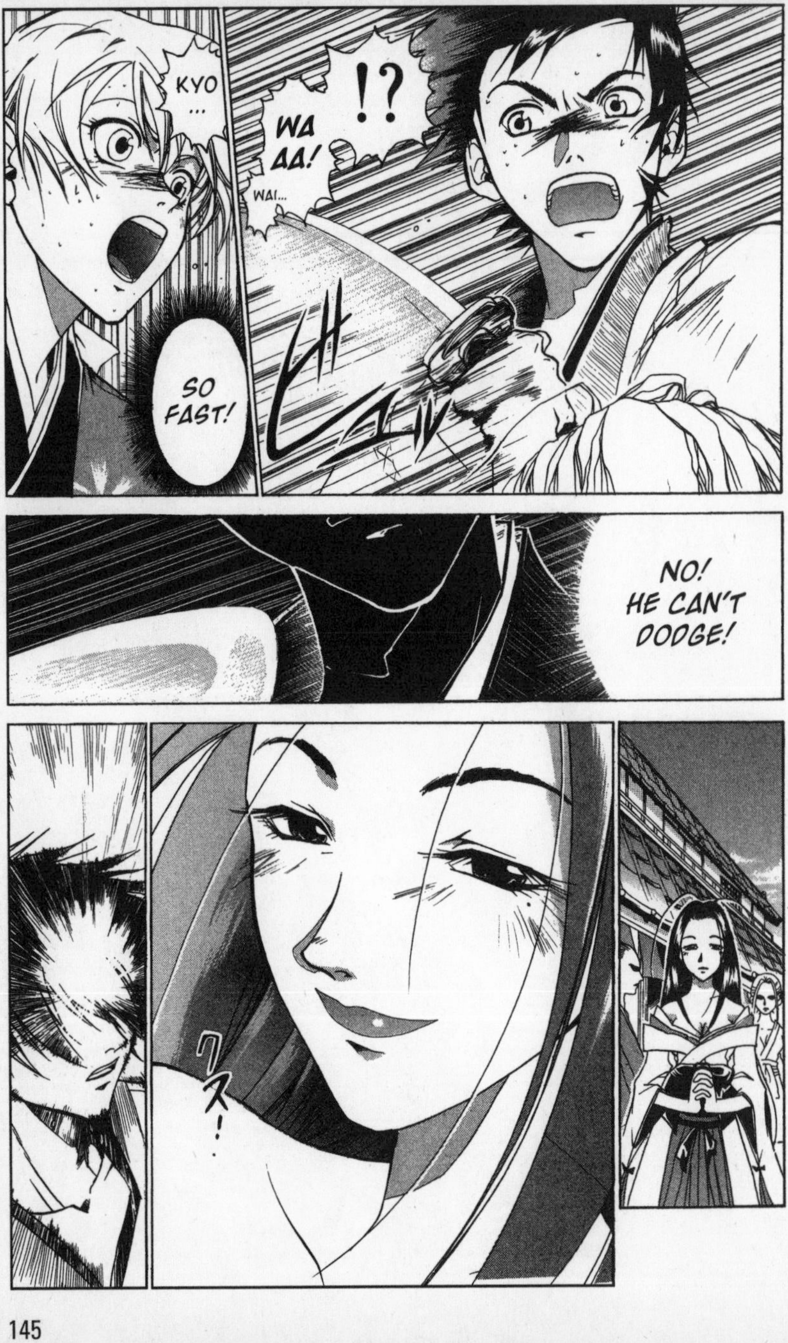
!?
WA AA!
WAI...
KYO ...
SO FAST!
NO! HE CAN'T DODGE!
クス!

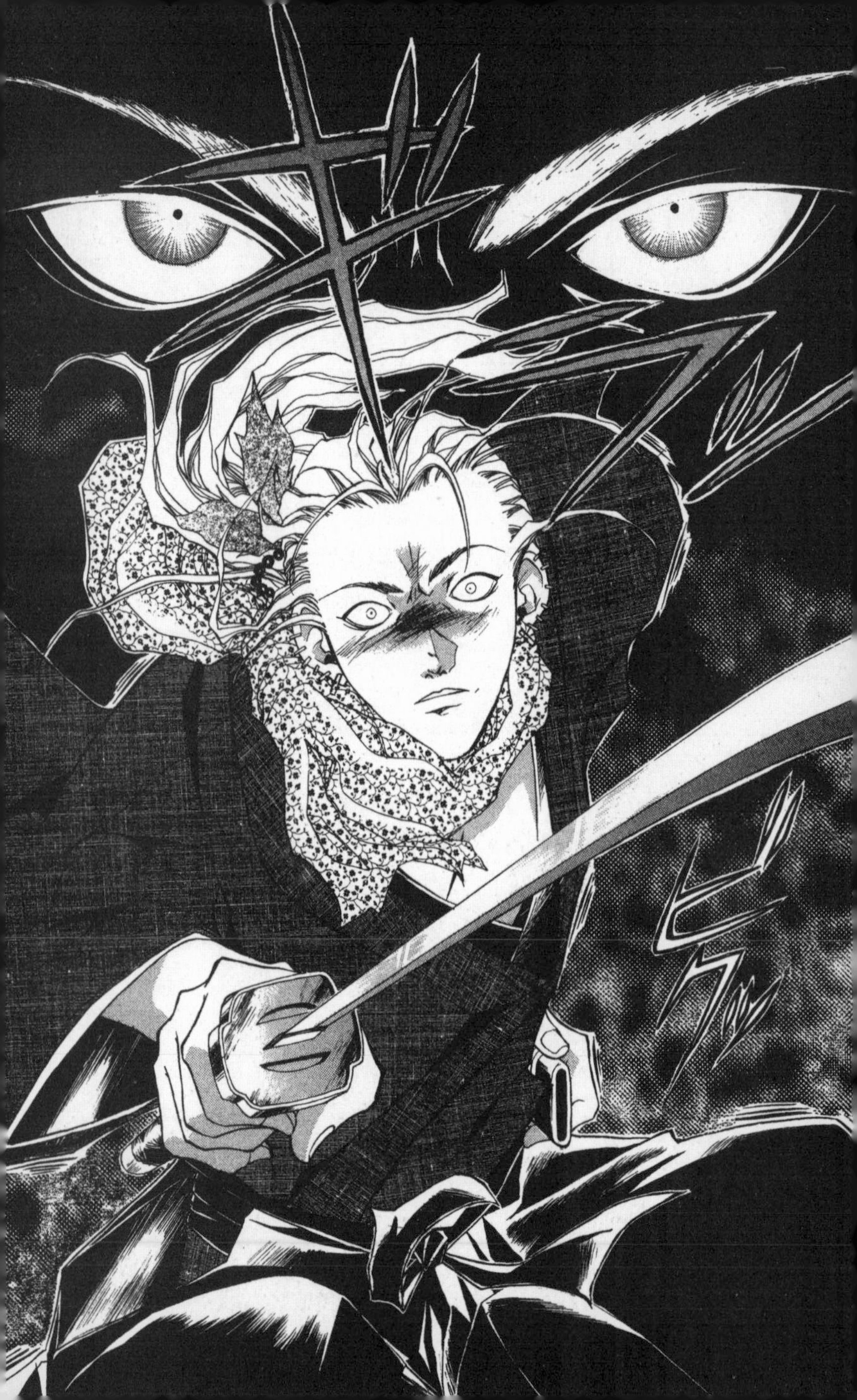

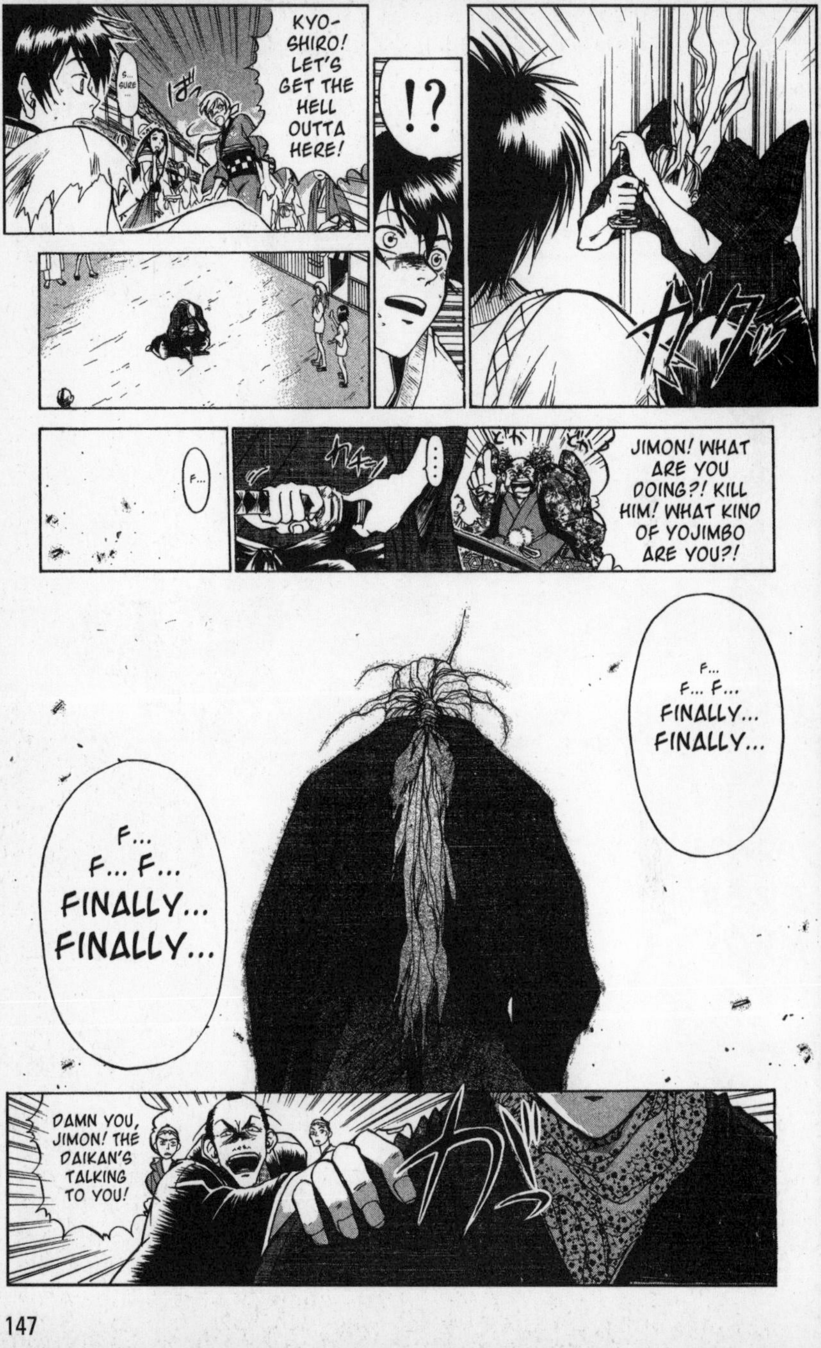
!?
KYO-SHIRO! LET'S GET THE HELL OUTTA HERE!
S... SURE...
JIMON! WHAT ARE YOU DOING?! KILL HIM! WHAT KIND OF YOJIMBO ARE YOU?!
...
F...
F... F... F... FINALLY... FINALLY...
F... F... F... FINALLY... FINALLY...
DAMN YOU, JIMON! THE DAIKAN'S TALKING TO YOU!

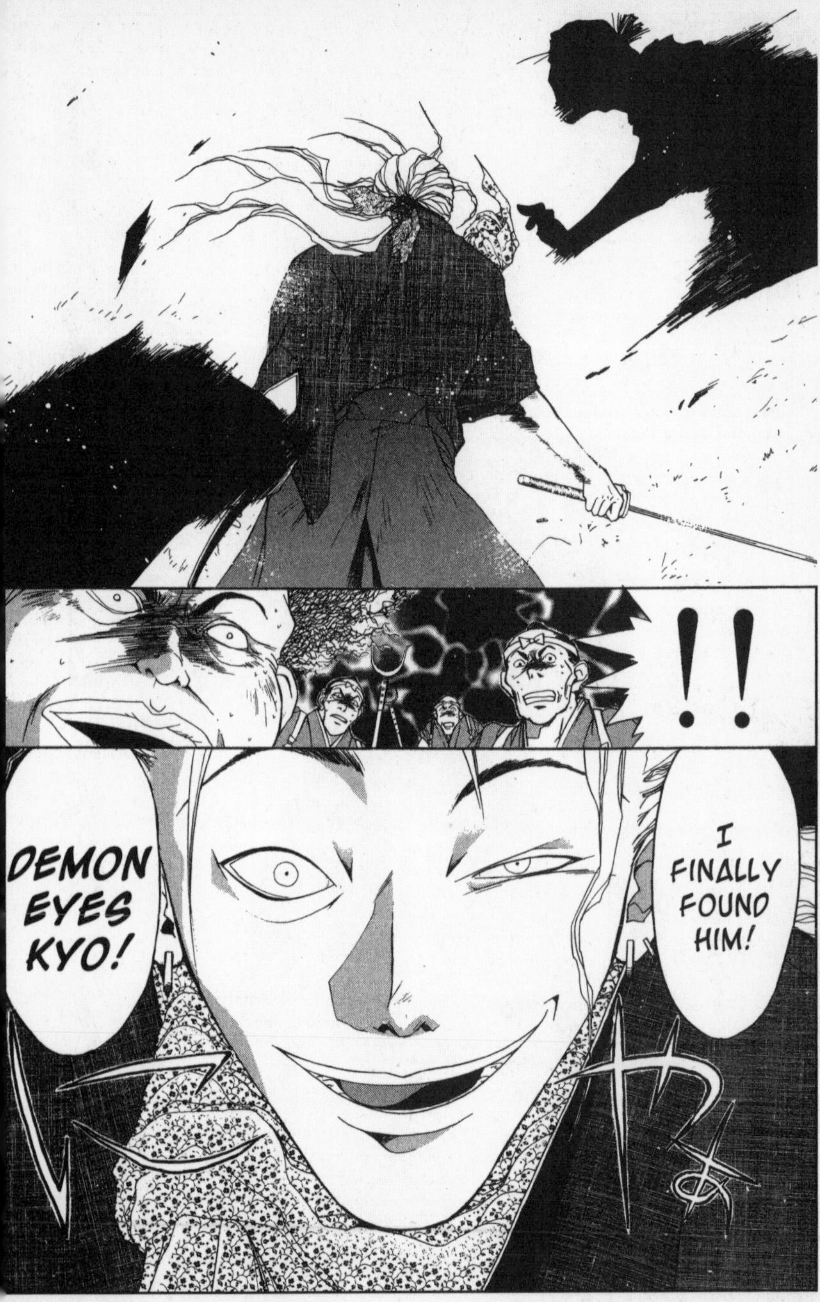
!!
I FINALLY FOUND HIM!
DEMON EYES KYO!

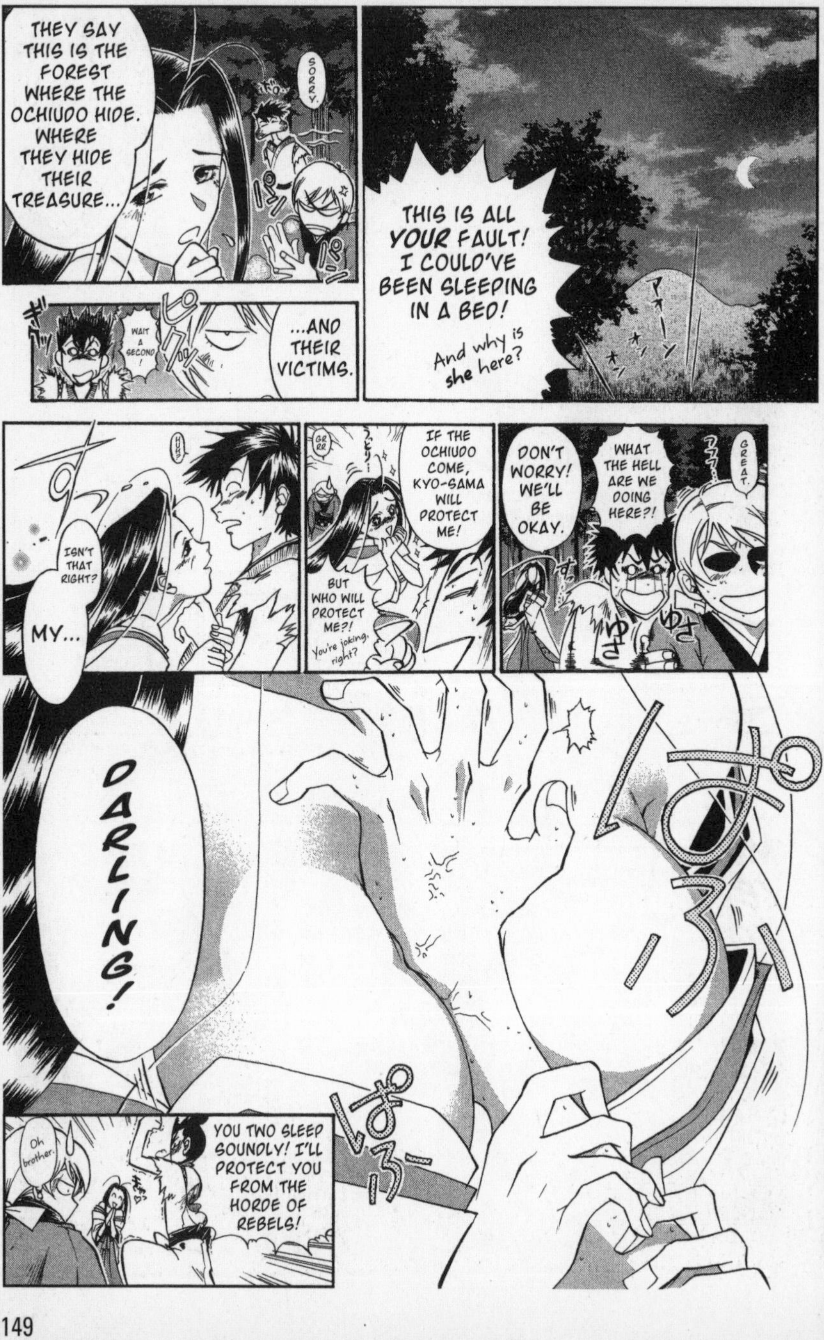
THIS IS ALL YOUR FAULT! I COULD'VE BEEN SLEEPING IN A BED!
And why is she here?
THEY SAY THIS IS THE FOREST WHERE THE OCHIUDO HIDE. WHERE THEY HIDE THEIR TREASURE...
SORRY.
...AND THEIR VICTIMS.
WAIT A SECOND!
GREAT.
WHAT THE HELL ARE WE DOING HERE?!
DON'T WORRY! WE'LL BE OKAY.
IF THE OCHIUDO COME, KYO-SAMA WILL PROTECT ME!
GRR
BUT WHO WILL PROTECT ME?!
You're joking, right?
HUH?
ISN'T THAT RIGHT?
MY...
DARLING!
YOU TWO SLEEP SOUNDLY! I'LL PROTECT YOU FROM THE HORDE OF REBELS!
Oh brother.

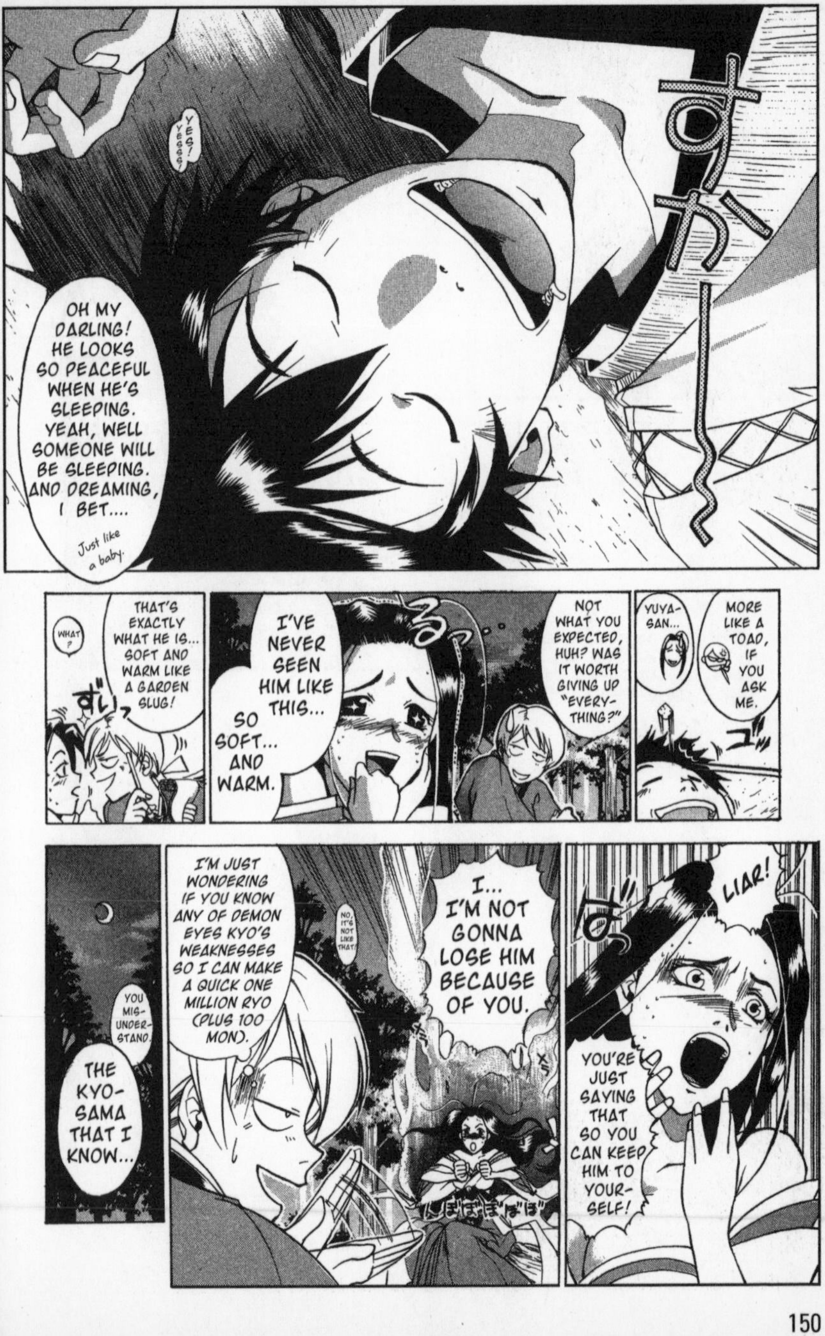

YES! YESS!
OH MY DARLING! HE LOOKS SO PEACEFUL WHEN HE'S SLEEPING. YEAH, WELL SOMEONE WILL BE SLEEPING. AND DREAMING, I BET....
Just like a baby.
MORE LIKE A TOAD, IF YOU ASK ME.
YUYA-SAN...
NOT WHAT YOU EXPECTED, HUH? WAS IT WORTH GIVING UP "EVERYTHING?"
I'VE NEVER SEEN HIM LIKE THIS...
SO SOFT... AND WARM.
THAT'S EXACTLY WHAT HE IS... SOFT AND WARM LIKE A GARDEN SLUG!
WHAT?
LIAR!
YOU'RE JUST SAYING THAT SO YOU CAN KEEP HIM TO YOURSELF!
I... I'M NOT GONNA LOSE HIM BECAUSE OF YOU.
NO, IT'S NOT LIKE THAT!
I'M JUST WONDERING IF YOU KNOW ANY OF DEMON EYES KYO'S WEAKNESSES SO I CAN MAKE A QUICK ONE MILLION RYO (PLUS 100 MON).
YOU MISUNDERSTAND.
THE KYO-SAMA THAT I KNOW...

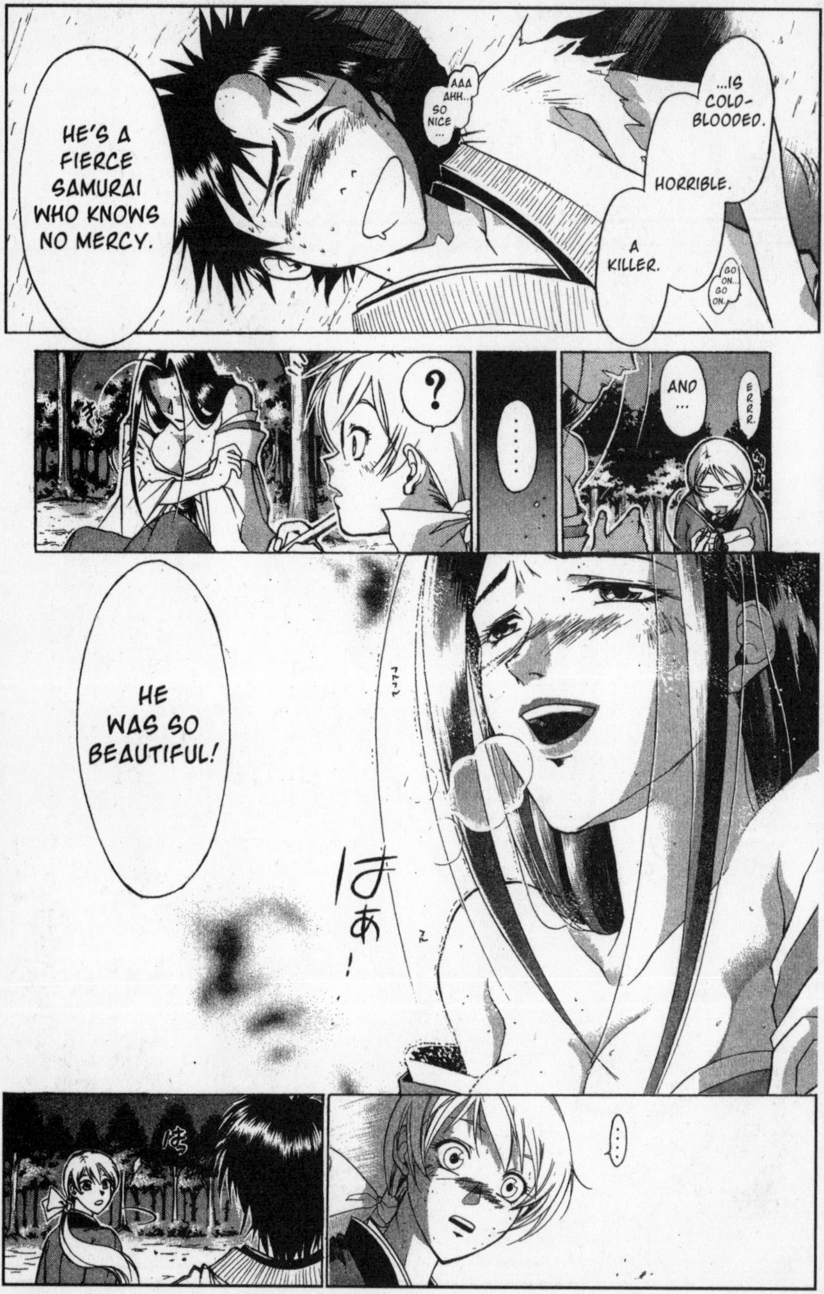
...IS COLD-BLOODED.
HORRIBLE.
A KILLER.
GO ON... GO ON.
AAA AHH... SO NICE ...
HE'S A FIERCE SAMURAI WHO KNOWS NO MERCY.
AND ...
ERRR.
......
?
HE WAS SO BEAUTIFUL!
はあ!
....

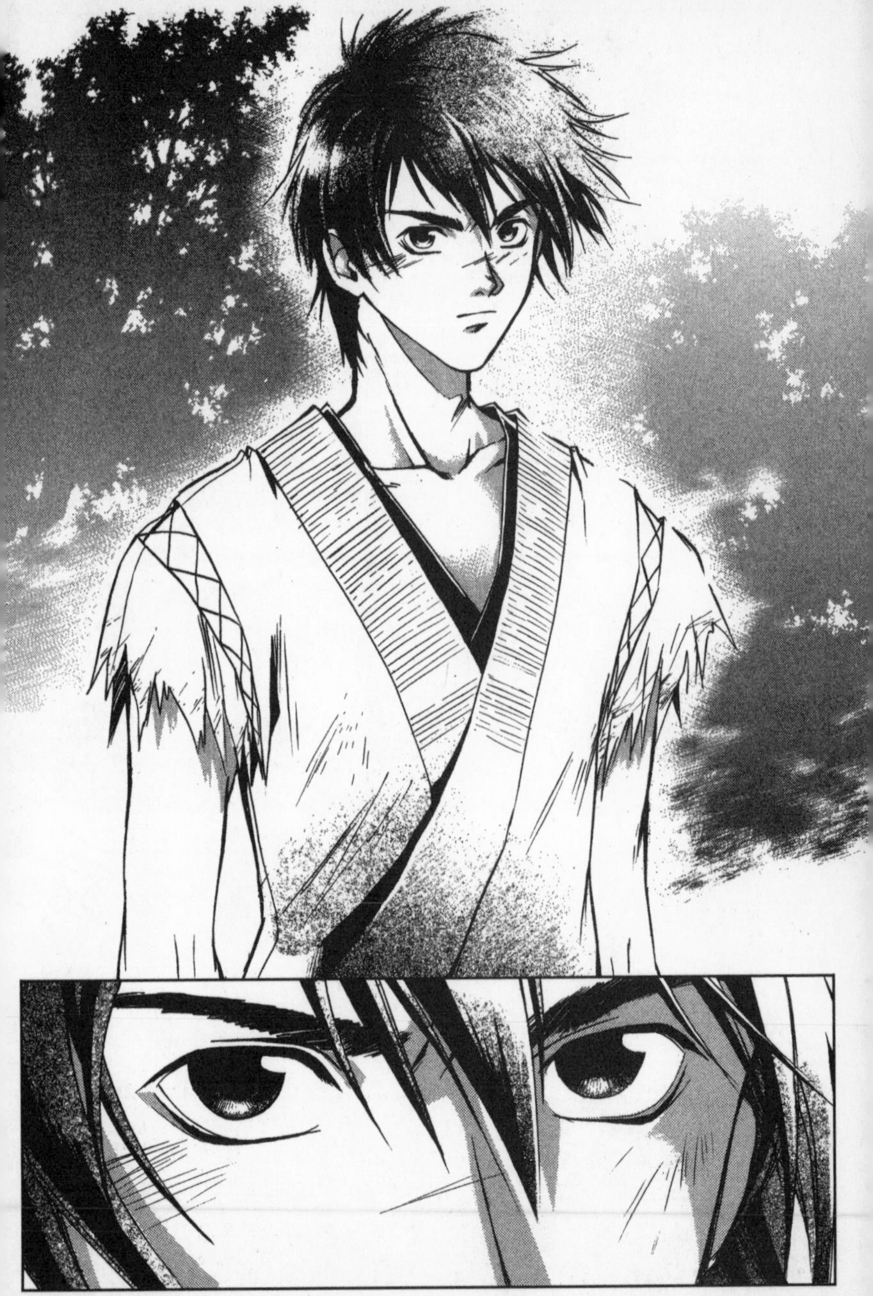

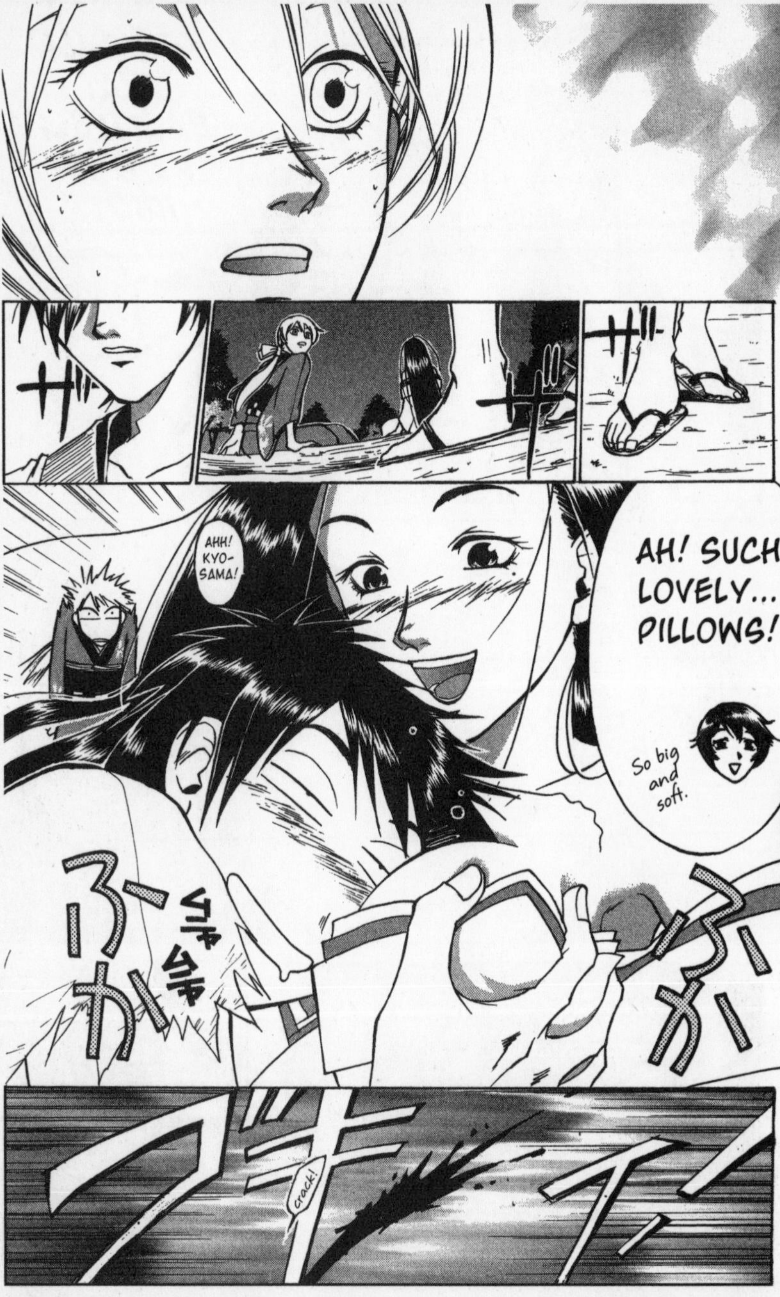
AH! SUCH LOVELY... PILLOWS!
So big and soft.
AHH! KYO-SAMA!
crack!

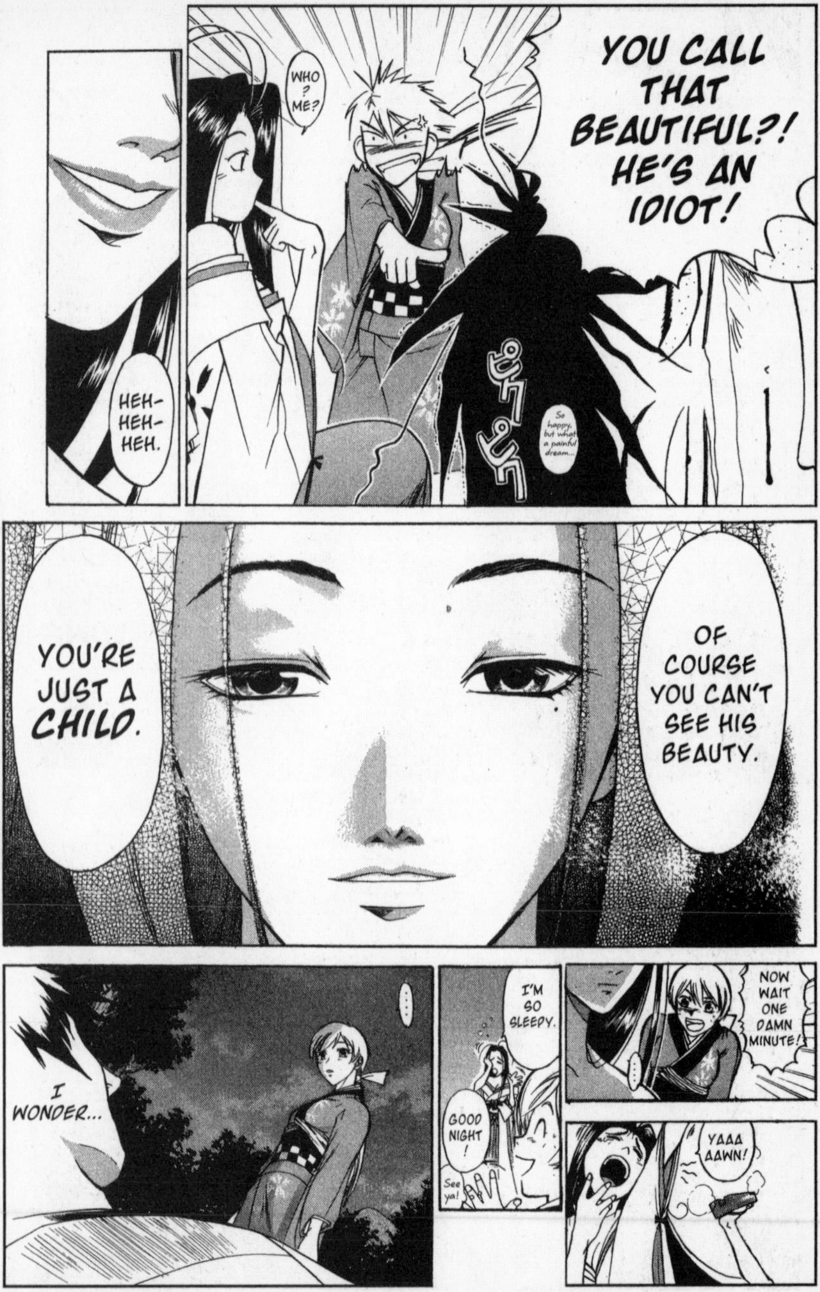
YOU CALL THAT BEAUTIFUL?! HE'S AN IDIOT!
WHO? ME?
So happy, but what a painful dream...
HEH-HEH-HEH.
OF COURSE YOU CAN'T SEE HIS BEAUTY.
YOU'RE JUST A CHILD.
NOW WAIT ONE DAMN MINUTE!
...
YAAAAAWN!
I'M SO SLEEPY.
GOOD NIGHT!
See ya!
...
I WONDER...

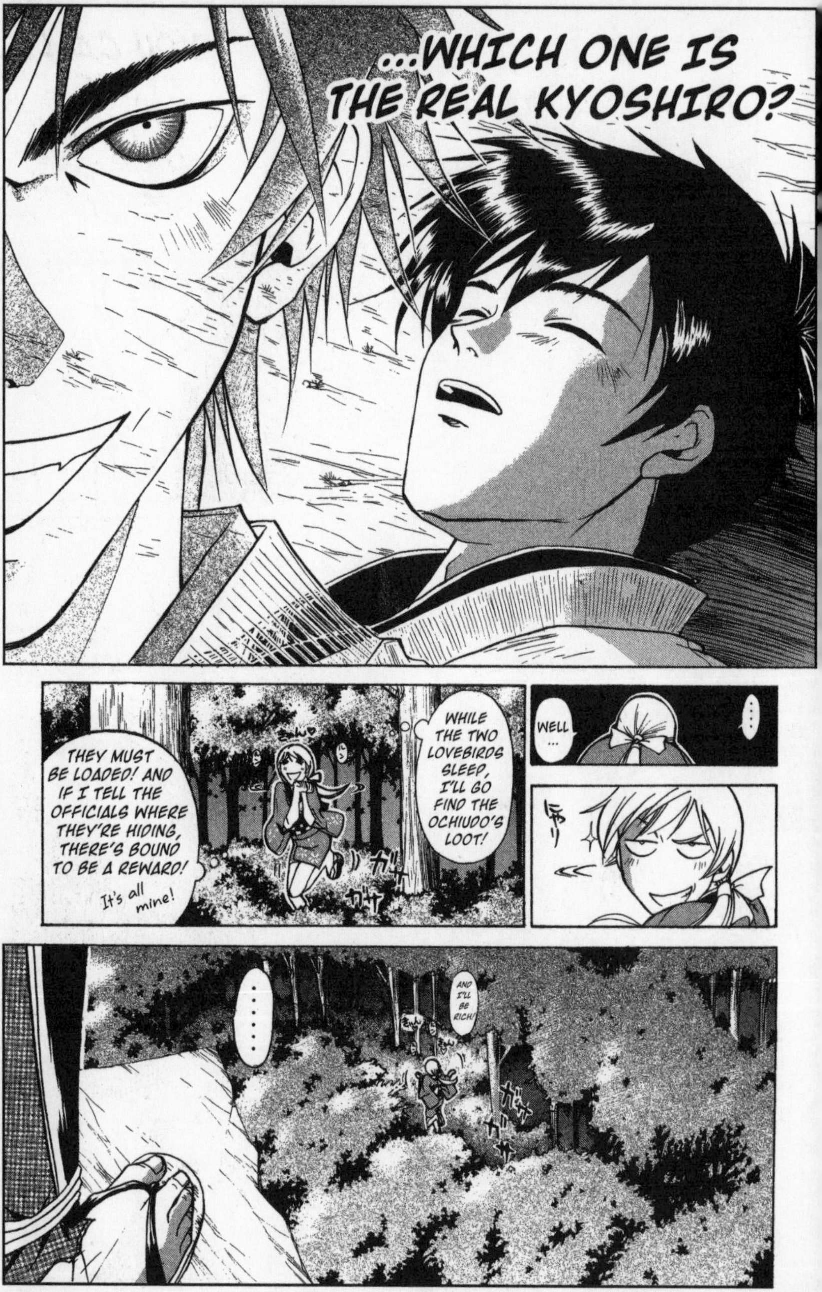
...WHICH ONE IS THE REAL KYOSHIRO?
....
WELL ...
WHILE THE TWO LOVEBIRDS SLEEP, I'LL GO FIND THE OCHIUDO'S LOOT!
THEY MUST BE LOADED! AND IF I TELL THE OFFICIALS WHERE THEY'RE HIDING, THERE'S BOUND TO BE A REWARD!
It's all mine!
AND I'LL BE RICH!
......

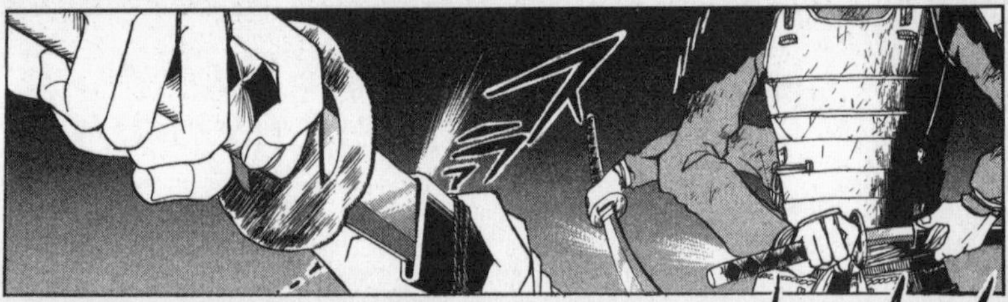
スラ
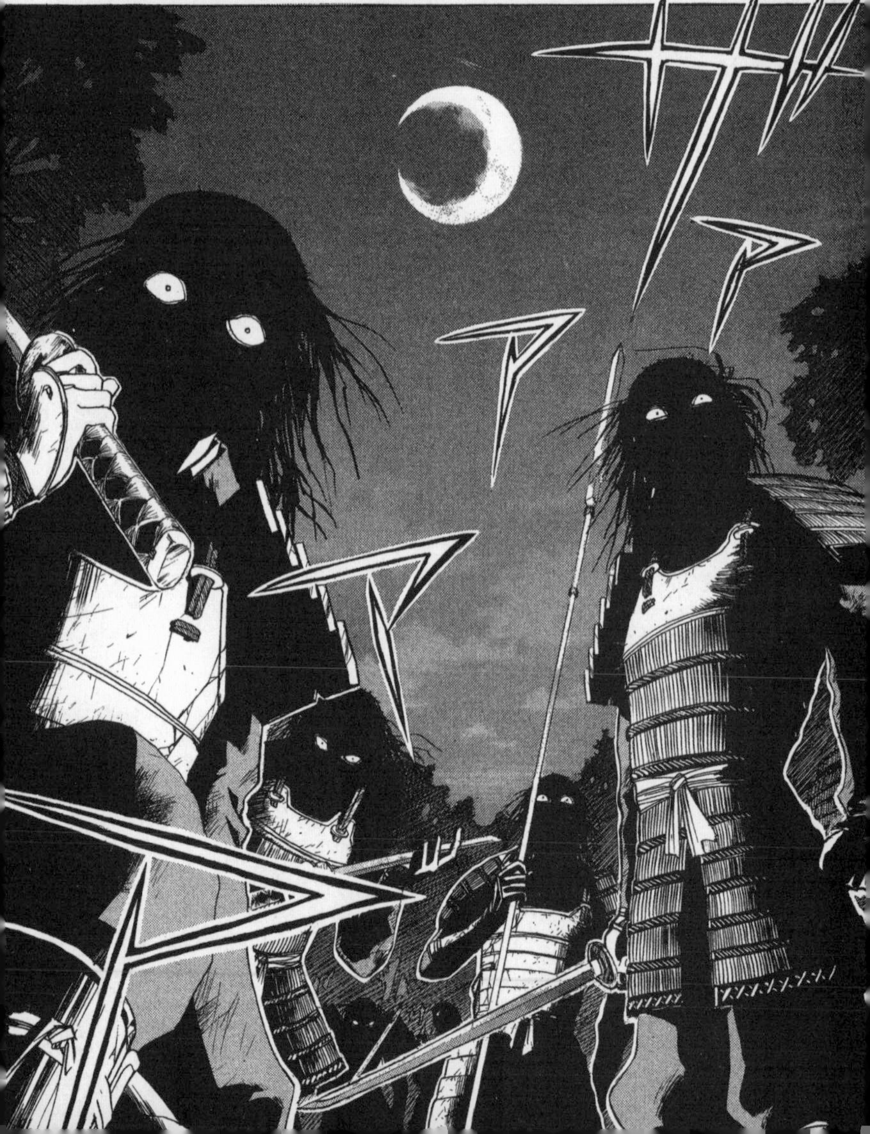
ザァァァァ

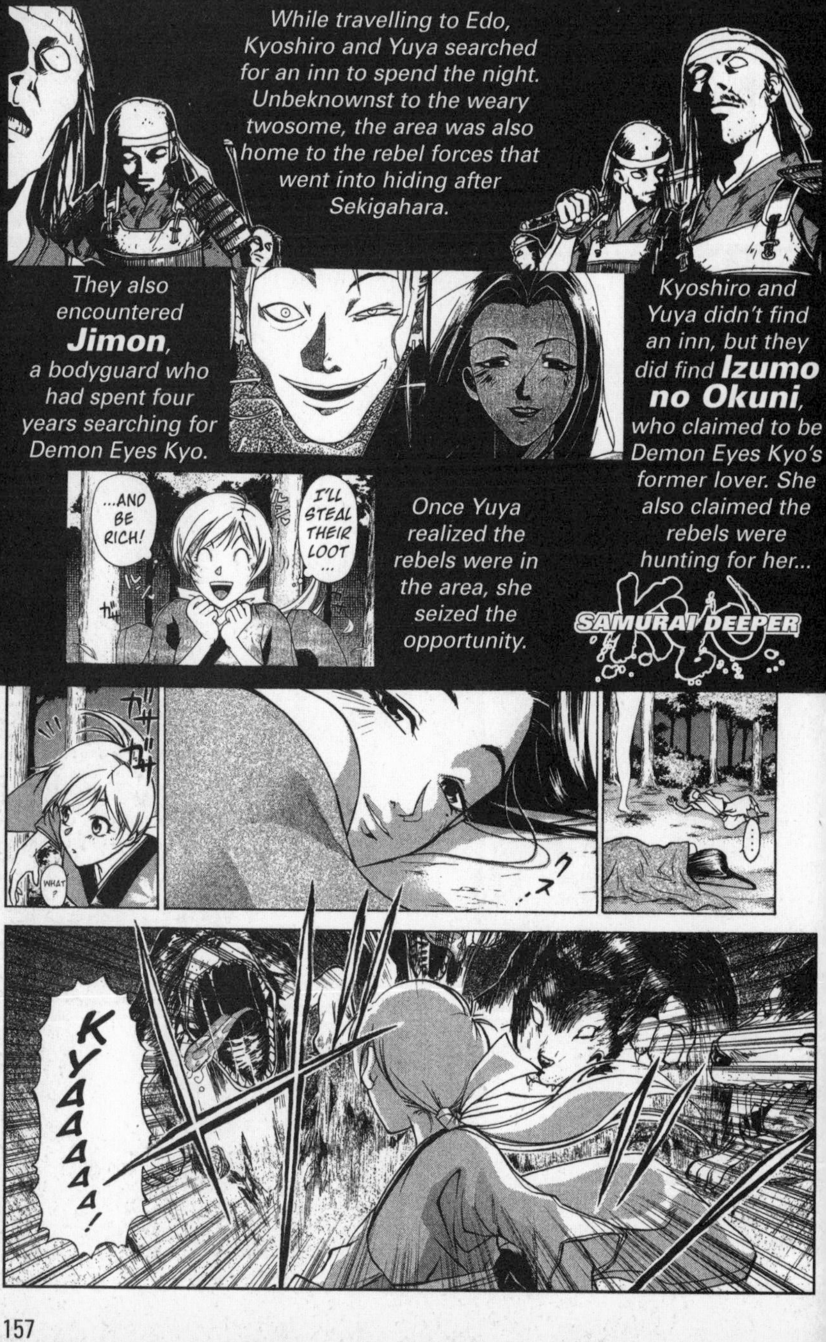
While travelling to Edo, Kyoshiro and Yuya searched for an inn to spend the night. Unbeknownst to the weary twosome, the area was also home to the rebel forces that went into hiding after Sekigahara.
Kyoshiro and Yuya didn't find an inn, but they did find **Izumo no Okuni**, who claimed to be Demon Eyes Kyo's former lover. She also claimed the rebels were hunting for her...
They also encountered **Jimon**, a bodyguard who had spent four years searching for Demon Eyes Kyo.
Once Yuya realized the rebels were in the area, she seized the opportunity.
I'LL STEAL THEIR LOOT...
...AND BE RICH!
SAMURAI DEEPER KYO
...
!!
WHAT?
KYAAAAAA!

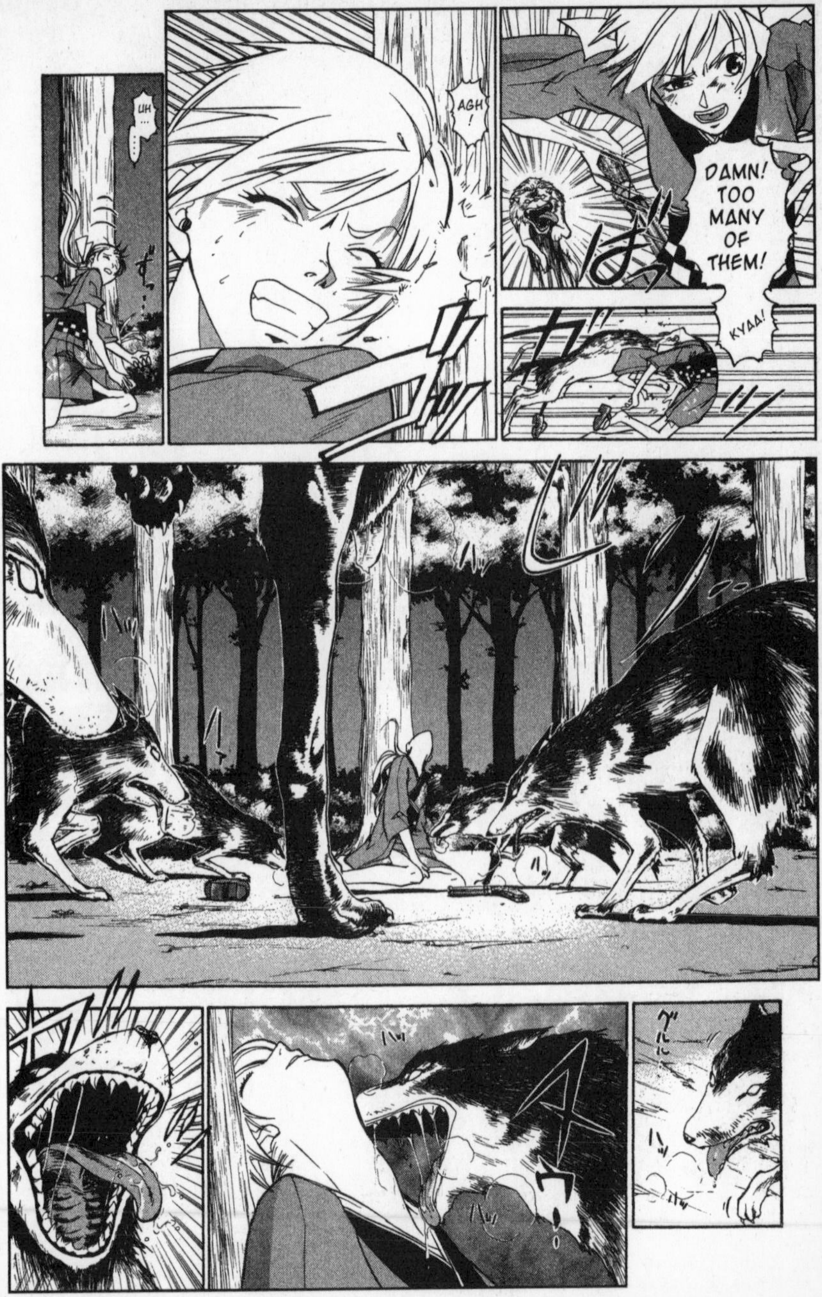
DAMN! TOO MANY OF THEM!
KYAA!
AGH!
UH ... ...

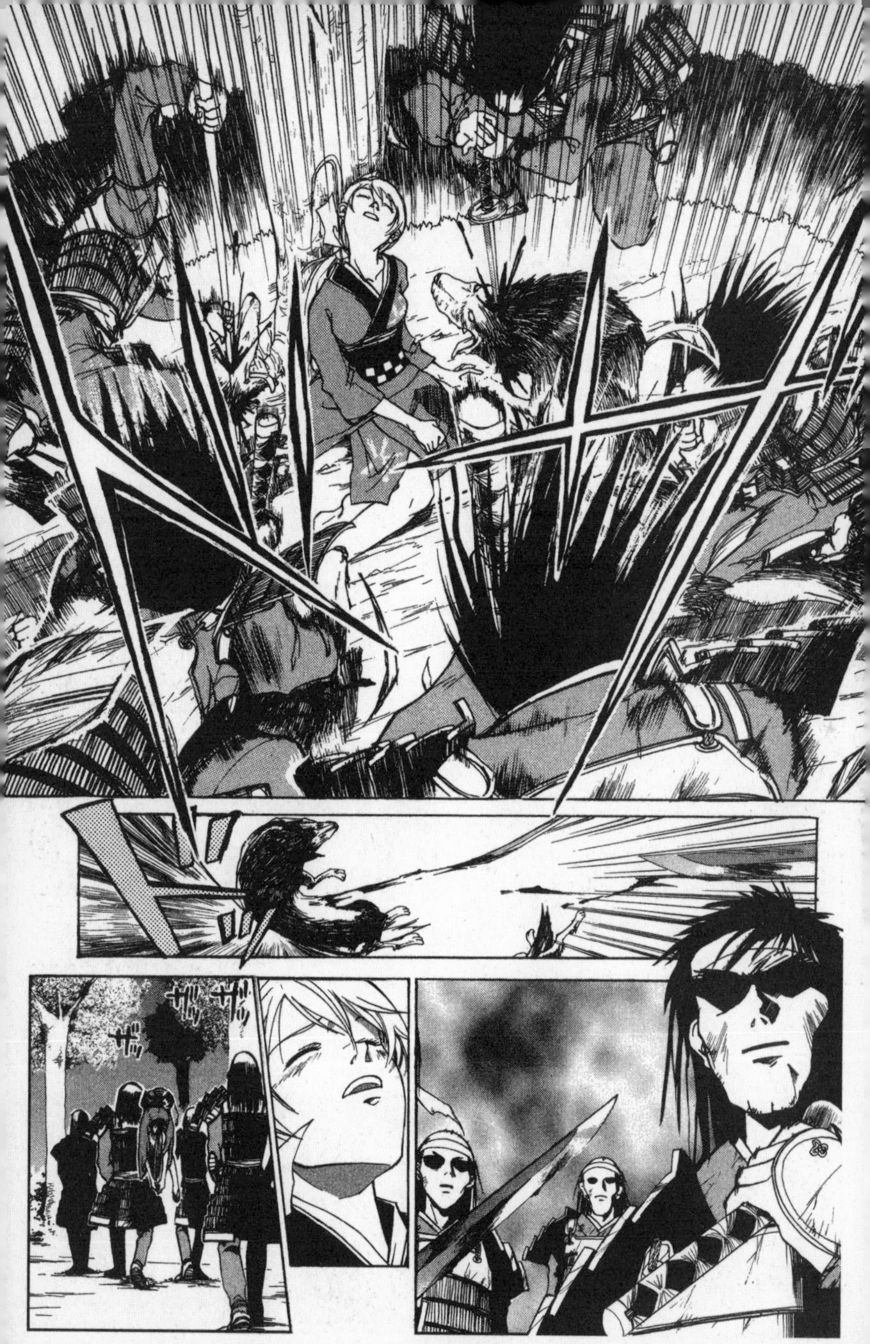
ザッ
ザッ
ザッ

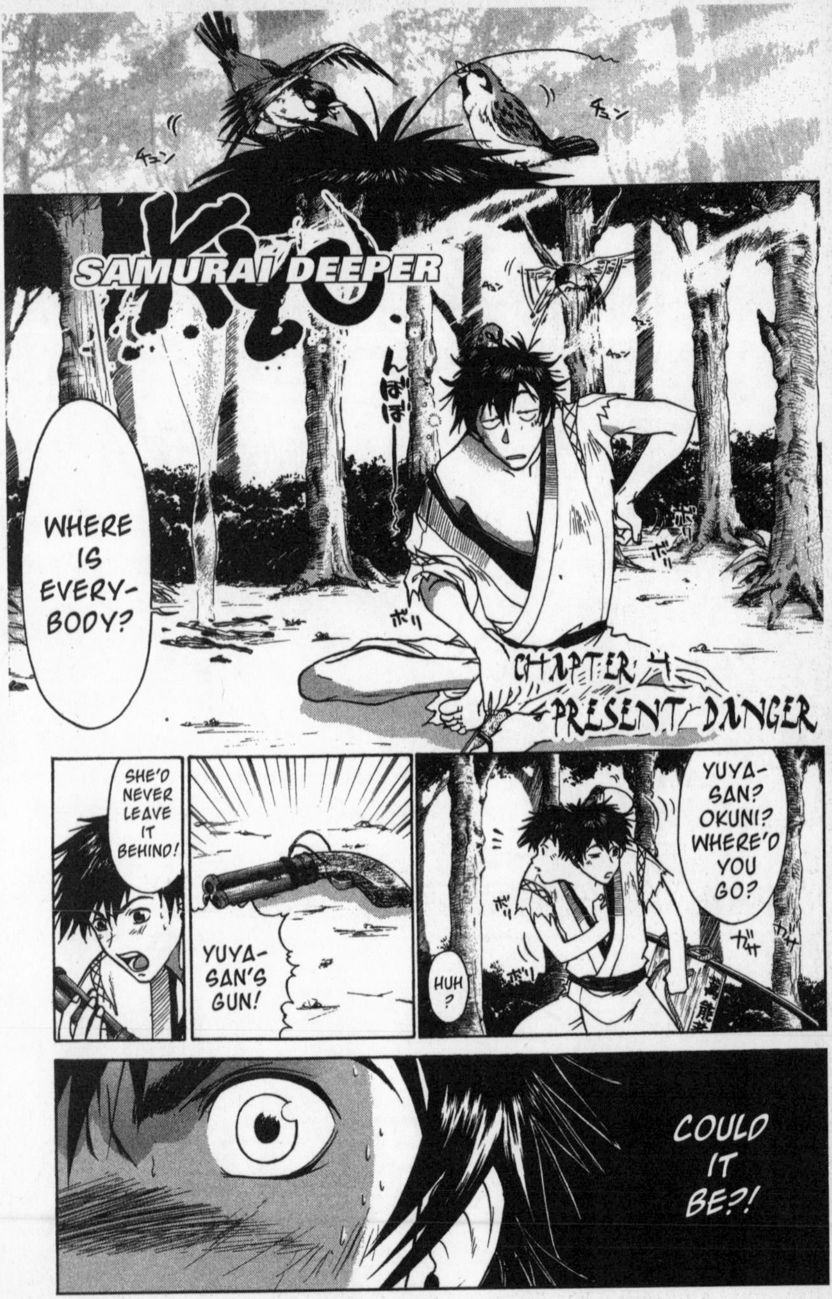
SAMURAI DEEPER KYO
CHAPTER 4 PRESENT DANGER
WHERE IS EVERY-BODY?
YUYA-SAN? OKUNI? WHERE'D YOU GO?
HUH?
YUYA-SAN'S GUN!
SHE'D NEVER LEAVE IT BEHIND!
COULD IT BE?!

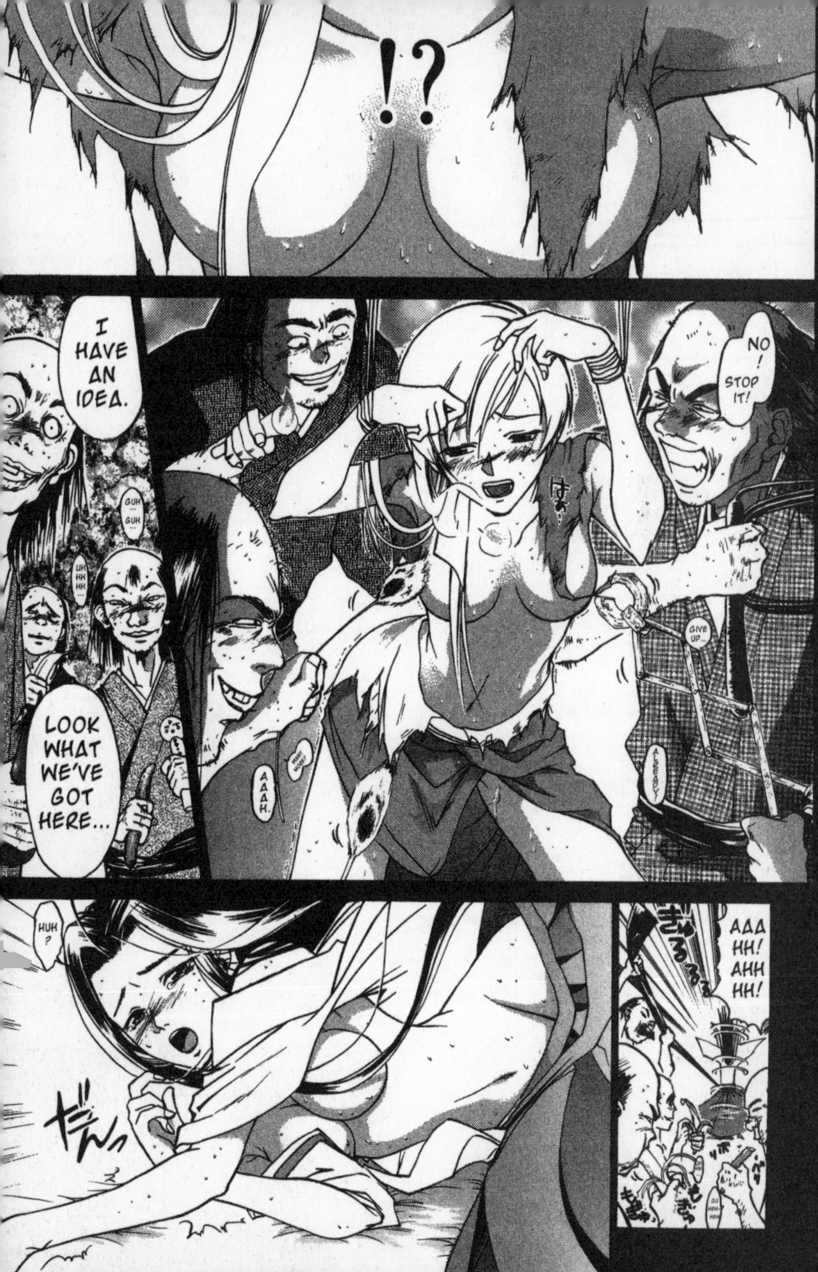
!?
NO! STOP IT!
GIVE UP...
ALREADY!
I HAVE AN IDEA.
GUH... GUH...
UH HH HH...
AAAH.
LOOK WHAT WE'VE GOT HERE...
AAAHH! AHHHH!
HUH?

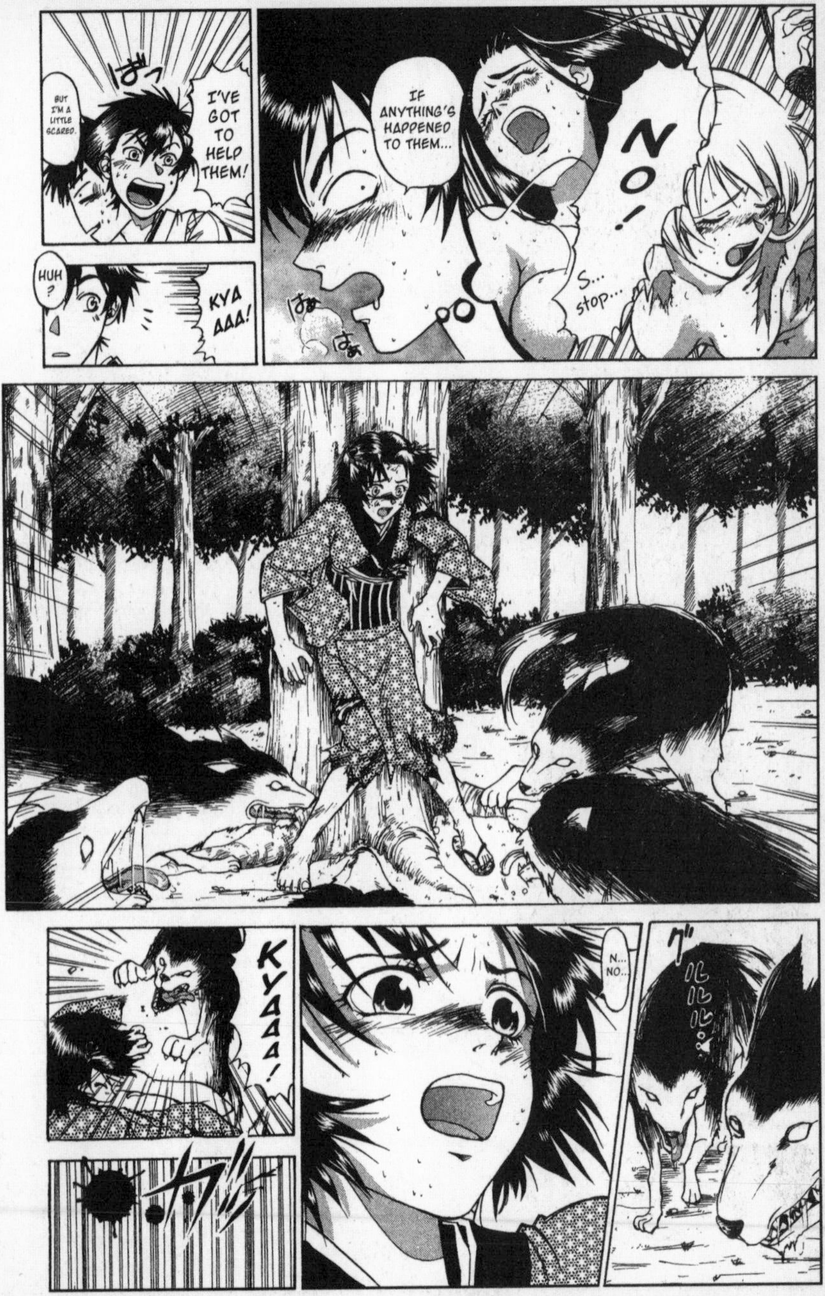
NO...!
S... stop...
IF ANYTHING'S HAPPENED TO THEM...
はぁ はぁ
ばっ
I'VE GOT TO HELP THEM!
BUT I'M A LITTLE SCARED.
KYAAAA!
HUH?
グルルル...
N... NO...
KYAAAA!
ガブ!!

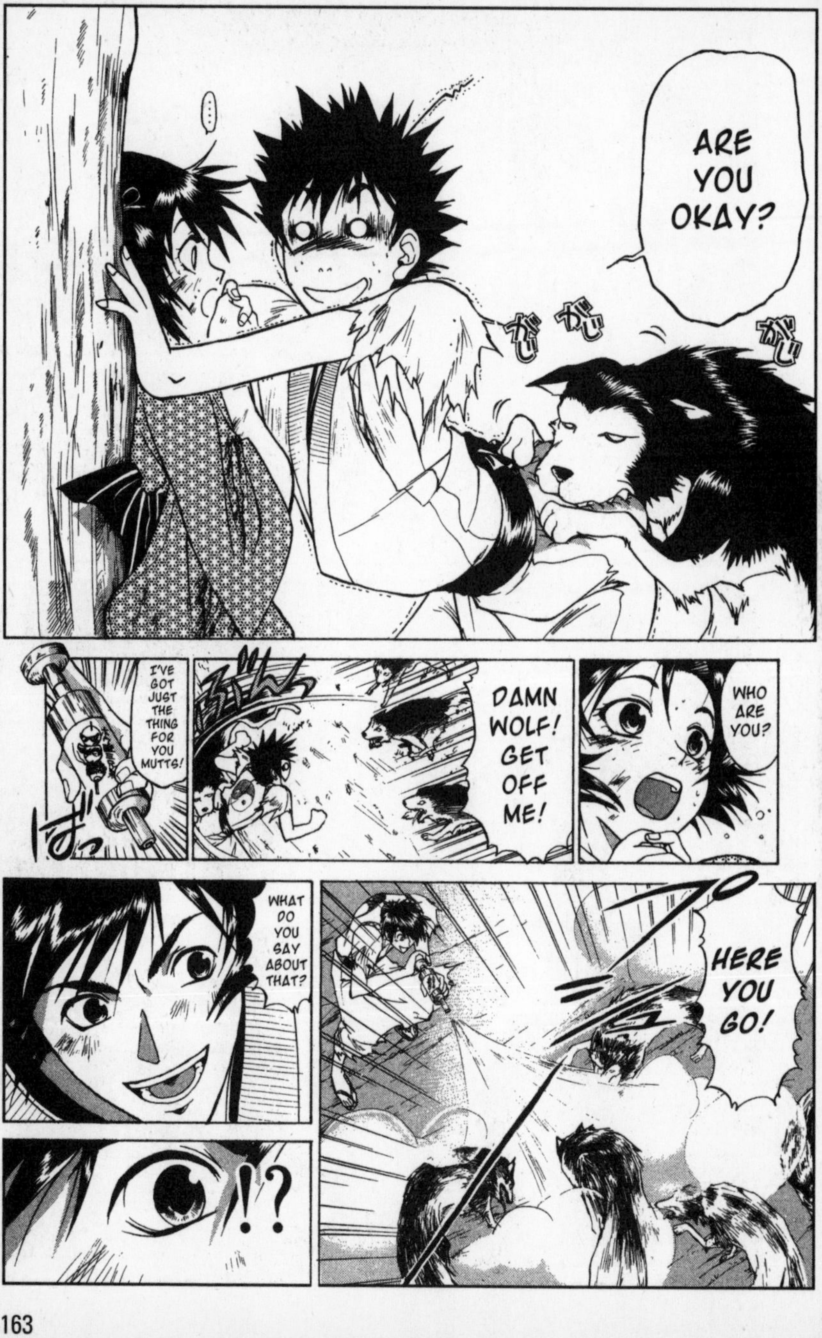
ARE YOU OKAY?
...
がじ
がじ
がじ
WHO ARE YOU?
DAMN WOLF! GET OFF ME!
I'VE GOT JUST THE THING FOR YOU MUTTS!
HERE YOU GO!
WHAT DO YOU SAY ABOUT THAT?
!?

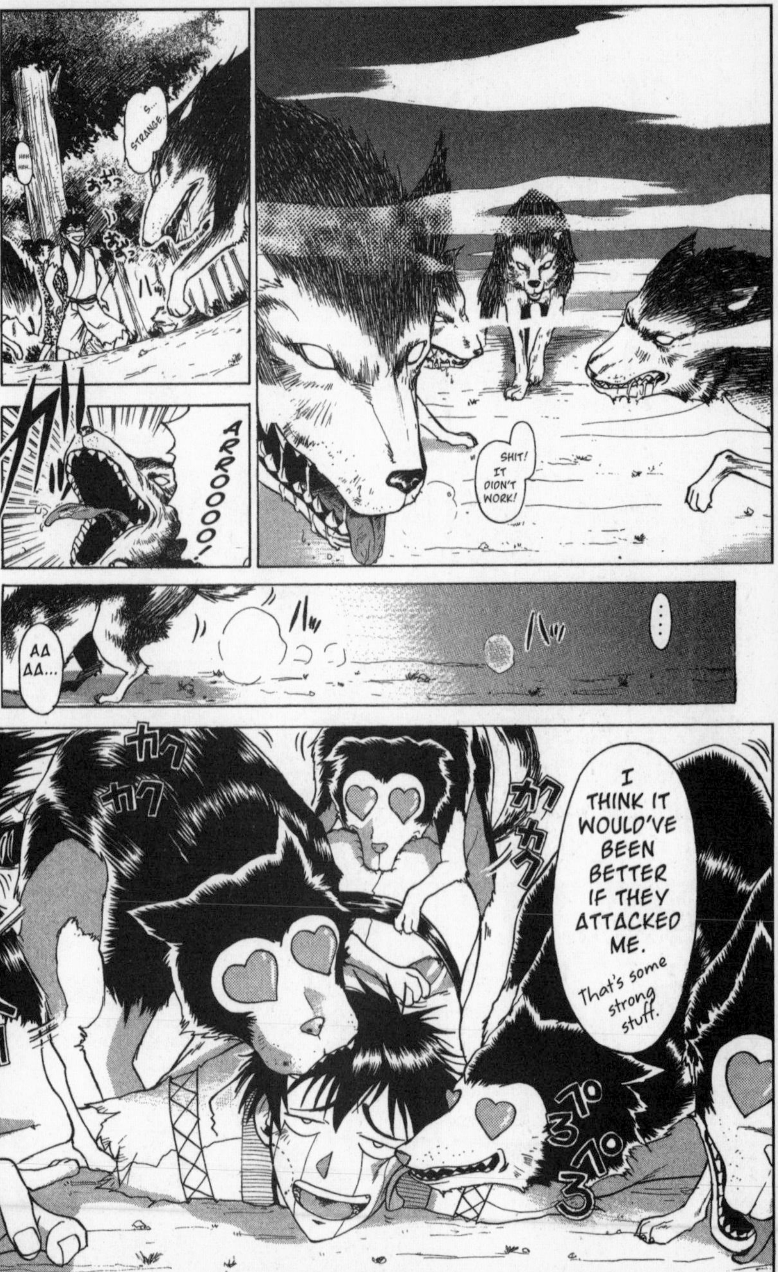
SHIT! IT DIDN'T WORK!
S... STRANGE...
HNH HNH.
ARROOOOOO!
...
AA AA...
I THINK IT WOULD'VE BEEN BETTER IF THEY ATTACKED ME.
That's some strong stuff.

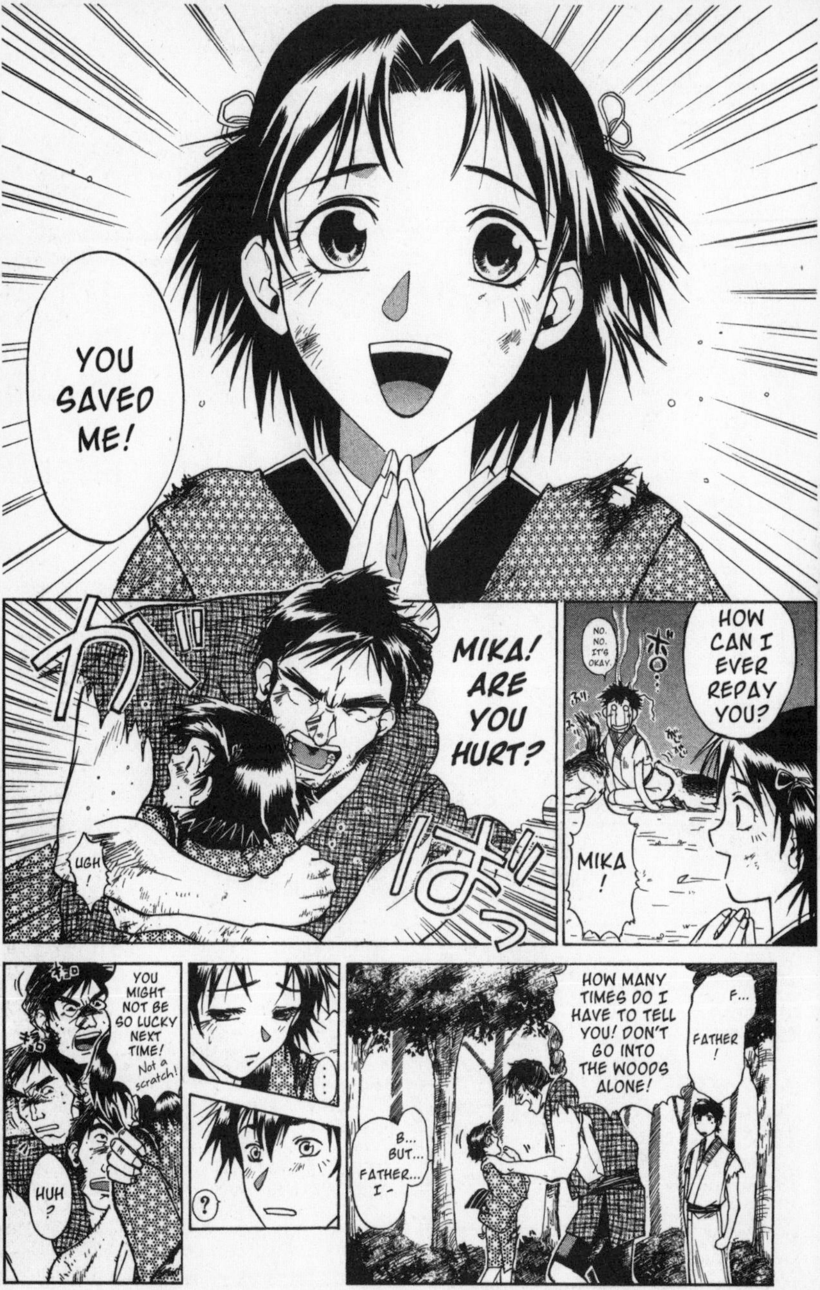
YOU SAVED ME!
HOW CAN I EVER REPAY YOU?
NO. NO. IT'S OKAY.
MIKA!
MIKA! ARE YOU HURT?
UGH!
F... FATHER!
HOW MANY TIMES DO I HAVE TO TELL YOU! DON'T GO INTO THE WOODS ALONE!
B... BUT... FATHER... I -
...
?
YOU MIGHT NOT BE SO LUCKY NEXT TIME!
Not a scratch!
HUH?

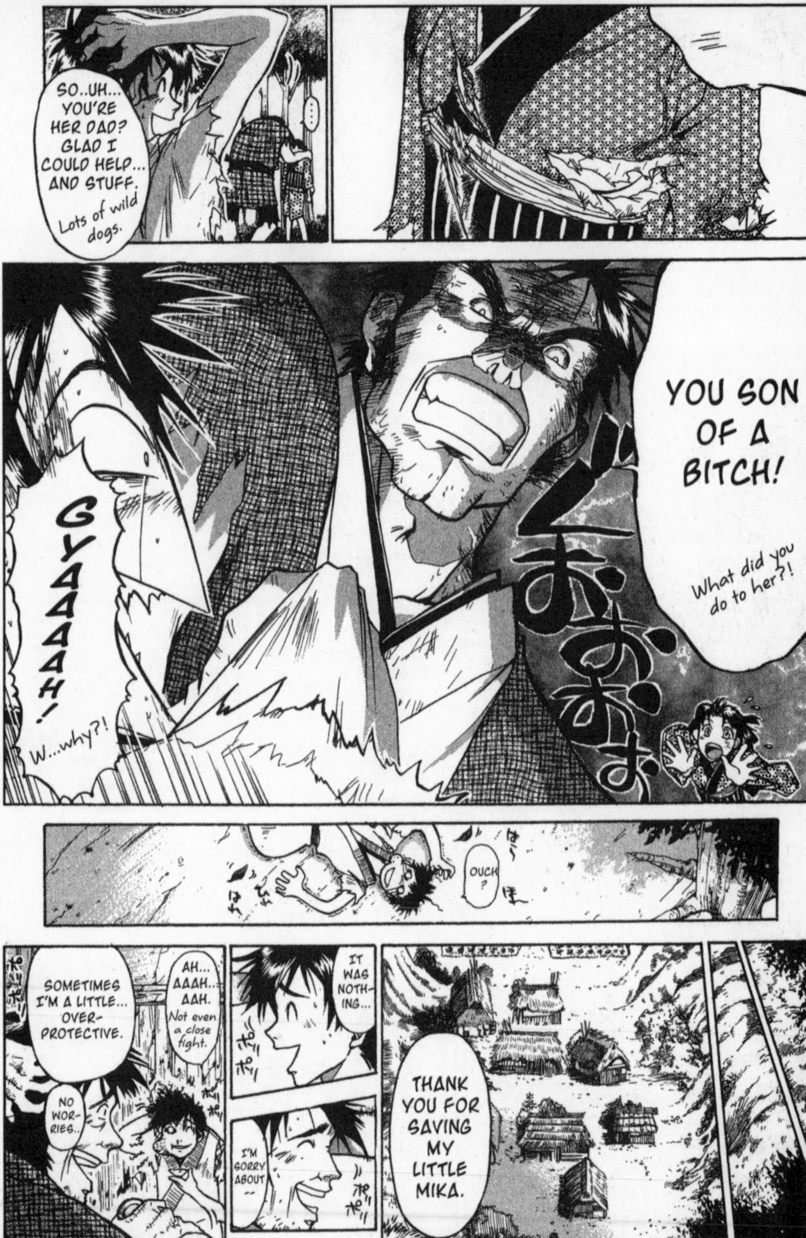
...
SO...UH... YOU'RE HER DAD? GLAD I COULD HELP... AND STUFF.
Lots of wild dogs.
YOU SON OF A BITCH!
What did you do to her?!
おおおおお
GYAAAAAAH!
W...why?!
OUCH?
THANK YOU FOR SAVING MY LITTLE MIKA.
IT WAS NOTHING...
I'M SORRY ABOUT --
AH... AAAH... AAH.
Not even a close fight.
SOMETIMES I'M A LITTLE... OVER-PROTECTIVE.
NO WORRIES...

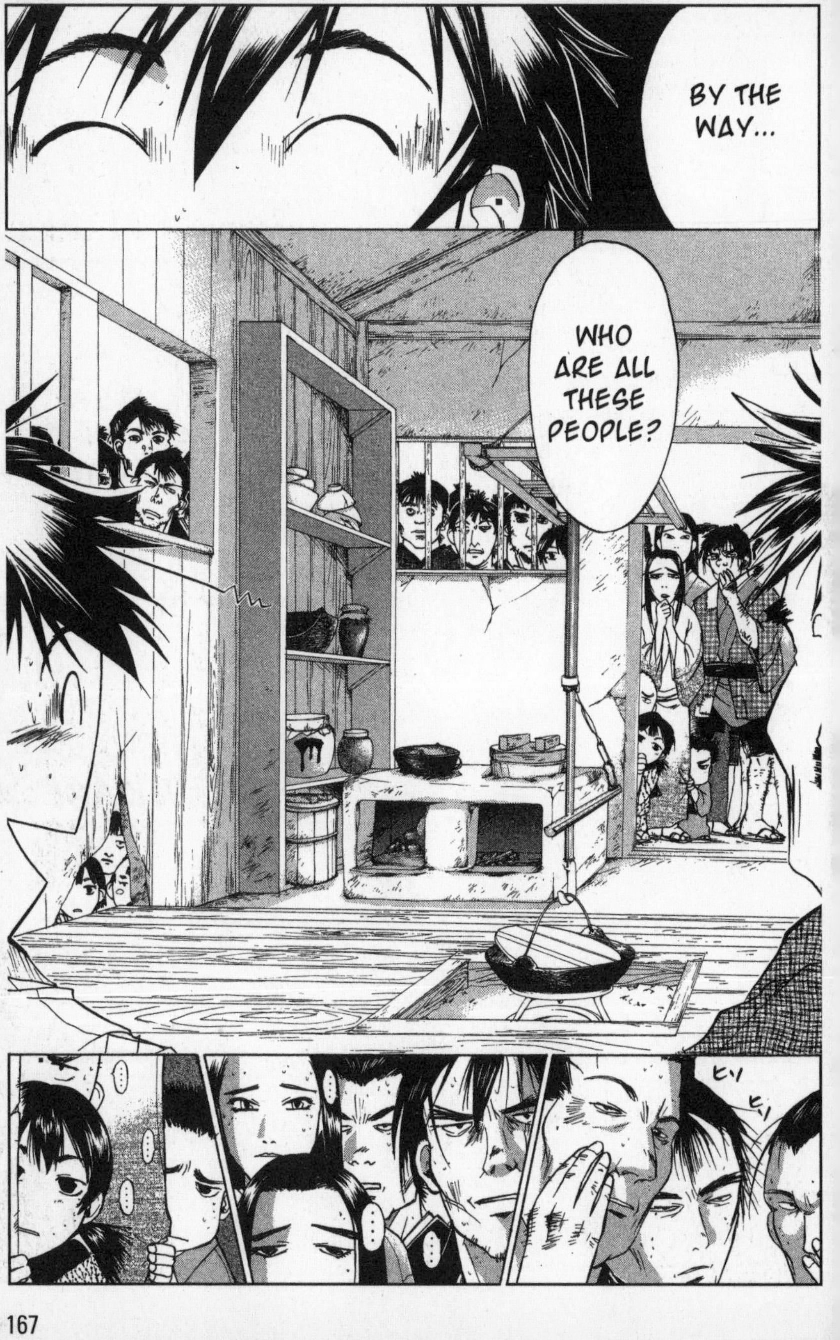
BY THE WAY...
WHO ARE ALL THESE PEOPLE?
ヒソ
ヒソ
...
...
...
...
...

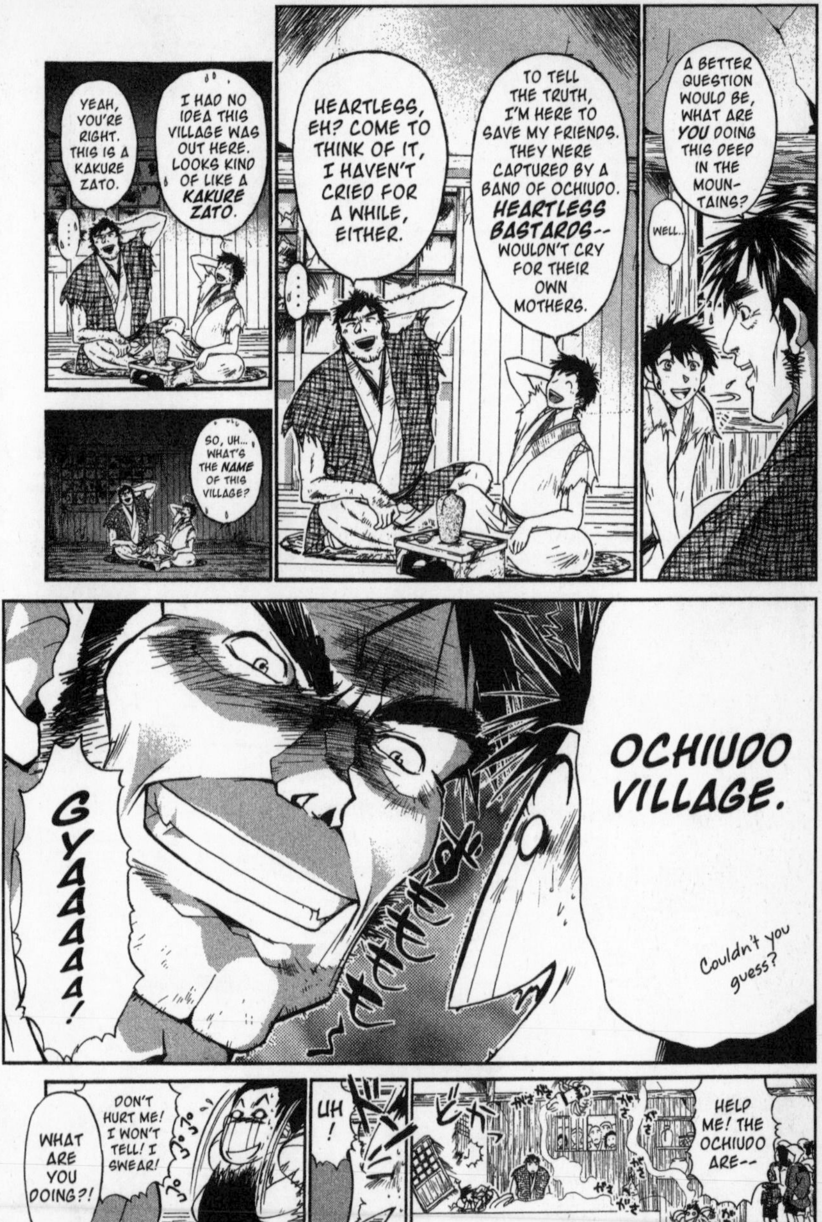

I HAD NO IDEA THIS VILLAGE WAS OUT HERE. LOOKS KIND OF LIKE A KAKURE ZATO.
YEAH, YOU'RE RIGHT. THIS IS A KAKURE ZATO.
...
TO TELL THE TRUTH, I'M HERE TO SAVE MY FRIENDS. THEY WERE CAPTURED BY A BAND OF OCHIUDO. HEARTLESS BASTARDS-- WOULDN'T CRY FOR THEIR OWN MOTHERS.
HEARTLESS, EH? COME TO THINK OF IT, I HAVEN'T CRIED FOR A WHILE, EITHER.
...
A BETTER QUESTION WOULD BE, WHAT ARE YOU DOING THIS DEEP IN THE MOUNTAINS?
WELL...
SO, UH... WHAT'S THE NAME OF THIS VILLAGE?
OCHIUDO VILLAGE.
Couldn't you guess?
GYAAAAAA!
WHAT ARE YOU DOING?!
DON'T HURT ME! I WON'T TELL! I SWEAR!
UH!
HELP ME! THE OCHIUDO ARE--

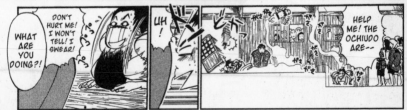

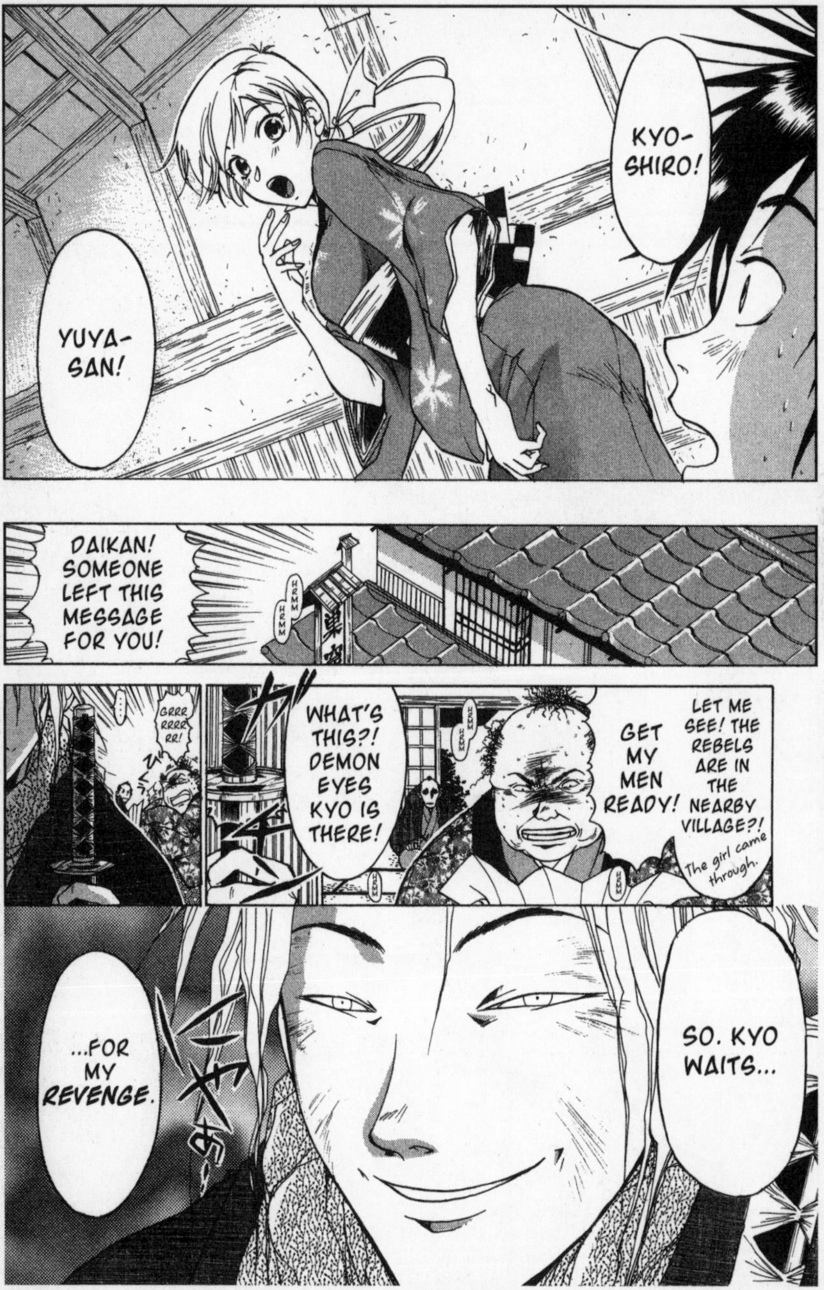
KYO-SHIRO!
YUYA-SAN!
DAIKAN! SOMEONE LEFT THIS MESSAGE FOR YOU!
HRMM HRMM
LET ME SEE! THE REBELS ARE IN THE NEARBY VILLAGE?!
The girl came through.
GET MY MEN READY!
HRMM
WHAT'S THIS?! DEMON EYES KYO IS THERE!
HRMM HRMM
...
GRRR RRRR RR!
SO. KYO WAITS...
...FOR MY REVENGE.

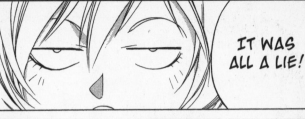

IT WAS ALL A LIE!
THE OCHIUDO ARE MORE DESTITUTE THAN I AM.
IN FACT, THEY'RE HARDLY REBELS. I MEAN, THEY MAY HAVE BEEN AT ONE TIME.
BUT LOOK AT THEM NOW. JUST HARMLESS FARMERS. EVERYTHING WE HEARD WAS UNTRUE.
Only their looks are hard.
THEY SAVED ME FROM A PACK OF WOLVES AND FED ME.
This place is just perfect.
I SEE...
じーー
I WAS SO WORRIED THEY TORTURED YOU! I WAS COMING TO SAVE YOU!
Sorry.
I was worried.
WHAT ABOUT OKUNI? DID SHE COME HERE, TOO?
I DON'T THINK SO.
WHAT HAPPENED TO HER?
I HATE YOU!

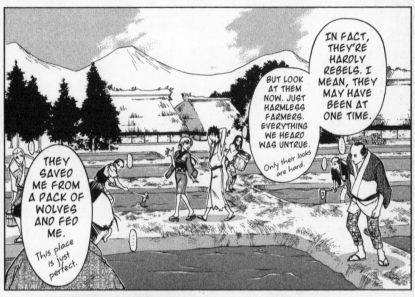

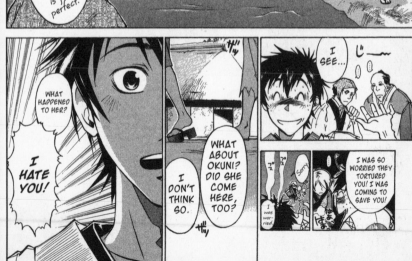

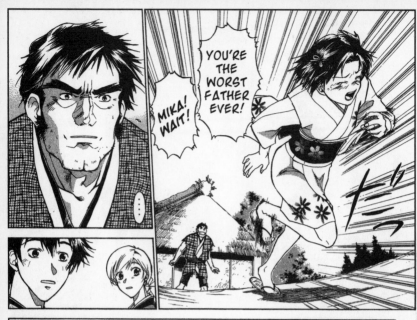

YOU'RE THE WORST FATHER EVER!
MIKA! WAIT!
ダーッ
....
MIKA-CHAN?
YOU RAN AWAY SO QUICKLY... IS SOMETHING WRONG?
ひょいっ
YUYA-SAN...
I HATE THIS PLACE! I WANT TO LEAVE!
AND I TOLD MY FATHER --
WHY WOULD YOU WANT TO LEAVE THIS VILLAGE?
Nothing but perverts out there.
BELIEVE ME, THE WORLD OUTSIDE IS MUCH WORSE!
NO!

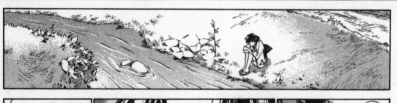

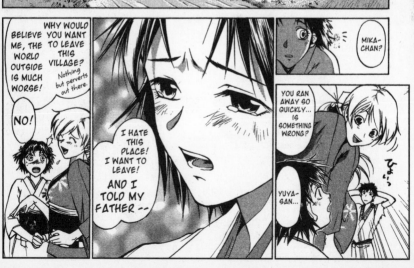

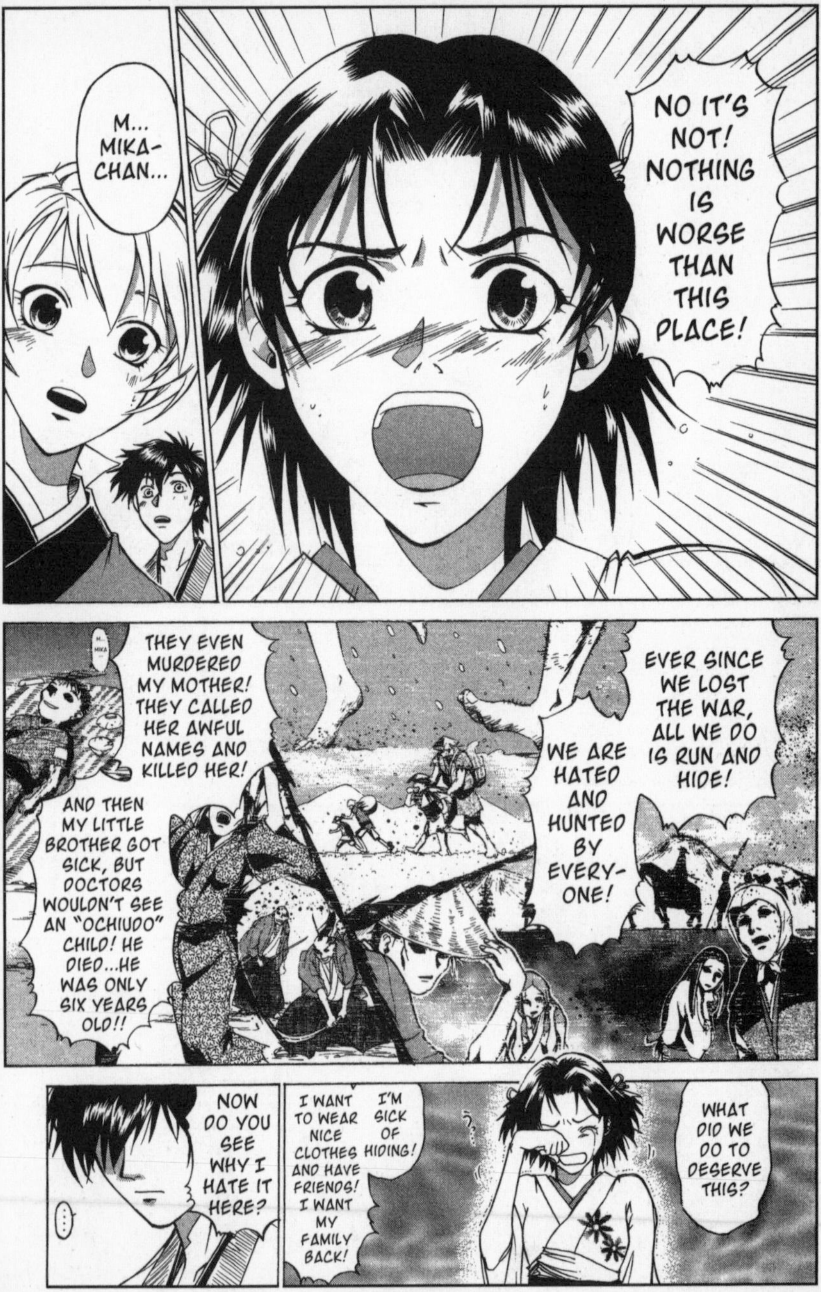
NO IT'S NOT! NOTHING IS WORSE THAN THIS PLACE!
M... MIKA-CHAN...
EVER SINCE WE LOST THE WAR, ALL WE DO IS RUN AND HIDE!
WE ARE HATED AND HUNTED BY EVERY-ONE!
THEY EVEN MURDERED MY MOTHER! THEY CALLED HER AWFUL NAMES AND KILLED HER!
M... MIKA ...
AND THEN MY LITTLE BROTHER GOT SICK, BUT DOCTORS WOULDN'T SEE AN "OCHIUDO" CHILD! HE DIED...HE WAS ONLY SIX YEARS OLD!!
WHAT DID WE DO TO DESERVE THIS?
I'M SICK OF HIDING!
I WANT TO WEAR NICE CLOTHES AND HAVE FRIENDS! I WANT MY FAMILY BACK!
NOW DO YOU SEE WHY I HATE IT HERE?
...

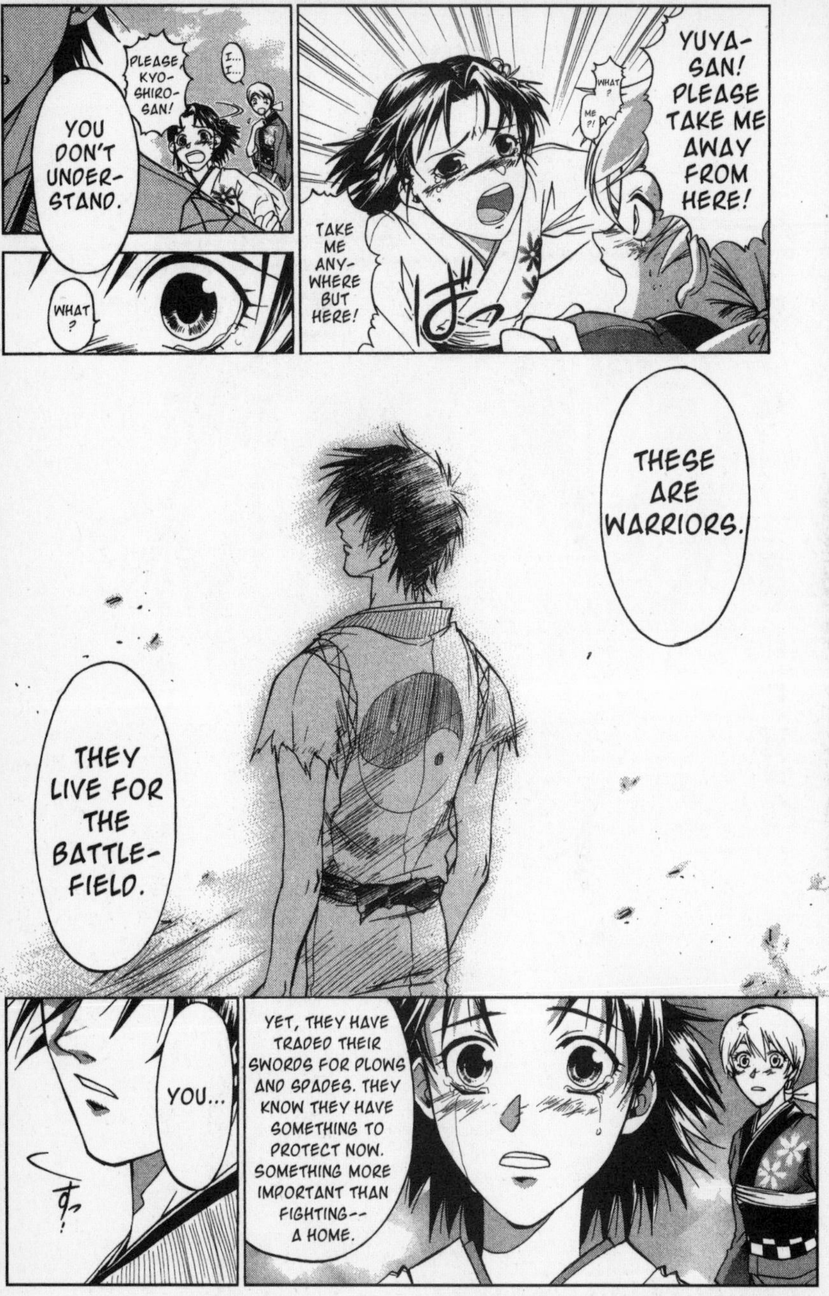
YUYA-SAN! PLEASE TAKE ME AWAY FROM HERE!
WHAT?
ME?!
TAKE ME ANYWHERE BUT HERE!
I... I...
PLEASE KYO-SHIRO-SAN!
YOU DON'T UNDERSTAND.
WHAT?
THESE ARE WARRIORS.
THEY LIVE FOR THE BATTLEFIELD.
YET, THEY HAVE TRADED THEIR SWORDS FOR PLOWS AND SPADES. THEY KNOW THEY HAVE SOMETHING TO PROTECT NOW. SOMETHING MORE IMPORTANT THAN FIGHTING-- A HOME.
YOU...

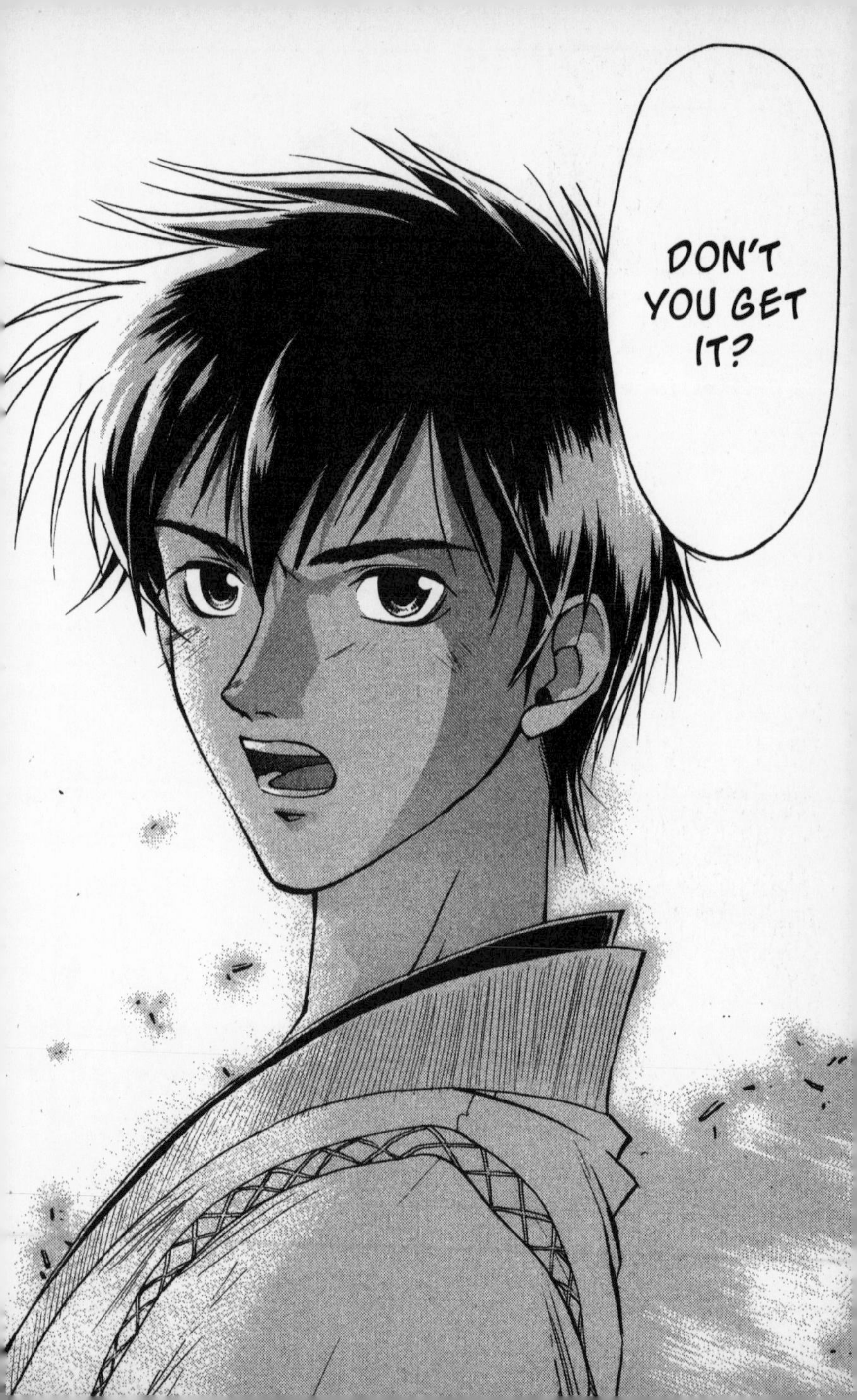
DON'T YOU GET IT?

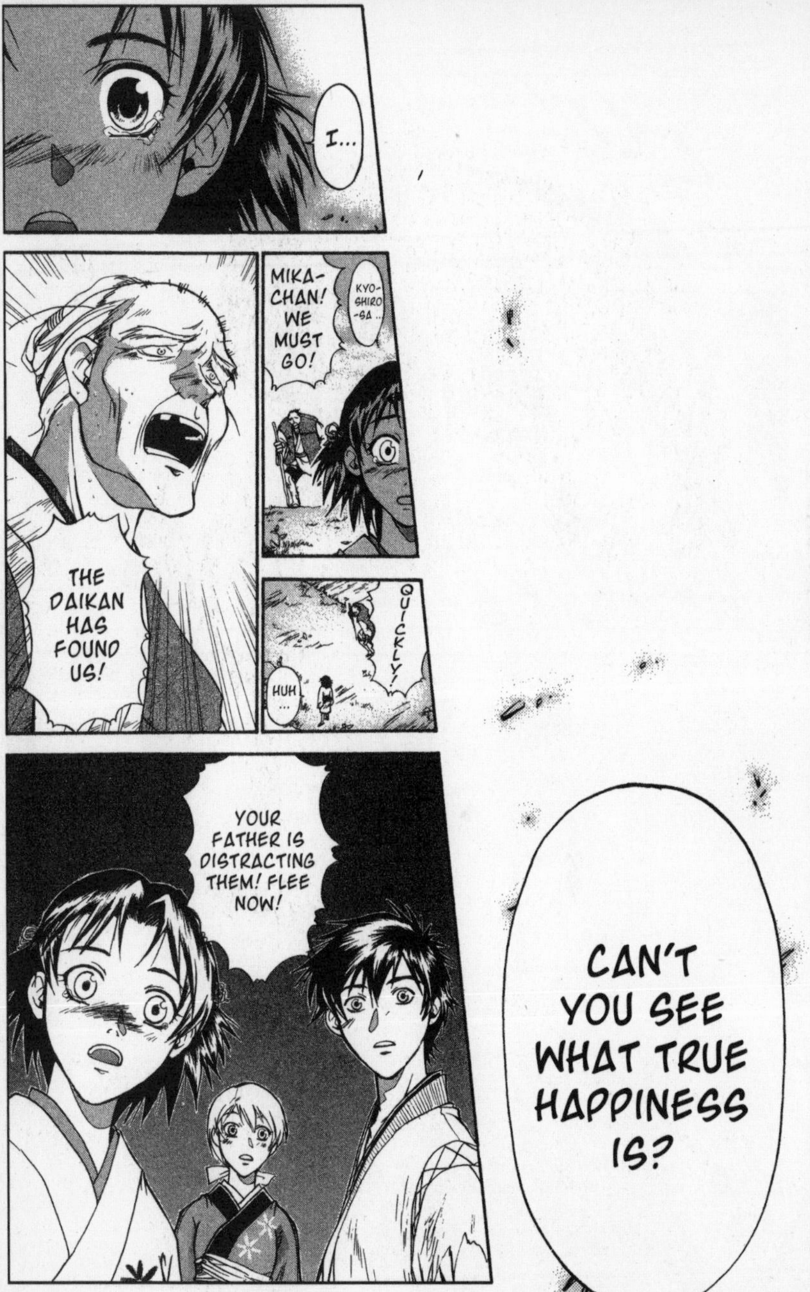
I...
KYO-SHIRO-SA...
MIKA-CHAN! WE MUST GO!
QUICKLY!
HUH...
THE DAIKAN HAS FOUND US!
YOUR FATHER IS DISTRACTING THEM! FLEE NOW!
CAN'T YOU SEE WHAT TRUE HAPPINESS IS?

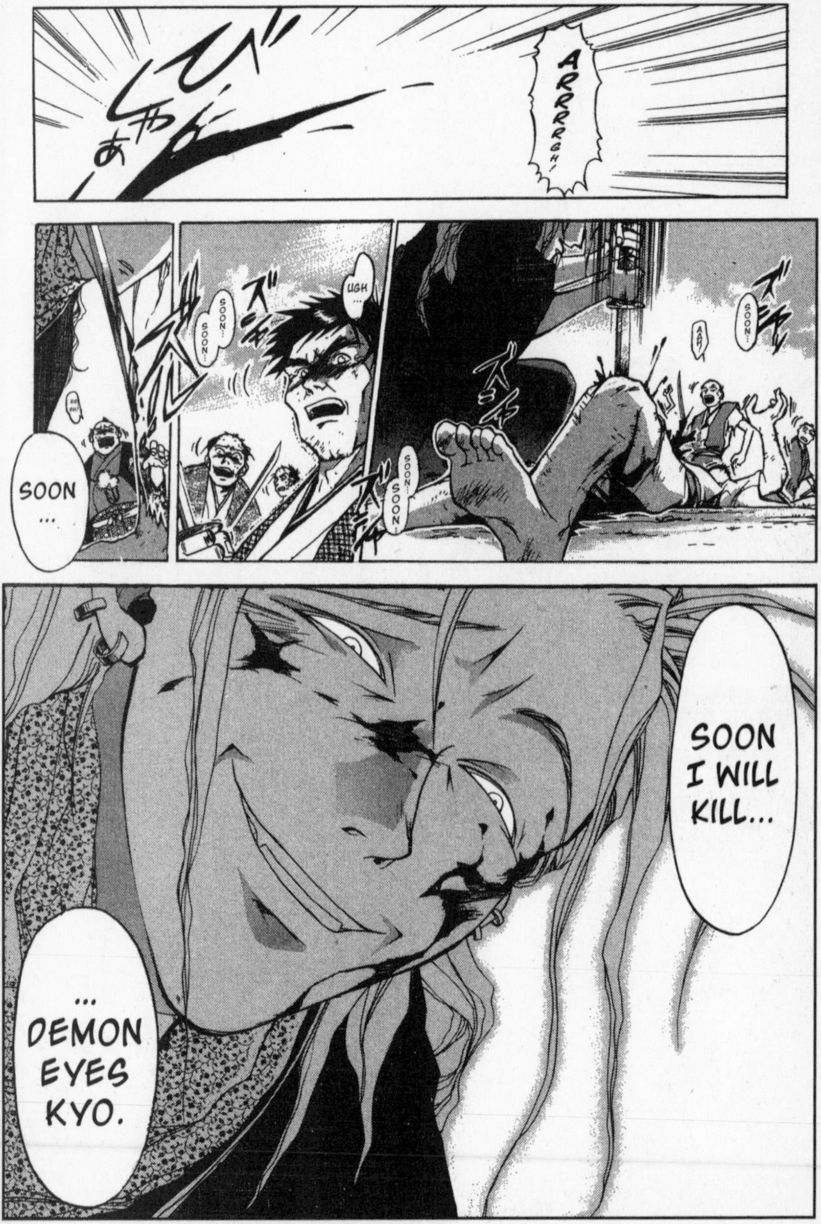
ARRRRRGH!
SOON...
AH!
SOON... SOON...
UGH...
SOON... SOON...
SOON ...
SOON I WILL KILL...
... DEMON EYES KYO.

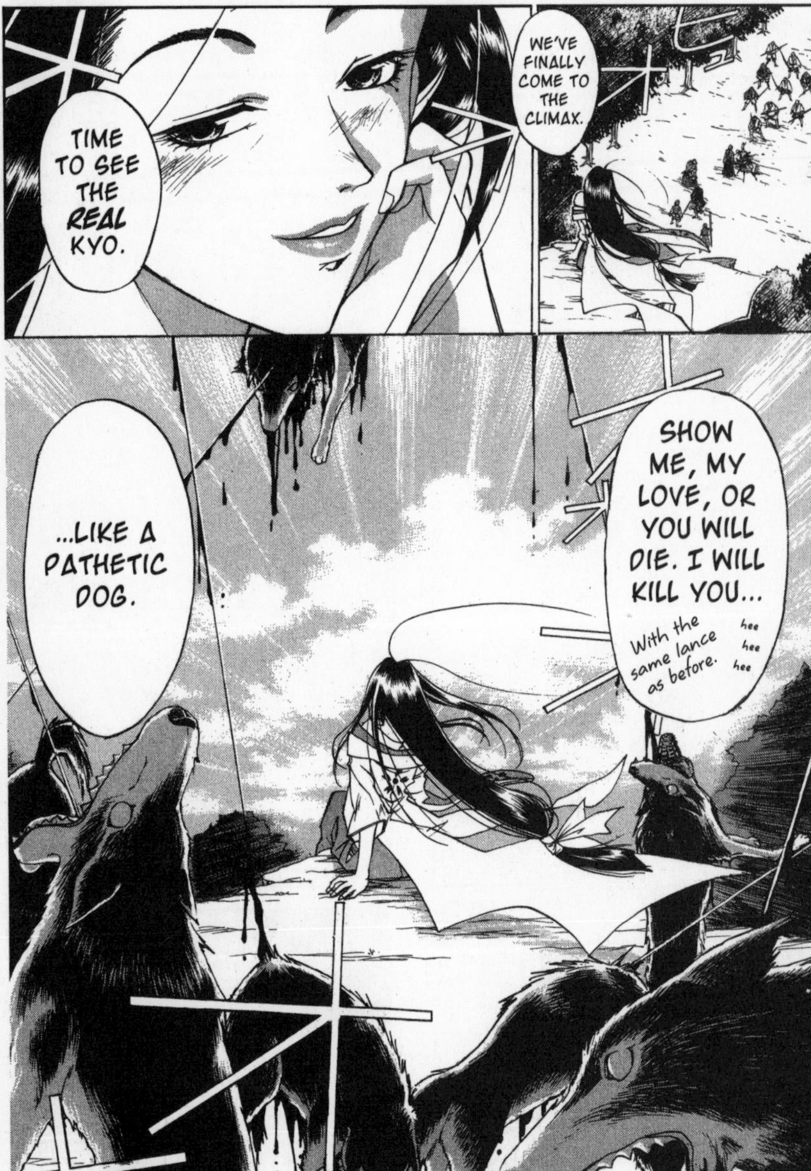
WE'VE FINALLY COME TO THE CLIMAX.
TIME TO SEE THE REAL KYO.
SHOW ME, MY LOVE, OR YOU WILL DIE. I WILL KILL YOU...
With the same lance as before.
hee hee hee
...LIKE A PATHETIC DOG.

Kamijyo Circumstances

Secret Language

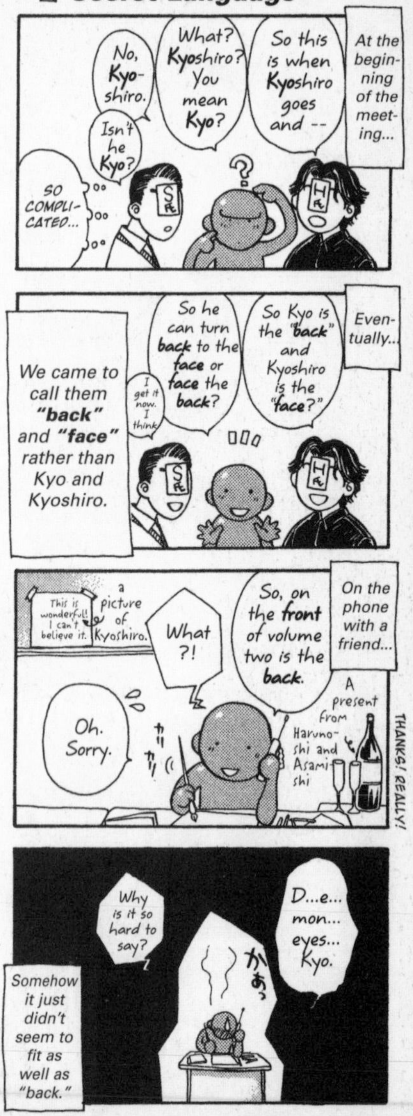

At the beginning of the meeting...
So this is when Kyoshiro goes and --
What? Kyoshiro? You mean Kyo?
No, Kyo-shiro.
Isn't he Kyo?
SO COMPLICATED...
Eventually...
So Kyo is the "back" and Kyoshiro is the "face?"
So he can turn back to the face or face the back?
I get it now. I think.
We came to call them "back" and "face" rather than Kyo and Kyoshiro.
On the phone with a friend...
So, on the front of volume two is the back.
What?!
a picture of Kyoshiro.
This is wonderful! I can't believe it.
A present from Haruno-shi and Asami-shi
THANKS! REALLY!
Oh. Sorry.
D...e...mon...eyes...Kyo.
かあっ
Why is it so hard to say?
Somehow it just didn't seem to fit as well as "back."

Izumo no Okuni

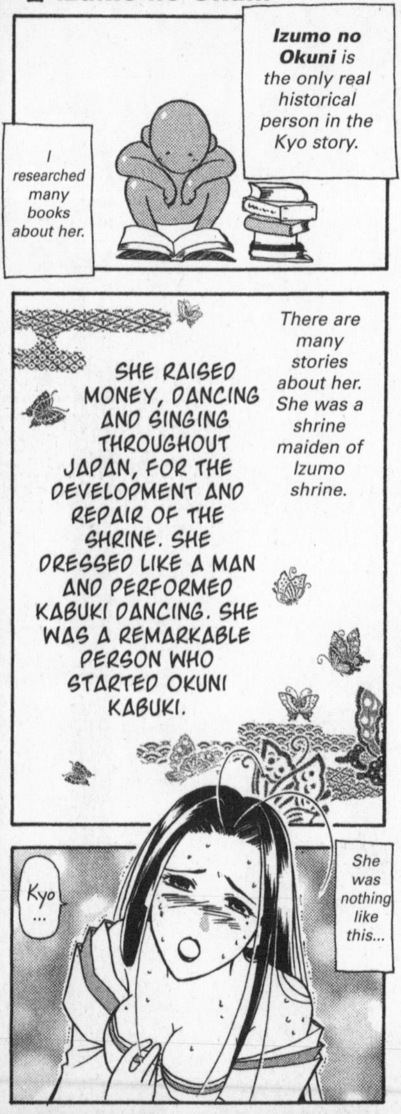

Izumo no Okuni is the only real historical person in the Kyo story.
I researched many books about her.
There are many stories about her. She was a shrine maiden of Izumo shrine.
SHE RAISED MONEY, DANCING AND SINGING THROUGHOUT JAPAN, FOR THE DEVELOPMENT AND REPAIR OF THE SHRINE. SHE DRESSED LIKE A MAN AND PERFORMED KABUKI DANCING. SHE WAS A REMARKABLE PERSON WHO STARTED OKUNI KABUKI.
She was nothing like this...
Kyo ...

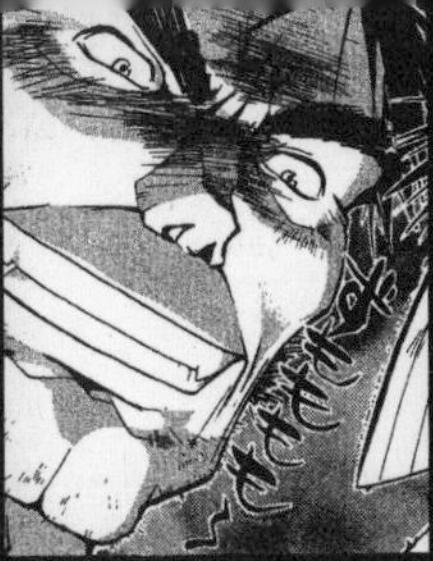

While searching for Yuya and Okuni, Kyoshiro saved **Mika** from a pack of wild dogs. To show his gratitude, her father invited him to the **Ochiudo's Kakure Zato**.

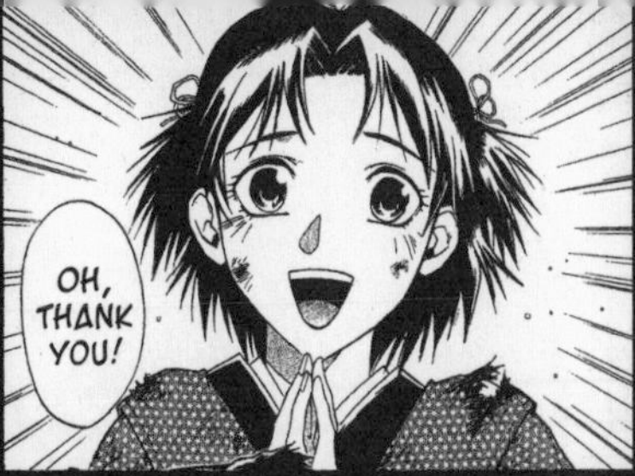
OH, THANK YOU!

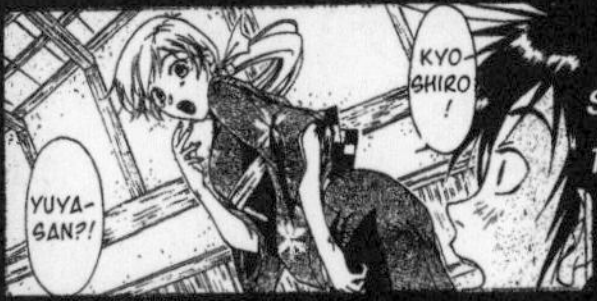
KYO-SHIRO!
YUYA-SAN?!

He was surprised to find **Yuya** already there.

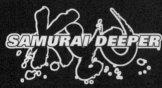

SAMURAI DEEPER KYO

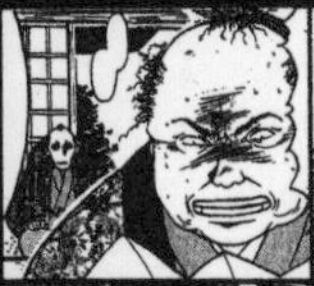

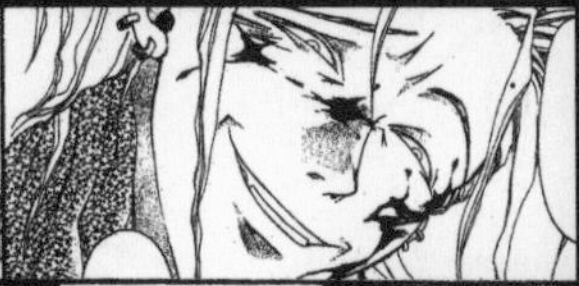

But their rest would be short. The Daikan and **Jimon** learned of the rebels' hideout...

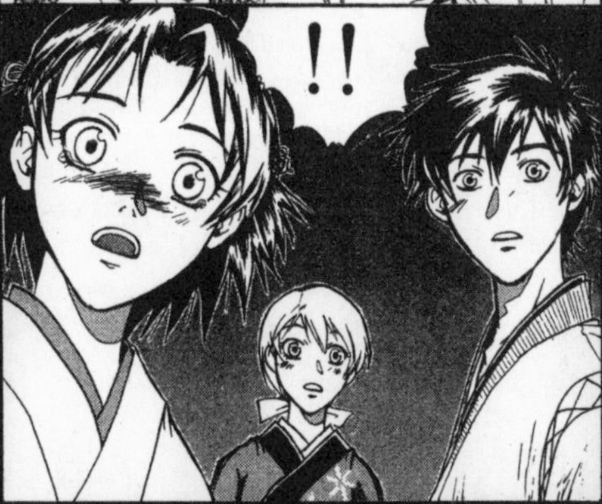
!!

And hurried to destroy the rebels once and for all...

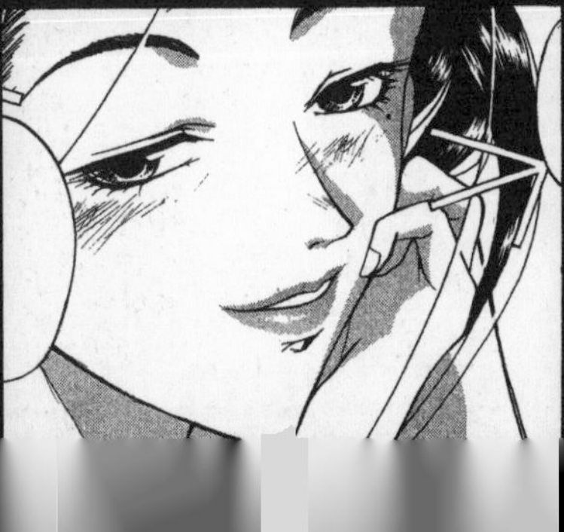

Meanwhile, **Okuni** watched the whole scene from afar...her thoughts her own.

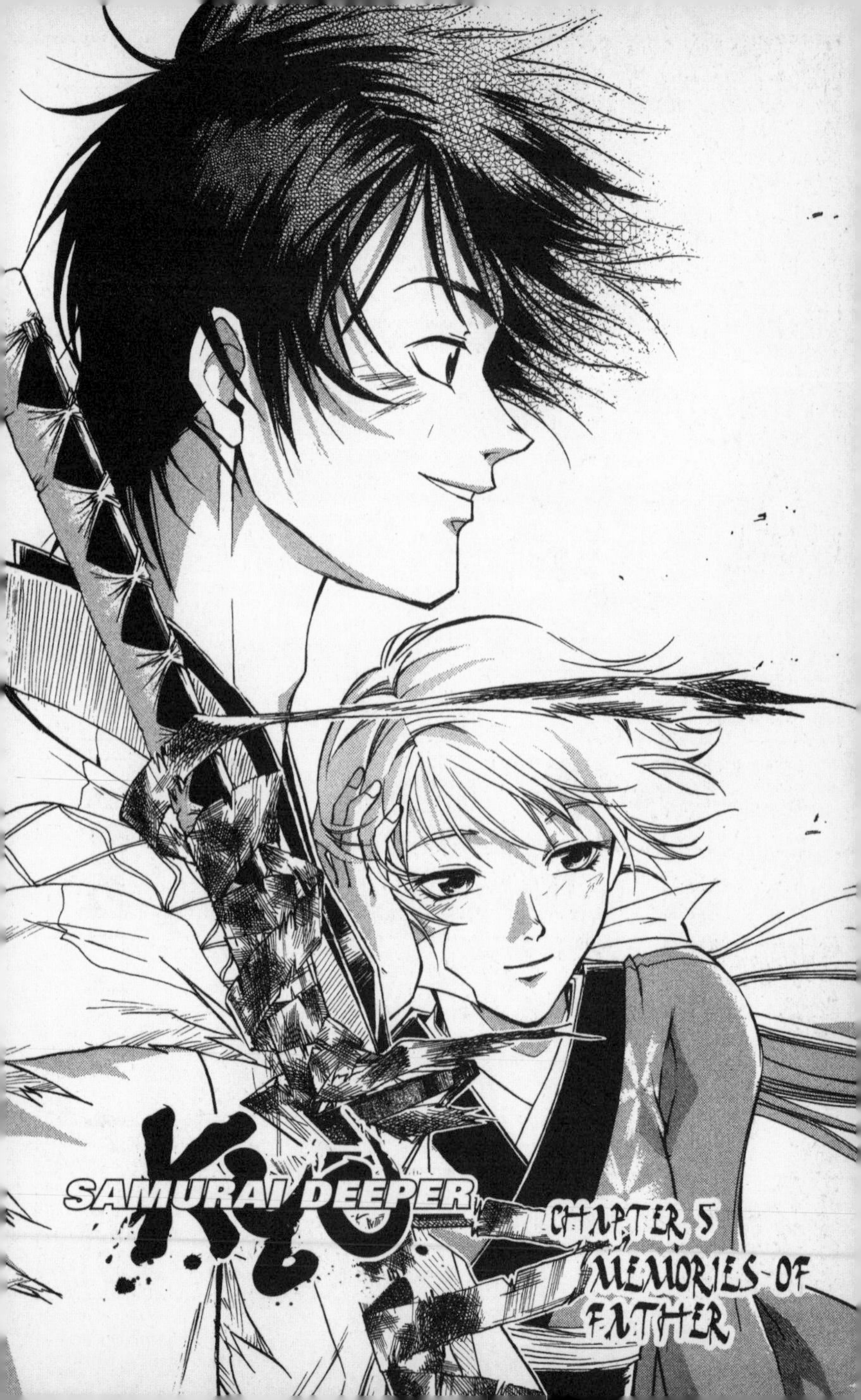
SAMURAI DEEPER
KYO
CHAPTER 5
MEMORIES OF FATHER

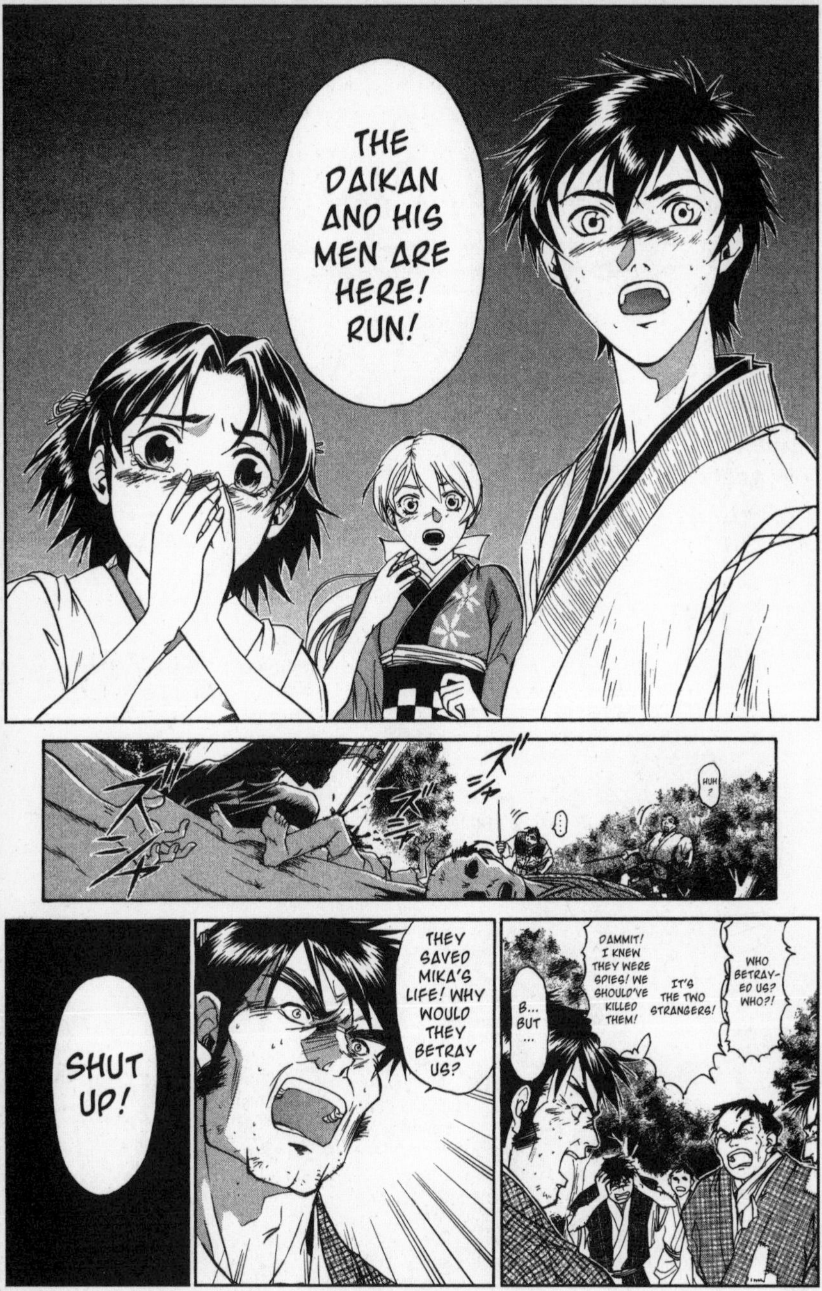
THE DAIKAN AND HIS MEN ARE HERE! RUN!
HUH?
...
WHO BETRAY-ED US? WHO?!
IT'S THE TWO STRANGERS!
DAMMIT! I KNEW THEY WERE SPIES! WE SHOULD'VE KILLED THEM!
B... BUT ...
THEY SAVED MIKA'S LIFE! WHY WOULD THEY BETRAY US?
SHUT UP!

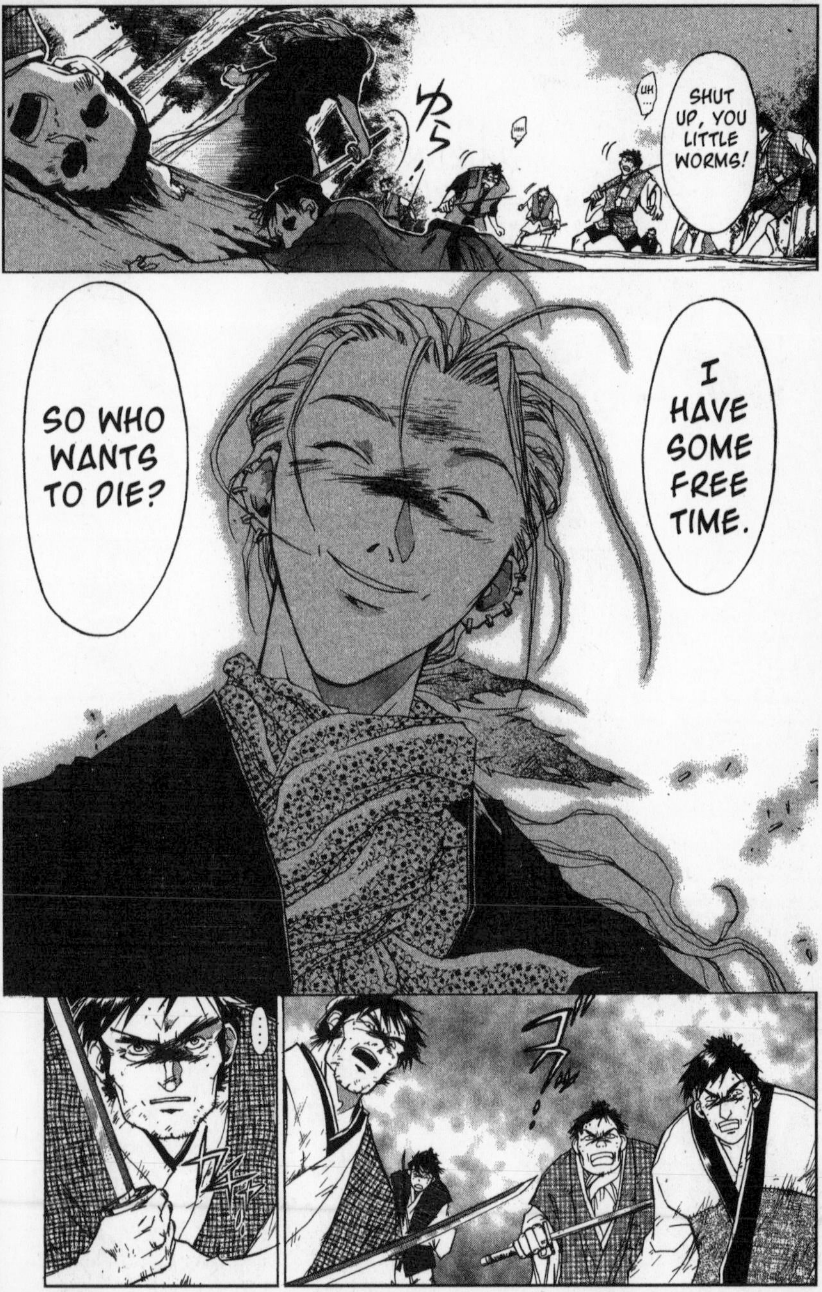
SHUT UP, YOU LITTLE WORMS!
UH...
ゆら
I HAVE SOME FREE TIME.
SO WHO WANTS TO DIE?
...

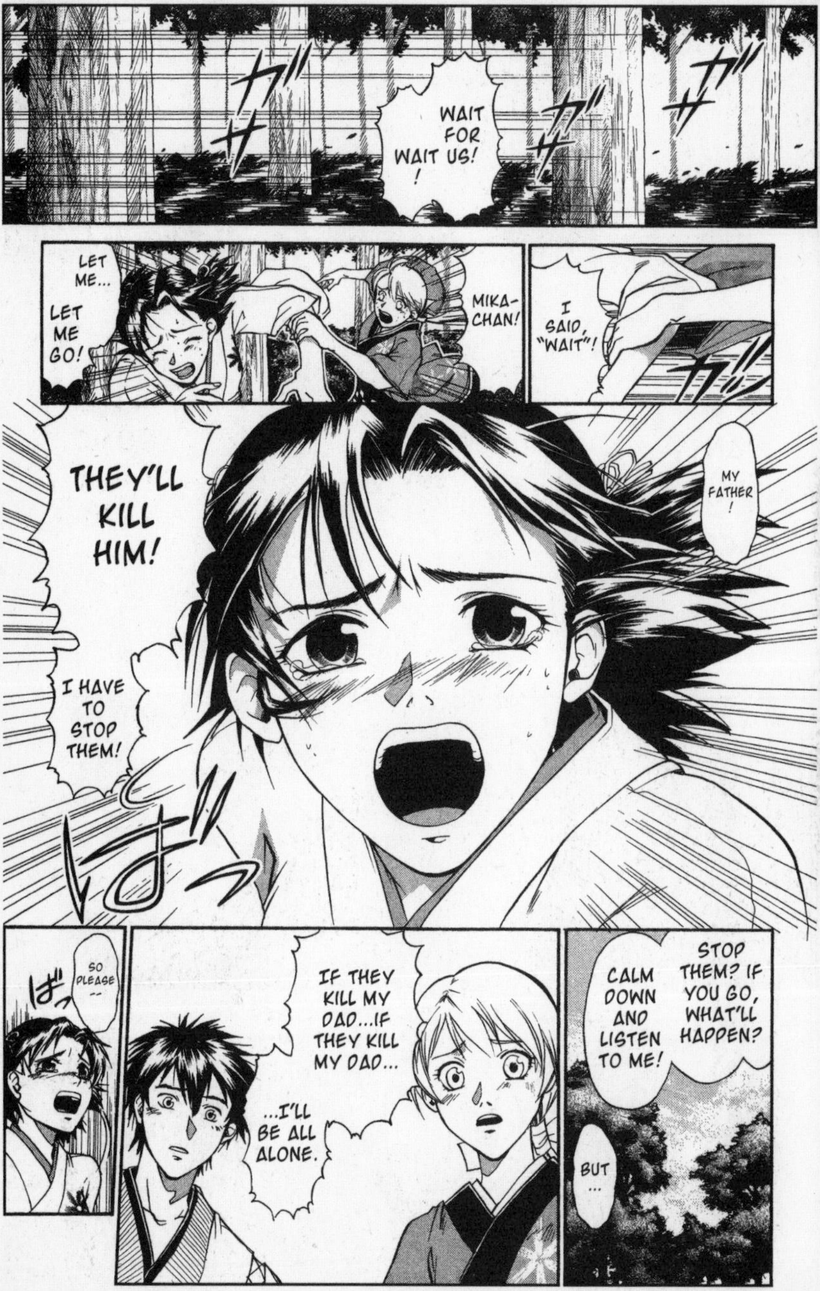
WAIT FOR US!
WAIT!
I SAID, "WAIT"!
MIKA-CHAN!
LET ME...
LET ME GO!
MY FATHER!
THEY'LL KILL HIM!
I HAVE TO STOP THEM!
STOP THEM? IF YOU GO, WHAT'LL HAPPEN?
CALM DOWN AND LISTEN TO ME!
BUT...
IF THEY KILL MY DAD...IF THEY KILL MY DAD...
...I'LL BE ALL ALONE.
SO PLEASE --

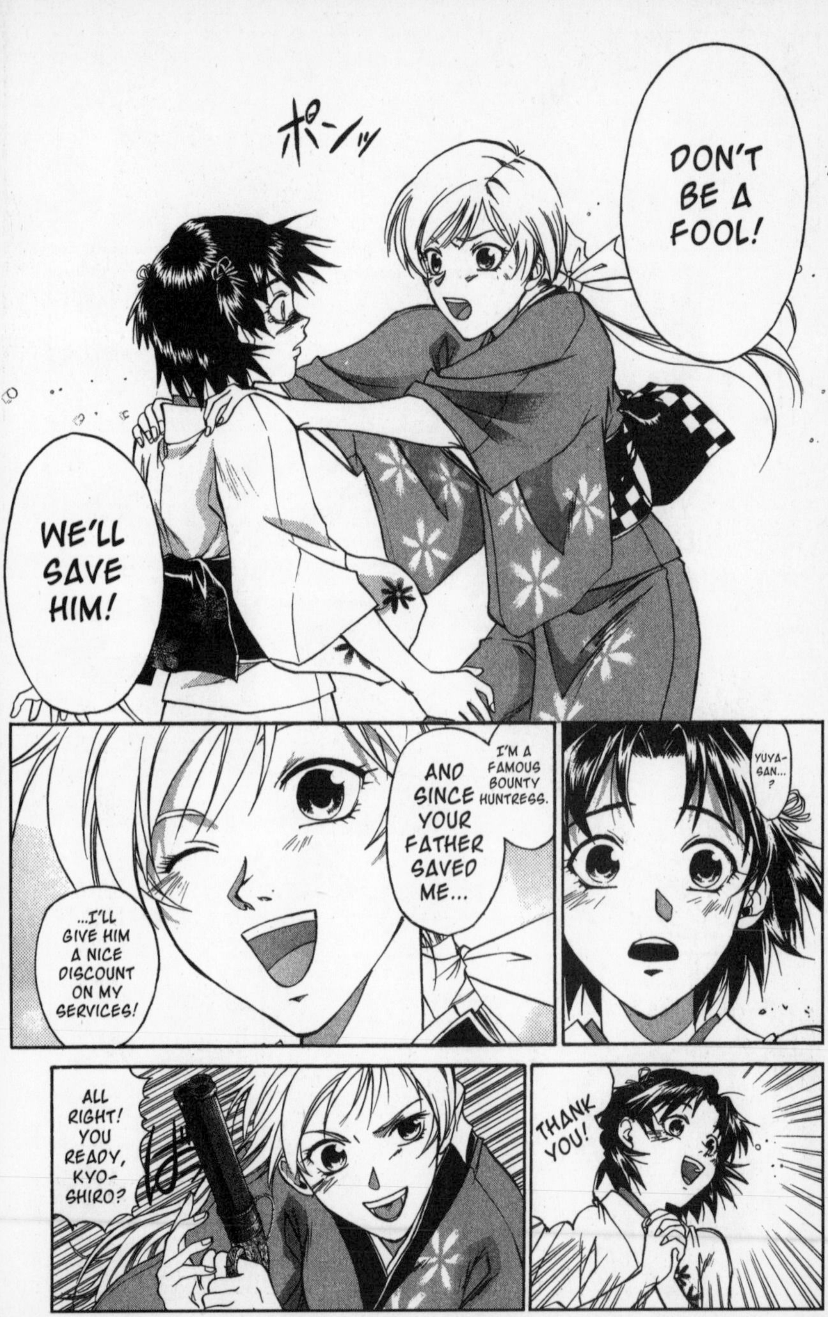
ポーンッ
DON'T BE A FOOL!
WE'LL SAVE HIM!
YUYA-SAN...?
I'M A FAMOUS BOUNTY HUNTRESS.
AND SINCE YOUR FATHER SAVED ME...
...I'LL GIVE HIM A NICE DISCOUNT ON MY SERVICES!
THANK YOU!
ALL RIGHT! YOU READY, KYO-SHIRO?

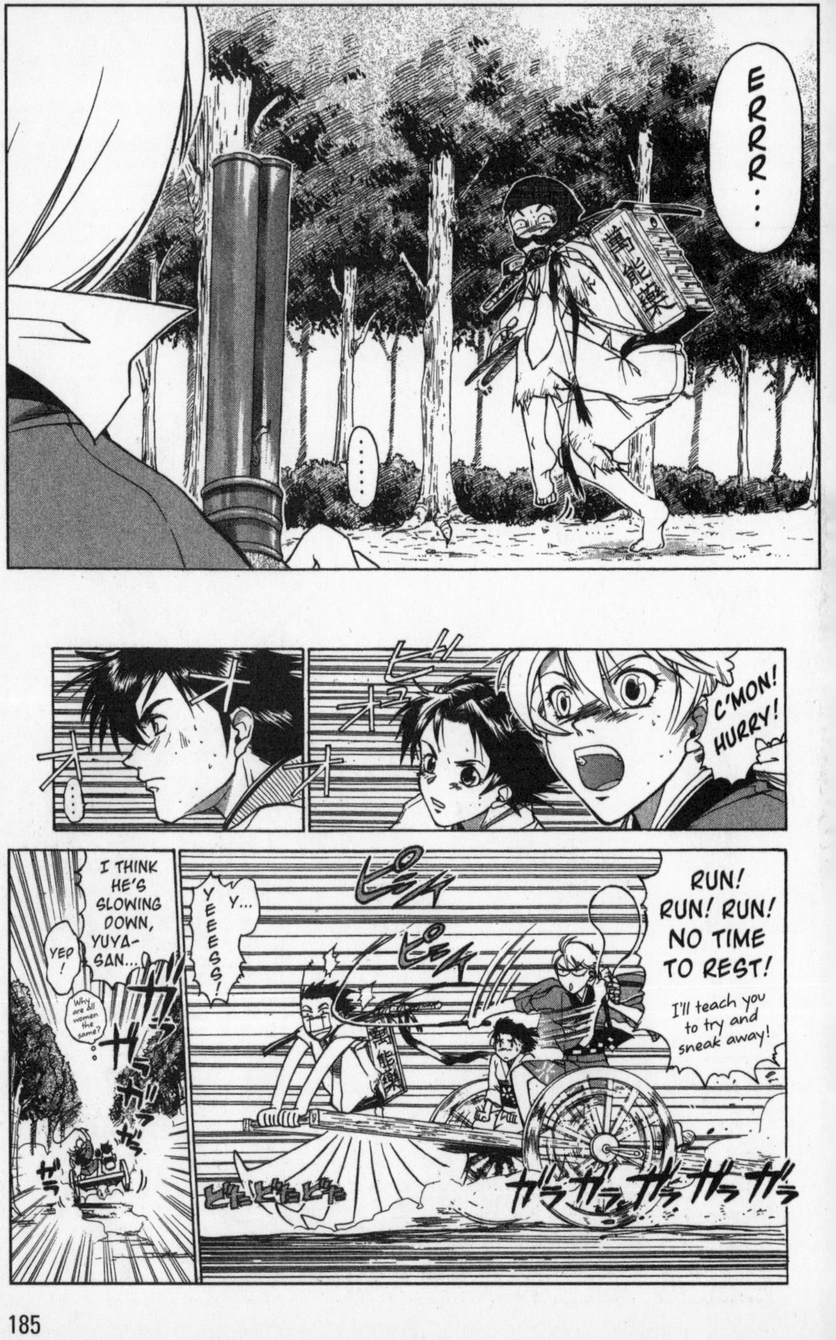
ERRR...
......
C'MON! HURRY!
...
RUN! RUN! RUN! NO TIME TO REST!
I'll teach you to try and sneak away!
Y... YEEEESS!
I THINK HE'S SLOWING DOWN, YUYA-SAN...
YEP!
Why are all women the same?

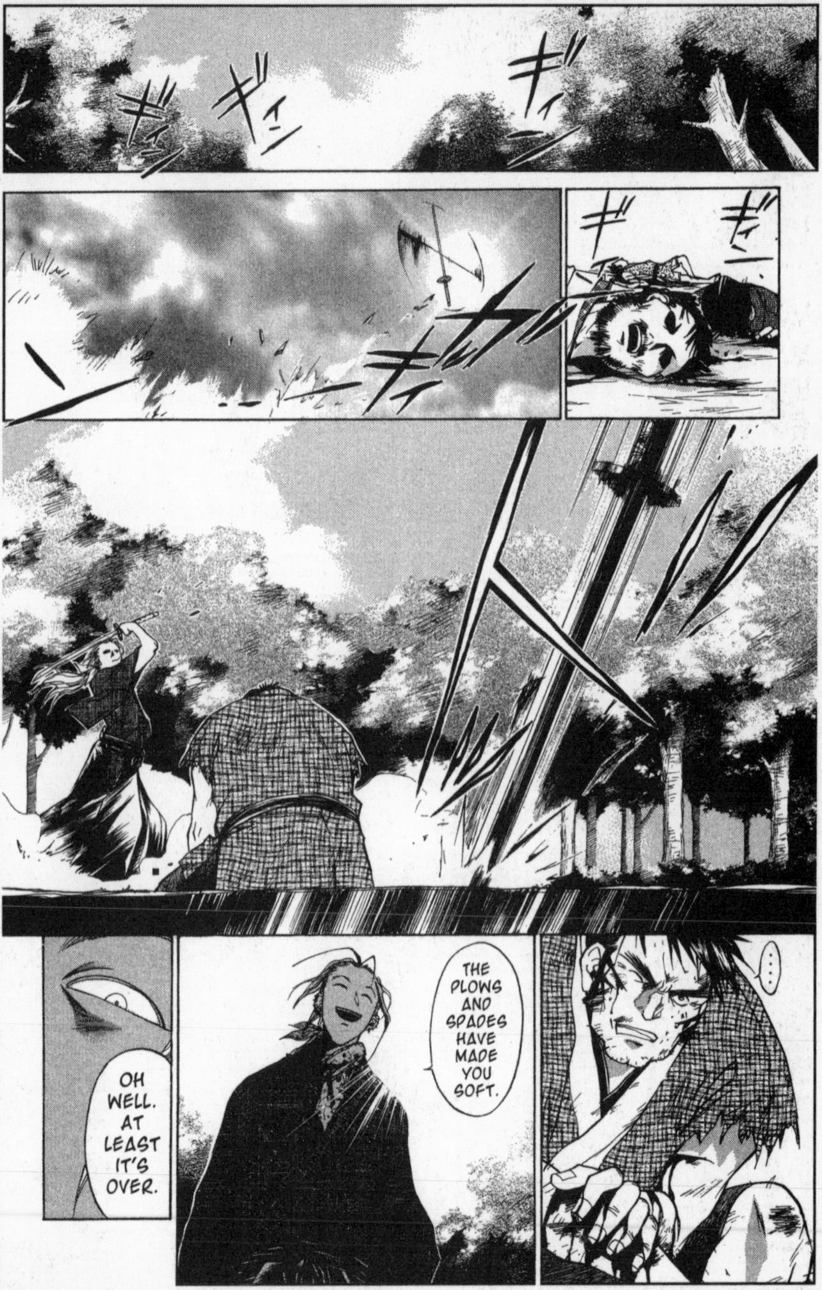
...
THE PLOWS AND SPADES HAVE MADE YOU SOFT.
OH WELL. AT LEAST IT'S OVER.

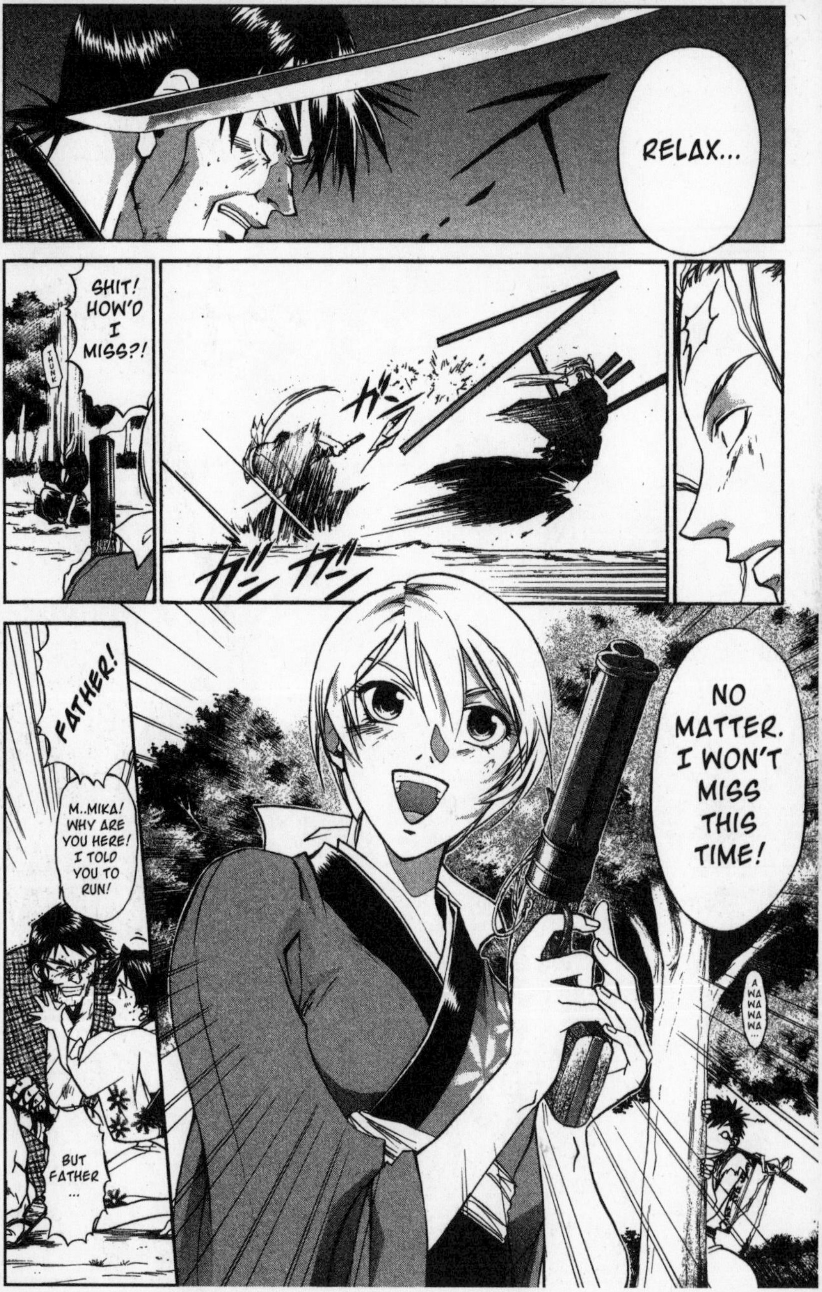
RELAX...
SHIT! HOW'D I MISS?!
THUNK
NO MATTER. I WON'T MISS THIS TIME!
FATHER!
M..MIKA! WHY ARE YOU HERE! I TOLD YOU TO RUN!
A WA WA WA WA...
BUT FATHER ...

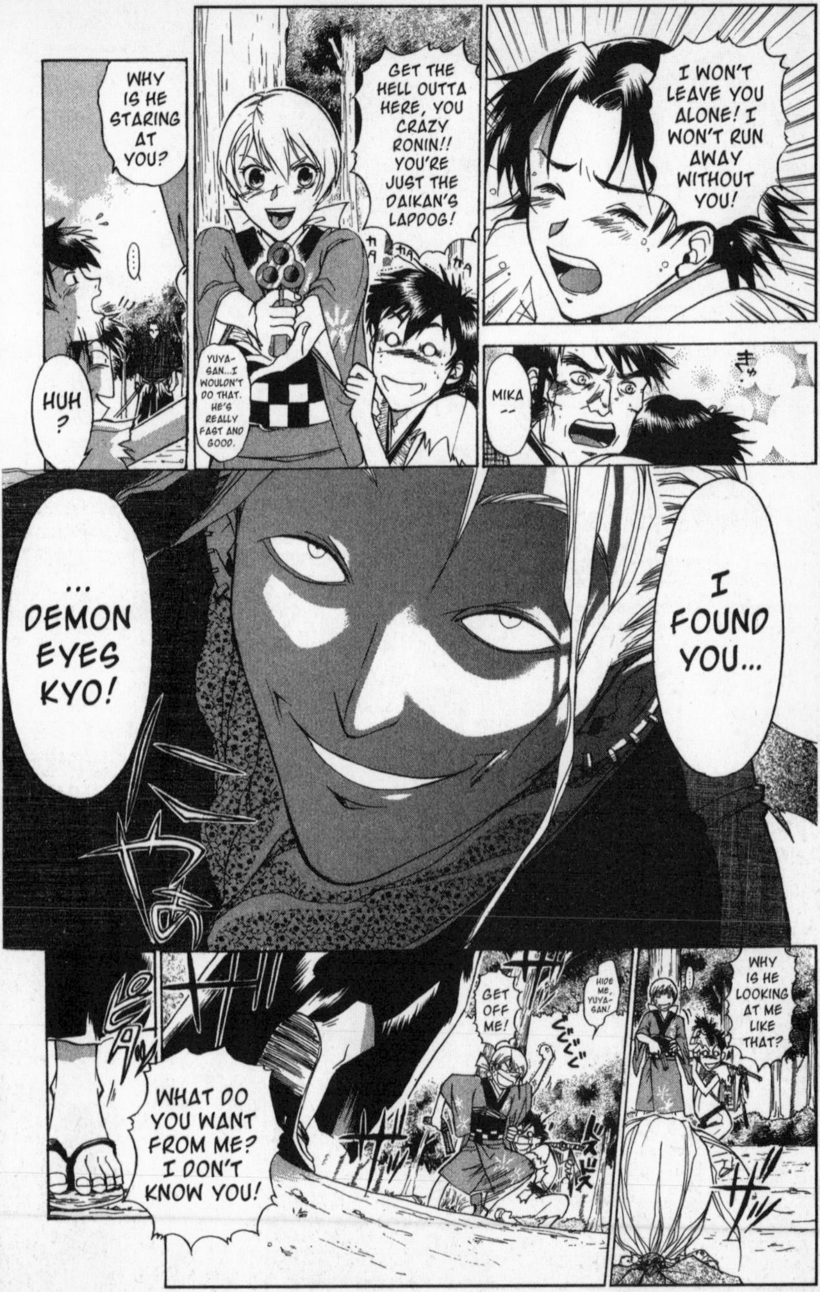
I WON'T LEAVE YOU ALONE! I WON'T RUN AWAY WITHOUT YOU!
MIKA--
GET THE HELL OUTTA HERE, YOU CRAZY RONIN!! YOU'RE JUST THE DAIKAN'S LAPDOG!
YUYA-SAN...I WOULDN'T DO THAT. HE'S REALLY FAST AND GOOD.
WHY IS HE STARING AT YOU?
...
HUH?
I FOUND YOU...
...DEMON EYES KYO!
WHY IS HE LOOKING AT ME LIKE THAT?
HIDE ME, YUYA-SAN!
GET OFF ME!
WHAT DO YOU WANT FROM ME? I DON'T KNOW YOU!

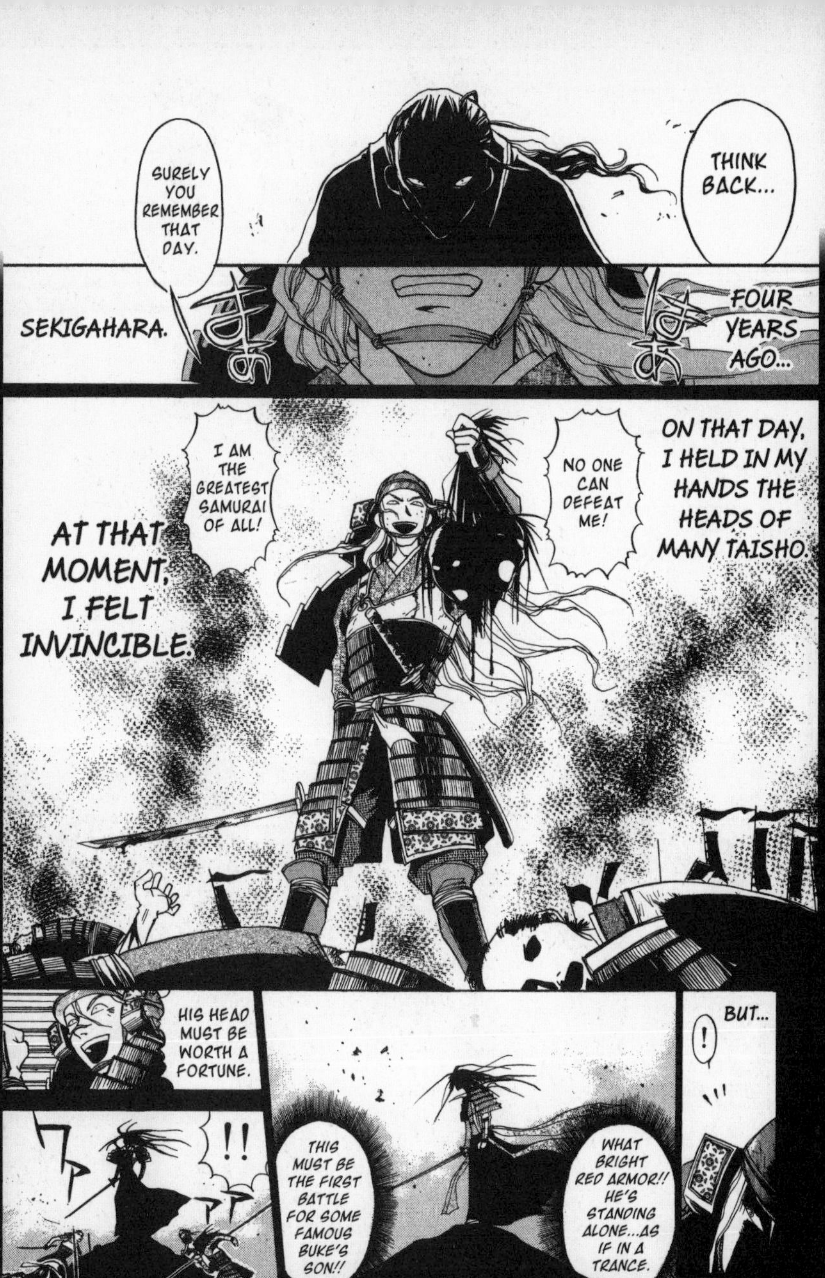
THINK BACK...
SURELY YOU REMEMBER THAT DAY.
FOUR YEARS AGO...
SEKIGAHARA.
ON THAT DAY, I HELD IN MY HANDS THE HEADS OF MANY TAISHO.
NO ONE CAN DEFEAT ME!
I AM THE GREATEST SAMURAI OF ALL!
AT THAT MOMENT, I FELT INVINCIBLE.
BUT...
!
WHAT BRIGHT RED ARMOR!! HE'S STANDING ALONE...AS IF IN A TRANCE.
THIS MUST BE THE FIRST BATTLE FOR SOME FAMOUS BUKE'S SON!!
HIS HEAD MUST BE WORTH A FORTUNE.
!!

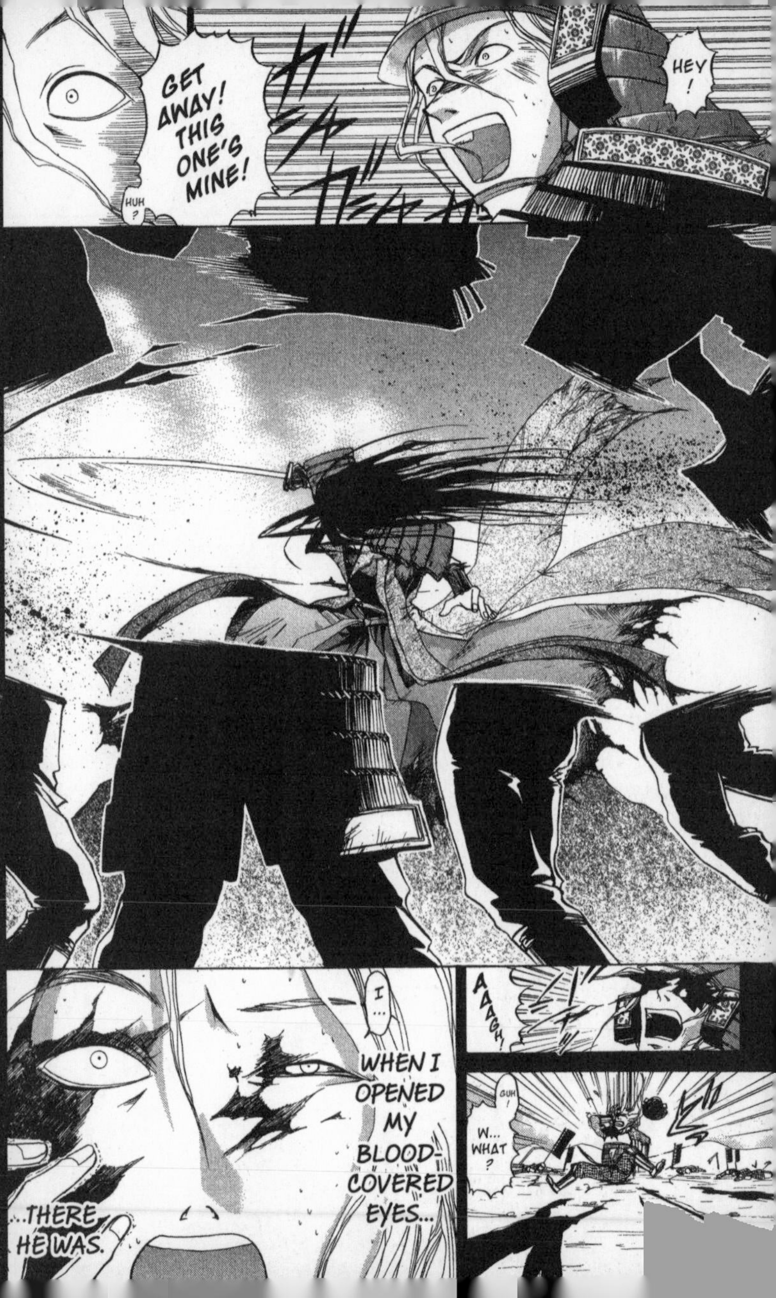
HEY!
GET AWAY! THIS ONE'S MINE!
HUH?
AAAGH!
GUH!
W... WHAT?
I...
WHEN I OPENED MY BLOOD-COVERED EYES...
...THERE HE WAS.

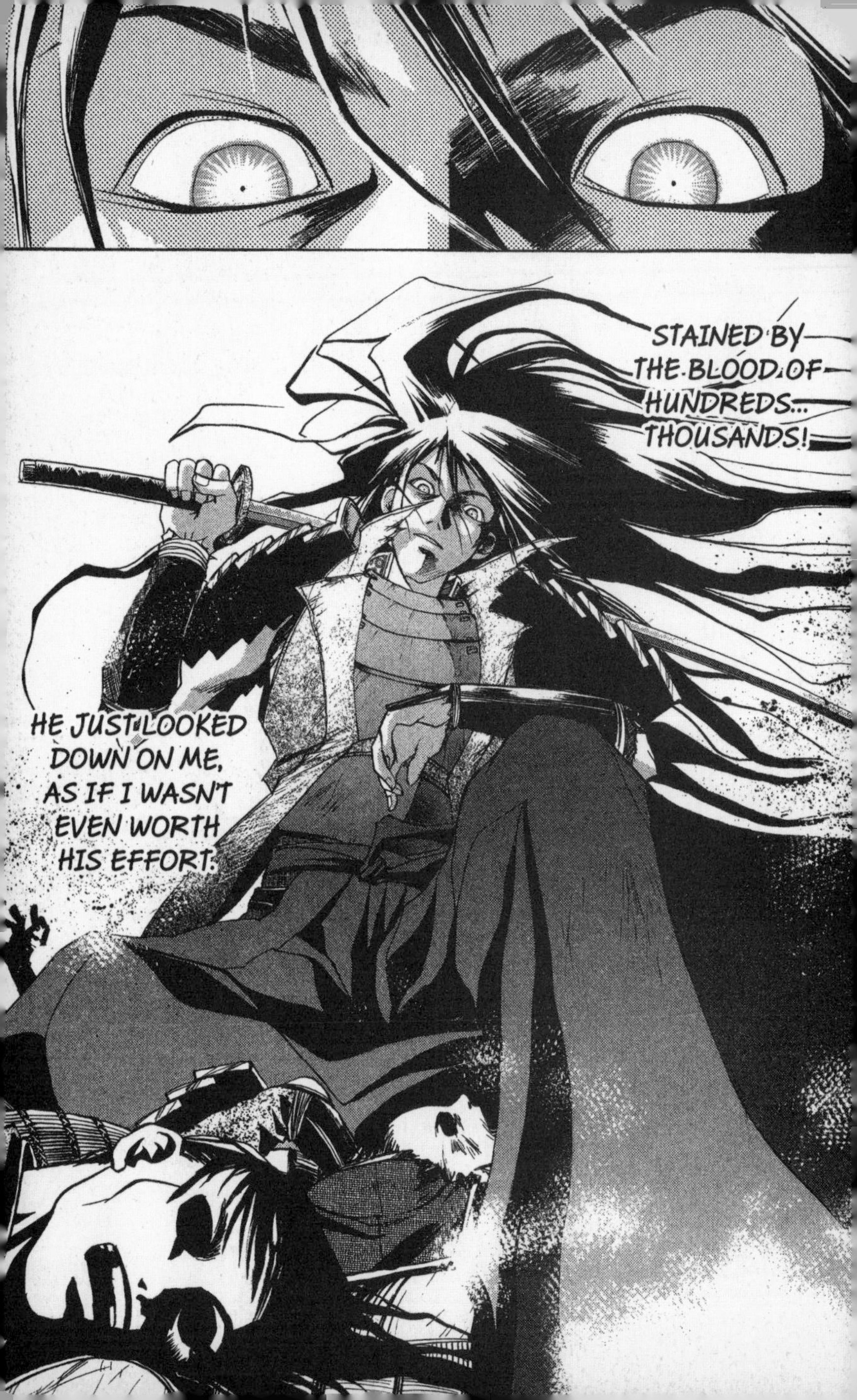
STAINED BY THE BLOOD OF HUNDREDS... THOUSANDS!
HE JUST LOOKED DOWN ON ME, AS IF I WASN'T EVEN WORTH HIS EFFORT.

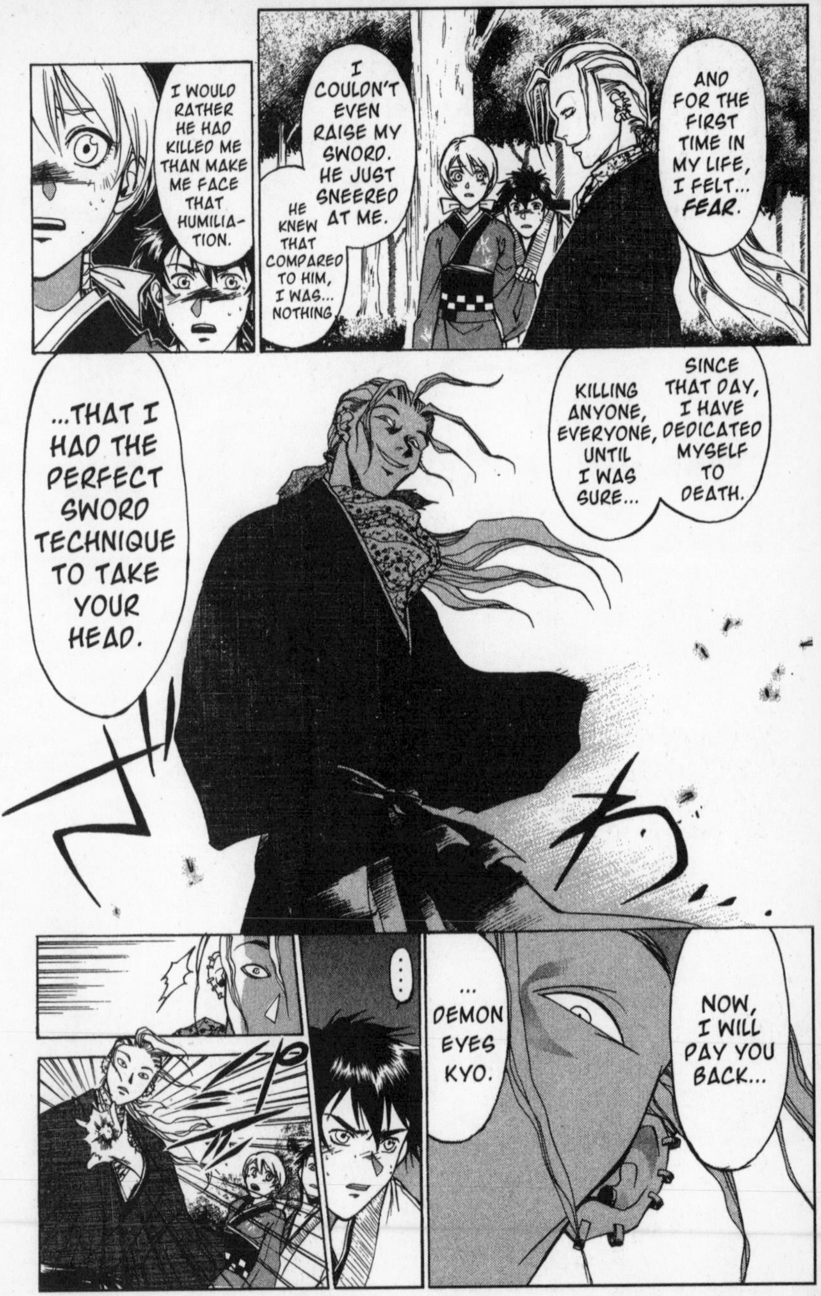
AND FOR THE FIRST TIME IN MY LIFE, I FELT... FEAR.
I COULDN'T EVEN RAISE MY SWORD. HE JUST SNEERED AT ME.
HE KNEW THAT COMPARED TO HIM, I WAS... NOTHING.
I WOULD RATHER HE HAD KILLED ME THAN MAKE ME FACE THAT HUMILIATION.
SINCE THAT DAY, I HAVE DEDICATED MYSELF TO DEATH.
KILLING ANYONE, EVERYONE, UNTIL I WAS SURE...
...THAT I HAD THE PERFECT SWORD TECHNIQUE TO TAKE YOUR HEAD.
NOW, I WILL PAY YOU BACK...
... DEMON EYES KYO.
...

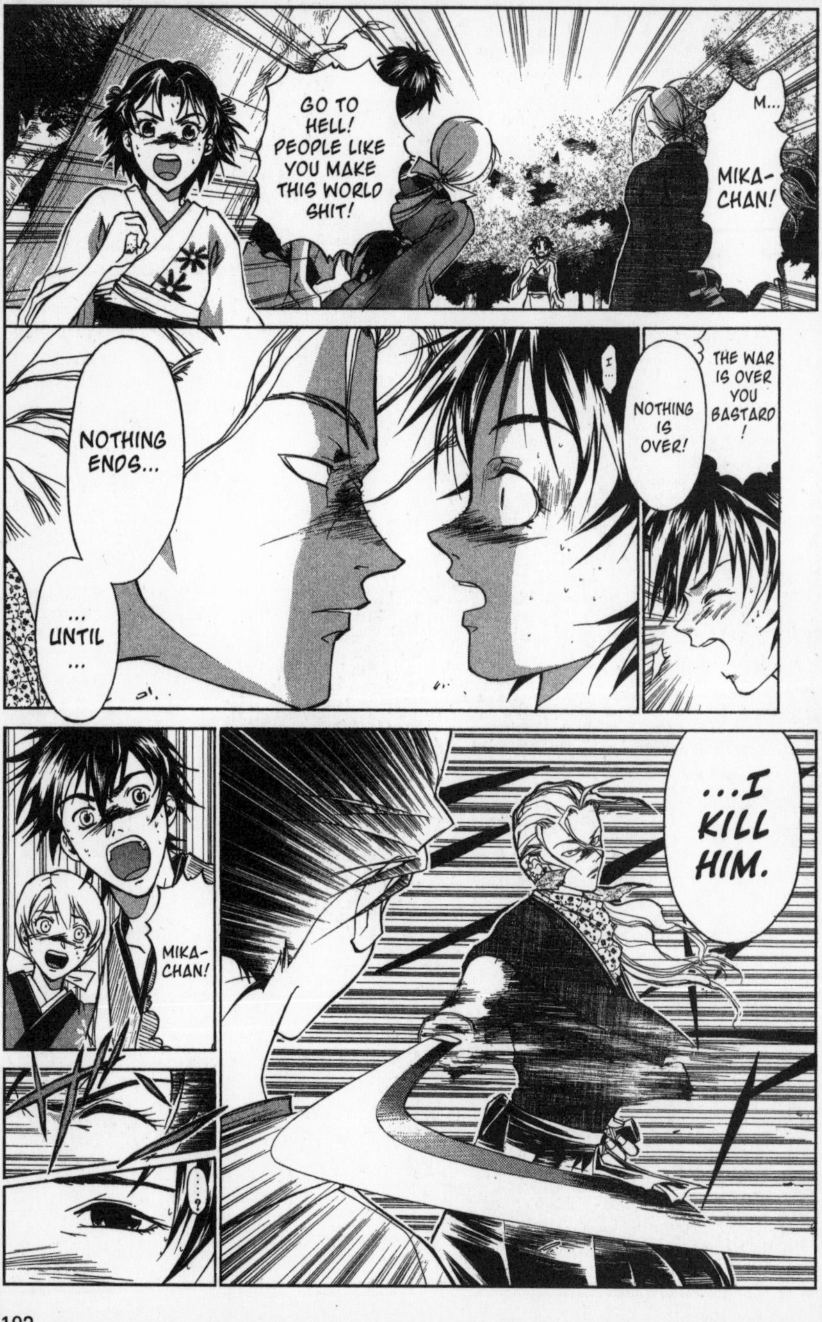
M...
MIKA-CHAN!
GO TO HELL! PEOPLE LIKE YOU MAKE THIS WORLD SHIT!
THE WAR IS OVER YOU BASTARD!
NOTHING IS OVER!
I...
NOTHING ENDS...
...UNTIL...
...I KILL HIM.
MIKA-CHAN!
...?

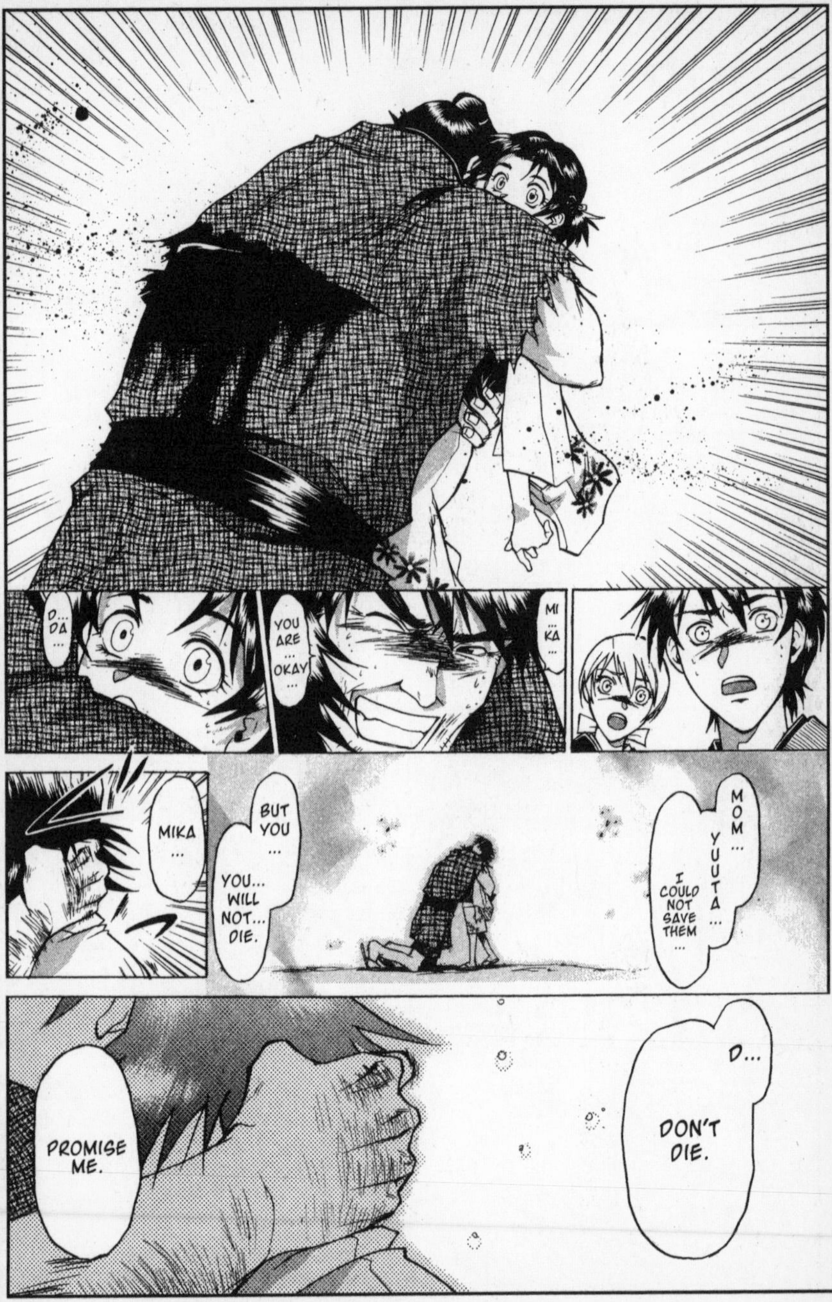
MI... KA...
YOU ARE... OKAY...
D... DA...
MOM... YUUTA...
I COULD NOT SAVE THEM...
BUT YOU... YOU... WILL NOT... DIE.
MIKA...
D...
DON'T DIE.
PROMISE ME.

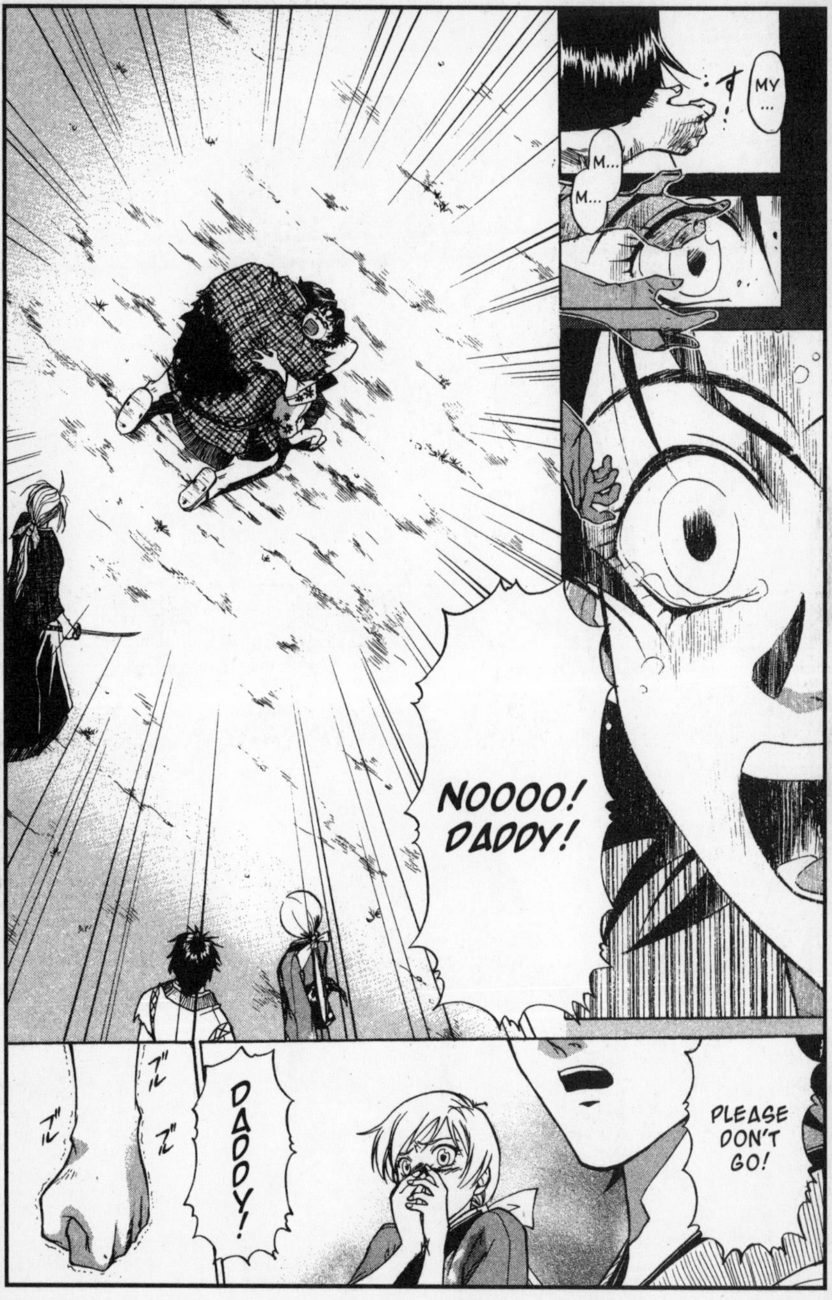
MY ...
M... M...
NOOOO! DADDY!
PLEASE DON'T GO!
DADDY!

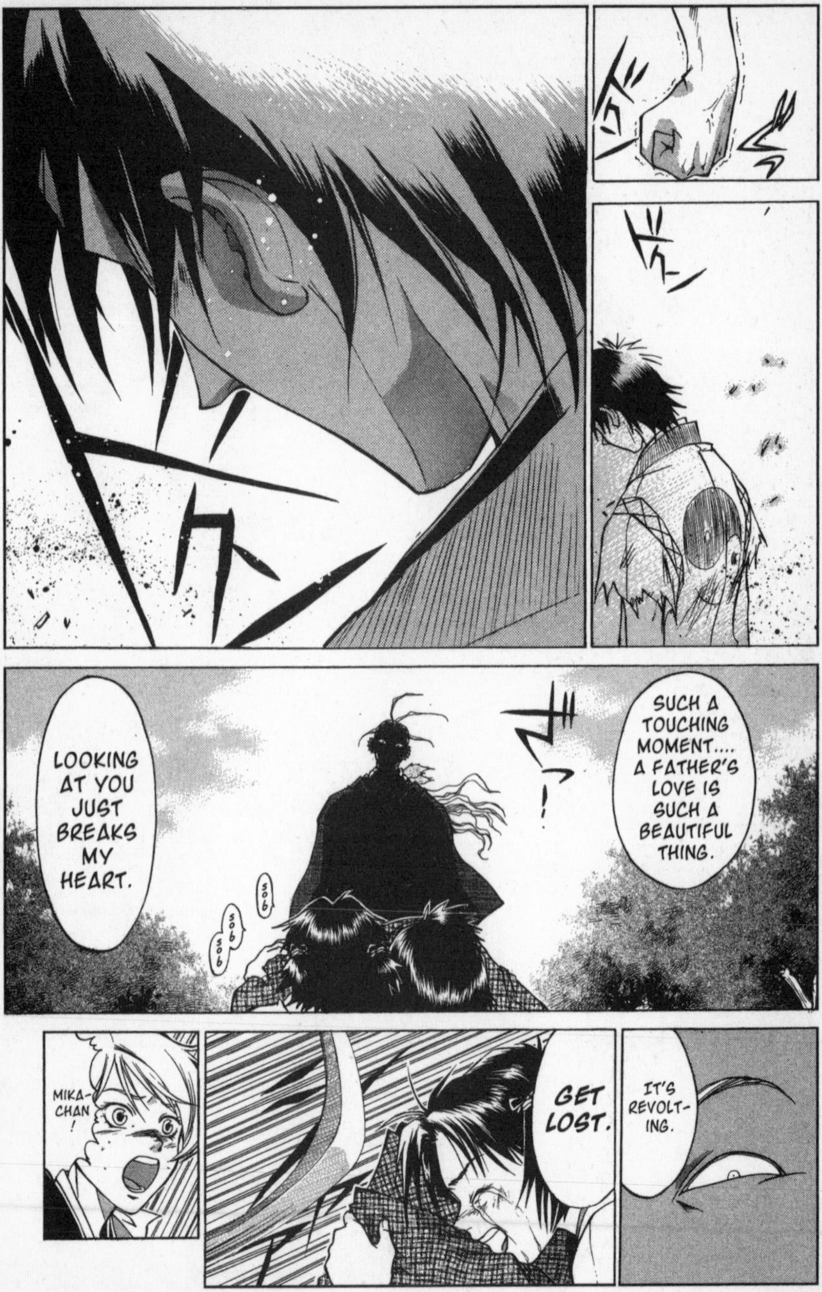
SUCH A TOUCHING MOMENT.... A FATHER'S LOVE IS SUCH A BEAUTIFUL THING.
LOOKING AT YOU JUST BREAKS MY HEART.
SOB SOB SOB
IT'S REVOLT-ING.
GET LOST.
MIKA-CHAN!

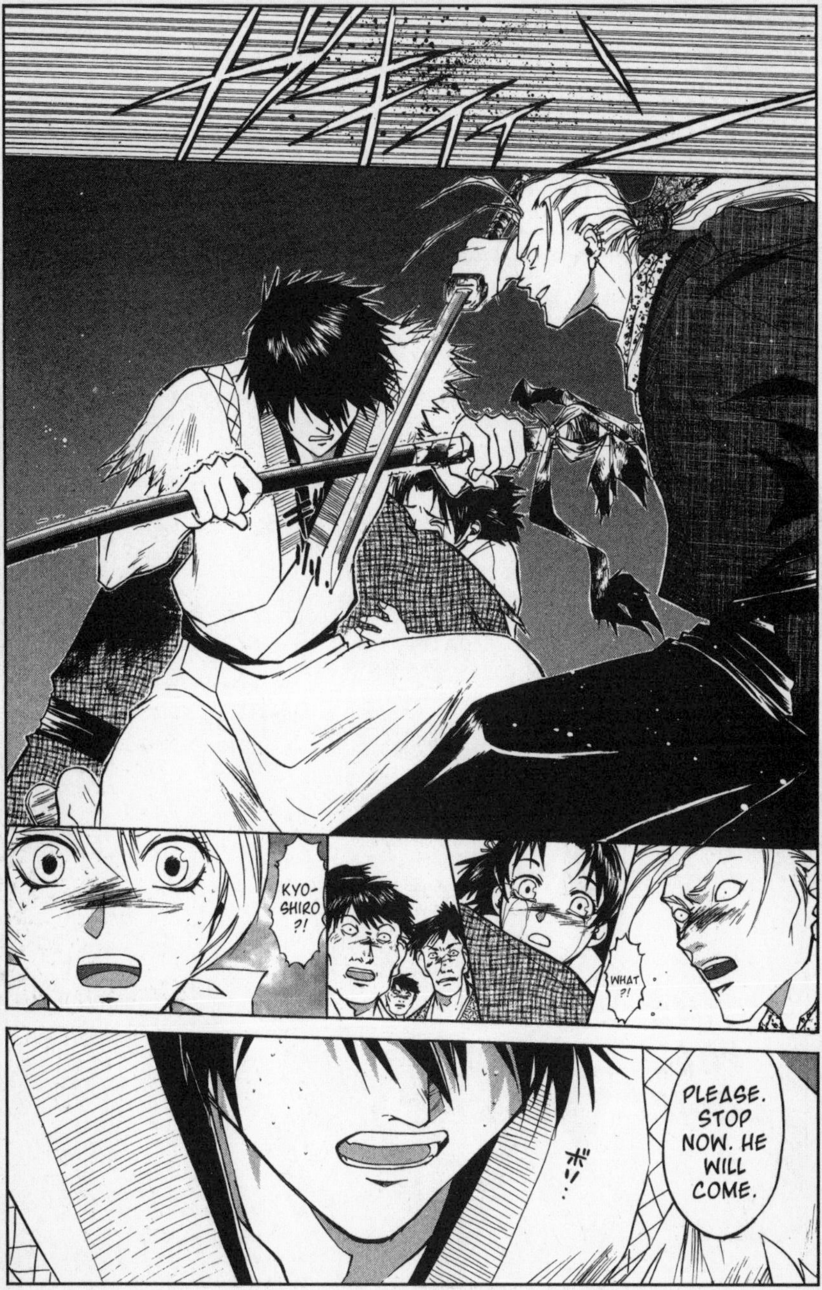
WHAT?!
KYO-SHIRO?!
PLEASE. STOP NOW. HE WILL COME.

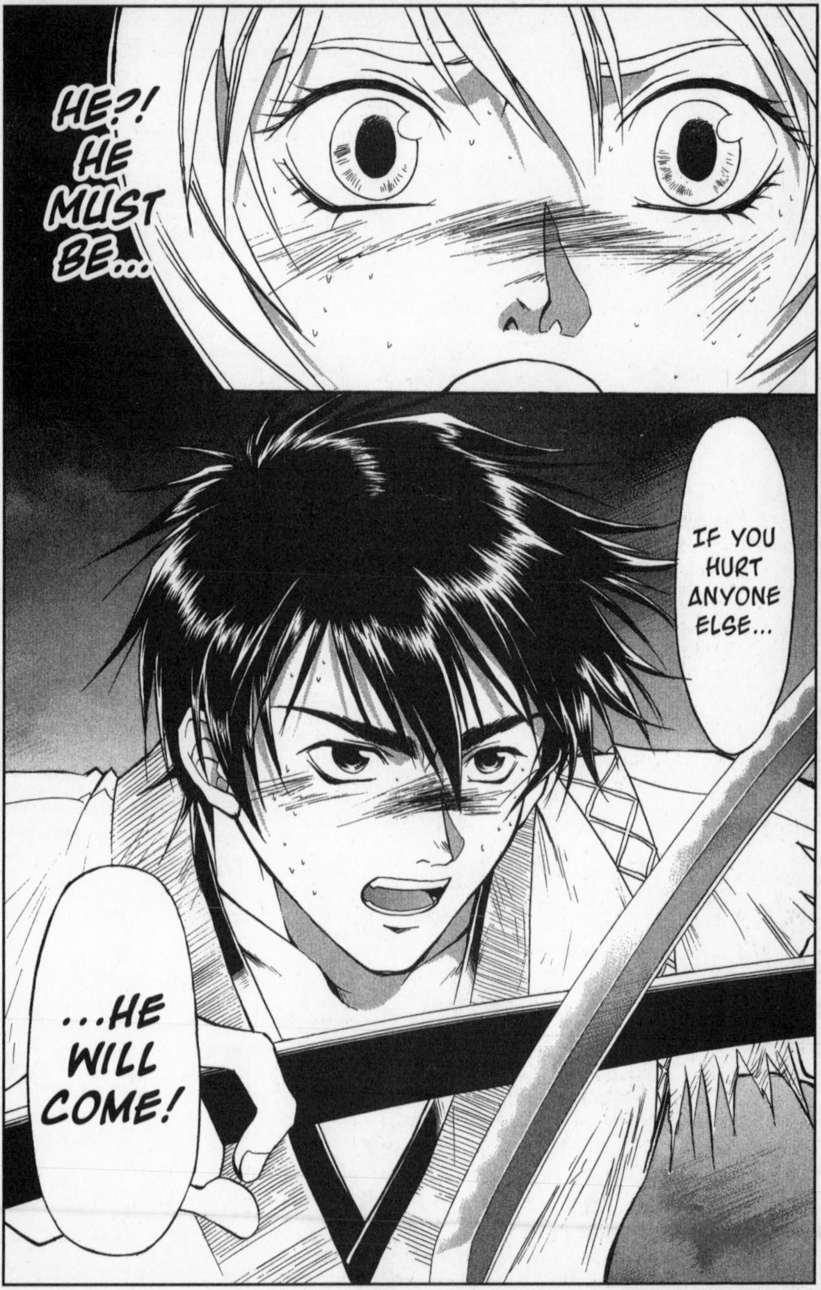
HE?! HE MUST BE...
IF YOU HURT ANYONE ELSE...
...HE WILL COME!

TO BE CONTINUED...

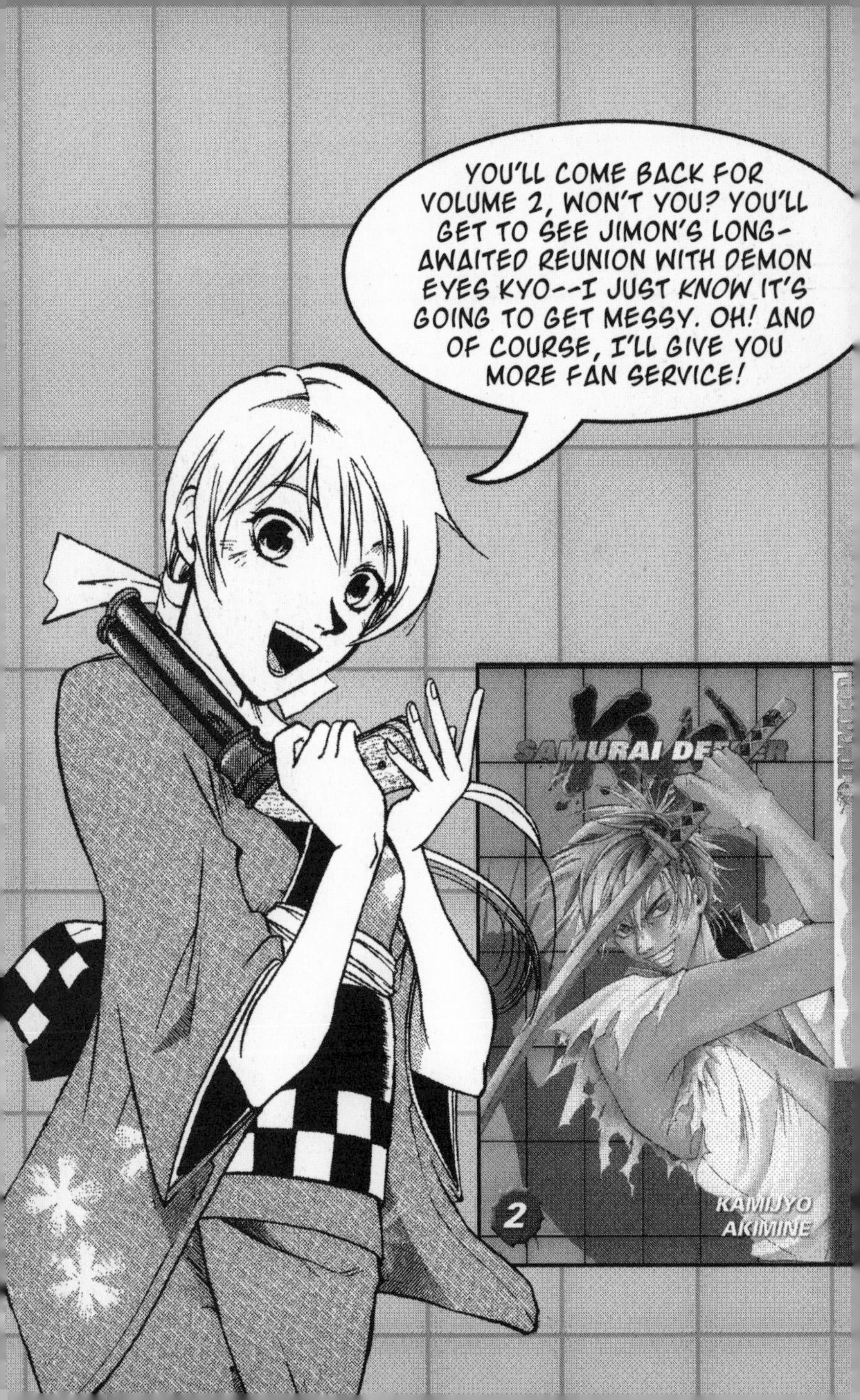
YOU'LL COME BACK FOR VOLUME 2, WON'T YOU? YOU'LL GET TO SEE JIMON'S LONG-AWAITED REUNION WITH DEMON EYES KYO--I JUST KNOW IT'S GOING TO GET MESSY. OH! AND OF COURSE, I'LL GIVE YOU MORE FAN SERVICE!
2
KAMIJYO AKIMINE

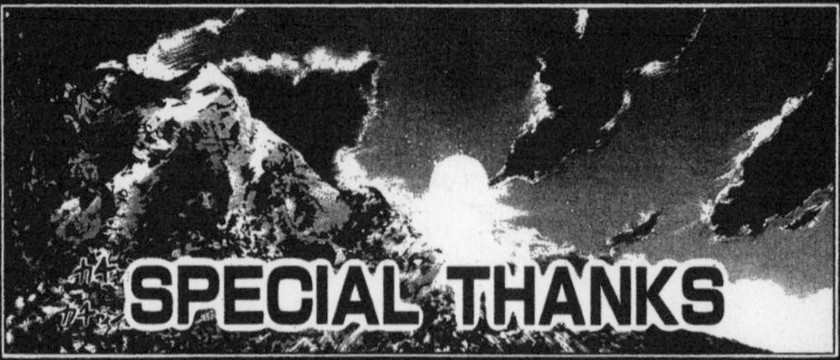
SPECIAL THANKS

YUZU HARUNO
(The chief staff)
HAZUKI ASAMI
SHINZIN ASHI 1430GOH
TAKAYA NAGAO
SHO YASHIOKA
AKIRA SHIKIBU
CHIKA OGAKI

AND
YOU

⬇ Yuzu Haruno

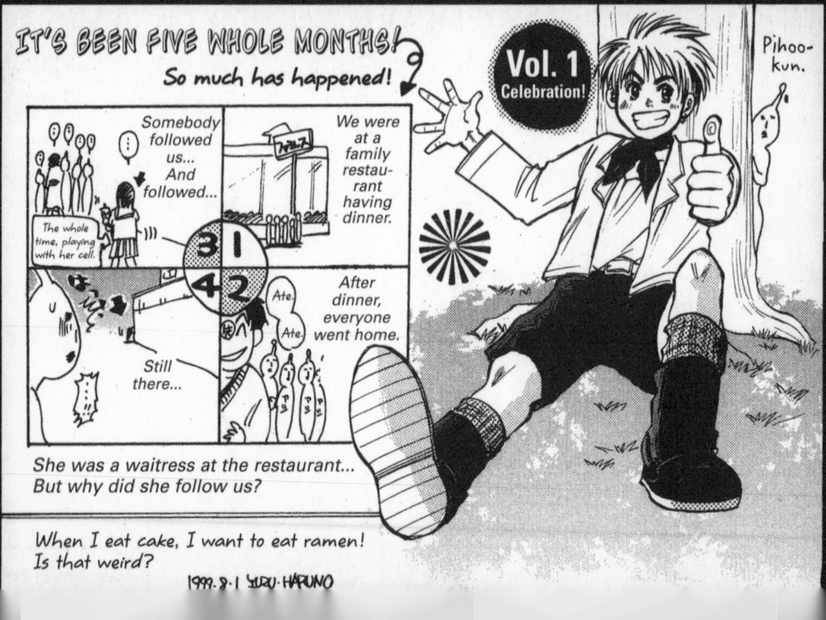
IT'S BEEN FIVE WHOLE MONTHS!
So much has happened!
Vol. 1 Celebration!
Pihoo-kun.
We were at a family restaurant having dinner.
After dinner, everyone went home.
Ate.
Ate.
Somebody followed us... And followed...
The whole time, playing with her cell.
Still there...
She was a waitress at the restaurant... But why did she follow us?
When I eat cake, I want to eat ramen! Is that weird?
1999.8.1 YUZU·HARUNO

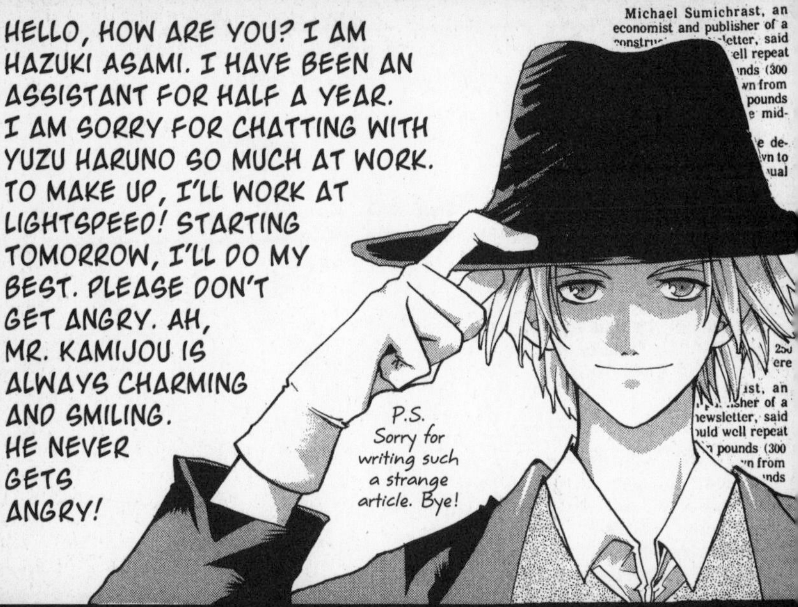
HELLO, HOW ARE YOU? I AM HAZUKI ASAMI. I HAVE BEEN AN ASSISTANT FOR HALF A YEAR. I AM SORRY FOR CHATTING WITH YUZU HARUNO SO MUCH AT WORK. TO MAKE UP, I'LL WORK AT LIGHTSPEED! STARTING TOMORROW, I'LL DO MY BEST. PLEASE DON'T GET ANGRY. AH, MR. KAMIJOU IS ALWAYS CHARMING AND SMILING. HE NEVER GETS ANGRY!
P.S. Sorry for writing such a strange article. Bye!
Michael Sumichrast, an
economist and publisher of a

⬆ Hazuki Asami ⬇ New Assistant #1430

IRREGULAR SERIES

ASSISTANT DIARY

BY NEW ASSISTANT #1430

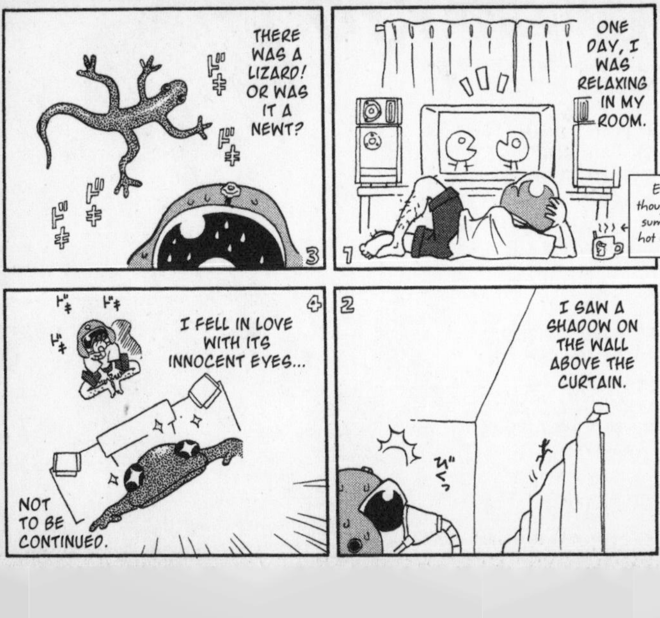
ONE DAY, I WAS RELAXING IN MY ROOM.
Even though it's summer, hot coffee
I SAW A SHADOW ON THE WALL ABOVE THE CURTAIN.
THERE WAS A LIZARD! OR WAS IT A NEWT?
I FELL IN LOVE WITH ITS INNOCENT EYES...
NOT TO BE CONTINUED.

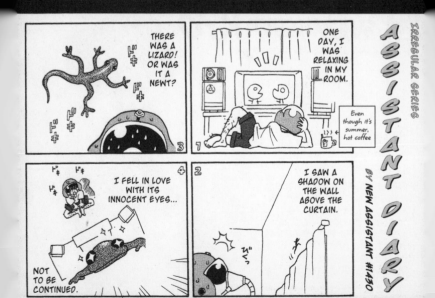

CORNER FOR FUNNY STUFF!

- A FRIEND OF MINE SAID "MAINICHI HONETA" INSTEAD OF "MAINICHI HONEBUTO!"

- IN A COMMERCIAL FOR EDWIN JEANS, BRAD PITT PLAYS A HITCH-HIKER WHO TRIES ALL DAY TO GET SOMEONE TO STOP. WHEN SOMEONE FINALLY DOES PICK HIM UP HE SAYS, "EDWIN." DON'T AMERICANS USUALLY SAY "THANK YOU"? WELL, HE'S STILL COOL ANYWAY.

BULLETIN BOARD

To Tadashi Kanzaki:
Good luck at the Aadonto Hair Festival this year! I'll do my best as a model, too!

PRESENTS BY TAKAYA NAGAO

THE BIG QUESTION:
IF KYO CARRIED HIS SWORD AT HIS WAIST...

Guh! Ugh! It's too long to pull out!

↑ What will happen?

↑ **Takaya Nagao**   ↓ **Sho Yashioka**

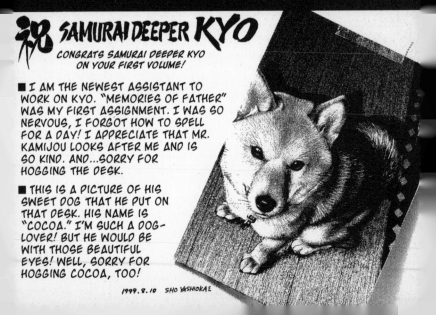

SAMURAI DEEPER KYO

CONGRATS SAMURAI DEEPER KYO ON YOUR FIRST VOLUME!

■ I AM THE NEWEST ASSISTANT TO WORK ON KYO. "MEMORIES OF FATHER" WAS MY FIRST ASSIGNMENT. I WAS SO NERVOUS, I FORGOT HOW TO SPELL FOR A DAY! I APPRECIATE THAT MR. KAMIJOU LOOKS AFTER ME AND IS SO KIND. AND...SORRY FOR HOGGING THE DESK.

■ THIS IS A PICTURE OF HIS SWEET DOG THAT HE PUT ON THAT DESK. HIS NAME IS "COCOA." I'M SUCH A DOG-LOVER! BUT HE WOULD BE WITH THOSE BEAUTIFUL EYES! WELL, SORRY FOR HOGGING COCOA, TOO!

1999.8.10   SHO YASHIOKA

GLOSSARY

Bansho – A guard house at the entrance to a village.

Buke – The samurai/warrior class. Can also refer to a specific samurai family.

Daikan – A magistrate. A local government administrator.

Daimyo – A feudal lord.

"Dani Daikan" – Dani is a pejorative term meaning "tick-like." A fitting insult for a bloated, lazy, thieving daikan.

Edo Era – (1603-1868) Japan's "golden era" of political and economic stability following the civil wars of the Sengoku era. Samurai Deeper takes place at the start of the Edo Era.

Fumikomi – A quick fighting step to close ground.

Kakure Zato – A hidden village. The tradition of Kakure Zato is rich in Japanese folklore.

Kengi – Sword technique.

Maii – The distance between two sword fighters. Without enough maii, a swordsman can't take a proper swing. Too much maii and a hit can't connect with sufficient force.

Miko – "Shrine Virgins." Young women who assist with sacred duties at a Shinto Shrine.

Mon – A small silver coin or copper coin.

Ochiudo – A fugitive samurai. Considered to be a rebel or a brigand.

Oneechan & Oniichan – Affectionate terms for big sister and big brother.

Ryo – A gold coin of about 15 grams.

"SATSUJIN KEN MUMYO JINPU RYU MIZUCHI" – "Without Light, Let the Divine Wind Flow – Deadly Sword Technique"

Sekigahara – The greatest battle in Japanese history which took place in fall of 1600 and ended the years of civil war in Japan. Following Sekigahara, all Japan would be ruled by one Shogun.

Sengoku era – A time of civil war in Japan that lasted from 1467-1568. It was a warlike age—the heyday of the Samurai.

Shauku/Sun/Bu – Units of measurement from old Japan. One shaku equals approx.11.92 inches; 10 Sun = 1 Shaku; 10 Bu = 1 Sun.

Tachikaze – A special term for the wind given off from the swing of a sword.

Taisho – A general or lord. One step below a Daimyo in feudal Japan.

Tokaido-cho – The main trade road that runs along Japan's coast.

Yojimbo – A bodyguard.

BULLETIN BOARD

CHALLENGE AKIMINE KAMIJYO!

Think you can draw better than the manga-ka? Then send us your illustrations of Kyo!

We'll publish them in upcoming volumes, along with fan art from Japanese readers. Illustrations should be drawn in ink in black and white on clean, unlined paper.

Send mail to:
TOKYOPOP
5900 Wilshire Blvd., Ste. 2000
Los Angeles, CA 90036
Attn: *Samurai Deeper KYO* Fan Mail

You can also send your questions for Kamijyo-san or the TOKYOPOP editors!

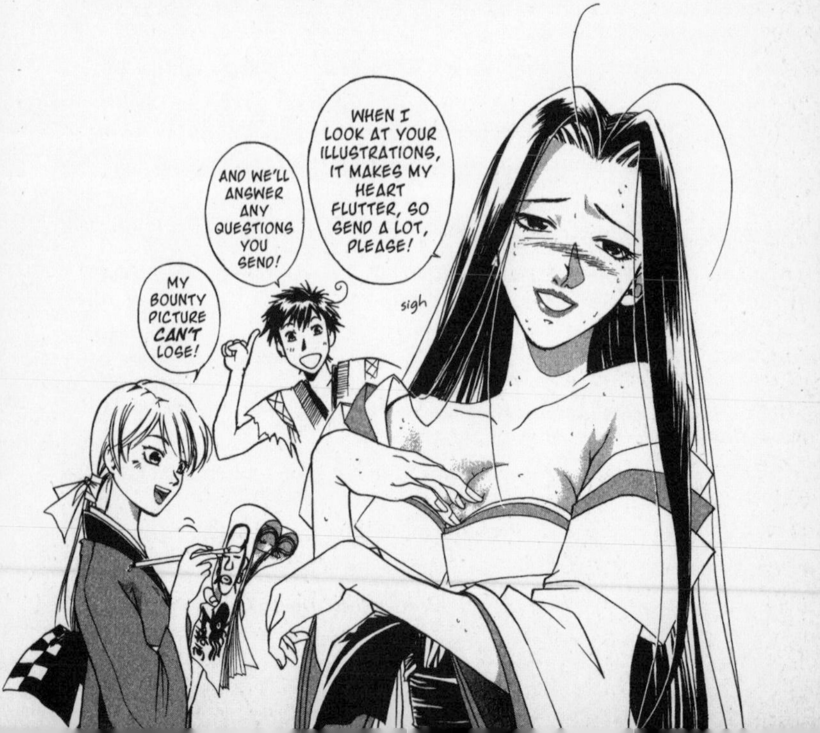
WHEN I LOOK AT YOUR ILLUSTRATIONS, IT MAKES MY HEART FLUTTER, SO SEND A LOT, PLEASE!
sigh
AND WE'LL ANSWER ANY QUESTIONS YOU SEND!
MY BOUNTY PICTURE CAN'T LOSE!

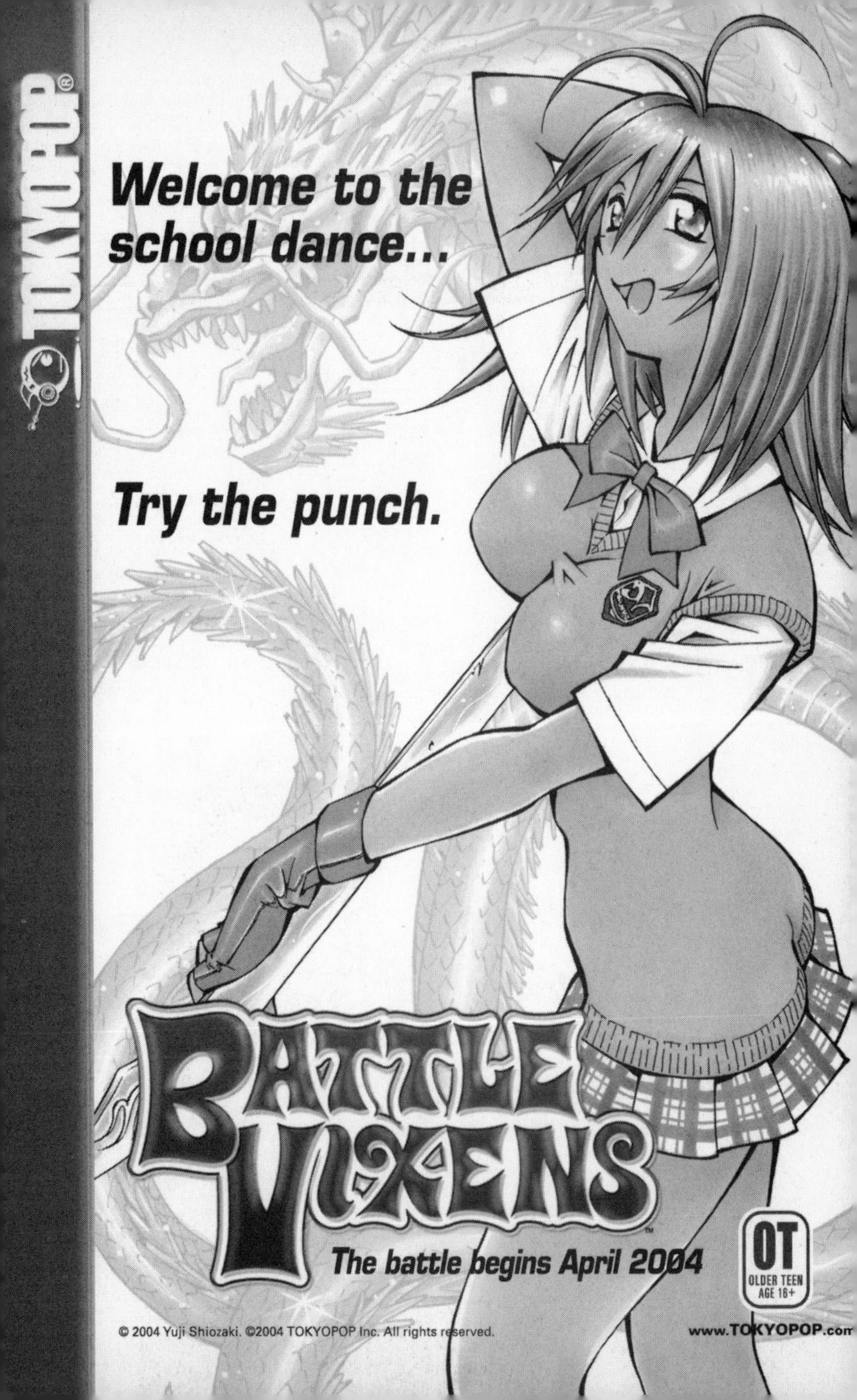
TOKYOPOP
Welcome to the school dance...
Try the punch.
BATTLE VIXENS™
The battle begins April 2004
OT
OLDER TEEN
AGE 16+
© 2004 Yuji Shiozaki. ©2004 TOKYOPOP Inc. All rights reserved.
www.TOKYOPOP.com

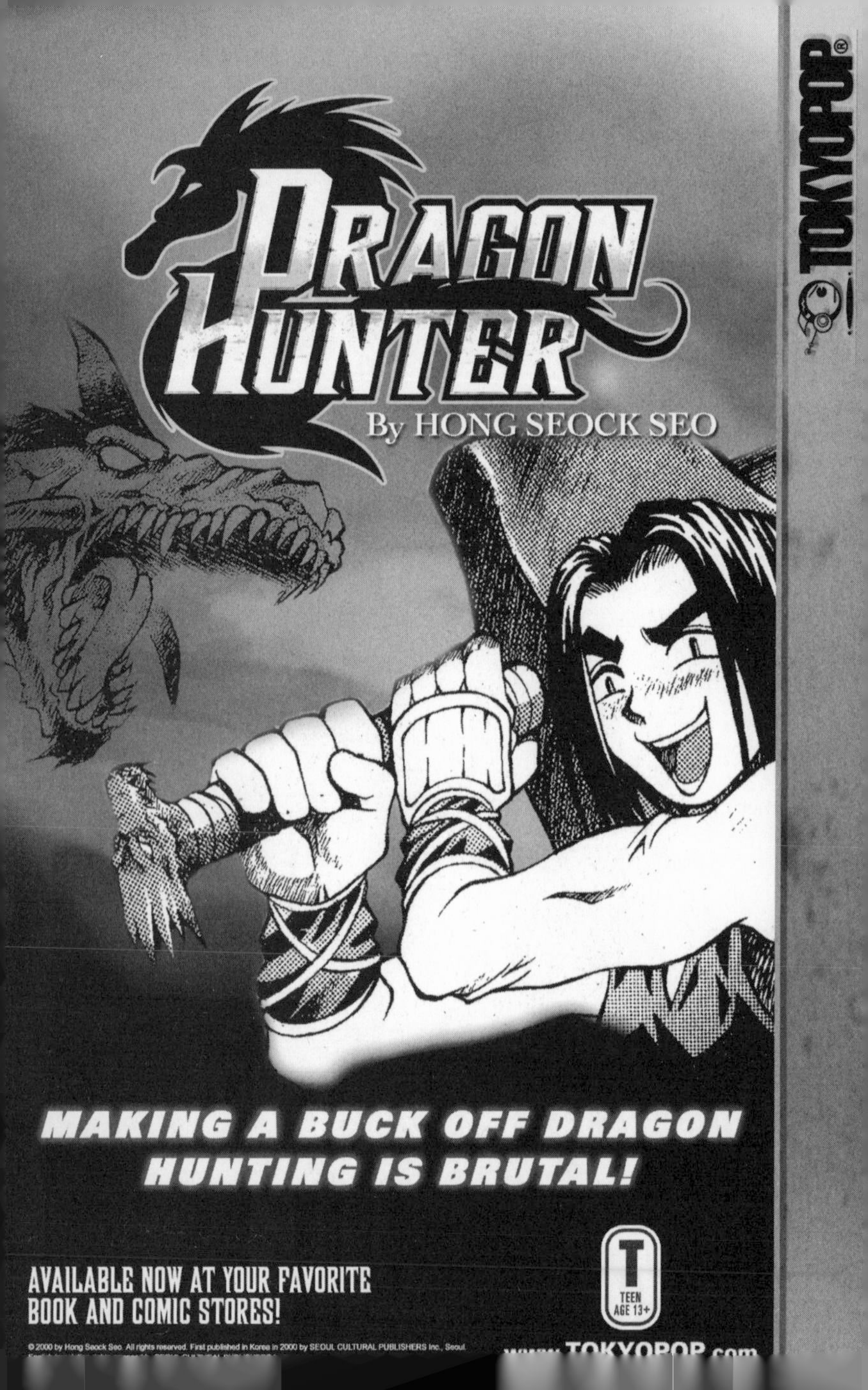
TOKYOPOP
DRAGON HUNTER
By HONG SEOCK SEO
MAKING A BUCK OFF DRAGON HUNTING IS BRUTAL!
T TEEN AGE 13+
AVAILABLE NOW AT YOUR FAVORITE BOOK AND COMIC STORES!
© 2000 by Hong Seock Seo. All rights reserved. First published in Korea in 2000 by SEOUL CULTURAL PUBLISHERS Inc., Seoul.
www.TOKYOPOP.com

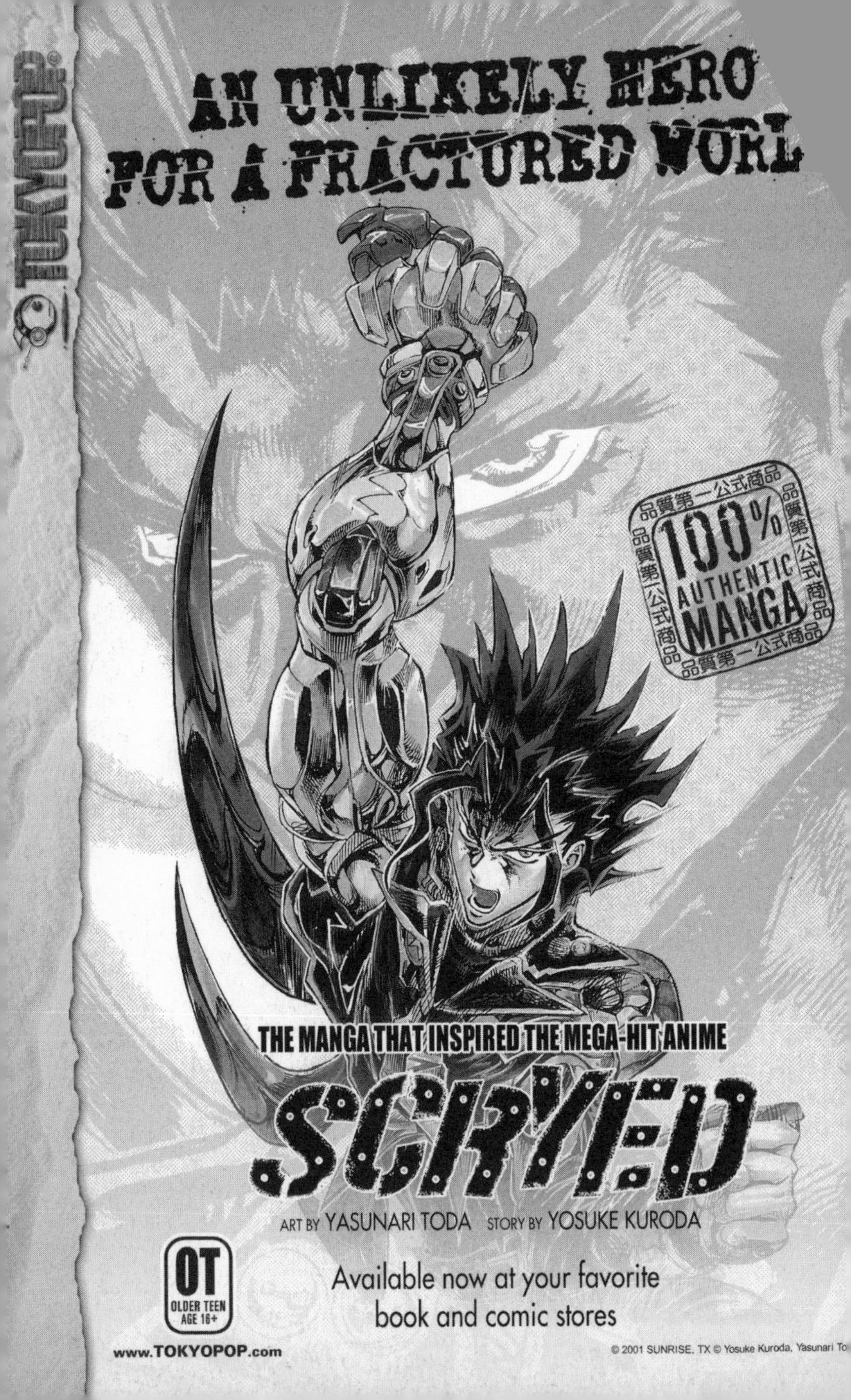
TOKYOPOP
AN UNLIKELY HERO
FOR A FRACTURED WORL
品質第一公式商品
100% AUTHENTIC MANGA
THE MANGA THAT INSPIRED THE MEGA-HIT ANIME
SCRYED
ART BY YASUNARI TODA STORY BY YOSUKE KURODA
OT
OLDER TEEN
AGE 16+
Available now at your favorite
book and comic stores
www.TOKYOPOP.com
© 2001 SUNRISE, TX © Yosuke Kuroda, Yasunari To

STOP!

This is the back of the book.
You wouldn't want to spoil a great ending!

This book is printed "manga-style," in the authentic Japanese right-to-left format. Since none of the artwork has been flipped or altered, readers get to experience the story just as the creator intended. You've been asking for it, so TOKYOPOP® delivered: authentic, hot-off-the-press, and far more fun!

DIRECTIONS

If this is your first time reading manga-style, here's a quick guide to help you understand how it works.

It's easy... just start in the top right panel and follow the numbers. Have fun, and look for more 100% authentic manga from TOKYOPOP®!

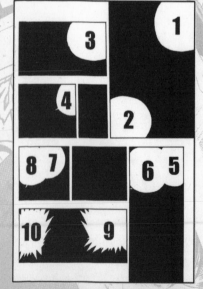